Workshops
for the Handicapped
in the United States

Publication Number 814

AMERICAN LECTURE SERIES®

A Monograph in

The BANNERSTONE DIVISION *of*

AMERICAN LECTURES IN SPECIAL EDUCATION

Edited by

MORRIS VAL JONES, Ph.D.

Speech and Hearing Center
Sacramento State College
Sacramento, California

Workshops for the Handicapped in the United States

An Historical and Developmental Perspective

By

NATHAN NELSON, Ph.D.

Associate Professor of Rehabilitation Services
DePaul University, Chicago, Illinois

Formerly, Chief Rehabilitation Workshop Consultant
California Department of Rehabilitation

CHARLES C THOMAS • PUBLISHER

Springfield • Illinois • U.S.A.

Published and Distributed Throughout the World by
CHARLES C THOMAS • PUBLISHER
Bannerstone House
301-327 East Lawrence Avenue, Springfield, Illinois, U.S.A.
Natchez Plantation House
735 North Atlantic Boulevard, Fort Lauderdale, Florida, U.S.A.

*With THOMAS BOOKS careful attention is given to all details of
manufacturing and design. It is the Publisher's desire to present books that are
satisfactory as to their physical qualities and artistic possibilities and
appropriate for their particular use. THOMAS BOOKS will be true to those
laws of quality that assure a good name and good will.*

Printed in the United States of America
RN-1

To my wife,
Helen Ewing Nelson,
*Gallant Advocate of the
Consumer Interest,
This book is dedicated.*

INTRODUCTION

A LITTLE-NOTED but significant development in the United States has been the growth of workshops for the handicapped. These are programs whose primary purpose is to provide work for handicapped and disadvantaged persons — work as a source of gainful employment or as a means of helping to solve human problems.

Since 1950, more than a thousand work places have been created by such organizations. Called most often merely "workshops," the recent rapid increase in their numbers suggests that they arise to meet a need, an increasing need.

They are arising to meet a need of some of our least successful people. The unsuccessful people who come to workshops have not been able to find jobs elsewhere because they are physically or mentally handicapped, have educational limitations, or are socially unacceptable. They include the mentally retarded, the cerebral palsied, the orthopedically handicapped, the deaf, the blind, the epileptic, the mentally ill, and the aging. More recently the drug addicts, the penal offenders, the educationally and culturally deprived, the ethnically stigmatized or alienated, and the socially unadaptable have also been coming to workshops.

The workshop offers opportunity to those who have not found it previously in a land which boasts that it provides opportunity for all. It is designed to help the persons employed, not to maximize profits.

The story of workshops in the United States has not been told. Some organizations have told the story of their own particular organization. There have been accounts of workshops for special disability groups. Occasionally a public agency or a voluntary health agency has reviewed workshop activities from the particular view of that agency. This book represents an effort to tell the story of workshops generally: sheltered workshops, rehabilitation workshops, rehabilitation work centers, rehabilitation industries, work adjustment centers, and work training centers, among others. Whatever the differentiating nomenclature suggests, they all have the common aim of helping people through the provision of real work. They appeal to the creative instincts of man to bring forth constructive responses. They replace frustration with a sense of confidence which in turn releases added capability.

The purpose of this book is to set forth how workshops have developed to help handicapped persons solve their employment and work-related problems, to describe how they function, to make some suggestions for their general improvement, and to forecast their future opportunities. The scope of the account is restricted mainly to programs which use substantial paid work. Activity centers having exclusively recreational, social, or arts and crafts programs are not covered. Medical rehabilitation centers which have vocational assessment programs not based on paid work are also excluded.

A definitive or comprehensive account has not been attempted. The attempt here is to include the major aspects of workshops in a general summary. Much of what has been published about workshops has appeared in specialized articles in professional periodicals. Here those aspects of the specialized literature judged to contribute most significantly to illuminating major workshop problems and the few books which have been written in the field are collated. The author has added his own observations made from experience over the last twenty years in the field.

It is hoped that an account of workshops may help those who plan social programs for the country to visualize the delivery of more comprehensive systems of human services in a more effective manner. When workshops succeed in their goal of helping people by providing gainful employment, they also relieve society of some of the costs of public assistance, of mental hospitals, and of custodial and penal institutions. When workshops succeed in their goal, they also lessen the financial and social burdens being carried by the families of handicapped persons. But most important of all, workshops help create well-being in frustrated and defeated persons whose problems are not being met by other social programs. Thus the role of workshops must be reckoned with by those interested in an adequate social blueprint for the country.

It is hoped that the founders of the many new workshops not yet in existence will benefit from an account of the experiences of their predecessors, and that workshop staffs may find the accounts of others' experiments useful in their development of new techniques and methods.

It is hoped too that this account may help those who use workshop services. Counselors in public and private rehabilitation, special education, mental health, and social welfare programs may find here new ways to help their students and clients.

Finally, a general review of workshop developments may serve as a guide to future students of workshops. Perhaps this account may inspire more interest in research in the field. Possibly even it may suggest comparative analyses of North American and European workshop systems to investigators here and abroad.

ACKNOWLEDGMENTS

IT is generally believed that a book is the creation of the person whose name is shown on the title page as the author. If that is usually so, this book is an exception. It was created by hundreds of people. They are the handicapped persons working in workshops, workshop foremen and their supervisors, and the many others who appreciate the value of workshops. They told me what to say, and I have tried to write it down.

Among the many people who influenced the making of this book, a few deserve special mention. The first, Andrew Marrin, was chief of the Vocational Rehabilitation Service of California when this book was conceived and started. Marrin enabled employees in a government bureaucracy to be innovative and creative. Under his leadership, the writer was able to conceive and operate the first public consultation program for workshops in the United States.

Morris Val Jones, the editor of the book, became interested in the workshop consultation program and as a result became acquainted with the writer. He suggested that I write a book about workshops. In the years that followed, he has provided patient guidance and many invaluable suggestions. The organization of the subject matter was conceived by him.

As groups of chapters were finished, they were reviewed by persons whose knowledge of the subject matter I value. They are William Button, William Gellman, Paul Lustig, Helen Ewing Nelson, Theodore Pezman, and Antonio Suazo. I appreciate their creative criticism. The book is undoubtedly better than it would have been without their analysis. They are not, of course, responsible for the final version of the text.

I am grateful to Dominic G. Parisi, Director of the Administration Studies Center, DePaul University, for his encouragement and support in the completion of the book.

I have been most fortunate in my secretaries, Vergie Erhardt and Dianne LeMonnier. They cheerfully compensated for my editorial deficiencies.

I am also grateful to James R. Flynn and Stella Cross, who did the index.

To each mentioned, I am grateful.

N. N.

CONTENTS

PART ONE

The Development of Workshops for the Handicapped

PART TWO

Workshops Today — Their Nature and Characteristics

PART THREE

The Future of Workshops

Workshops for the Handicapped in the United States

Part One

The Development of Workshops for the Handicapped

"Open your eyes and look for some man, or some work for the sake of man, which needs a little time, a little friendship, a little sympathy, a little sociability, a little human toil. Search and see if there is not some place where you may invest your humanity."

— Albert Schweitzer

I

THE ROLE OF WORKSHOPS FOR THE HANDICAPPED AND DISADVANTAGED

W ORKSHOPS for handicapped and disadvantaged persons come into being to provide work programs that meet needs which are not being met by other institutions and which a sufficient sector of society wants met.

Originally workshops came into being as adjuncts to existing institutions: the workshop's services supplemented the ongoing services of the sponsoring institution. Because objectives of the sponsoring institutions differed and because the goals society held for given groups of handicapped persons varied, workshops have exhibited great variety during their development. Yet their common and central purpose has been the creation of programs to enable handicapped and disadvantaged persons to work and to acquire the benefits that come from work.

THE LACUNAE INTERPRETATION OF WORKSHOP DEVELOPMENT

The principle institutions whose functions workshops have augmented or extended were the educational system, the church and moral improvement societies, health organizations, social welfare agencies, public and private vocational rehabilitation agencies, and the business and industrial sectors of the nation. During workshop development, some workshop roles have diminished, i.e. that of abettors of religious or moral ideals; some new roles have been added, i.e. that of providers of opportunity for disadvantaged ethnic and cultural groups. The predominant emphases of workshops from time to time have varied, depending upon the awareness of problems of various disability groups and social philosophy about work and the needs of handicapped persons in American society.

5

The roles workshops undertook have been influenced by the recognition among segments of the nation that other existing social organisms were not enabling handicapped persons to participate as fully as possible in American life. The workshops created programs to provide handicapped persons opportunities to participate in the vocational life of the country to the extent and in such a manner that such sectors indicated and supported.

Since a workshop typically is brought into being to supplement the services of an existing institution or institutions, each workshop organization has generally been able to select one, several, or many of the neglected social lacunae, depending upon the organization's mission and support. If it chose to compensate exclusively for the lapses of one type of institution, it could specialize in that institutional framework and serve that unmet need in depth. For example, if it tried to correct educational deficits, it might attempt to enhance occupational skills by on-the-job training and teaching of an elementary academic proficiency. If it attempted to cover a number of major neglected work-related areas of life, the chances were it would deal with each relatively superficially. Although some did attempt to serve many such neglected areas in depth and comprehensively, these have been the exceptions. Typically, a workshop chooses to serve one type of need in depth predominately or to serve a large number of needs more superficially. In general, workshops develop vertically (specialized) or horizontally (comprehensive), depending on whether they attempt to serve one or several institutional lacunae.

Since there is a relationship between the functions exercised, the source of financing, and the objectives of the interrelated agencies, a review of the way in which workshops filled the empty space in American institutional scope and function can provide an overview of their development. Through such an outline, a better understanding of the dynamics of their current role may hopefully be reached. Perhaps also such an approach can provide a base for planning their future. To present such an outline is the purpose of this chapter. In it may be found the lacunae interpretation of workshop development — an analysis of the ways in which workshops used work and work environment to meet the needs of handicapped persons which other social institutions neglected.

THE EDUCATIONAL ROLE OF THE WORKSHOP

The first American workshop in the Perkins Institute for the Blind near Boston was started as a supplementary vocational education program in 1838, about two hundred years after the settlement of the country and sixty-two years after the Declaration of Independence. Two questions may set the stage for an account of the development of workshops as an educational institution. Why was the program started at this time? Why was it started as a vocational education program?

The answer to the first question is that the essential and sufficient conditions for the establishment of such a program did not exist until that time. Information about workshops was not available until the European workshops were started in the last years of the eighteenth century and the beginning of the nineteenth century. In the United States, the idea that free education should be available to all was getting general acceptance in the northern states during the first half of the nineteenth century. It was therefore considered desirable to make education available to the blind, a disability group that was getting much attention at the time. Through education, the chances for success in life would be enhanced, thus giving the blind more opportunity to share the benefits of American society in keeping with the emerging principles of American democracy.

THE ROLE OF WORKSHOPS IN VOCATIONAL TRAINING

The choice of the vocational education content of the early programs in the nineteenth century is probably due to the example of the English workshops and of the manual labor schools which sprang up in the first half of the nineteenth century in the United States. The latter schools (such as the Oneida School of Science and Industry at Whitesborough, New York, and the Worchester Manual-Labor High School in Massachusetts, which were modeled after the ideas of Emanuel Fellenberg of Switzerland) were for nonhandicapped persons, but they provided occupational skill training and some made payments to students. Their existence may have made the vocational training of the blind more acceptable in light of the new principles of equal educational opportunities for all (1).

The manual labor schools did not flourish, but the workshops for the blind as vocational education facilities continued to grow and spread throughout the land. As a rule, however, the early workshops for the blind were not successful in achieving the original objectives of their founders, the provision of employment in industry through training in occupational skills. They became predominately places of employment for blind persons. From this failure some have concluded that skill training is not appropriate in a workshop setting (2), but it is possible that the failure may have resulted from the stereotyped types of training given in skills not greatly needed in industry, the lack of work readiness of the blind to accommodate easily to industry without preliminary personal adjustment training and special accommodations, and the psychological unreadiness of industry to accept blind workers during the nineteenth and first half of the twentieth century.

In any case, although occupational skill training was not emphasized generally as a principal means of enabling handicapped persons to work in industry by the early workshops for the blind, some other workshops provided on-the-job training in many occupational areas; and many others provided such training in a few occupational areas during the first half of the twentieth century. On-the-job training was used extensively as a means of preparing for work projects in workshops, and when such projects were industry related, jobs in industry sometimes resulted from training for the work of the shop. With the advent of financing from the state-federal vocational rehabilitation programs in 1920, skill training was encouraged. With the advent of training services grants under the Vocational Rehabilitation Amendments of 1965, training in occupational skills for placement in industry became an important function of the workshops in the training services program.

The workshops developed vocational training programs for two general reasons: general public vocational training programs were not available to handicapped persons, or they were not suited to their needs. Although the idea that general education should be available for all was accepted everywhere but in the South by 1850, vocational training, with the exception of agricultural education and some highly technical education programs, was not available to most persons, whether handicapped or not, until well into the twentieth century. When vocational education gradually became more prevalent after the passage of the Smith-Hughes Act in 1917, trade schools were not generally able to accommodate to the individual and special needs of handicapped persons. The mentally retarded, the orthopedically handicapped, and other handicapped persons found that vocational schools either refused them admittance or were often unsuited to their needs.

The vocational schools serving the general public were often unsuited to the needs of the handicapped for two general reasons. They often failed to provide the special techniques required to teach handicapped persons, or they did not accommodate sufficiently to the secondary needs of handicapped persons for training in work habits and social efficiency. As a result, workshops and some vocational rehabilitation centers have undertaken the role of vocational educators and have exercised the role with varying degrees of success to the present time. This role was most frequently exercised in combination with other roles.

THE ROLE OF THE WORKSHOP IN SPECIAL EDUCATION

Although generally the people of the United States accepted early the principle of free and universal education, in practice some groups of citizens were excluded from suitable educational opportunities throughout its history. Among these were various groups of handicapped persons. Handicapped persons who resided in institutional facilities usually received educational attention earlier in our history than those who lived at home. During the nineteenth century most of the latter, with the exception of some blind and deaf persons, had to take their chances of getting an education through the general instruction of public or private schools. Some handicapped persons, such as many of the mentally retarded, were denied admission to public schools because it was believed they could not benefit from academic instruction. Others who could not get to school because of severe orthopedic handicaps did not receive any instruction. At the beginning of the twentieth century, it could hardly be said that all severely handicapped persons who lived at home had an equal chance at a suitable educational opportunity.

During the first half of the twentieth century in various parts of the United States, local school systems began providing special programs for handicapped persons and began providing for the education of some of the excluded handicapped groups. The existence of these special programs in some places and not in others made parents of handicapped persons aware that their children were not getting the educational opportunity that should be available to them. Before the middle of the twentieth century, these parents, especially the parents of the mentally retarded and the cerebral palsied, formed organizations and established their own schools for their children. These schools usually tried to serve many functions, including those of the regular general schools — academic proficiency, vocational efficiency, and social efficiency. In addition, they usually included recreational and self-care programs and after 1950 included workshops. The workshops very soon became the predominant programs. They often maintained the original objective, which was to provide special education programs suitable to the needs of students. These workshops assumed the responsibilities of special education in the public schools.

By the middle of the twentieth century, public school systems were assuming more responsibility for the education of these handicapped persons. For the mentally retarded, this process began with the more able group academically (the educable retarded), and later extended to the less able academically (the trainable retarded). The schools or classes established by the parent groups that lasted longest were mostly for the trainable retarded, since those classes were the last to be taken over by the public schools. When the public schools took over the training of the educable retarded, the privately operated schools retained some of their educational functions and added others, including paid work programs. Thus they became hybrid organizations of school, work, social, and recreational activities, but they were designated as workshop schools or by general names such as opportunity centers. As the young adults in them reached their maximum educational potential, the educational activities of the workshop school were decreased, and the paid work activities increased, while the social and recreational activities were continued. Finally in some instances, the education activities, with the exception of the vocational and homemaking activities, were diminished. A workshop for the mentally retarded was the result.

At the present time, many of the workshops for the mentally retarded or school workshops are at various stages of the progression described. The same is true for similar programs for other disabled persons, such as the cerebral palsied. Depending upon the stage of development, the programs may be assuming the responsibilities of public special education or adult education programs. Workshop organizations are operating classes which are similar to those provided by public special education programs and adult education programs. Workshops are providing half-day programs on their work floors for handicapped persons enrolled in public schools. Finally, workshops are attempting to remedy the educational deficits which affect the ability to work for handicapped persons past the school age who do not have available or cannot benefit from adult education classes.

THE WORKSHOP AS A BASE
FOR SPIRITUAL REHABILITATION

The last decades of the nineteenth century were turbulent years in the economic life of the United States. Vast fortunes were made by entrepreneurs while recurrent economic crises created unemployment, distress, and misery for handicapped and underprivileged persons. Philanthropy became stylish and private charitable organizations multiplied. The humanitarian agencies often attempted to restore the fortunes of the handicapped and needy by leading them into the paths of moral virtue. Evangelical religious groups sought to "save the souls" of unfortunate victims of economic distress while at the same time restoring them to material well-being. Remedial social services for people were closely allied in the public mind with the development of correct moral attitudes and spiritual values.

To cope with the problems of the poor and the handicapped, the humanitarian and religious organizations devised programs to ameliorate their economic condition and to reverse the deterioration of their spiritual condition, which was conceived as being the source of their unfortunate circumstances. It was hoped that through a religious or moral appeal they might restore both spiritual nobility and material well-being. In their efforts to achieve their economic goals, they found that the traditional approaches of charity and philanthropy were generally ineffective and that some measure of economic self-sufficiency had to be established before moral improvement could be expected. They therefore sought new ways to help restore the poor to economic self-sufficiency so that spiritual values might be restored. The establishment of workshops was one outcome.

The humanitarian organizations which developed workshops learned that it was very difficult to get acceptance of religious or ethical ideals by men who were jobless, hungry, and miserable. They also learned that the meager allowances of public assistance programs or private charity did not provide an adequate economic base from which to elevate man's moral character. The men they sought to help needed work, and since the organizations could not find work, they created it. They created it in workshops through renovation of discards, then service work, and finally subcontract work. Having provided a man with work, they then sought to improve his behavior or save his soul. Their objective, however, was always to rehabilitate the man spiritually. Work was merely a means towards that end.

Over the years, the workshops that used work as a means of moral improvement found that men accepted the work they offered more readily than spiritual guidance. They found that a man became a good worker much more readily than he changed his moral character or religious belief. As a result, over the years the spiritual role of these workshops receded into the background, and they assumed other vocational roles, retaining their spiritual missions as secondary objectives. There are, of course, outstanding exceptions, workshops which still try to influence men in moral or religious directions, but only a few workshops now consider their role to be that of saving men's souls.

A second reason for the general disappearance of the spiritual role as such is that styles change in social thinking and terminology as well as in clothes. By the middle of the twentieth century, spiritual objectives were not fashionable. Social reformers no longer try to save men's souls or elevate their characters. They try to modify their behavior. So it appears that the spiritual role of the workshop may still be carried on in workshops in its modern equivalent. However, most workshops have substituted the standards of society for the ideals of religious goals. The attempt to get an individual to conform to the social standards may be the modern version of "saving his soul." This many of the workshops try to do, though not always with the recognition that they are thereby trying to impose moral precepts of conduct as did the workshops of the nineteenth century.

The spiritual or moral role of the workshop has been exercised in three general ways. First, it was carried on for many years at the end of the last century and the beginning of this century directly with the frank expression of religious or moral goals which could not be achieved in other ways by traditional institutions. Second, the role has more recently been carried on at times by some workshops indirectly as a secondary one. Third, the moral role has been carried out covertly with moral values disguised as social criteria. In any case, the role has not been an unqualified success. Workshops generally have not been as successful in supplementing the efforts of the church and of moral reformers as they have been in achieving other work related goals.

THE WORKSHOP AS A PUBLIC HEALTH ORGANIZATION

While the moral reformers and religious organizations were trying to save the poor and handicapped, the growing charitable agencies at the end of the nineteenth century found a more attractive object for their attention, the orthopedically crippled and disabled, especially crippled children. During the nineteenth and the first half of the twentieth century, this concern was expressed in the growth of orthopedic hospitals and clinics. But these medical programs could effect maximum physical recovery only. The crippled person still remained disabled, dependent, and without a satisfactory way of life. Early in the twentieth century, a few voluntary agencies began schools, training centers, and social and recreational centers for crippled children, but these facilities did not serve the needs of the adult disabled person who needed work or work activity.

THE WORKSHOP AS THE THIRD PHASE OF ORTHOPEDICS

Early in the twentieth century, workshops began to train the orthopedically handicapped for employment. In the 1920's, curative workshops were established to provide preparation for work in industry by using occupational training or work tolerance training or both. The renovating shop operated by religious organizations, which had previously served principally the needy, began serving large numbers of the orthopedic handicapped. In many of these groups of shops, the orthopedically handicapped remained in the shops for long-term employment when they did not find jobs in industry.

With the passage of the workmen's compensation laws in the second decade of the twentieth century, large numbers of occupationally injured disabled adults were expected to seek the services of the workshops, but the numbers who sought services were few. The same was true for the disabled soldiers returning from World War II. Few disabled men with pensions from the government or from workmen's compensation found the early workshops attractive, but publicity about their existence encouraged the growth of workshops for the orthopedically handicapped. Later in the 1930's and 1940's, a scattering of workshops for the orthopedically handicapped sprang up in various parts of the country, providing principally occupational training, occupational therapy, placement, or sheltered employment. These consisted of freestanding workshops or units in rehabilitation centers. They served mainly persons injured in accidents, with congenital conditions, or those with orthopedic defects. During the first half of the twentieth century, workshops, with some exceptions, were serving principally the blind or the orthopedically handicapped.

Thus, early in their history, workshops moved into the area of providing services to the orthopedically handicapped after maximum physical recovery had been achieved. To paraphrase Howard Rusk, these workshops assumed the role of carrying out the third phase of orthopedic rehabilitation. This role has generally been continued by these workshops to the present day, though many assumed additional roles in later years.

THE WORKSHOPS AND TUBERCULOSIS REHABILITATION

The concern for tuberculosis which swept the world in the early part of the twentieth century created a new role for workshops. When the persons infected by tuberculosis recovered from the active form of their disease and returned to their jobs, the work pressures often resulted in a reactivation of their condition. It was evident that a period of adjustment in activity was needed between release from the sanitarium and return to the job. Initially, physical hardening programs were instituted in sanitarium programs. Later, following European precedent, workshops for the recovered tuberculosis patients were started in large cities, beginning with the Altro Workshop in New York in 1915. These workshops were successful in assisting the tuberculosis ex-patient make the transition between the sanitarium and the job.

The tuberculosis rehabilitation programs established a new role for workshops in health services — the role of the work conditioner. It differed in emphasis from the role of the workshop which used work to improve physical function in the orthopedically handicapped. It used work to enable the tubercular to meet work demands. By gradually increasing work pressures, the workshop for these people conditioned its individuals for work. When the incidence of tuberculosis diminished, the workshops applied the techniques developed to cardiac patients and other disability groups as well as the recovered tuberculosis patient. Most of the ex-patients recovered their ability to work. A few, however, did not recover the ability to tolerate a full day's work under normal pressures, and long-term work programs were set up to prevent deterioration and to preserve mental health.

THE WORKSHOP AND CHRONIC ILLNESS

By the middle of the twentieth century, the incidence of tuberculosis had declined, and the workshops organized for the tuberculous individuals began serving new groups of individuals with other disabilities. These included cardiac patients, the mentally ill, and sometimes the mentally retarded. In serving the cardiac patients and mentally ill, some shops found themselves rendering recurrent services. They began rendering long-term services to them. About the same time, hospitals serving the chronically ill or the aged started workshops in their facilities. Community shops also established workshops for persons with mental illness or other chronic disease. Later workshops began providing long-term services to alcoholics, drug addicts, delinquents, and public offenders.

The chronic disability groups being served varied in their needs, but what they had in common was a need for long-term or recurrent services. Many handicapped persons had the ability to work but could not work at a level acceptable to industry. Others were unstable in attendance or erratic at work. At the level at which they could work and to the extent that they could work, work activity was beneficial to their physical condition or to their mental health. Thus these workshops assumed the role of a supplementary public health facility for chronic illness and mental health programs which lacked paid work programs.

THE LONG-TERM WORKSHOP FOR
PERSONS OF LOW POTENTIAL

Somewhat analogous to the needs of the chronically ill were the needs of certain groups of the mentally retarded, cerebral palsied, uncontrolled epileptics, and others. Among these groups were some individuals who would remain low producers even with the best of services. Though their productivity was not great, work benefited them greatly by developing more mature social and personal relationships, by developing self-sufficiency, and by enabling them to lead generally happier lives. The small earnings they made had value to them which transcended the economic worth of their wages.

The workshop here assumed a role that could not be undertaken by the school, by the hospital, by the church, or by industry. It was also a role which was not assumed by the traditional private voluntary agencies on a large scale. That workshops were able to assume this role, albeit belatedly, was due to the growth of a new group of private voluntary agencies for the mentally retarded, cerebral palsied, and epileptics after 1950. The growth of these shops is of paramount importance in the history of workshops in the United States. They were soon to include the largest numbers of workshops in the country in any single group.

THE ROLE OF THE WORKSHOPS
IN VOCATIONAL REHABILITATION

The fragmentary rudiments of vocational rehabilitation services were initiated in the United States principally by private voluntary agencies and by a few state programs during the course of the nineteenth century. They were offered mainly in schools, hospital clinics, and workshops. They consisted predominately of vocational training, special education, medical and medically related services, and sheltered employment, the main service in workshops. The private rehabilitation services were usually neither extensive nor comprehensive until after World War I, when they became excellent in quality in some parts of the country. During the period before World War I, workshops were generally isolated from other agencies, rendering occupational training but mostly sheltered employment to blind and orthopedically handicapped persons.

In 1920, a national vocational rehabilitation system was established with the passage of Public Law 236, the Civilian Vocational Rehabilitation Act. Under its provisions, the states could secure federal funds by matching with state funds and could operate public vocational rehabilitation programs within the framework of the federal law. It defined vocational rehabilitation as the provision of counseling, vocational training, and placement. The workshops in existence at the time and until the middle of the twentieth century could offer little to the state programs except an occasional opportunity to train handicapped persons in vocational training programs not available in trade schools or other vocational training facilities. Some state programs used workshops, however, as a place of employment for severely handicapped persons not considered capable of absorbing training or working in private industry. The workshops continued their existing programs without a great deal of coordination with the state vocational rehabilitation agencies.

The state agencies in their early history were influenced by the prevailing vocational guidance practices of the time. These practices placed great reliance on intelligence and apptitude testing together with counseling "to place the right man on the right job." While this approach was useful for nonhandicapped, intelligent, well-adjusted young adults with good educations, it had the effect of highlighting the verbal and abstract deficiencies of the blind, deaf, mentally retarded, the multiply handicapped, and the culturally and educationally deprived without emphasizing the capabilities of these disability groups in informal work settings. Neither did these practices address themselves to the handicapped person's ability to adjust to the requirements of employment, to tolerate work pressures, or to produce adequately. By 1950, it had become apparent that psychometrics and counseling alone could not tell the vocational rehabilitation counselor if the marginal, educationally and culturally deprived, mentally retarded or men- tally ill applicant was ready for vocational rehabilitation.

THE WORKSHOP AS VOCATIONAL EVALUATOR

It became apparent that it was the workshop which was potentially best suited to make the assessment the state public agencies needed for severely handicapped clients. Testing a handicapped person on real work following psychological tests could get a more accurate measure of his potential to work generally than psychological testing alone achieved. By recording his production, workshops could estimate the percent of standard production in industry he could achieve. By observing his work habits and behavior, they could measure his distance from satisfactory work adjustment. By observing and recording his performance and behavior over a period of time, they could measure his ability to improve in both. These ratings of employ- ability and of capacity to improve were invaluable to the state agencies. Subsequent experience showed that they purchased this service from workshops in greater amounts than any other single service.

THE WORKSHOP AS CONDITIONER AND ADJUSTOR

Another problem facing the rehabilitation counselor was that handicapped persons who were well trained in occupational skills sometimes lost their jobs because they could not produce enough or they could not adjust to the requirements of work. Here again workshops were best suited to handle these problems. Their abilities varied. Some workshops were best able to engender work efficiency and productivity, some specialized in work adjustment, and still others combined both capabilities. While the quality of workshop services differed from place to place, at any given location in the country the workshops were often the best resource in the community to handle the problems of the ineffective and maladjusted handicapped worker.

THE WORKSHOP AS AN AGENT OF THE
STATE VOCATIONAL REHABILITATION AGENCY

Although the workshops were needed by the state vocational rehabilitation programs, the high cost of the assessment and adjustment programs made them difficult to finance. Assessment costs in particular were high, since the individual often remained in the shop for a brief period during which time his productivity was low. Income for these or other purchased services was uncertain, since the state agencies usually paid on an individual fee-for-service basis at the time. Workshops were often unable to establish the desired services unless they could support them with their own earnings from work income or from private charitable grants. Since private grants were infrequent, it became apparent that public government grants to workshops would be necessary if the workshops were to meet the needs of the state programs.

In response to these needs and others of vocational rehabilitation generally, Congress passed the Vocational Rehabilitation Amendments of 1954. The Act provided that federal funds could be made available to private nonprofit workshops through or with the approval of the state agencies for specific purposes and for limited times. Two direct methods of providing assistance were set up: "extention and improvement" projects when state agencies were authorized to enter into joint projects with workshops, and "establishment" grants whereby buildings could be expanded and modified and new equipment provided to develop additional workshop capacity. More useful, however, were the research and demonstration project grants, which paid the cost of staff in new programs. The selected demonstration projects, in particular, were of great importance in developing services. They enabled workshops to start new programs based on prototype projects developed elsewhere. The recently established workshops for the mentally retarded benefited greatly from the special demonstration projects.

The purpose of the projects funded under the 1954 amendments was to create new or additional services for the use of state vocational rehabilitation agencies. Thus, workshops funded under most provisions of the amendments committed their programs to performing adjunctive or supplementary services for state agencies. They often served primarily handicapped persons sponsored by state agencies because these brought in additional money.

As agents of the state programs, they tailored their programs to serve handicapped persons sent them by those agencies. These were in the main individuals who could benefit by relatively short-term services and could then be expected to move into competitive employment or productive employment in workshops. Thus, large numbers of severely handicapped individuals who had not been able to work productively previously were able to engage in employment as a result of the state agency — private workshop partnership. However, workshops in the state agency orbit did not as a rule develop long-term programs for the most severely handicapped, who needed to remain in workshops for an extended or indefinite period of time without the prospect of substantial earnings.

THE WORKSHOP AND LONG-TERM
REHABILITATION SERVICES

Not all workshops receiving state-federal funds were dependent on such support for a major portion of their finances. One group of large workshops who received state-federal funds also developed considerable private charitable financial support. Some of these workshops used private funds to develop rehabilitation programs for handicapped persons needing services of long-term or indefinite duration. Another group which received little or no public money also maintained long-term rehabilitation programs. These two groups provided extended employment to individuals to improve their functioning at work in the shop and their physical and mental health.

Thus, workshops played a number of roles in vocational rehabilitation. Many workshops' efforts were primarily ancillary to the state vocational rehabilitation programs. Some workshops which were agents for the state agencies operated short-term services for potentially productive individuals referred by state agencies and also operated independently financed long-term rehabilitation services for individuals with little productive potential. Other workshops provided primarily long-term rehabilitation services to handicapped persons with low productive potential and little connection with state agencies.

THE WORKSHOP AS A SOCIAL WELFARE AGENCY

Many organizations used the workshop to achieve objectives other than employment. Early workshops attempted to enhance the moral virtue of the poor or handicapped. Later sponsoring groups found that work in shops produced secondary social benefits such as better relationships with the families of the worker or more satisfactory social relationships generally. A few workshops were started as programs where the work place would be used as a base or "launching pad" from which desirable social welfare objectives could be achieved or social deterioration prevented.

The workshops which saw their role as that of solving social problems attempted to work with the same kinds of social problems that were undertaken in social welfare agencies. They used the background of the shop to bring these problems to the treatment level. Many handicapped persons of low intellect or who were socially deprived had family, personal, and social problems about which they were not willing to "talk" in the formal dyadic office setting, but they were eager to go to a workshop to work. There they felt more comfortable in revealing their problems to persons they got to know well over a long period of time in an informal work environment. Their problems could then be handled in an informal manner by persons they saw as related to the work process. The method was effective to the extent that it was compatible with the cultural or ethnic backgrounds of the handicapped persons served.

Another social welfare role played by some workshops is that of social prevention. It is like the role that Bertram Black, former director of Altro Workshop, envisions as "tertiary prevention" in mental health (3). For some persons, long-term employment in the shop produces social stability. When they leave the shop, they get into trouble, either landing in prisons or mental hospitals, or leading lives of petty crime, nomadism, alcoholism, or addiction. When they work in the shop, the social lapses are less frequent. The money they make is usually not great, but they find satisfaction in the workshop as a combined employment and social environment. Some have considered that these shops perform a custodial function. A more perceptive view is that these workshops engage in the role of social prevention of personal delinquency.

THE WORKSHOP AS EMPLOYER

The final role of the workshop is that of employer. In an economy where the objective of business is to make a profit, there are some handicapped and disadvantaged persons who do not produce enough to warrant employment. For these individuals, some workshops have provided an opportunity to work for wages, usually at rates commensurate with productivity. The role of the workshop as a provider of long-term employment has existed since the first workshop began in the United States and will probably continue as long as the present socioeconomic form of organization exists in the United States.

The nonprofit workshops providing employment for handicapped persons should be distinguished from the profit-making companies in the United States who hire disabled persons exclusively. The latter employ disabled persons whose productivity has not been hampered greatly by their disability. These companies benefit by their lack of prejudice against disabled persons to acquire good employees who cannot find work elsewhere because of the unwarranted prejudices of other business organizations. The nonprofit workshops should also be distinguished from units of disabled workers in industrial plants which generally hire nondisabled persons. These disabled workers are also able to produce at average levels of expectancy.

The workshop which emphasizes employment trains persons for jobs in the shop and also provides secondary benefits of a social nature. It sometimes makes allowances for workers which are not tenable in a profit-making organization. Its main role, however, is to provide work for pay. Its most important by-product is the dignity and satisfaction it provides its workers. Some social theorists have suggested ways that money can be provided to substitute for wages, but there appears to be no adequate substitutes which have been suggested for the satisfactions handicapped persons secure from working as productively as they can.

NOTES

1. Cubberly, E. P.: Public Education in the United States. Boston, Houghton Mifflin Company, 1934.
2. ten Broek, J. and Matson, Floyd: Hope Deferred, Public Welfare and the Blind. Berkeley and Los Angeles, University of California Press, 1959, pp. 249-268.
3. Black, B. J.: A workshop in a changing world. Rehabilitation Literature, August, 1965.

II

THE ORIGIN OF WORKSHOPS

THE ORIGINATORS – OUR EUROPEAN ANTECEDENTS

DURING most of history, society not only refused to give handicapped persons the help they needed, but discriminated against them. Physical prowess and mental agility were essential in man's early struggle for survival, wealth, and power. The handicapped could not contribute readily to primitive society's most urgent needs, and as a consequence were generally treated with cruelty or contempt. In primitive and ancient times they were destroyed, sold as slaves, or allowed to become beggars. The few exceptions were those who excelled in the arts, philosophy or religion. In some Asian countries, special occupations were reserved for them. However, most handicapped persons have had little chance of leading rewarding lives.

In Europe during the Middle Ages, man's attitude toward the handicapped changed from general hostility and contempt to charity and benevolence. Many handicapped persons were beggars and others received alms from religious organizations. Some lived in asylums or hospitals where they were given work. The most famous of these was the Quinze Vingts, which was established for the blind in Paris in 1254. At the end of the sixteenth century St. Vincent de Paul established workshops where the old and infirm were given work to ameliorate their physical condition and to enliven their spirits. These establishments may be considered the first workshops, since they were the first to provide work programs designed to benefit the handicapped.

With the breakdown of the feudal economy and the loss of the minimal security it provided people, the burden of providing poor relief from voluntary offerings proved too great for the religious institutions of Western Europe. Local government was faced with the problem of providing for the poor, both "sturdy" and

24

"impotent." During the first quarter of the sixteenth century, leading thinkers addressed themselves to the problems of the poor and disabled. John Major in France, Martin Luther in Germany, and Ulrich Zwingli in Switzerland developed new theories for the care of the poor. The most influential, however, was the Spanish humanist, Juan Luis Vives. In 1526, he published *On the Subvention of the Poor,* in which he held that recipients of assistance should be put to useful employment as a contribution to their support.

Vives' ideas were accepted widely in Western Europe. His principles were applied with modifications in England in the seventeenth and eighteenth centuries. Local communities established houses of correction, working schools, workhouses or houses of industry. Planned for the unemployed poor, these included some disabled. The purpose of these establishments in most instances was to discourage the poor from seeking assistance and, when seeking it was unavoidable, to require them to contribute their labor to its cost. The workhouses existed more to relieve the local treasuries than to help the handicapped or other poor. When they are classified as workshops this distinction should be made. They were not workshops for the handicapped in the sense that they were operated in the interest of the handicapped.

In 1784, Valentin Haüy, influenced by the revolutionary ideas about the rights of man, established a school and workshop for the blind in Paris. His purpose was to train the blind in skills that would enable them to earn a living after leaving the school and shop. Although he was not successful in his industrial objectives, his intent to help blind men and women lead rewarding lives through training for employment marks his effort as a notable attempt to establish a workshop operated in the interest of the handicapped. Haüy's example was followed in other countries on the continent of Europe, in the United Kingdom, and later led to the establishment of the first workshop for the blind in the United States of America.

Though Haüy's influence benefited the blind in the United States, it did not carry over to persons with other handicaps. The force of American social philosophy and customs worked against the establishment of constructive workshop programs for the handicapped in the early history of the United States. Until the second half of the twentieth century, no national government financial support was available for workshops. The initiation of workshop programs was to depend upon small, dedicated groups of private individuals who were interested in helping persons with special disabilities or in the salvation of impoverished, troubled, or socially disadvantaged persons.

THE FIRST AMERICAN WORKSHOPS

Workshops for the Blind

The first workshops in the United States were started in connection with schools for the blind following English and continental precedents. After the founding of Haüy's school in Paris, six institutions for the blind were started in the United Kingdom from 1791 to 1827. Those at Edinburgh and Dublin had workshops (1). The next decade saw three schools for the blind established in the United States: the New York Institute for the Blind, the Pennsylvania Institute for the Blind, and the Perkins Institution for the Blind near Boston, Massachusetts. All three schools tried workshop programs. The shops at the Pennsylvania and New York schools were given up after a number of years, but the Perkins workshop lasted 114 years until 1951 (2).

The workshop at the Perkins Institute was the first in the United States. It was founded by Samuel Gridley Howe, a physician, who was the first director at Perkins. Before starting the school, Howe traveled in the United Kingdom and on the continent to visit schools for the blind. In 1837, he brought to Perkins a blind instructor from the Edinburgh Institute for the Blind, John Pringle. Pringle was probably the first workshop director in the United States. Under his supervision, the shop manufactured mattresses, cushions, pillows, brushes, brooms, chair bottoms (caning) and floor mats. The products found a market and the shop set off to a good start (3). Pringle's first workers were the young students at the school. In 1840, adults were allowed to work at the shop, and some of them resided at the school.

Howe's purpose in establishing the shop was to train the blind so that they could work in their home communities. However, he found that the blind workers preferred to remain in the shop where they could work and live under the same roof. In 1851, he established a separate shop a few blocks away from the school and required that the workers live away from the institution. In this he was successful, but the blind still failed generally to find jobs in private industry (4).

The subsequent history of the shop is a record of recurrent financial troubles. In 1851, Howe arranged to have the shop run as a private venture by its manager, but this arrangement was given up after a few years' trial. The shop lost money on its industrial operations. The losses varied from ten cents for every dollar of wages paid to one dollar for every dollar of wages paid. The losses vexed the trustees, whose main interest was in the original objectives of educating the young blind students. In 1935, legislation was passed in Massachusetts giving blind-made products preference in state and local government purchases. This aid increased the volume of business, but losses continued (5), and the shop was finally closed in 1951.

In spite of the financial difficulties at Perkins, and the closing of the shops in New York and Pennsylvania, other schools for the blind in Maryland, Illinois, and Louisiana established workshops in the second half of the nineteenth century. Like Perkins and the schools in New York and Pennsylvania, they suffered similar financial losses and ultimately gave up their shops. It became apparent that private schools for the blind were not successful in operating and financing workshops (6). As a rule, future workshops for the blind were not connected with schools for the blind.

The first workshop for the blind operated independently of a school was the Pennsylvania Working Home for Blind Men, established by Hinman Hall at Philadelphia in 1874. Its objectives were stated as "the organization of Workshops and a Home for homeless Blind Mechanics, teaching useful trades to blind persons, giving employment also to those blind men who leave homes, and the selling of manufactures." The first "manufactures" were brooms, mattresses, harnesses, rugs, and "segars." The Workingman's Home served as an example for many future workshops for the blind. Hall had been influenced not by Howe and the Perkins' experience, but by his teacher, William Chapin, principal of the Pennsylvania School for the Blind at Overbrook (7).

Chapin had been corresponding with Elizabeth Gilbert, a blind woman who started the first English workshop independent of a school in London in 1854. Previous shops had served primarily graduates of the schools. Chapin championed the idea of an independent workshop. Hall carried it out by starting a workshop which manufactured products, as did the English and continental shops, but he added a sales appeal by selling them as "blind-made" products (8). Chapin also stressed the need for homes for the blind. Hall combined the ideas of a workshop and a home into a working home. He thus set a precedent which was followed for many decades. In doing so, he rejected the advice of Howe (9). Apparently, experience has shown that Howe was right. Institutional residence in work homes has not proven desirable for most blind persons, and the practice has diminished.

The workshops which have been described were operated with money raised principally from private sources. The first workshop financed entirely by public funds was the Industrial Home of Mechanic Trades for the Blind in Oakland, California, established by the California Legislature, March 5, 1885 (10). A study had been made previously by a committee, which crossed the Isthmus of Panama and sailed by ship to Philadelphia to visit the Pennsylvania Working Home for Blind Men. The committee took sketches of the arrangement of the machinery at the Working Home and made what is probably the first workshop layout in the United States (11).

Soon after the study was made, the "Regan Place" in Oakland, a house of eighteen rooms with barn and stable, was obtained and on August 10, 1888, the first blind men were admitted to the home. It was not to be "an asylum, but rather as a school from which many may graduate in rotation." One of the first students, Joseph Jenkinson, "showed such great aptitude for broom making he returned to Santa Cruz to go into business for himself." In December 1887, the notation was made that "five men are now engaged outside the home" (12). Yet in the same year, the governor of California stated the home "has not achieved its original objectives" (13). The objective was the preparation of the blind for an occupation in industry.

With the advent of the California shop in Oakland, later to be called the California Industries for the Blind, the national pattern of private and public workshops for the blind was established. By 1900, several more workshops for the blind were started, and by 1920, twenty more were established (14). In 1934, there were about seventy specialized industrial establishments for the blind in the United States (15). As far as can be ascertained, their objectives appear similar: to provide training in occupational skills to enable the blind to find employment in industry, and when outside industrial placement proves impossible, to provide employment in the shop so that the blind may earn wages for their support. It appears that the shops were often not successful in achieving the first purpose. There is no indication that the numbers placed in industry were large. Probably most of the shops became places where the blind found employment. Nor does it appear that the blind were always able to support themselves from their wages. When the public assistance costs and the subsidies to the workshop are totaled, the savings to the public were not usually impressive. Thus, with the exception of some in industrial training schools, the early workshops for the blind in the main became providers of homes and sheltered employment or of sheltered employment (16).

Providing employment in workshops for the blind first required work to be done and second, money to cover the operating deficits. Money was usually forthcoming for the blind, sometimes from public sometimes from private sources, though getting it was not always easy. Work was more difficult to obtain, and in the first quarter of the twentieth century, the workshops made few products in small quantities (17). Many of the products had been copied from those made in the workshops of Europe in the nineteenth century (18). Although much discussion took place about occupations for the blind (19), as a rule the familiar few products were maintained as staples with infrequent attempts to increase the number of products. Finally in 1938, the friends of the blind, led by the American Foundation for the Blind, prevailed upon Congress to pass the Wagner-O'Day Act, which made it mandatory upon government to purchase designated products from workshops for the blind (20).

The purpose of the Wagner-O'Day Act was to bring orders for products purchased by the federal government into the shops so that more blind persons could be employed. To funnel the government orders into the shops, a private nonprofit organization, the National Industries for the Blind, was created. It handled the orders for products listed on the schedule of blind-made products. As the number of products listed on the schedule increased, the shops developed skills in manufacturing to government specifications. These skills were then used in making products for other markets. The improved efficiency resulted in higher wages for blind workers. The National Industries for the Blind reported that the average hourly wages of employees in affiliated workshops was 1.67 dollars per hour in 1969 (21).

Many of the smaller workshops did not affiliate with the National Industries for the Blind. In 1961, there were approximately 120 workshops for the blind, employing nearly 4900 workers, of which the majority were blind (22). In June 1969, the shops affiliated with the National Industries for the Blind numbered sixty-five, and they employed more than 4500 blind workers (23). Both groups trained the blind for jobs in industry but they were primarily places of employment for blind people. It was this group of 120 workshops that gained preeminence in the public conception of workshops and first led to acceptance of the label of "sheltered workshop" as the traditional designation for workshops for the handicapped.

In the 1960's, the shops affiliated with the National Industries for the Blind expanded their products considerably and have initiated new marketing methods such as rack-selling of Skilcraft products. Principal additions have been in the consumer products such as whisk brooms, sponge mops, clothes lines, plastic dust pans, fly swatters, and dish glow cloths. New items were added to the schedule of blind-made products such as construction workers' aprons, tool bags, helmet covers, litter covers, field pack suspenders, and disposable paper pillow cases. On April 16, 1968, the General Services Administrator committed the United States Government to purchase all its ballpoint pens and ballpoint pen refills from the NIB shops. These approximated seventy million annually worth 3,300,000 dollars. In addition, the government gave the NIB a contract for one million sanitation hats for civil defense. Also, the Industries has developed extensive subcontracts with major industrial firms including IBM, Proctor & Gamble, Boeing, General Electric, American Sugar Refining, Schenleys, Seagrams, National Distillers, and Eaton Manufacturing Company (24).

In the 1960's there was also a movement to bring more rehabilitation services into the workshop because of a changing emphasis in this direction together with support from state rehabilitation agencies in the form of training fees (25). Thus both in range of products and in rehabilitation services, blind workshops have expanded in recent years. However, not all workshops for the blind have experienced these changes. A group still works with the traditional products. A substantial number lack rehabilitation services. The latter are places where blind persons can work indefinitely under uninspiring conditions with little challenge.

THE RENOVATORS – SPIRITUAL AND MATERIAL

Four religious organizations seeking to bring about the salvation of the poor and handicapped early saw the need to meet the material needs of the destitute first, and for this reason they began to engage in the collection, renovation, and distribution of old clothing and household furnishings. As a result of these activities, they developed services for handicapped persons and probably have served more of them than all other workshops combined, They are the Society of St. Vincent de Paul, the Salvation Army, the Volunteers of America, and the Goodwill Industries of America. Later the Deseret Industries of the Church of Jesus Christ of Latter-Day Saints joined in providing similar services.

The Society of St. Vincent de Paul

The first national religious society in the United States which aided needy and handicapped persons through use of discards was probably the Society of St. Vincent de Paul. The Society had been founded in Paris by Frederic Ozanam in 1833, and in 1845, the first conference, or local service unit, was started in St. Louis, Missouri. Another was started in New York City the following year, and others followed in Buffalo, Milwaukee, and New Orleans. The rules of the Society stated that each conference was to have "the keeper of the clothes room" and these early local units gave old clothes to poor people. It is not known when the "central clothes rooms" gave way to the larger Salvage Bureau. In Philadelphia in 1911, the Salvage Bureau had forty fulltime employees. In Detroit in 1917, the Central Clothes Bureau had four stores and gave away 31,500 articles in response to 3,881 requests. By 1963, the Society had salvage bureaus in fifty-one cities with more than 118 stores (26).

The purpose of the Society is to help the needy both spiritually and materially. Much stress is placed on Ozanam's admonition that giving humiliates the poor unless accompanied by respect. Those who could afford to pay for the articles made available by the Society were charged a token or nominal price according to their resources. As a result of this policy, a business of collecting, cleaning, and repairing household discards grew up, though the extent to which repairing was done varied from conference to conference. In any case, these activities required the services of full-time paid employees. In 1963, the salvage bureaus employed 1,335 permanent employees. Of this number, forty-nine were handicapped and the rest were hired because they were needy or had skills essential to the operations. Besides these, there were the sales people and other employees of the stores. Stores in the western region alone employed 1,403 persons, of which 549 were handicapped (27). Though some training took place in the large salvage operations, in general, the conferences provided employment for needy and handicapped persons as a by-product of the Society's mission to help the poor.

The Salvation Army

Whereas the Society of St. Vincent de Paul got into the collection and distribution of discards gradually in response to the needs of the poor for clothes and household furnishings, a second religious organization became renovators of discards on the basis of a predetermined blueprint. The plan was visualized by William Booth, the English founder and first General of the Salvation Army. In 1891, he published *In Darkest England and the Way Out,* in which he described far-reaching remedies for many of the social and economic ills of the world. To attack the employment problems of the poor he proposed an interrelated system of shelter depots, household salvage bureaus, and cooperative industrial factories and villages (28).

Booth's industrial experiments were not successful, but his ideas about the salvage of discards proved sound. He proposed to establish in every city a force of organized collectors who would pick up discards from receptacles placed for their disposal. He refused to compete with the Sisters of the Poor or others who were collecting household articles. "The unoccupied wilderness of waste," he said, "is wide enough an area for the operations of our brigade." The collected items were to be cleaned and repaired and given or sold to the poor. Thus work was to be created for those who wanted to work and could not find employment. He laid to rest the argument that the renovation of discards would diminish the demand for new goods by pointing out that economy is a spur to trade as the money saved on the reclaimed articles would be expended for other products (29).

The Salvation Army had been established in the United States for eleven years when William Booth wrote *In Darkest England* for the guidance of the world activities of the Army. His son, Ballington Booth, who headed the Salvation Army in the United States at the time, followed his father's suggestions, and the first shelter depot was established in an old church at Bedford and Downing Streets in New York City in 1891. Another began in Buffalo, New York, two years later. Following Ballington Booth's resignation in 1896, Fred Booth-Tucker became General, and undertook a vigorous "Work for the Workless Program." Men with push carts were sent out in New York to collect paper and salvagable materials. The success of Booth-Tucker's push led other units to start new salvage brigades. By 1898, salvage operations had been added in Chicago, Illinois; Waterbury, Connecticut; Houston, Texas; San Francisco, California; and Seattle,

Washington (30).

As the salvage collections grew, a system of stores was developed to sell the articles. In 1929, there were thirty-five stores in New York City alone. The salvage operations proved profitable and provided considerable sums for the other charitable activities of the organization (31). In time the salvage operations, the stores, and the shelter depots were combined to form the Men's Social Service Centers. There homeless, troubled men were helped to work out their personal problems. To gain their board and room, the men worked in the salvage operations. In 1965, there were 144 such centers in the United States.

William Booth's main purpose was to help troubled people find salvation. He considered the work provided in the salvage operations as a means toward that objective. He made it a rule that the men were not paid for their work but were provided room and board at the shelters. When they found the strength to face their problems, they were expected to make their own way in the world (32). The Salvation Army in the United States has followed the spirit of his rule, though the men have been given gratuities for incidentals, and some have later been hired as employees at regular wages. The Salvation Army may be considered to have operated the first work program in the United States which announced a policy that limited the worker's stay to a time when an objective was accomplished (33). However, as the Men's Social Service Centers accepted only homeless and unattached men who needed shelter as well as rehabilitative services, they became places of help for men with alcoholic and other personal problems. In 1961, they served 57,000 men, of whom about 80 percent were alcoholics. This number may be contrasted with the estimated 20,000 to 30,000 men with drinking problems treated in all outpatient clinics in the United States in 1959. While these statistics are not precise, they tend to reinforce the conjecture that the centers serve more alcoholics than any other organization in the United States (34).

The Volunteers of America

The third organization which used a program of renovation and resale of discarded material to provide work for disadvantaged and needy men was the Volunteers of America. In 1895, Ballington Booth, then head of the Salvation Army in the United States, was ordered by his father, William Booth, to leave his post and report for a transfer to a new assignment. Rather than to obey the order, Ballington Booth resigned from the Salvation Army in 1896 and subsequently founded the Volunteers of America (35). He carried over into the new organization many of the principles and methods of the Salvation Army. As a result the salvage program of the Volunteers of America has had many similarities with that of the Salvation Army.

The first salvage program of the Volunteers of America began in Bridgeport, Connecticut, in 1899, when Bacheller and Speer started the first "Industrial Home." Men who applied "were obliged to work in the woodyard as a test of their worthiness" for which they got a meal and a night's lodging. They were also given clothing when necessary. In the first year, eighty-nine men were given employment (36). Subsequently, work programs were started in Philadelphia, Chicago, Baltimore, Easton, Pennsylvania, and Portland, Oregon. By 1952, there were sixty-eight salvage programs in the United States operated by the Volunteers of America.

While the programs of Volunteers of America were similar to those of the Salvation Army, and there is the same emphasis on spiritual guidance, there appears to be more emphasis in later years on developing skills among the men in the salvage programs. For example, training in cabinetmaking, upholstery, and radio repair has been given. Apparently, the brief-stay policy of the early years gave way to longer stays during which men learned skills.

The Goodwill Industries of America

Edgar James Helms, who founded the Goodwill Industries of America, lived to see the organization he started serve more disadvantaged persons than any other workshop organization in the United States. In 1895, he was called to the ministry of the Morgan Chapel in Boston, a church made famous by Henry Morgan who was a dedicated but unorthodox pastor who had spent his life fighting vice, ignorance, and poverty. Helms soon became convinced that something had to be done to relieve the awful conditions of misery and poverty of the people of the slum neighborhood where the church was located if they were to lead religious lives. His approach, though similar to his predecessors, differed in the added emphasis which he placed on the necessity of finding or creating work which would provide income for the impoverished as an alternative to charity or public assistance (37).

During the first years of his ministry, Helms had been able to raise money from the rich of Boston and with it buy clothes and household necessities for the poor. During the depression of 1902, larger numbers of unemployed, desperate people came to him for help. When he turned to the rich for help, he found that they were no longer able to give money as freely, so he asked them for their unneeded clothing. The story is told that Helms walked the streets of Boston with a burlap sack over his shoulder, filling it with cast-off clothing. After a conductor refused to let him on the street car because of the size of his pack, he took to carrying his discards in a wheelbarrow. In any case, he collected a large supply of clothes and scattered them on the pews of his church. He then invited the poor to come and take what they wanted. The riot which ensued convinced him that there should be a more dignified way to make clothes available to the poor. He subsequently started a small store where for a token price any one could choose to buy any article available.

Yet, providing clothing alone did not solve the many other problems of the poor. Many of them came to Helms for help in getting work. Since jobs were not available, he put them to work on the discards he collected. He wrote, "We gave work to the poor people by having them cleanse, renovate, and make new articles from our old ones sent in. We sold these for small sums to the poor, and used the income to pay wages to the destitute whose labors made these articles serviceable. In this way began our Goodwill Industries (38).

Helms's decision to pay wages to the workers from the income on the sale of the articles had far-reaching consequences. It meant that the wages paid had a relationship to the value which the labor added to the articles sold. Consequently, good business practice had to be honored. To help him, he enlisted Fred C. Moore, a business man, who became his right-hand man. Helms thus early combined social conscience with business acumen to create "a business with a heart," and set the example of blending business and humanitarian skills which has proven essential to effective and financially sound workshop programs in the United States.

Helms encountered financial problems and the opposition of some people who disapproved of his methods, but in general, his public support grew and his operations expanded. In 1905, the reconditioning program was incorporated as the Morgan Memorial Cooperative Industries and Stores. He had laid a firm foundation for his programs, and his lead set an example which future Goodwill Industries could follow.

The first organization to follow his example was the Mission Society of Brooklyn. In 1915, the Mission Society set up a similar program and called it the Goodwill Industries.

Similar programs named Goodwill Industries were started in San Francisco and St. Louis in 1916, and in Los Angeles in 1917. In 1918, the Methodist Century Campaign raised money to start Goodwill programs in thirty-five cities in the United States. To promote this expansion the Bureau of Goodwill Industries of the Board of Missions of the Methodist Church was established, and Helms was made its executive-secretary. By 1923, there were twenty-six Goodwill Industries in the United States, and by 1934 there were fifty-six.

The depression of the early 1930's and the extensive unemployment which followed resulted in more adequate federal and state programs for the relief of destitution in the United States. With this development the Goodwill Industries shifted their emphasis towards helping handicapped and the aged and other disadvantaged persons. In previous years the needy had been taught skills in the repair of shoes, clothes, furniture and household appliances. Now the handicapped were taught these skills. With this new development, the state vocational rehabilitation programs began using Goodwill Industries as training facilities. Around the middle of the twentieth century, some Goodwill Industries added subcontracting activities to their programs, diversifying and increasing the number of training and work opportunities which were available. The handicapped trained in Goodwill Industries, got jobs in industry, or remained as employees.

The diversification of the types of activities in the Goodwill Industries and their use of training facilities by other organizations led to further expansion of services to more persons and in many instances to more comprehensive programs. From Helms's small start in 1902, the Goodwill Industries had by 1968 grown to a chain of 135 workshops serving the largest number of handicapped persons in a single workshop organization in the United States. That year, Goodwill Industries provided help to 91,596 persons, of which 63,637 received rehabilitation services, 45,152 were provided employment in Goodwills, and 6,629 were placed in industry. Total wages paid to handicapped persons amounted to 35,286,916 dollars (39). It had changed from an evangelical missionary society manned principally by ministers to a vocationally oriented service organization staffed by industrial and rehabilitation specialists. Still it adhered to its spiritual goals in its religious services. Its success may be attributed to its principal emphasis upon realistic solutions to the practical problems of earning a living.

The Deseret Industries

In the history of the westward expansion of the United States, no episode is more stirring than the settlement of the arid, uninhabited sections of the western United States by the pioneers of the Church of Jesus Christ of the Latter Day Saints. After establishing themselves in Salt Lake City, Utah, they established prosperous settlements through Utah and in Idaho and Arizona. A tenet of their belief was to take care of the unfortunate among their church members, and this led to informal social programs in the beginning and later to a formal organization of the welfare program in 1936. The primary purpose of the welfare program was to set up a system "under which the curse of idleness would be done away with, the evils of a dole abolished, and independence, industry, thrift, and self-respect be once more established among our people. The aim of the Church is to help the people to help themselves" (40). To carry out these principles, the Church engaged in business projects to provide work for its people and in 1938 established the Deseret Industries.

The basic objective of the Deseret Industries has been to provide useful work opportunities for Church members who, through age, physical, mental or other handicaps, are unable to obtain gainful employment in regular industry. The program was patterned after the Goodwill Industries. In 1966, there were eight separate Deseret Industries. Four were in Utah at Salt Lake City, Ogden, Provo, and Logan. Two were in California, at Colton and Los Angeles. The two others were at Mesa, Arizona, and Pocatello, Idaho. In 1963, the Deseret Industries served 661 persons.

THE EARLY FREESTANDING WORKSHOPS

About two decades after the Society of St. Vincent de Paul started its first service unit, and before the Salvation Army came to the United States, a local society in Boston dedicated to moral purpose started a workshop for the needy. The workshop ultimately became the Community Workshops of Boston.

The leader of the group was Mrs. James T. Fields, a woman prominent in the social and cultural life of Boston. In 1877, she organized a group of citizens which took the name of the "Co-operative Society of Visitors among the Poor in Boston." The society's purpose was "the amelioration, moral and physical, of the poor, by teaching them habits of temperance and cleanliness, giving sewing to poor women from a workroom and finding employment for men." As part of its program the society established a workroom where the women did hand sewing (41).

For their sewing the women were paid wages. It was possible to work at home as well as in the shop. Mrs. Field's visitors brought the work to those unable to come to the shop. Training in sewing skills was given by the superintendent of the workroom. Placement on a casual basis was done by the visitors. The shop used a "work test" to determine willingness to work and a method of developing capacity, imparting instruction, and fostering habits of industry. The questions used in the test were, Is a girl persistent and regular in her work? Is she patient in learning to sew? Is she willing to redo poor work? Is she neat in appearance, orderly with work materials, and respectful in demeanor? These questions suggest that the work test was quite different from the work trial in connection with public assistance programs or tests of occupational skill. It was probably the first instance of evaluation for work habits in a workshop in the United States (42).

In the beginning, wages were paid from charitable contributions and the clothing and sheets produced were given away free to needy families and to hospitals. Later when the shop experienced financial difficulties, the products were sold at less than cost. After a time, the original sponsors withdrew and the workshop became known as the Co-operative Workrooms. The work aspects of the program were emphasized and the visiting diminished in importance. In 1914, the shop introduced power sewing and subcontracts were brought into the shop. The purpose then was to train the handicapped for outside employment. In 1917, the name was changed to the Co-operative Workrooms for Handicapped Women. Hand sewing was eliminated. In 1939, the shop merged with the Christopher Shop to become Community Workshops, Inc. (43).

In 1942, another freestanding community workshop similar to the Boston Community Workshops was started in Binghamton, New York. The shop was typical of a number of industrially oriented workshops which started in the second quarter of the twentieth century and increased in numbers after 1950. The Sheltered Workshop for the Disabled, Inc., of Binghamton served principally physically handicapped in the beginning and later accepted limited numbers of persons with other disabilities. Its purpose was "to employ handicapped persons who are not capable of adjusting industrially on a competitive basis. To evaluate and train disabled persons to become capable of competitive employment by increasing physical improvement and endurance, developing interest, skills, work habits, and psychological adaptation (44).

By 1959, the shop had classified its workers as evaluatees, trainees, permanents, labor pool, and subsidy. The labor pool workers were those who had left the shop of their own accord but who were willing to work on a temporary basis. The subsidy group of workers were persons with severe disabilities, incapable of industrial production in the workshop setting, who work twenty hours a week every other week. Trainees and permanents received paid vacations and holidays, limited medical care insurance, health and accident insurance, life insurance, and Social Security participation. Subsidy workers received all the above except life insurance.

Some of the essential operating philosophy of the shop as stated in 1959 was as follows (45):

1. The same standards must be carried out that are found in business and industry.
2. A workshop must have the support of industry to survive.
3. Pity cannot be a part of any successful workshop program.
4. The entire program of the Sheltered Workshop cannot be generalized but must be shaped to fit the needs of the individual and the community.
5. Teach the handicapped worker that he must accept the responsibilities of a wage earner and a good citizen.
6. A workshop can be self-supporting, if operated on a business basis; that is, meeting production schedules, doing superior work, maintaining a low cost and low rate of rejection; in other words, doing a better than average job.
7. Measure success in terms of regained self-respect and independence of the disabled.

The Sheltered Workshop for the Disabled, Inc., of Binghamton as described in 1959, and the Community Workshops, Inc., of Boston as it existed in 1963, illustrate the form general service freestanding community workshops took in the United States. The community workshops served persons with all disabilities. They had varied industrial activities and a range of rehabilitation services without specialization in one or two. They offered a short-term stay with movement out of the shop, but they also provided long-term employment. These workshops were neither auxiliary to a resident institution such as an outpatient rehabilitation center, nor a unit of a national voluntary health or workshop agency. They were supported by charitable contributions from a variety of sources but derived most of their income from the work they did.

The community workshops did not achieve their characteristic features until about 1960. Because of their evolution from other types of workshops such as the workshops for the tubercular or development through combinations of existing workshops, it is difficult to identify them and determine their number. It is estimated that there were about forty-five in the United States in 1960 (46). They will probably increase both in number and in importance in the future.

THE WORK PROGRAMS FOR THE TUBERCULAR

Another group of local workshops which later served all disabilities were the workshops for the tubercular. They began as a result of an innovation in the use of work which was introduced in the early years of the twentieth century in programs for the tubercular. Workers in tuberculosis rehabilitation had ruefully observed ex-patients of hospitals and sanatoriums suffering recurrences of their disease because they were unable to stand the pressures of a full workday. Hence, programs were established to provide a graduated hardening to the requirements of work activities. The object was to develop in the worker a tolerance to work which would enable him to return to a job in industry without jeopardy to his health. The programs took place in both rural and urban settings.

In the first half of the twentieth century, rural programs in such places as Glen Lake in Minnesota, Saranac Lake in New York, and Lake Tomahawk in Wisconsin were operated under medical supervision. Work in connection with the facility or its environs was used to accustom the worker gradually to increasing activity. The outdoor work was usually in agricultural pursuits, sawmill or wood-cutting activities, grounds maintenance and mechanical repair or servicing. Some programs also had classes in occupational skills where work tolerance or conditioning was attempted. The Rutland Training Center did work-conditioning through skill training classes alone. Wages were not paid as a rule, though at Lake Tomahawk, a state facility, credit was given for labor up to the cost of maintenance.

As the drugs for treating tuberculosis became more effective towards the middle of the century, some of the organizations for the tubercular began serving other disabilities. Often their facilities were used for rehabilitation centers, vocational training centers, or workshops (47).

The typical pattern was to start the shop for the tubercular and gradually accept more of other disabilities. The urban workshops for the tuberculous, such as those at Boston, Hartford, New York and Honolulu, gradually took on activities more typical of other workshops in the United States. As they began serving persons with other disabilities, the emphasis on work tolerance gave way to a more comprehensive approach which included skill training, training in work habits, short- and long-term employment, and supportive services from professional staff.

The first urban workshop for the tubercular was the Altro Workshop in New York, established in 1915. Its initial purpose was to provide graduated work to prevent relapses in ex-patients who wished to remain in New York City. In 1948, it accepted persons with cardovascular conditions and applied to them work tolerance procedures similar to those used for the tubercular. In 1953, it began a rehabilitation program for mentally ill persons who needed a bridge from the mental hospital to private employment.

Edward Hochhauser, the first director of Altro Workshops, describes its program for the period to 1954 as follows:

> It is a scheme for hardening through productive work where the hazard of exacerbation of the disease is greatly reduced, and the psychological value of earning on a competitive basis is retained. It establishes the habits and rhythms of normal employment. Simulating industry in equipment methods, it provides work and rest under careful medical supervision. While it sells competively and pays prevailing union rates for work produced, it sacrifices economy in production for the welfare of its patients.

The work of the shop consisted mainly of garment manufacturing. It relied heavily on medical and supporting professional staff, principally social workers for decisions relating to its shops' workers. It was the recipient of a considerable subsidy from the New York Federation of Philanthropies (48).

After the introduction of mental patients in 1953, the shop developed a total approach which included the involvement with the person's medical condition, work and economic life, and family and social situation (49). A workshop for the tubercular whose history differed greatly from that of the Altro Workshop was the Sheltered Workshop of the Boston Tuberculosis Society. Starting in 1923, it found less need for services to the tubercular, and later admitted persons with many other types of disabilities, though the tubercular continued to be significant among their beneficiaries. It developed a program of work evaluating, training in work habits, and transition and sheltered employment. It relied heavily on "junior staff," a cadre of the most efficient of its handicapped workers. Under a federal certificate, it paid wages less than the minimum established for industry generally. It assumed the characteristics of a general service workshop such as the Boston Community Workshop. In 1962, the Boston Tuberculosis Society decided that the need for workshop services for the tubercular was not great enough to justify the money spent, and the shop was closed (50).

Another workshop which began as a program for the tubercular and subsequently proved very successful in serving all disabilities is Lanakila Crafts in Honolulu, Hawaii. Starting in 1939 with support from Oahu Tuberculosis and Health Association, it was incorporated in 1959 as an independent organization. It takes pride in being able to cover its operating costs from its sales and fees. In 1965, it served 394 physically and mentally handicapped persons.

Lanakila Crafts differs from most other workshops which started as shops for the tubercular in its emphasis on prime manufacturing for the retail trade rather than on subcontracts. Starting with the hula skirt, it manufactured more than forty curio products in 1964. It provides evaluation, personnel and work adjustment, sheltered employment, and placement. It is dedicated to the following philosophy: "There is perhaps no greater service than that which enables those needing help to help themselves (51).

In less populous areas, the workshops for the tubercular often took persons with other disabilities when they began. In New York State several were started. The workshop at Albany, New York, begun in 1955, took the tubercular as the largest single group, but it also served cardiacs and cerebral palsied; those with multidisabilities exceed the first three named groups in number. The program started with a work tolerance regime on medical prescription and followed with other services. The object was to move people on to competitive employment (52).

NOTES

1. Armatage, T. R.: The Education and Employment of the Blind. London, Harrison and Sons, 1886, pp. 93-102.
2. Best, H.: Blindness and the Blind in the United States. New York, MacMillan Co., 1934, pp. 310-311, 496. Hemphill, J. S.: The Perkins Institution Workshop. The Lantern, p. 3, December 15, 1951.
3. Hemphill, J. S., op.cit., pp. 3-4.
4. Ibid., p. 4. Best, op.cit., p. 496.
5. Hemphill, op.cit., pp. 4-6, 8.
6. Best, op.cit., pp. 499-500.
7. Barrett, R. E.: The Paths of Employment. Indianapolis, Speech to the American Association of Workers for the Blind, July, 1957, pp. 1-6.
8. Ibid., pp. 2-3. Armitage, op.cit., pp. 92-110, 125-157, 72.
9. Howe, S. G.: Report . . . 1894. Outlook for the Blind, pp. 43-45, April, 1908.
10. The Industrial Home for the Adult Blind, Its History While Under the Jurisdiction of a Board of Directors, 1885-1890. In files of the California Department of Rehabilitation, p. 1. Saunders, J.: Broom making, Outlook for the Blind, pp. 12-13, April, 1908.
11. Boston, R. (Pennsylvania Working Home for Blind Men): Personal communication, January 18, 1965.
12. The Industrial Home for the Adult Blind, op.cit., pp. 3-8.
13. Best, op.cit., p. 506.
14. Directory of Workshops for the Handicapped. Washington, Department of Health, Education, and Welfare, 1961.
15. Best, op.cit., p. 508.
16. Ibid., pp. 505-508.
17. Goodpasture, R. C.: Operation Bootstrap. New York, National Industries for the Blind, 1965, p. 2.
18. Armitage, op.cit., pp. 59-63, 92-109, 125-155.
19. Occupations for the blind. Outlook for the Blind, Vol. II, No. 1, p. 187; Vol. XXII, No. 3, pp. 33, 41, 37; Vol. XXIII, No. 3, p. 51.
20. 52 Stat. 1196; 41 U.S.C., 46-48, Goodpasture, op.cit., pp. 2-3.
21. Annual Report – 1969. New York, National Industries for the Blind, 1970.
22. Directory of Workshops for the Handicapped, op cit.
23. Annual Report – 1969, op.cit.
24. Annual Report – 1969, op.cit. Blind Manpower for Government and Industry. New York, National Industries for the Blind (undated). New Horizons for the Blind in American Industry. New York, National Industries for the Blind (undated).
25. Richterman, H. (of National Industries for the Blind): Personal communication, October 17, 1969.
26. Taylor, T. R.: How help can bring honor with giving. The Register, The St. Vincent de Paul Supplement Issue, p. 10, September 17, 1961.

27. Salvage Bureau Personnel. Society for St. Vincent de Paul Administrative Records, p. 2. Store Bureau Activities of the Society of St. Vincent de Paul in the Western Region. Western Region Administrative Records, April 24, 1963, pp. 1-2.
28. Booth, W.: In Darkest England and the Way Out. New York and London, Funk and Wagnalls, 1891, pp. 115-120.
29. Ibid., pp. 117-125.
30. Wisbey, H. A., Jr.: Soldiers without Swords. New York, MacMillan, 1955, pp. 1-128.
31. Sandull, R.: The History of the Salvation Army in the United States. 1883-1953. New York, Thomas Nelson and Sons, 1955, Vol. III, p. 127.
32. Booth, op.cit.,
33. Wisbey, op.cit., p. 103.
34. Katz, L.: The Salvation Army Men's Social Service Center, Quarterly Journal of Studies on Alcohol, p. 324, June, 1964.
35. Wisbey, H. A., Jr.: History of the Volunteers of America. Western Area Headquarters L. H. pp. 1-70, 1954. Wisbey, H. A.: Soldiers without Swords. New York, MacMillan, 1955, pp. 110-117. Sandull, op.cit., Vol. IV, pp. 335-359.
36. Quoted from Volunteers Gazette, March 3, 1900. In Wisbey, H. A., Jr.: History of the Volunteers of America, op.cit., p. 73.
37. The account of Dr. Helms's activities is taken mainly from Beatrice Plume's Edgar James Helms, The Goodwill Man, Minneapolis, T. S. Dennison, 1965, pp. 92-213.
38. Ibid., p. 129.
39. Foreword. Statistical Report, 1968. Washington, Goodwill Industries of America, 1969.
40. The Welfare Program of the Church of Jesus Christ of the Latter-Day Saints. Salt Lake City, The Church of Jesus Christ of the Latter-Day Saints, 1964.
41. McCann, R. V. (Ed.): Sheltered Work Shops in Massachusetts: A Descriptive and Functorial Study. Boston, Massachusetts Rehabilitation Commission on Vocational Rehabilitation Administration, 1963, pp. 158-159.
42. Ibid., pp. 159-160.
43. Ibid., pp. 163-164.
44. Seventeen Years of Progress. Binghamton, Sheltered Workshop for the Disabled, 1959, p. 3.
45. Ibid., pp. 16-20.
46. Directory of Workshops for the Handicapped, op.cit.
47. The story of these centers may be found in Pearce, K. R.: Rehabilitating the Tuberculous in Hennepin County. New York, National Tuberculosis Association, 1942, pp. 5-12. Holland, H.: Rehabilitation at Lake Tomahawk State Camp. New York, National Tuberculosis Association, 1945, pp. 1-32. White, H. L. and Maloney, R. T.: The Training Center

plan for the Rehabilitation of the Tuberculous at Rutland Training Center. New York, National Tuberculosis Association, 1946, pp. 1-5. McCann, R. V., op.cit., p. 1.

48. Hochhauser, E. and Henkel, C.: History, philosophy, and operations of the Altro Workshops. The British Journal of Physical Medicine, pp. 3-7, January, 1954.

49. Black, B.; Meyer, H. J. and Borgatta, E. F.: Altro Health and Rehabilitation Services: Case study of a protected workshop., the Journal of Social Issues Vol. XVI, No. 2, pp. 40-46, 1960.

50. McCann, op.cit., pp. 2-12.

51. Helping Hands to Help Themselves. Honolulu, Lanakila Crafts, 1964. Annual Report 1965. Honolulu, Lanakila Crafts, 1966.

52. Proceedings of the First Institute on Sheltered Workshops in New York. New York, State Committee on Tuberculosis and Public Health, 1957, pp. 13-15.

III

THE MIDDLE PERIOD-
THE EXPANSION OF WORKSHOPS

WORKSHOPS IN REHABILITATION CENTERS

IN the early decades of the twentieth century, while the already established types of workshops were growing in numbers and expanding their operations, a new idea about the way rehabilitation services for the handicapped could be organized gained acceptance in the United States. It was held that if most of the main services that a handicapped person needed would be given by one facility, he would benefit more than if services were given him by several organizations separately. The organization or place where the many services were to be given was called a rehabilitation center. As a result of this conception, many rehabilitation centers were started.

In 1964, 723 such facilities responded to an inquiry of the staff of the Directory of Rehabilitation Centers. However, few of these centers gave all the principal services needed. Most of them emphasized either medical services or vocational services, although psychological and social services were usually given as well. Of the 390 centers which completed the Directory of Rehabilitation Center's questionnaire, seventy-four had workshops (1).

The Vocationally Oriented Rehabilitation Center Workshops

The workshops in a vocational rehabilitation center whose origins go back farthest are those found in the Vocational Guidance and Rehabilitation Services of Cleveland, Ohio. As far back as 1890, the Sunbeam Circle, a group of volunteer women, held bazaars and sold their handiwork for the benefit of crippled children. In 1901 they started a kindergarten for young crippled children, and in 1910 they began the Wilson School for Crippled

Children, where older girls were taught sewing, and older boys, manual trades.

During the years between 1901 and 1910, the Sunbeam Circle experimented with summer school sewing classes to determine if a permanent sewing shop would be feasible. The products of the classes were sold at the club's bazaars, which later became known as the Sunbeam Sales. In 1915, the Sunbeam Circle set up a training and work room for sewing and a sales room. This work room and store is the ancestor of the workshops and sales program of the Vocational Guidance and Rehabilitation Services (2).

The Sunbeam Circle continued to expand its activities and in 1918 became the Association for the Crippled and Disabled. It accepted adults and its services became more comprehensive. By 1922, it included a social service department, the orthopedic center, and a homebound and workshop program, with wages based on productivity.

In 1933, Bell Greve became the director of the Association for the Crippled and Disabled. The services were increased and in 1939 the name was changed to the Cleveland Rehabilitation Center. In 1956, the Cleveland Rehabilitation Center and the Vocational Guidance Bureau of Cleveland were merged to form a new agency, the Vocational Guidance and Rehabilitation Services. In 1965, the center had four workshops which engaged in subcontracting and manufacturing of products. Their major purpose was to provide work evaluation and work adjustment. Medical evaluation, vocational and psychological testing, vocational counseling, physical therapy, vocational training, and home activities were available in the program. The shops provided work experiences and build-up for transition to employment.

The Institute for the Crippled and Disabled of New York

Soon after Sunbeam Circle set up their workshop in 1915, another vocational rehabilitation center was founded which was to play an important role in rehabilitation centers, the Institute for the Crippled and Disabled of New York. Founded in 1917 as the Red Cross Institute for the Crippled and Disabled, it achieved its own corporate identity in 1920. It developed a comprehensive program of medical, psychological, and vocational services and did much to spread the concept of a comprehensive rehabilitation. In 1927, it started a subcontract workshop. In 1937, power sewing was brought into the workshop. In the early years the workshop served large numbers of physically handicapped. In 1955, when it served 104 persons, the trend was to serve greater percentages of other disabilities and the more severely handicapped.

In 1965 it served 250 persons, taking persons with any disability except blindness, deafness, and mental retardation. The shop did principally subcontract work and paid its workers on a piece work basis. The principal operations were power sewing, fabrication processing and assembly, direct mail services, packaging heat sealing, inspection, collation, sorting, soldering, stapling, and banding and pasting. This work is utilized for vocational evaluation, work hardening and work adjustment, and vocational training (3).

The League for the Handicapped of Detroit

A third vocational rehabilitation center which operated a workshop as well as other rehabilitation programs has been the League for the Handicapped of Detroit. This voluntary agency was started in 1920 to help homebound and other physically handicapped persons. It began by selling products made by homebound persons but soon developed subcontracting and industrial salvage work programs for ambulatory physically handicapped persons. In the course of its history, it developed social services, a prevention of blindness service, a hearing center, and vocational adjustment and placement services. In 1964, it had several branch workshops including two in local hospitals. These served 262 handicapped persons. The organization served persons with all kinds of handicaps including the blind, the deaf, the mentally retarded, the epileptic, and the mentally ill (4).

THE MEDICAL REHABILITATION CENTER WORKSHOPS

Shortly after the vocational rehabilitation centers began starting workshops, another group of rehabilitation centers began including workshops in their facilities. These were the private, voluntary rehabilitation centers which emphasized medical procedures as a means of restoring handicapped persons to their fullest potential. Most of these centers which included workshops were outpatient centers. They fell generally into three groups: those operated by units affiliated with the National Society for Crippled Children and Adults, those called Curative Workshops and having similar characteristics, and those operated by independent groups of citizens that were not affiliated with any national organization nor followed any national pattern of organization.

The Easter Seal Workshops

The largest number by far were affiliates of the National Society for Crippled Children and Adults. The first unit of this organization was founded by Edgar F. Allen in Elyria, Ohio, after the death of his child because of lack of medical care. In 1908, he was able to start a hospital and to secure care for crippled children. He interested the Rotary Clubs of Ohio in his project. In 1918, the Ohio Society for Crippled Children and Adults was established. The program spread and in 1921, the National Society for Crippled Children and Adults was started. Societies for Crippled Children and Adults, after 1934 sometimes called Easter Seal Societies, raised money from private contributions to provide medical care for the physically handicapped, established medical facilities, operated homebound programs, and financed research in disabling conditions (5).

In the 1940's and 1950's many of the societies began establishing workshops. Sometimes they established workshops which existed alone without connections with rehabilitation centers. An early example was the establishment of the Lawrence L. Frank Sheltered Workshop in Los Angeles in 1947. The workshops sponsored by the Alabama Society for Crippled Children and Adults with the cooperation of the State Vocational Rehabilitation Agency was a later example of a group of Easter Seal workshops without rehabilitation center affiliation.

The majority of Easter Seal sponsored workshops were parts of outpatient rehabilitation centers which provided medical services.

These workshops usually did subcontract work for private employers. Originally, they served principally physically handicapped persons who were receiving or had received services from the rehabilitation centers. Sometimes the handicapped person spent only part of his day in the workshop while receiving various therapies in the rehabilitation center. The position of the workshop in the organizational structure varied, but it usually started out as an additional unit of the rehabilitation center, and later achieved a more independent position.

The 1964 Directory of Rehabilitation Facilities shows seventy-one rehabilitation centers affiliated with the National Society for Crippled Children and Adults. Of these, sixty-one had vocational programs, in which there were approximately twenty-five workshops. There are no exact figures for numbers of persons served; however, if the Department of Labor average in certificated shops is used as a base, there were approximately nine hundred certificated persons served in these workshops in 1964 (6). The National Society reported that there were twenty-nine workshops in comprehensive rehabilitation centers in the spring of 1966. There were another twenty-one Easter Seal affiliated workshops which were not part of a comprehensive center. These twenty-one Easter Seal workshops were serving 1300 handicapped persons in 1966 (7).

Workshops in the "Curative Workshops"

A second group of medically oriented centers were the "Curative Workshops." They were started soon after the first World War. They took their names from the curative workshop instruction units of physical reconstruction sections of military hospitals which were called "Curative-Workshops" (8). They were not usually workshops, although they later included workshops in their programs. They provided outpatient restorative medical services at first and later added social, psychological, and vocational programs.

The first was the Curative Workshop of Milwaukee, Wisconsin. It was started in 1919 by Mrs. Elizabeth Davis, and the Milwaukee Junior League, a women's voluntary service organization. In the early years it provided occupational and physical therapy. After 1926, when it became a Community Fund Agency, it provided social and home occupational therapy services. In 1931, the Junior League gave up sponsorship and the workshop incorporated separately. In the following years many different programs were added: a nursery school for cerebral-palsied children, a cardiac activity control program, a medical social service program, professional training programs, a research program, a psychological program, a day care center, and a vocational program.

The vocational program began in 1945 with an experimental work adjustment program. Simulated work activities in occupational therapy were provided to orient handicapped persons to work situations. This program was designed for those with acute or short-term disabilities. After 1950, the Curative Workshop began serving larger numbers with chronic and multiple disabilities. In 1955, an occupational evaluation laboratory was established to help handicapped persons who could not return to their former employment arrive at realistic vocational goals. It used principally standardized job performance tests. In the same year, a vocational department developed services which would prepare severely handicapped persons to meet the requirements of competitive employment. Work adjustment, tutorial vocational training, on the job and "sheltered work" training were given to develop work confidence, acceptable work habits, and work tolerance. In 1962, the activities in the Industrial Work Adjustment Unit were incorporated separately as a subsidiary of the Curative Workshop. This was necessary, since special accounting was needed for insurance coverage and subcontract work. Between 1955 and 1962, the Curative Workshop had developed vocational activities which had become workshop services. In 1965, the Milwaukee Curative Workshop served 217 persons in workshop programs (9).

The Curative Workshop of New York, started in 1924, followed a somewhat different pattern. Although its purpose was restorative and therapeutic, it early developed a work-oriented program. By 1926, it had developed a subcontract program. It was supported by fees from the New York State Vocational Rehabilitation Service, from insurance companies' payment for injured workers' services, and from public offerings. Its first director was a man with industrial experience (10).

The majority of the curative workshops, however, followed the pattern of the Curative Workshop of Milwaukee. Their initial staffs were drawn from medical settings. In 1954, there were twenty-seven institutions in the United States which took the name of Curative Workshop (11). Many changed their names to rehabilitation centers as they expanded their range of services. In 1965, there were four Curative Workshops in the United States that had workshops in the programs. Three were in Wisconsin at Milwaukee, Green Bay, and Racine. The other was at Philadelphia, Pennsylvania. They were private voluntary organizations rendering primarily restorative medical services but with social, psychological, and vocational programs as supplementary programs. The workshops were originally part of the vocational program. It is estimated that the four workshops in the Curative Workshops served less than four hundred in 1964 (12).

WORKSHOPS IN FREESTANDING
OUTPATIENT REHABILITATION CENTERS

In addition to the workshops in the "Curative Workshops" and those in Easter Seal Centers, a small group of workshops were established in private outpatient rehabilitation centers which were not affiliated with national, voluntary agencies. The centers were usually started by groups of people who organized for the specific purpose of operating medically oriented rehabilitation centers. The workshops in these centers usually started as part of the centers' medical program, and sometimes were extensions of the occupation therapy programs. As the workshop developed, it usually became more autonomous. As a rule they emphasized subcontracting from industry. In the early 1950's, they served principally the physically handicapped, but gradually extended their services to the mentally retarded and the mentally ill.

It is difficult to identify workshops in these centers because there is no listing of them. The trend since 1950 has been for medically oriented rehabilitation centers to affiliate with hospitals. Sometimes the workshop separated from the center when the hospital affiliation was made. An example was the establishment of the San Francisco Community Rehabilitation Workshop after the Morrison Center for Rehabilitation affiliated with the Presbyterian Hospital in 1962. It is estimated that there were about a dozen workshops in freestanding outpatient rehabilitation centers in 1966.

Rehabilitation Institute of Kansas City

An outstanding example of a workshop in a freestanding outpatient rehabilitation center is the Work Evaluation and Adjustment Unit of the Rehabilitation Institute of Kansas City. This workshop started on a small scale when the Institute was founded in 1947. In 1957, it was expanded to include the Work Evaluation and Adjustment Unit. The work of the shop is mainly subcontracts, but it does manufacturing in the electronic industry. The shop has a large industrial and professional staff. It provides short- and long-term evaluation, work adjustment, and extended employment. In 1966, extended employment was provided a small group which constituted about 25 percent of the clientele. The number served varied between sixty and eighty persons. Persons with all disabilities are accepted. More than half of those served have physical disabilities. Those with emotional conditions and the mentally retarded are also served. More than 60 percent of those who come to the shop are found jobs or made ready for employment (13).

NOTES

1. Directory of rehabilitation centers. Journal of Rehabilitation, pp. 65-70, May-June, 1964.
2. The story of the Vocational Guidance and Rehabilitation Services is taken from Sunbeam's 75th Anniversary. Cleveland, Vocational Guidance and Rehabilitation Center, 1965.
3. The account is based on Rehabilitation Trends, Midcentury to 1956. New York City, Institute for Crippled and Disabled, 1955. Also, Rosenberg, B., (Director of Vocational Services of I.C.D.): Personal communication, September 27, 1965.
4. This account is based on the annual reports of the League for the Handicapped for 1960 and 1964, Detroit, Detroit League for Handicapped.

5. Obermann, C. E.: A History of Vocational Rehabilitation in America. Minneapolis, T. S. Denison, 1968, pp. 105-108.

6. Directory of rehabilitation facilities. Journal of Rehabilitation, pp. 25-64, May-June, 1964. Sheltered Workshops Certificated by the Wage and Hour and Public Contracts Division of the U. S. Department of Labor. Section of Handicapped Workers Problems, Branch of Special Minimum Wages, Office of Wage Determination and Research, Wage and Hour and Public Contract Department, U. S. Department of Labor, Washington, D. C., June 30, 1964. Directory of Workshops of the Handicapped. Washington, Department of Health, Education, and Welfare, 1961.

7. Bader, E. J., (Director, Care and Treatment Service, National Society for Crippled Children and Adults): Personal communication, March 17, 1966.

8. Harris, G.: The Redemption of the Disabled. New York, D. Appleton, 1919, pp. 6-7, 13, 206-210, 129.

9. Curative Workshop of Milwaukee Chronological History of the Agencies Growth and Development. Milwaukee, Curative Workshops of Milwaukee, 1965. Allegressa, T. S. (Executive Director, Curative Workshops of Milwaukee): Personal communication, March 21, 1966.

10. Sullivan, O. M. and Snortium, K. O.: Disabled Persons, Their Education and Rehabiliation. New York, Century, 1926.

11. Curative Workshops of Milwaukee, Chronological History of the Agency's Growth and Development, op.cit., p. 5.

12. This estimate is based on the report of the Wage and Hour Division of the Department of Labor of June 1964. Also, Allegressa, T. S.: Personal communication, March 21, 1966.

13. Shepherd, V.: Personal communication, July 1, 1966. Shephard, V.: The Role of the Rehabilitation Center in the Rehabilitation Process. Kansas City, The Rehabilitation Institute, 1965, p. 5. The Rehabilitation Institute, Annual Report, 1962. Kansas City, The Rehabilitation Institute, 1962.

IV

THE LATEST PERIOD-
THE FLOWERING OF WORKSHOPS

THE EXTENSION OF SCOPE AND FUNCTION

FROM 1950 to 1965, twice as many workshops were started than in all the previous history of workshops in the United States. Single disability shops were established for the mentally retarded, cerebral palsied, the epileptic, and the mentally ill. New techniques were developed for the new groups served, and new methods of services were developed for those served previously. The older existing workshops accepted the new groups for services and utilized the new methods.

THE JEWISH VOCATIONAL SERVICE WORKSHOPS

The first group of shops which were started in this period were the Jewish Vocational Service workshops. Jewish community agencies in the United States developed workshops as a result of their vocational guidance and placement programs. Before World War I, there were few public programs which provided vocational guidance and placement. After World War I, professional knowledge and techniques in vocational guidance were developed, and Jewish agencies established specialized vocational services for Jewish young people and the aged and handicapped. In time the services became generally available on a non-sectarian basis. The agency which provided these services was most often called the Jewish Vocational Services.

The Jewish Vocational Service Agencies found that the persons who needed their help most were the aged, the immigrants, and after World War II, the refugees from the Nazi-dominated countries of Europe. Some of these persons were not able to get or hold jobs even when they had occupational skills which might

57

have made them useful employees. The difficulty often was that they did not look, act, or respond as was expected of satisfactory employees. Jewish community agencies first set up workshops to provide employment and financial assistance for them in a manner that would maintain their dignity and self-respect. They found that through work and the work environment it often became possible to modify some of the personality and behavioral difficulties that made the handicapped person an unacceptable employee. As a result, the Jewish Vocational Service agencies developed workshop programs which, while they differed in many specific respects, were alike in their principal emphasis on work adjustment processes and related services which helped apparently unemployable persons to become acceptable workers.

Not all Jewish agency workshops, however, emphasized vocational adjustment as a principal service in their programs. The Vocational Rehabilitation Center of Pittsburg and the Jewish Vocational Service Workshop of Milwaukee both provided adjustment services but added many other types of rehabilitation services. Some, such as the Utility Workshop of the Family Service Agency of San Francisco, continued to provide employment to aged persons. Others, such as the workshops of the Federation Employment and Guidance Service of New York, were used as a part of a more comprehensive vocational rehabilitation program for the aged handicapped and persons with other handicapping conditions. The majority of the Jewish Vocational Service agencies, however, stressed work adjustment services in their workshops, and it is for this area of service that they were best known.

The Jewish Vocational Service of Chicago first developed and explained the uses of work adjustment in the United States. In 1951, the Agency, under the direction of William Gellman, started the Vocational Adjustment Center. Its purpose was to help the apparently unemployable handicapped person enter into competitive employment. This was done by using work and the work situation to enable the apparently unemployable person to become productive, to behave appropriately, and to conform to work requirements (1). Since the specific objective was employability, whether or not it had been achieved might be determined after a given amount of time. Gellman found that after a given length of time some handicapped persons became employable (2) and that those that did not were not helped substantially by further stay in the shop. As a consequence, the Chicago shop limited the stay of its workers. This limited-stay characteristic was applied in popular usage to classify workshops as either "transitional" or "terminal." Gellman and his associates, however, went on to define the Chicago workshop as a vocational adjustment workshop in which the staff utilized work activity and the work setting as a means of assessing, improving, or maintaining a disabled person's employability level (3).

By 1962, there were seventeen agencies which were affiliated with the Jewish Occupational Council, the national organization of the Jewish Vocational Service Agencies. In 1960, the Jewish Vocational Service workshops served 1,630 persons. The average attendance per day was 976 persons. The average length of stay was approximately four months. In only two shops could all persons remain indefinitely. Thus the Jewish Vocational Service workshops were mainly highly specialized vocational adjustment workshops which served relatively few persons but served them intensively and contributed greatly to their rehabilitation.

Though the numbers they served were relatively small, the contribution of the Jewish Vocational Service agencies to the development of the vocational rehabilitation of disadvantaged persons was great indeed. Before the Jewish Vocational Service started their programs, workshops had developed principally occupational training, work conditioning, and long-term employment as basic workshop services. Although earlier shops had no doubt helped their workers develop good work habits, this had been done informally and without a clearly defined rationale. The Jewish Vocational Service workshops developed and defined work adjustment as an additional workshop service. They developed a rationale for work adjustment, described its definitive characteristics, and demonstrated its effectiveness. In doing so they added a new and significant means of rehabilitating disadvantaged persons, of helping people who find it difficult to adjust to the requirements of work.

In addition to the contributions indicated above, Jewish

agencies made other organizational and conceptual innovations. The Jewish Vocational Service of Milwaukee under the leadership of Michael Galazan developed extensive demonstration and permanent programs through a network of cooperative relationships with public and private agencies. As a result, the agency was enabled to provide comprehensive services for large numbers of handicapped persons of all disabilities and especially young adults from the school system without regard to disability. The Philadelphia Jewish Vocational Services varied its techniques somewhat from the typical Jewish Vocational Services pattern by stressing work competence skills, by substituting industrial experienced personnel for psychologist as foremen, and more recently by exploring innovative approaches dealing with new groups of disadvantaged persons.

WORKSHOPS SPONSORED BY PARENT GROUPS

The sponsors of workshops in the first half of the twentieth century were usually professional persons and volunteers who developed programs for handicapped persons with whom they had no family connections. In the first two decades of the second half of the century, a large number of new workshops were started by groups which consisted at first largely of parents of handicapped children and young adults. The initial interest of the parents in these groups was to provide services for their children. The impact of the parent groups and the service programs they established had a substantial effect upon the development of workshops in the country. The parent groups were also successful in securing national and state legislation and financing of service programs geared to the needs of their children. As a result many existing workshops developed new or expanded programs to meet the expectations of parent groups. What final effect the influence of the parent groups will have on the development of workshop programs remains to be decided in the future. It is clear, however, that workshops have been and will continue to be affected by the steps which the parents of severely handicapped persons took to solve the problems of their children.

At the beginning of the twentieth century, the future of a

severely handicapped child was unpromising indeed. He had little chance for an appropriate education, a job, or a satisfactory social life. He would probably be a burden to his parents all his life. About the only course open to a parent wishing to obtain services for his child was to place him in a public or private residential school or hospital for the physically handicapped, mentally ill or mentally retarded. To the perceptive parent, hospitalization was not a satisfactory solution. He doubted that his child's care in the hospital was as good as it should be. He was troubled because it seemed to him that a better way should be found to enable his child to live a more useful and a happier life at home. He felt frustrated because neither he nor society could discover an answer to his dilemma. The parent that could accept hospitalization found himself suffering from the social stigma that then was attached to the putting of one's child in an institution. At the time the unhappy parents could do little to help their children or themselves. They bore their burden in quiet desperation.

In the first several decades of the twentieth century, progress was made in the medical sciences, innovations appeared in public and private education, some of the voluntary health agencies were established, and laws were passed instituting public vocational rehabilitation and public health programs. It seemed to the troubled parents that these developments should result in help for their children. They were disappointed. They thereupon got together to find ways to help their children themselves. The organizations for the cerebral palsied and the mentally retarded were the initial result.

To understand the programs of the parent organizations, it is necessary to know the reasons why they did not benefit from existing public and private service programs for handicapped persons. The progress in medical services was directed mostly towards acute and chronic conditions which benefited from medication or surgery. When occupational and physical therapy programs were developed, they were seldom prescribed for static conditions by private physicians available to most parents. The voluntary health agencies were interested primarily in helping with physical conditions that responded quickly to conventional medical procedures. The public health agencies, though more responsive in some places, as a whole responded to the usual medical practice in their areas and provided services accordingly. The public vocational rehabilitation agencies usually rejected their severely handicapped children if they could not benefit from conventional medical procedures or if they could not be trained for remunerative employment in generally available trade schools or on-the-job training programs in industry. The public schools occasionally developed special programs for the severely handicapped and the mentally retarded but these programs were in the minority. As a rule neither public or private social case work agencies or recreation programs had provided services for the severely handicapped and the mentally retarded. Thus the parent groups found that the existing agencies for the handicapped did not have a place in their programs for the most severely handicapped or for most mentally retarded children and young adults.

The existing public and private agencies not only refused to provide services as a rule to the most severely handicapped and most of the mentally retarded, but they were unwilling or unable to experiment with the new and different kinds of services that their children needed. The professional personnel of agencies seemed too ready to decide that nothing could be done for their children. Subsequent experience has shown that public and private agencies were as a rule indeed conservative in their policies and judgments. The fact that the judgments of the parents were at times more correct than those of the agencies and their professionally trained personnel had little influence on the public and private agencies at the time.

Finding their requests generally rejected by public and private agencies, the parent organizations adopted a twofold program. They established programs under their own sponsorship and control that duplicated those of public and private agencies when those programs did not serve their children. They carried on educational programs to enlighten the public and political programs to require public agencies to serve their children.

Since their political activities took long periods of time before the goals were reached, they started varied and extensive programs with their own resources. They established educational classes, day care centers, socialization and recreational programs, family casework and counseling services, diagnostic programs, self-care programs and workshops. They needed all or most of these kinds of programs. Their resources were meager at first, so they often put these different programs together in various combinations based not upon the nature of the services but depending upon the extent of their resources at the time.

WORKSHOPS FOR THE CEREBRAL PALSIED

In the 1940's parents of cerebral-palsied children began meeting to discuss how they might best solve the problems of their children. These meetings often led to the formation of local organizations to sponsor services for the cerebral palsied. The local societies joined together in 1948 to form the United Cerebral Palsy Associations, Inc., a national organization. Each local group remained autonomous and developed local service programs, which differed from place to place. Some local groups provided workshop services by paying for units for the cerebral palsied in existing workshops. Other local societies developed workshops for the cerebral palsied. A third group established comprehensive rehabilitation services in which a workshop was but one unit.

One of the earliest of the metropolitan societies which established a workshop was the United Cerebral Palsy of King's County at Seattle, Washington. This group of parents first met in 1942 to plan a school for spastic children. They started the school in 1944. In 1947, state legislation was passed providing funds for the education of the cerebral palsied, and the group turned its attention to the establishment of a workshop for the cerebral palsied.

The workshop was begun in 1952 with an enrollment of twenty-two adults in 7,260 square feet of space. It was staffed by a director and an occupational therapist. In 1954, it turned to subcontracts for work and doubled its enrollment. An important contractor was the Boeing Aircraft Co., and its work and that of other contractors made it necessary to have more space. In 1959, a new wing of 6,000 square feet was added and a machine shop was built on the grounds. By 1965, the shop served 114 persons at a time, but persons with other disabilities as well as cerebral palsy were served. In that year it was probably the largest workshop operated by a cerebral palsy organization in the country, and possibly the only one operating a major machine shop for the cerebral palsied (4).

Another group of cerebral palsy organizations financed workshop units in rehabilitation centers or in other workshops. Typical of this group was the United Cerebral Palsy organizations of San Francisco and New York. The San Francisco group first secured workshop services by financing a unit in the Disabled Employees Workshop in 1952, then financed a unit in the Morrison Center for Rehabilitation in 1957 (5), and finally financed services in the San Francisco Community Rehabilitation Workshop in 1962. The New York organization in 1955 sponsored a Work Classification and Evaluation Project that was later financed in part by the Federal Vocational Rehabilitation Administration and co-sponsored by three other community agencies. This workshop unit was managed by the Institute for the Crippled and Disabled in New York until 1960. In that year, the Cerebral Palsy Association of New York sponsored a new program at the Institute which was named The Cerebral Palsy Training Workshop (6). In these workshop units only the cerebral palsied were served.

Some United Cerebral Palsy organizations operated workshops in their own vocational or rehabilitation facilities. The United Cerebral Palsy Association of Philadelphia, for example, began a vocational program in 1956. This program consisted of an eight-week medical, psychological and social evaluation followed by work sample testing and exposure to simulated job situations. In 1958, a workshop was established. It served those who needed personal adjustment and long-term employment. To remain in the shop indefinitely, the handicapped person had to be able to produce at 10 percent of normal production or better. The workshop did subcontract work. In 1965, the shop served about sixty handicapped persons, of which number about 70 percent would be kept by the shop indefinitely (7).

A similar program, but with more extensive medical services, was established by the United Cerebral Palsy Association of Los Angeles. In 1954, the organization started an industrial training workshop. Its purpose was to place cerebral palsied in industry through a realistic work training experience under conditions similar to those found in industry. To provide such an environment, subcontracts in drill sharpening, soldering, cable harness assembly, and deburring were taken. The shop had a capacity to serve seventy handicapped adults. Although placements were made, the shop developed a large group of workers who remained in the shop indefinitely. Later the shop was taken over by an independent sponsoring group.

Cerebral Palsy Association operations differed in various communities. Their administrative control of the workshops or workshop units varied. As a rule, however, the organization made sure it controlled the intake policies of the programs it sponsored. Thus the parent organization usually determined who was admitted to the program and sometimes decided who could be released from it. In many instances, however, a small percentage of handicapped persons with disabilities other than cerebral palsy was admitted. A few cerebral-palsied groups combined efforts with other organizations for handicapped persons or with other community groups to serve persons having varying disabilities. In 1965 and in 1966, efforts were under way to combine with other workshop organizations to develop multidisability workshops.

The workshop programs of the cerebral palsy organizations were initially directed towards movement of the cerebral palsied into jobs in industry. However, the population of the workshops became static as the workshops filled up with cerebral-palsied workers who could not move into industry. In the early 1960's, the workshops provided sheltered employment to a majority of their handicapped workers. In 1966, there were 884 cerebral-palsied persons in workshops for whom wage certificates were issued by the Department of Labor (8). It is estimated that there were more than 1,000 cerebral-palsied workers in approximately thirty workshops for the cerebral palsied in the United States in the beginning of 1966. In addition, there were about ten vocational units in rehabilitation centers, some of which were becoming workshops (9), and several dozen informal part-time work programs which were called workshops.

WORKSHOPS FOR THE MENTALLY RETARDED

One of the most important developments in workshops in the twentieth century was the establishment of several hundred workshops for the mentally retarded. These were the largest single groups of shops started in the second half of the century. They enhanced supportive services and added new services. Preexisting workshops had used social work and psychological and vocational counseling services, for example, but the programs for the retarded intensified these services and added substantial socialization, recreation and self-care programs. The addition of these services left less time for work. At times, they turned the emphasis of the shops to nonvocational objectives. Yet in such instances the parent groups continued to regard their programs as workshops. The existence of hundreds of different kinds of programs which resembled conventional workshops, yet were different from them, raised questions about the identity and objectives of workshops.

Workshops for the mentally retarded came into being through many routes. Often they developed from classes that parent groups conducted for severely mentally retarded minors when public school systems failed to provide educational services. Sometimes the arts and crafts activities for retarded children of custodial, recreational or socialization programs developed into paid work when the retarded children became adults. Sometimes workshops for the mentally retarded were set up with paid work, usually subcontract work, from the beginning. Where paid work was initiated at the start, it was at times the major activity of the shop, and at other times a secondary or inconsequential part of the program. As these various types of programs moved towards an emphasis on paid work they often retained services which were residuals from their initial programs. There was a reluctance to drop the services of the original programs because the mentally retarded had many needs. They tried to serve as many needs as possible in the programs they sponsored. Thus, in workshops for the retarded, there was much greater variability in objectives and variety of services than was characteristic of previous workshops.

Early group services for mentally retarded children and young adults were developed by informal groups of parents who operated their programs with much devotion and energy but in the beginning without conventional organizational discipline. Programs were started by volunteers in homes, school classes, and recreational settings without designation of administrative responsibility. These early programs rarely kept records and are difficult to describe or classify. As the organizations grew they developed more formal administrative structures and more distinct programs. Their local literature grew; it was primarily educational or promotional, not historical. Thus it is difficult to develop a comprehensive account of workshops for the mentally retarded from existing records. The best that can be done until more research is carried out is to describe some workshop programs whose history is available. Such an account will be illustrative rather than comprehensive.

Mentally retarded persons were put to work in supervised settings long before the parent organizations began workshops. In the last half of the nineteenth century, they worked in residential colonies and in the twentieth century in state hospitals and residential schools as well. Work in these settings was usually part of residential care. Work was used in two ways: to keep the retarded occupied usefully, or to train them in occupational skills needed in the institutions or colonies where they resided, and which could be used elsewhere as well. A few mentally retarded persons also worked in existing workshops before 1950.

In the 1930's, parents of the mentally retarded began discussing ways to establish workshops in local communities for mentally retarded adults living at home. Beginning in 1951, workshops serving mentally retarded only were established by organizations often consisting mainly of parents of the retarded. These workshops usually emphasized services to the severely retarded (10). About the same time existing multidisability workshops began serving severely retarded adults in separate units in their shops and larger numbers of moderately retarded adults integrated with persons having various disabilities.

The San Francisco Workshop

An early development of workshop services for the mentally

retarded took place in San Francisco, California. Two subcontract workshops had existed in San Francisco for many years, the Disabled Employees Workshop Incorporated since 1936, and the Utility Workshop since 1943, but neither they nor the Goodwill Industries usually served severely mentally retarded persons prior to 1951. During 1947 and 1948, a community committee was set up to plan for the establishment of a community workshop which would serve all handicapped persons. After this plan fell through, small groups of parents of retarded children met to establish a workshop for the retarded. These meetings led to the founding of San Francisco Aid Retarded Children, and in 1951 a workshop was started (11).

Between 1951 and 1953, the San Francisco shop was conducted by volunteers on a part-time basis. Some of the volunteers were parents of the retarded in the shop. The board of trustees included parents whose children were in the workshop. Other trustees were parents of mentally retarded children who attended public school classes for the retarded, or were in Sonoma State Hospital. One of the first projects was the sorting of newspapers for florists. Later the shop got subcontracts. In 1953, the Adult Education Division of the San Francisco Unified School District furnished an instructor and the shop became a full-time operation. From 1956 to 1965, the Aid Retarded Children received a series of grants from the federal government which helped to expand the program in several directions.

In the initial period between 1951 and 1957, retarded persons of various levels of severity were served in one workshop by the staff and volunteers. With the first grant in 1956, social and psychological services were added to vocational services. During the period of second grant it was recognized that one program would not serve the needs of all levels of the retarded. Subsequently, the retarded were served in different programs, depending principally upon level of severity of retardation. The most severely retarded were served in a work activity center, the Adult Training Center, which was supported and operated by the Aid Retarded Children. The less severely retarded who were not expected to work in industry but needed long-term workshop employment were served separately. After 1963, this group was placed in the

San Francisco Community Rehabilitation Workshop and the Aid Retarded Children paid the costs. A third group of those who had possibilities of working in industry were referred to the San Francisco Community Rehabilitation Workshop by the California State Department of Rehabilitation which paid for the services to them. A fourth group was in the Independent Living Rehabilitation Program. This group consisted of those retardates who were not necessarily expected to work in industry but who could benefit from part-day work, homemaking training, arts and crafts, leisure time activities, and social case and social group work for them and their families. This group was housed in the San Francisco Community Rehabilitation Workshop and the Aid Retarded Children operated the program and paid the cost (12).

The Early Workshops for the Retarded

By 1953, there were six workshops for the retarded in the United States at San Francisco, New York City, Tampa, Denver, Minneapolis, and Newark. A survey made by the National Association for Retarded Children in 1957 disclosed there were 108 workshops for the retarded (13). These workshops developed in a number of ways. Some started as did the San Francisco program, which began with a simple work program and developed specialized units and comprehensive services. Some began with grant money or other public financing and developed varied types of comprehensive programs at the start. A third group began with work activity centers which emphasized social and recreational programs and developed work orientation later.

The Massachusetts Workshops for the Retarded

Between 1955 and 1962, eight chapters of the Massachusetts Association for the Retarded started group services for the retarded. These group programs were named variously as workshops, vocational adjustment centers, or training centers; but they were regarded by their sponsor as workshops. A different type of program that served retarded persons was the Rutland Training Center. This organization was started in 1923 for the tubercular, later served many disability groups, and in 1962, about 50 percent of its trainees were retarded persons. As a group, the Massachusetts centers emphasized, with some exceptions, social rather than vocational skills, paid no wages since their activities did not provide a means of payment, and usually provided no basis upon which vocational or rehabilitation assessment could be made. They were illustrative of the different kinds of programs from which many workshops for the mentally retarded evolved.

The centers of the Massachusetts Association for the Retarded were at Boston, Barnstable, Reading, Framington, Salem, Weymouth, Springfield, and Worcester. In 1963, the centers served 174 retarded persons with an average enrollment of nineteen. Most of the trainees were severely retarded, but the moderately and minimally retarded were served at several centers. Three centers did evaluation, but only one stressed work evaluation. Four centers provided skill training. The principal activity in seven centers was arts and crafts. Three centers had no other activity than arts and crafts. Rutland ran a printing business, at Barnstable there was boat storage and repair, and the Framington center produced a company newspaper and a weekly newsletter. Two centers had sporadic subcontracts. All the centers had social training or adjustment programs. Four centers did placement of trainees. Most of the directors were educators. The floor supervisors were usually chosen for their skill or knowledge of arts and crafts. A few centers had part-time trained personnel from the helping professions.

The above description highlights the condition of new centers in ferment and transition which was characteristic of many new centers in the United States at the time. A federally sponsored study of the Massachusetts centers made in 1962-1963 by Richard McCann and his associates indicates that several centers were giving careful attention to adding services which are among those offered by the traditional sheltered workshops. Those services include transitional and long-term employment by subcontracting or manufacturing and the payment of wages. The same study group asked the centers to make self evaluations. They report:

> In our interviews with directors and other staff members ... the
> information they have provided and particularly the problems they

have singled out, have highlighted the precarious course run by agencies whose objectives are to serve the community, but which have only tenuous ties to that community.

The changes in program affected in the recent past and projected for the immediate future depict ways in which these centers have strengthened — or intend to strengthen — the effectiveness of their services and thus establish more fruitful relationships with the community at large, as well as with its several specialized aspects, the rehabilitative and medical, industrial, financial and educational (14).

The same could have been said of other programs of the associations for the retarded in the United States during that period.

Government Financial Support

The initial experience of the workshops for the retarded during the 1950's made it clear that few local organizations sponsoring workshops could finance them adequately. The federal government gave some aid to the organizations for the retarded. The 1954 amendments to the Vocational Rehabilitation Act authorized the Vocational Rehabilitation Administration to make grants to non-profit agencies in support of research and demonstration projects. In the first ten years following the passage of the Act, 151 grants were made in support of programs for the mentally retarded. One of the early demonstration grants to a workshop was given to the Association for the Help of Retarded Children of New York City, which had started a workshop in 1953. This demonstration project was used as a prototype for a group of selected demonstration projects, and forty-five organizations were given grants to repeat the demonstration from 1958 to 1965. The majority of these grants went to new workshops for the mentally retarded exclusively. The workshops in which demonstrations were made were called Occupational Training Centers for the Mentally Retarded. This label, shortened to work training centers, became popular as a designation for workshops for the retarded during this period.

The title of the New York project is illustrative of the purpose of the forty-five workshops which got the grant. It was "To demonstrate that special sheltered *workshop training* can rehabilitate mentally retarded *young adults* whose employment had previously been considered impossible" (15). The employment was not necessarily in industry but more often was provided in a workshop. Additional purposes of the grant were to provide facilities for the severely mentally retarded and to increase the number of previously unemployable retarded adults being prepared for remunerative employment.

The partial financing of workshops by the federal government had a stimulating effect on the workshops for the retarded, but the limited duration of the grants made the benefits temporary. A few states provided permanent partial support of workshops for the retarded. In 1964, Wisconsin led by paying part of the costs of operating such workshops. Louisiana followed by paying the costs of staff in one workshop and of several activity centers. Later the Louisiana Division of Vocational Rehabilitation assumed the operation of four workshops. In 1965, the Tennessee Division of Vocational Rehabilitation participated in the financing of ten workshops administered by the Tennessee Association for Retarded Children and assumed their operation in 1965. In some states hospitals and residential schools for the retarded set up workshops. In California, workshops for the mentally retarded were developed in state hospitals informally at first, and after 1966, officially. The state provided small sums to private shops which provided long-term services to severely retarded persons (16).

In Missouri in 1965, legislation was passed providing for the payment of a per diem rate of two dollars per day for each retarded person in an approved workshop. The money was provided by the State Board of Education. In 1966, nine community workshops were established as a result of this act. The shops served three hundred moderately retarded and other handicapped young adults who had productive capacity but who could not work in competitive business. Many more workshops were expected to be started as a result of this legislation. In addition to the workshops subsidized by this act, there were programs for trainable retarded at the Goodwill Industries of Greater Kansas City. Similar demonstration grants were given to the Goodwill by the federal government as a selected demonstration project (17).

The growth of workshops serving exclusively or primarily the retarded had a twofold effect on the organization of workshop services for the retarded. Many multidisability shops began serving larger numbers of moderately retarded persons. Some workshops exclusively for the mentally retarded began serving persons with other disabilities. The nature of the sponsoring groups of shops for the retarded changed. Some organizations which just had consisted mainly of parents took more nonparents into the organization. Some sponsoring groups were formed which had few or no parents in the leadership roles. Some organizations of parents of the retarded joined forces with other groups in the community interested in other disabilities. After 1963, the pattern of shops providing services for mentally retarded persons had changed materially; however, the workshops sponsored by parent organizations were still in the majority.

Types of Workshops

To estimate the numbers of workshops for the mentally retarded, it is necessary to classify them into three groups. The first group may be called workshops *exclusively* for the retarded. In this group of shops admission is possible only if a person is retarded. The second group might be called workshops *primarily* for the retarded. In this group the majority are retarded, but some persons are admitted with other handicapping conditions. A third group might be classified as workshops *including* retarded persons. This group serves many disabilities but includes a substantial minority of retarded persons.

There is still another set whose classification as a workshop group is in doubt. They are often designated as activity centers for mentally retarded persons. Here the emphasis is on nonwork-related activities such as socialization, recreation, self-care training, and personal relationships. Work for wages is nonexistent or only an insignificant part of the day's schedule.

Numbers of Shops for the Retarded

Using the above classifications, and excluding the activity centers, some estimates can be made of numbers of shops in the

United States at the end of 1965. It is estimated there were over 155 workshops exclusively for the retarded. If to this group were added the workshops primarily for retarded persons, the two groups would exceed 300 shops. If the workshops which included the retarded persons were added to the first two groups, the three groups would total more than 500 workshops. In January 1966, there were 8,662 retarded persons in workshops for whom the Department of Labor issued work certificates (18). If the division into levels of retardation which exists in California workshops is the same for the country as a whole, then about half of the 8,662 would be severely retarded, and the rest would be moderately and minimally retarded (19).

By March, 1968, the Department of Labor had certified 468 workshops for mentally retarded persons whose work was covered by the Fair Labor Standards Act. These were probably shops exclusively or primarily for the retarded. At the time, 13,722 mentally retarded persons were certified by the Department of Labor. These figures would not include mentally retarded private workshops doing noncovered work, or twenty-five workshops in state hospitals or schools for the mentally retarded, which were not covered at the time. It is estimated that there were approximately 18,000 mentally retarded persons in workshops in the United States in the beginning of 1969 (20).

WORKSHOPS FOR THE AGED

Probably the largest group of people in the United States who need workshop services are the aged. In 1960, there were 23,702,000 people in the country over sixty years of age. Of these, 6,445,000 were working. In the same year, there were 16,500,000 over sixty-five, of whom 2,425,000 were working (21). Many in the nonworking group had adjusted to retirement and had no need for workshops. A third group, however, had not been able to adjust to retirement. Among this group there were many who needed workshop services (22). How many could have benefited is not known, but it is likely that the aged in workshops up to the present time constitute but a small portion of the aged who could lead happier lives if they worked in workshops.

The aged are served by workshops in a number of ways. Some aged persons are provided work in workshops in connection with the homes in which they reside. Others are provided work in workshops not connected with homes but which serve only the aged. Another group is provided services in workshops which accept persons on the basis of many other handicaps, but these workshops have special programs or group services for the aged. The final group are those aged who are taken into general workshops serving persons with many disabilities, and no special treatment is given them which differentiates them from other workers.

The first program to serve the aged, among other handicapped persons, was probably the Society of St. Vincent de Paul. The Salvation Army and the Volunteers of America followed. The Goodwill Industries began services to the aged as early as 1902 and employed more aged persons in 1967 than any other group of workshops. The principal objective of the above workshops in respect to the aged was to provide work and pay to the aged. The objectives of the workshop programs in the homes for the aged were more varied. In addition to pay, it was intended that employment would sustain the physical or mental health of the aged and occupy their time more happily. It is not known when the homes for the aged initiated workshop programs. There were about two dozen homes for the aged that paid wages in 1966 in programs which could be identified as workshops.

The first nonresident workshop serving the aged was probably the Utility Workshop of San Francisco, California. It was started in 1943 by the San Francisco Committee for Service to Refugees of the Jewish Welfare Federation, but was later taken over by the Jewish Family Service agency. During and after the Second World War, the Jewish agencies found it extremely difficult to find work for the many Jewish refugees from Europe. The older workers in particular were hard to place. At the time work was plentiful, but employers would not hire some of the refugees, so the Utility Workshop was started to provide work for them, especially the older refugees. About 10 percent of those provided work in the shop later got jobs in industry, but the rest remained in the shop indefinitely. As a result, the shop became a place of work for the aged, most of whom were over sixty-five. The wages were low, but the old people got a feeling of being useful and enjoyed the pleasure of social contacts with other workers. The general feeling of contentment led to better health, as evidenced by fewer requests for medical care (23). In 1966, the shop served about forty aged persons, including some that were not refugees.

The need to provide services for the refugees from Europe was recognized during the Second World War by the Jewish Vocational Services of many major cities in the United States. Since the older refugees were more difficult to place, some Jewish Vocational Services admitted them into their workshop for various services, often with the definite understanding that they might remain in the shop indefinitely if necessary. Some times the Jewish Vocational Service provided workshop services for homes for the aged, as in Chicago, Illinois. Eight other workshops of the Jewish Vocational Service accepted the aged in 1961 (24). Thus, some of the workshops which were identified as being "transitional" workshops found themselves providing long-term employment to the aged.

The involvement of the Jewish Vocational Services with the aged made them aware that vocational rehabilitation services for them lagged behind availability of services for other groups of handicapped persons. In 1951, the Detroit Jewish Vocational Service developed a special program for the aged (25). The major expansion of more intensive services for the aged, however, came as a result of a survey of federal grants to workshops interested in the aged. In 1957, the Federation Employment and Guidance Service of New York was given a grant to demonstrate the feasibility of providing vocational rehabilitation services to the aged. The project originally defined the aged as those sixty years of age or over, but the definition was changed later to include those fifty-five and over. Workshop services played an important part in the project.

The aged who needed workshop services entered a three-week workshop evaluation where they engaged in paid work under supervision. Some of those who went to work evaluation received thirteen weeks personal adjustment training. Of the first 700 aged persons served in the project in the four years between 1957 and

1961, 490 or 70 percent were able to work. About 123, or 25 percent, spent some time in the workshop after the evaluation and personal adjustment period in temporary or long-term employment. The Federation believed that a large number needed workshop employment and would have accepted it if there had been a workshop closer to their home. For this reason, the Federation developed two neighborhood branch workshops out of the downtown area (26).

Following the success of the New York Project, the Vocational Rehabilitation Administration made thirteen grants to agencies for demonstration projects for older disabled workers. Among these were six grants to workshops: five to Jewish Vocational Service workshops in Kansas City, Missouri; Miami, Florida; St. Louis, Missouri; Philadelphia, Pennsylvania; and Chicago, Illinois; and to the Kiwanis Opportunity Workshop in Milwaukee, Wisconsin. Thus from 1960 to 1966, there was further demonstration of the feasibility of rehabilitating aged persons in workshops for employment in industry or in the workshop (27).

Helpful as the federal efforts were to demonstrate what could be done with the aged, the workshops' services for the aged have not increased in keeping with the numbers of aged and their need for services. In 1966, there were fewer than two dozen workshops serving the aged exclusively. There were about 1,000 aged persons in their shops. In 1960, 270 workshops indicated that they would accept the aged in their shops, but many seldom served the aged, and some served them intermittently and in small numbers. The largest numbers were probably served by the Goodwill Industries of America, and they served about 8,000 at a time in 1967. In California in 1964, the aged constituted 3.8 percent of the workshop population. In all, probably the aged get less service from workshops in proportion to their numbers and need than any other group of handicapped persons (28).

WORKSHOPS FOR THE EPILEPTICS

Most handicapped persons in workshops were unable to work in industry when they sought admission to the shops. The same cannot be said of many epileptics who are in workshops. Since the middle of the twenty century, many epileptics who have been well controlled by medication have been able to work without significant lowered productivity, substantial time loss, or substantial disturbance of work routines. The principle obstacle to the employment of the epileptic has been the misunderstanding and apprehension of the employer and his employees. The frustration resulting from this and other kinds of personal rejection has at times increased maladjustment and emotional disturbances among epileptics. Consequently, many epileptics needed workshops to provide work until they could get jobs, to prepare them for work if they needed adjustment or training for work, and to help them overcome emotional disturbances which made it difficult for them to work.

The recognition of these problems led a group of men at the Central Seizure Center of the Veterans Administration at Sawtelle near Los Angeles, California, to resolve that a program should be developed to help service-connected epileptic veterans. In 1948, an Epilepsy Program Committee was formed, and it was successful in establishing an Epilepsy Research Program under John D. French in 1949. The purpose of the project was to make a medical, sociological and economic investigation of the problems of epileptics, but a workshop was to play a large part in the research activities (29). As an outgrowth of the experimental workshops came the workshops for the epileptics in the United States.

The director of this pioneer workshop for epileptics was Frank Risch, a psychologist who also served the Epileptic Research Program. The rationale of the workshop was that the men should be given the opportunity to experience the work conditions that would confront them in industry. The goal was the placement of the epileptic in private industry. To achieve the goal, the shop set up a woodworking and assembly section, a machine shop, a processing section, and a finishing section consisting of packaging, sanding, painting, and drying units. The shop served an average of thirty-six men the first year under the supervision of a manual arts therapist. The average wage was 75 cents an hour. In 1951 an administrative officer and a shop foreman were assigned. In the next few years the shop developed a substantial subcontract program.

Among the epileptics assigned to the shop were some with severe psychiatric disturbances. It was soon observed that when a worker was assigned to a job which suited his unique needs, a marked improvement in his social and job adjustment occurred. It was assumed that the particular circumstances of the tasks assigned reinforced his defense mechanisms and sublimated his ill-repressed destructive or hostile drives. The effect of suitable work was considered to reduce anxiety, irritability and antagonism, and to develop a more socially adaptable individual. This result could not be produced by verbal suggestion, since the interview could not provide the performance equivalent which was anxiety reducing. As a result of observation of repeated instances where work created dramatic changes in behavior, the staff developed a theory of work as therapy which has to some extent influenced Veterans Administration workshops for the mentally ill.

Although the specific observation of therapeutic value of work was probably their most important early finding, the staff also developed the diagnostic value of work in testing the needs and postures of emotionally disturbed persons. The epileptic's reaction to the shop environment was used to judge his readiness for outside employment. This kind of assessment made over a long period of time by close observation of performance and behavior was judged to add predictive value to evaluations made by other means at various points in time.

The tentative conclusion of the workshop staff after the first two years of operation was that the workshop could contribute in several ways to the rehabilitation of the epileptic. It could provide good methods of assessment and prognosis. It could restore the apathetic epileptic's interest in work. It could restore his confidence in his ability to work. It could reduce the incidence of his seizures. It could at times get him ready for work. The workshop could contribute to improving the epileptic's functioning as an individual in society and at work.

One finding of the Epilepsy Research Program was that over three fourths of the epileptic veterans outside of the Veterans Administration facilities could engage in workshop activities with many of this number capable of holding jobs in industry (30).

Consequently, in February 1955, Risch and others interested in the epileptic organized a private nonprofit corporation named Epi-Hab which operated a workshop in Los Angeles. This was the first of five private nonprofit workshops for epileptics bearing the name of Epi-Hab. In addition to the shops in Sawtelle and Los Angeles, Epi-Habs were started in Long Island, New York, in 1957, Phoenix, Arizona, in 1958, and Evansville, Indiana in 1964. Several other workshops for epileptics were started, of which the largest was at the Academy of Seizures in Minneapolis, Minnesota.

Added support to workshops for epileptics was given by the Vocational Rehabilitation Administration. The Demonstration and Research Program of that organization in 1956 financed a project conducted by Epi-Hab of Los Angeles to demonstrate that epileptics can perform industrial and mechanical jobs from which they have been excluded. Epi-Hab of Phoenix, Arizona, and Long Island, New York, followed with prototype, or follow-up, projects. A project of another type was conducted by the Rehabilitation Institute of Kansas City beginning in 1963.

The feasibility of employing epileptics had been demonstrated, but the reluctance to hire epileptics remained. In 1964, the United Epilepsy Association of New York undertook a project to demonstrate methods of shaping employer attitudes through business associations. Finally, in 1966, the Epilepsy Association of America began a project to demonstrate how a voluntary health organization can develop local, state, and national programs to encourage the rehabilitation of epileptics (31).

WORKSHOPS FOR THE MENTALLY ILL

The mentally ill was the last large group of handicapped persons to be given special attention by workshops in the United States. Before the first World War the mentally ill and emotionally disturbed were served in small numbers by the religious organizations that operated workshops at the time, probably not as persons with a psychiatric diagnosis but because they had economic or personal problems. After the first World War they were probably served in larger numbers, but usually by workshops which served many disability groups. No special programs for the mentally ill were undertaken by multidisability workshops until the middle of the twentieth century. When groups of workshops serving the mentally ill exclusively developed, their numbers were small indeed. This history is in contrast to that of Western Europe where larger numbers of workshops for the mentally ill have existed since after World War I (32). Programs for the mentally ill in workshops are in their infancy in the United States.

Mentally ill persons were probably first put to work in large numbers in the mental hospitals of the United States. However, the work was usually institutional; the chores of housekeeping, maintenance, farming, food processing and feeding, and the like, were assigned to patients to reduce costs of operating the hospitals. Sometimes the desire to get the work done became more important than the need to help patients. There were rarely wages or a relationship between the work and a reward for its accomplishment. Since there were usually plenty of patients, the amount of work done mattered little, and there was no reason to make great efforts. Often work was not used to activate the patient to function better or to prepare him for a job in industry after his release from the hospital. Work in the hospital did not have the same meaning to patients as work in the outside world. Thus, until paid employment on work for the outside world was introduced into hospitals at midcentury, the establishments for the mentally ill could not be said to have had workshops.

The first workshops to serve the mentally ill in the nineteenth century were probably those operated by the Salvation Army and the Volunteers of America. These organizations may not have labeled the troubled persons they served by psychiatric terminology, but considerable numbers of them may have been persons who would now be classified as mentally ill or emotionally disturbed. Between 1905 and 1921, a half-dozen Goodwill Industries began serving some emotionally disturbed, probably without psychiatric designations. Between 1921 and 1950, about two dozen more Goodwills began serving some emotionally disturbed. During the latter period, a small number of multidisability workshops began accepting troubled people; the Detroit League for the Handicapped in 1921, the Rehabilitation Center of St. Louis in 1925, the Community Workshop of Boston and the

Vocational Rehabilitation Center in Pittsburg in 1940, and the Vocational Guidance and Rehabilitation Service of Cleveland in 1949, were the largest. During this latter period, a few emotionally disturbed persons were accepted in workshops for the blind when they were blind as well as emotionally disturbed. In addition, a small number of rescue missions without national affiliation provided work for emotionally disturbed persons in what may be considered workshops (33).

After 1950, several hundred more workshops began serving small numbers of emotionally disturbed persons. However, the majority of these workshops did not serve them because they were mentally ill. The single disability workshops accepted the mentally ill when they also had the disability which the shop served exclusively. These shops' personnel often found that the emotional disturbance was more of a handicap than the condition for which the workers were admitted. Other shops admitted the emotionally disturbed persons on the basis of a psychiatric diagnosis; however, these were a small minority of the total population of the shops. After 1953, a handful of community shops developed special programs for the emotionally disturbed persons. Beginning in 1956, Veterans Administration programs and later state programs developed workshops in mental hospitals, principally in Massachusetts, California, New York, and Illinois.

Probably the first program especially designed for the mentally ill in a community workshop was started by Altro Workshops of New York City in 1953. The intake for this project was limited to postpsychotics capable of benefiting from a workshop setting. The objective was to provide an intermediate program between the mental hospital and the outside world. Although Altro Workshops had divisions of garment manufacturing, business services, and machine shop and mechanical bench assembly, the work was not used for vocational training primarily. Rather, it was used to enable the postpsychotic to learn to work through trial and error without the consequences of error which exist in a job outside the workshop. The mentally ill were not segregated in a separate unit but were placed among the tubercular and cardiacs in any of the three divisions depending upon the individual's desires, aptitudes, and needs. The postpsychotic workers were surrounded by rehabilitation personnel who provided a "ring of protective services," which were considered necessary to the success of their rehabilitation. Nevertheless, the importance of work and money incentives in keeping patients interested in the program is recognized.

The program began in 1953 with a half-dozen patients from Hillside Hospital and later expanded to take referrals from aftercare programs of state hospitals, two state and veterans hospitals, and the psychiatric departments of two general hospitals. By 1960, the program had served 250 mentally ill persons, and was serving between 35 and 40 mentally ill persons at any given time. In November, 1966, Altro was serving 64 psychotics, 50 emotionally disturbed persons, and 21 mentally retarded adults. While working, they received the prevailing rate for work they did. The workshop phase lasts from six to twelve months (34).

In 1959, the Altro Workshops made use of control groups to test the results of its services to the mentally ill. Patients from the Bronx Aftercare Clinic who were judged likely to benefit from Altro's program were divided into two groups at random. The experimental group was referred for service while the comparison group was not given any service. The project was hampered by the small numbers of the intended population who accepted referral and who actually received service. Nevertheless, the project was completed. In respect to rehospitalization, it was found that 15 or 38 percent of the comparison group returned to the hospital while only 10 or 24 percent of the experimental or the group given service returned to the hospital. On the other hand, 25 or 62 percent of the comparison group did not return to the hospital while 31 or 76 percent of the experiment or served group did not return to the hospital. While the data was not considered statistically significant, the data suggests that Altro services reduced rehospitalization to a modest degree. The importance of the project lies in the willingness of Altro Workshops to test its effectiveness and the beginning of factual analysis in workshop programs (35).

WORKSHOPS IN MENTAL HOSPITALS

The history of workshops in mental hospitals begins a bit like a detective story. In the beginning, in some places those in authority would not admit the workshops existed; if they did admit workshops existed in mental hospitals, they usually refused to accept responsibility for them. Thus it is difficult to determine when workshops began in mental hospitals. Some hospitals had workshops in operation before they were officially recognized. These illegitimate workshops were called by names such as informal workshops, unofficial workshops, unbudgeted workshops and the most picturesque of all, bootleg workshops.

It is proposed to account for these illegitimate offsprings when their parents acknowledge them. This will not distort the narrative unduly, for they usually proved to be sturdy infants, and soon gained recognition for their undoubted virtues. However, since their status at birth influenced their growth and development, it is useful to inquire into the reasons they were disavowed by some hospital administrators. Also, the inquiry may throw some light on the reasons for the small numbers of workshops in mental hospitals in the United States.

One of the background factors that led mental hospital administrators to reject workshops in the first half of the twentieth century was the fear that industry would object if hospital patients were used to produce goods sold in the open market. After World War II, some administrators in particular were resistant to workshops for this reason. At midcentury and in the following decade, some hospital administrators continued to resist the starting of workshops without testing the public's reaction to their existence. Indeed, legal and technical objections were raised to workshops in mental hospitals which proved illusionary when the shops were started.

It appears that such resistance was often greater in hospitals in rural areas. These mental hospitals are often self-contained communities, remote from large centers of population, and in the past were usually inadequately financed and understaffed. Like the people of some small towns, the personnel of hospitals were well acquainted with each other and sensitive to each other's prestige, status, and self-interest. When expansion and recognition was sought by existing programs, it was easy to give lower priority to new programs like workshops which were not understood and therefore not appreciated. Furthermore, some medically trained superintendents did not feel comfortable with programs based on business operations. As a result, it was left, with some notable exceptions, to nonmedical or lower echelon personnel to start and develop hospital workshops in rural areas. These dedicated public servants soon found an important ally — the hospital patients (36). Because hospital patients responded so well to workshops, they were allowed to develop and were finally accepted by hospital administrators and their staffs.

Workshops in Veterans Hospitals

An early, officially acknowledged workshop in a mental hospital was started by John J. Brennan in the Veterans Administration Hospital at Bedford, Massachusetts, in 1956. He had previously started what was probably an informal workshop at Northhampton Veterans Administration Hospital in 1948. The Northhampton workshop was part of a threefold program to prepare patients to return to work in the community. The first two parts consisted of the Community Employment Project and the Day Work — Night Hospital Program in which patients worked in competitive industry. The workshop was called the Modified Community Employment Project because work in the form of subcontracts was brought into the hospital from the community. Patients worked on the subcontracts for standard earnings and met competitive quantity and quality standards. In 1954, Brennan began the first two mentioned projects at Bedford, without the workshop. However, some patients were unready for outside employment. In 1956, therefore, he started to bring work into the hospital and thus began the first official workshop. He called it the Modified Community Employment Project of the Northhampton Project.

Its principal objective was to prepare the patient to return to remunerative work in the community. To do so it was first necessary to restore his confidence in his ability to work. This required a simulated industrial setting where the stresses that exist in industry are present. Such stresses enable the patient to gain the tolerance for work he must have to bridge the gap between the hospital and the job. The workshop is therefore a learning and relearning situation. The patient learns to think in terms of the requirements of the shop and to avoid egotistical concerns. The shop is thus a performance and behavioral testing and proving grounds for productive, remunerative work. This coordination of realistic work activities for a clearly defined objective was in contrast with other workshops in mental hospitals which were to follow. The first mental hospital workshop was successful and continues to the present (37).

The first program to be called a workshop in a Veteran's Administration Mental Hospital was founded by Roy S. Hubbs at Palo Alto, California, in August 1957. This workshop, the Veteran's Workshop, was co-founded by E. Randal Free, who has been manager since its inception. The workshop received no budget assistance from the Veteran's Administration, but was given the use of space for its operations. A private nonprofit corporation was set up which provided the structure for the business transactions. This corporate form has proven useful in other workshops operated in government programs. Subcontracts were taken into the shop and the veteran patients were paid wages for their work. When Hubbs retired as Chief of Continuous Treatment Services in 1964, Joseph M. McDonough took over its professional direction. The workshop was probably the first in a mental hospital in the United States to demonstrate the effectiveness of a workshop through the use of matched control groups.

Before he started the workshop, Hubbs had been impressed by the undesirable sequence of events in institutional psychiatry: discharged patients' failure to hold gainful employment, the aggravation of financial difficulties, the increased domestic irritation, and the return of the patient to the hospital. Hubbs assumed the following hypothesis: remunerative work can provide ego satisfaction and result in an improvement of the psychiatric condition. The restoration of lost work abilities is the aim of the workshop, a protected environment where mild aberrant behavior is tolerated. By providing renumerative employment it increases the patients' self-confidence, skills, and mental equilibrium. It enables him to return to competitive labor market under circumstances favorable to continued employment.

From 1957 to 1962, Hubbs studied 48 patients in the workshop and 48 control patients who did not work in the shop. He found in the first nine months of the operation that one and one-half or more were working in industry from those who were in the workshop than those in the control group. By 1962, he found that 25 from the workshop group were gainfully employed and only 8 were working from the control group. He concluded that when the workshop is used to provide work and a livelihood to male patients unable to hold employment in the competitive labor market, it reduces the number of returns to the hospital except among those patients too ill or regressed to make an economic adjustment in any case. He estimated that 15 percent of released patients could benefit from a workshop program (38).

After the Bedford and Palo Alto experience, several other Veterans Administration hospitals tried paid work programs, usually on an informal or intermittent basis. Another large, permanent workshop in Veterans Administration mental hospitals was developed at Brockton, Massachusetts. This was the Community Hospital Industry Rehabilitation Program (CHIRP) started in 1961. The previous Brockton experience had indicated that many patients, including those who did well in industrial therapy, failed to find or keep jobs in industry. To reverse this trend, a hospital workshop was started where work conditions were as nearly identical to competitive industry as possible. In this case, the subcontracts operations were carried on by the hospital administration. Beginning with 21 discharged patients in 1961, the program grew to 229 in 1964. Nearly 400 patients were in the program in that year. Thirty-four companies have since provided subcontracts, and a large pharmaceutical firm provided a widespread educational and promotional program. By 1964, its sponsors believed that they had demonstrated the effectiveness of a reality-oriented transitional workshop for patients in a mental hospital (39).

The Veterans Administration mental hospital workshops described developed with a common emphasis on preparation for employment after leaving the hospital. The early development of workshops in state mental hospitals varied greatly from hospital to hospital. The principal difference consisted in providing benefits to patients in the hospital who were not ready to leave the hospital as well as those who were. Work was used to fill up the idle time in the patient day, to provide spending money for the patient, and to test his potential for activity, in contrast to the Veterans hospitals' emphasis.

WORKSHOPS IN STATE MENTAL HOSPITALS

New York

The first workshop in a state mental hospital was probably that started by Herman Denber in the Manhattan State Hospital at Wards' Island in New York City. Denber had visited workshops in European mental hospitals in 1954 and had conceived the idea of starting a workshop at Wards' island. However, it was April 1958 before he was able to get it in operation in the Research Division of the hospital.

Denber was impressed with the fact that in spite of chemotherapy, psychotherapy, and other therapies, the hospital patient's day was often a vacuum without purpose or activity. He reasoned that meaningful work would provide a realistic incentive to motivate the patient for his rehabilitation in the hospital and after his release. To provide the work, he secured subcontracts from industry. In general, the work proved satisfactory to most patients, although some wanted office work not available at the time. The shop at first served thirty-five patients a day, most of whom benefited from the experience. Some young patients were not happy with work and were terminated. It was found that a directive approach was most successful with schizophrenic patients.

Soon after starting the program, Denber secured a grant from the National Institute of Mental Health and was able to analyze the nature of his workshop. He determined that the workshop, as contrasted with other part-time treatment modalities, provided continuous movement, a continuum of positive factors, fixation and structured boundaries. He conceived it as a reality oriented environment, with wage incentives and perceptible goals. Supportive without creating dependency, it set boundaries for behavior that are flexible but rigid enough to integrate the disintegrated ego structure. He placed emphasis on the substitution of objects instead of human beings as attachments more suitable for schizophrenics until human relationship tolerance could be restored. Thus work projects should be selected in relationship to the patient's psychodynamic structure. He recognized, however, that practical considerations made such selection often impossible. Denber's suggestion on the suitability of work objects to the patient's psychodynamics is in contrast to the practices of community workshops for the mentally ill (40).

About the same time that Denber was starting the Manhattan workshop, another workshop in a mental hospital was started at Central Islip Hospital, Central Islip, New York. In 1959, a workshop was started at Middleton State Hospital and in 1962, a third at Rockland State Hospital at Orangeberg, New York. At Rockland the workshops were in the wards.

Apparently the legal status of workshops in state hospitals was in question in New York State at the time, and there was a question in the minds of some state agencies as to the propriety of labeling them as workshops. Subsequently, the decision of the Supreme Court in 1968, Maryland vs. Wirtz, indicated that work in mental hospitals was subject to minimum wage laws.

California — the Bootleg Workshops

The first workshop in a California state mental hospital was started at Napa State Hospital at Imola by Robert Cordial in 1960. Cordial, a recreational therapist, was probably the founder of the workshops in California mental hospitals. In 1962, after some experience with the Napa workshop, he wrote an outline or guide for the establishment of a workshop in a mental hospital.

Cordial's brochure described the aims of the workshop simply and clearly. "Our major goal," he wrote, "is to develop all requisites necessary to fulfill the job demands of a community industry. This will provide for equal opportunity in competing for job placement upon the patient's return to the community." In another place he stated, "We hope to establish a businesslike and realistic situation whereby a patient can earn and learn under the tutelage of skilled personnel." He also visualized the workshop as an important part of the treatment plan. He wrote, "The ability to earn money and have the choice of spending it is an integral part of the total therapeutic program which has as its emphasis the early return of the individual to the level of functioning, which would permit him to return to his family and get along in society."

Cordial foresaw the following advantages from a workshop in a state hospital.

1. It prevents the patient from retreating into a hospital-dependency type of relationship.
2. It decreases the problem of re-adaption to outside living in the community.
3. It enables the patient to keep a realistically oriented area of social-economic relationships, which are necessary for adequate adjustment in the community.
4. While in the hospital it helps the patient to maintain a sense of dignity and respect.

The example of the Napa State Hospital was followed in 1961 by Mendocino State Hospital near Ukiah, where Harold Dale Smith started a workshop along the lines of the Napa shop. The Napa and Mendocino shops served principally the mentally ill. In 1961 two state hospitals serving the mentally retarded started workshops. At Sonoma State Hospital at Eldridge, a workshop was operated under the direction of Harry Cusperson, and a workshop was started under the direction of Allan Toedter at Fairview State Hospital near Costa Mesa. The advent of the hospitals for the mentally retarded into workshop operation was to prove of great importance, for the future interest of the Department of Mental Hygiene centered on the workshops for the mentally retarded. The first two workshops are no longer in existence, the Mendocino shop closing in 1963 and the Napa shop, in 1967.

In 1962 the California Legislature increased the budget of the Department of Mental Hygiene to enable it to add services for the mentally retarded at Patton and DeWitt state hospitals. Among the services considered necessary were workshop services. The budget specifically authorized workshop positions in the two hospitals. Thus for the first time the Department of Mental Hygiene and the Legislature recognized the need for workshops and provided staff adequate to operate workshops in state hospitals. The personnel "package" consisted of a director (workshop manager), an occupational therapist, an industrial therapist, and three group leaders. The pioneer period when Cordial and Smith ran workshops by working out of classification and "bootlegging" help from other departments was over, at least for DeWitt and Patton.

Two more workshops were established in California state hospitals, one at the Porterville State Hospital in 1963, and the second at Agnews State Hospital near San Jose in 1966. The Agnews workshop was started as a result of a cooperative agreement between the Department of Rehabilitation and the Department of Mental Hygiene. The cooperative agreement was an arrangement whereby the two departments used their funds jointly to secure more federal funds to operate more extensive rehabilitation services in the hospital. The workshop was part of the expanded rehabilitation services. Department of Rehabilitation employees worked in the workshop as a result of this agreement, and the workshop had the benfit of budgeted positions.

In 1966, there were seven workshops in state hospitals in California. The workshops at DeWitt, Patton, and Agnews had budget positions for the workshops. The remainder at Napa, Sonoma, Fairview and Porterville had no budget positions and were operated by personnel in positions not budgeted for the workshops. Sonoma, Fairview, and Porterville serve principally the mentally retarded and the workshop populations are mainly mentally retarded. DeWitt, Patton, Napa, and Agnews serve principally the mentally ill, but the workshops at DeWitt and Patton were set up specifically for the mentally retarded. In 1966, the seven workshops served approximately five hundred patients (41).

Soon after the budgeted shops were established in 1963, the Department of Mental Hygiene made a study of the then existing workshops in state hospitals (42). The study made when some of the shops were new did indicate some of the directions the shops were taking. The three principal services found were work habit training, (tolerance, responsibility, and dependability), personal adjustment, and wages as a motivating agent to build self-esteem. The work consisted of subcontracts, (37%) repair and refinishing (34%), and services such as car washing and ironing (20%). Although subcontracts comprised only 37 percent of the man hours worked, they provided nearly two thirds of the income.

At the time of the survey, 49 percent of those served in the workshops were mentally ill, 33 percent mentally retarded, 10 percent epileptic, 6 percent alcoholic, and 2 percent cerebral palsied. Of this population, 38 percent were returned to the community in job placements, 15 percent were returned to other rehabilitation programs, 15 percent were found unable to make a workshop adjustment, and the rest were returned to the hospital for personal reasons, illness, and other reasons. Of the 38 percent returned to the community for work, 8 percent came back to the hospital. Of those returning to the hospital, 69 percent were unable to make an adjustment to the community, and 31 percent were unable to continue to work in job placements. In evaluating these results, it is well to remember that most of the shops were new and that only two had adequate staffs.

Massachusetts

The success of the paid employment programs in Veterans Administration hospitals apparently had no immediate influence upon the Massachusetts mental hospitals until the cause of the workshop was championed by Mrs. Edna Steen, President of the Brookline Association for Mental Health. Dismayed by the idleness she saw among mental patients in hospitals, and impressed by the results she saw in workshops in European mental hospitals, she inspired the creation of the workshop at the Metropolitan State Hospital in Waltham, near Boston, Massachusetts, in 1961. The Metropolitan workshop, while not the first workshop in a state mental hospital, was the first operated by a private nonprofit organization in a state mental hospital. The hospital supplied the space, utilities and patients, the Brookline Association for Mental

Health operated the workshop, and the Massachusetts Rehabilitation Commission utilized the shop for training of its clients and paid fees for the training services (43).

The workshop at Metropolitan was conceived as a bridge to the outside world to those that can leave the hospital, and as a place of work and source of money for those who cannot. The goals are to teach patients to assume responsibility in a socially acceptable manner, to enable them to learn to work with one another, and to provide a meaningful work experience which teaches skills and work habits in preparation for employment after discharge.

The administrative structure of the workshop is unique in several respects. The responsibility for the overall supervision of the workshop rests with a volunteer director who is employed as an executive by a large corporation and contributes time to the workshop program. He shares this responsibility with the executive director of the Brookline Association for Mental Health. Responsibility for the operation of the workshop remains with a full-time foreman who assigns the work, teaches the operations, and keeps time, production, and shipping and receiving records. A business agent is responsible for acquiring new contracts and for maintaining established contracts. He is responsible for flow of work and maintenance of production schedules. This responsibility places him over the foreman in line of authority. In addition, the hospital assigns a part-time social worker to the workshop, and the Massachusetts Rehabilitation Commission assigns a rehabilitation counselor full-time and a psychiatrist one-half day a week.

From May 1961 to May 1965, 153 patients were placed in the workshop. At the period's end, 20 were in the shop and 2 had died. Of the 131 who left the workshop, 77 were out of the hospital, a discharge rate of 59 percent. Of this discharged group, more than 60 percent were gainfully employed. The remainder are housewives, living with their families, or unaccounted for. Of the 54 still hospitalized, some have been transferred to Veterans Hospitals and many have left the hospital only to return. Many of them are in hospital industries. In evaluating these results, it is necessary to note that the shop is dealing with a chronic patient group characterized by multiple hospital admissions and long hospitalization. The expected normal discharge rate among a similar patient population has been much smaller.

The example of the Brookline Association for Mental Health was followed by others in Massachusetts, for example, the Norfolk Mental Health Association which sponsored a workshop in Redfield State Hospital at Westwood in 1963, and the North Shore Mental Health Association which started a workshop at Danvers State Hospital at Danvers in 1965. A variation of the approach was undertaken by a group of Boston businessmen at Boston State Hospital in 1964. The Massachusetts plan for a private nonprofit workshop in a state hospital, started by Mrs. Steen at Metropolitan, has been used at Mendocino State Hospital near Ukiah, California, and may influence newly established mental hospital workshops elsewhere.

A second workshop in a state mental hospital was initiated at Medfield State Hospital in 1963. The shop provides work experience similar to that in factories, a means of evaluation, and provides an opportunity to make money. The shop is a part of the hospital's rehabilitation work program project, which aims to prepare patients for employment in the community through the use of the shop and training in hospital jobs. The data available about results is stated in terms of the overall project. It shows that approximately nine times as many patients are working in outside industry from among the group that went through the work program compared with those that did not go through the work program (45).

A particularly interesting aspect of the Medfield program, which has been copied by other state hospitals, is their "step system," which sets up a series of incentives and rewards based on a series of graduated steps or stages. Not only productivity at work but other performance was rated in the steps. Among these were relationships with other workers, ability to use and follow directions, ability to work alone and to follow directions. Behavior was also rated in this system. The increasing requirements met in each step resulted in higher pay or more privileges.

At Boston State Hospital in 1964, a workshop program was started which was called PROP, Patients Rehabilitation Occupational Program, Inc. The program, though sponsored by a nonprofit corporation whose board consists of Boston volunteer businessmen, differs from the Metropolitan structure in that the hospital is more involved administratively. All employees are hired by the Hospital Superintendent's office, though PROP, Inc., pays the salaries of a floor lady, an assistant, and a bookkeeper. A coordinator and two shop supervisors are hired by the hospital, and two full-time volunteers supervise patients in the shops. The rehabilitation department of the hospital provides vocational counseling. psychological testing, job placement and follow-up.

The primary goal of the PROP program is the vocational rehabilitation of the patient – his ability to hold down a remunerative, productive and satisfying job. To secure this end, the program attempts to replace feelings of rejection and worthlessness with self-confidence, stagnation and apathy with identification with work, his supervisors, the product and his earning power. Patients are taught good work habits, good social and interpersonal relationship, and are made aware of the realities of life outside of the hospital. To create the industrial environment of a competitive world, the program has an industrial sewing shop, an assembly shop where assembly-line factory tasks are performed, a print shop, a press shop where laundry work is performed, a candy-packing shop, and a bookkeeping department where patients are prepared for clerical and bookkeeping work.

From January 1964 to October 1965, 176 patients were involved in the PROP activities. In October 1965, 75 patients were employed in the PROP shops. Twenty-two patients were working in outside industry. Eleven were living out of the hospital and not working. Twenty-six were working in other hospital jobs. Thirty were not able to work because of severity of physical or mental illness and 12 were transferred, living outside and their status was unknown. The patients indicated above were hospitalized for many years, some as long as twenty or thirty years and had no or limited work experience (46).

Illinois

A somewhat different development of mental hospital workshops took place in Illinois. Here workshops were set up in hospital wards, as was done at Rockford State Hospital, and in zone facilities as well as in separate hospital central and area shops. The zone facilities were mental health administrative and service centers which served designed geographic areas.

At the time this was written, the Illinois mental hospital workshops were expanding rapidly and were in an evolving stage. About a dozen facilities had workshops. The ward workshops in particular were expanding. In 1968, there were fifteen ward workshops in the Chicago State Hospital alone. Other workshops were at Manteno, Tinley Park, Madden, Anna, Jacksonville, Hines, Elgin, and Rockford.

Because of the newness of the programs, the objectives of the workshops varied from hospital to hospital. The ward workshops in particular have multiple and variable goals. They are used as tryout units to determine if a patient could benefit from the central workshop. They also received rejected patients from the central workshop who needed longer or different kinds of service. The ward workshops are also used to provide patients with pocket money. They provide activities for ward patients, help prepare patients for discharge by self-care instruction, and at times provide educational services for young patients. No predetermined standard goals or objectives existed in the ward workshops.

In the central workshops, the goals varied also. In the main, the objectives were evaluation, orientation to work, improvement of work habits and behavior, and improvement of productive capacity. In area shops or shops serving separate hospital programs, the objectives were varied, but the emphasis was on therapeutic gains.

In the zone facilities emphasis was on therapeutic gains from work and on adjustment to productive work levels in industry or in workshops. The zone workshops were closely integrated with the other services in the zone centers, and the workshop often served as an adjunct or auxiliary service to the other service programs of the facilities (47).

Summary

In spite of the slow start in creating workshops, many state hospitals did start some workshops. In 1967, the National Association of State Mental Health Directors made a survey of workshops in state mental hospitals for the President's Committee on Employment of the Handicapped. In the 271 state mental hospitals serving the mentally ill which were surveyed, 60 had workshops listed. The same group surveyed the workshops in 154 hospitals for the mentally retarded. In the latter group, they found 25 workshops for a total of 85 in state institutions.

No statistics are available on the numbers of mentally ill patients served in state mental hospitals. The state mental hospital workshops did not have to report to the Wage and Hours Division of the Department of Labor until the Maryland vs. Wirtz Supreme Court decisions in 1968. However, it appears the total numbers served in the shops were small although a few shops served large numbers. It is estimated that the sixty state hospital workshops served less than 6,000 in 1968, a small fraction of the numbers of mentally ill patients who could benefit from their service.

WORKSHOPS IN COMMUNITY MENTAL HEALTH FACILITIES

In contrast with the recent increase in workshops in mental hospitals, there has been but a slight movement in establishing workshops in community mental health programs. The workshops which are sponsored by organizations providing mental health services exclusively are few in number and serve small numbers in their shops. In light of the development of comprehensive mental health centers in the 1960's, such a condition is surprising. It is also in contrast with countries in other parts of the world, such as the Soviet Union, where workshops are an integral part of treatment of mental illness in connection with out-patient psychiatric clinics (48). It is anticipated that workshops will be used in connection with the mental health center programs, but whether such centers will establish workshops themselves or use other community workshops remains to be determined.

It is estimated that in 1965 there were about two dozen workshops outside of mental hospitals serving the emotionally disturbed exclusively in the United States (49). The workshops varied in size and sponsorship. The majority are privately sponsored, serve small numbers of emotionally disturbed persons, and are located in metropolitan areas. Typical of the privately sponsored workshops are Horizon House in Philadelphia, Pennsylvania; Prospect House in East Orange; New Jersey; and the Thresholds in Chicago, Illinois.

The first named workshop, Horizon House in Philadelphia, may be illustrative of the genre. The sponsoring organization provides a number of treatment services which include psychotherapy, social casework, and vocational guidance. As an adjunct to these services, the organization operates a workshop. The focus of the workshop program is on evaluation and personal adjustment. The intent is that the work program will contribute to the treatment program.

Services to the Emotionally Disturbed
in Multidisability Workshops

The largest increase in number of workshops which served the emotionally disturbed took place in multidisability workshops. This increase took place after 1950, when there were approximately 50 workshops serving the disability group. In 1965, there were over 443 (50). There was no national survey taken prior to 1965 giving disability information. In a California survey of 1958, however, approximately 10 percent of the existing workshops accepted the emotionally disturbed. In 1965, approximately 50 percent of the California workshops stated they served the emotionally disturbed (51). The numbers of persons served by these shops are not known precisely. However, of 490 reporting workshops serving the emotionally disturbed in a 1965 survey, the median number served daily in the shops was 11. Since the multidisability shops were the largest number in the group (443 out of 490), the figure reflects the small numbers served by them (52).

Summary

Workshop services for the emotionally ill are provided by three groups of workshops. They are multidisability workshops,

workshops in mental hospitals, and workshops in outpatient mental health facilities. A 1965 survey showed the largest number of reporting shops, 443, as multidisability workshops. There were approximately 60 workshops in state mental hospitals, and an unknown additional number of workshops in Veterans mental hospitals. Approximately 24 workshops were in outpatient mental health facilities. There were probably close to 550 workshops serving substantial numbers of the emotionally disturbed in 1965 and closer to 600 by 1969.

A 1965 survey indicates that 454 reporting workshops showed 12,535 emotionally disturbed persons in daily attendance. However, since the survey showed only 24 mental hospital workshops, and probably missed other workshops not shown on directories, the figure must be short of the total. It is estimated that close to 20,000 emotionally disturbed persons were served in workshops in the United States in 1969.

PUBLICLY SUPPORTED WORKSHOPS
IN THE UNITED STATES

It has been seen that the publicly supported workshops for the blind began in 1888 and that workshops in Veterans and state mental hospitals increased rapidly after 1960. Three other types of publicly supported workshops are found in the United States. They are state-operated workshops, and local workshops sponsored by county governments or by school districts. The numbers in the three groups are few. It is estimated that less than 10 percent of the workshops in the United States were operated by public organizations in 1967 (53).

State-operated Workshops

The first state system of workshops was established in South Carolina in 1959. The workshops are operated by the state agency for vocational rehabilitation. In 1969, there were ten workshops in the state which served approximately 1700 persons in the first half of that year. The shops serve clients of the state agency having all types of handicaps. The shops have evaluation, personal and work adjustment, and work experience services. They also have a Terminal Employment Section.

Although the workshops are operated by the state agency, each workshop has a community advisory board of local citizens and one agency representative. The board secures money locally which is turned over to the county treasurers for matching of federal funds. The board is responsible for the financing of the Terminal Employment Section and the business operations of the shop. The workers are paid from contract income. Staff are paid from state-federal funds, with the exception of the production supervisor and bookkeeper, who are paid from local funds or contract income (54).

A system of workshops similar to that of South Carolina was developed by the state vocational rehabilitation agency in Louisiana. Here the program began with a workshop for the mentally retarded in Baton Rouge in 1962. Originally the workshop was operated by a voluntary agency with the state agency supplying some staff members to operate the shop. Three more workshops for the mentally retarded were established: the Westbank Sheltered Workshop in 1966, the Monroe Sheltered Shop in 1967, and the New Hope Shop in 1968.

The primary objective is preparation for employment in industry. However, when employment in industry proves impossible, long-term training in the shop is undertaken. In 1967, seventy-nine mentally retarded persons were served in the four shops (55).

A larger program than that of Louisiana is operated by the Division of Vocational Rehabilitation of Tennessee. This program was started in 1962 as the Vocational Training Centers, funded in part by a federal grant from the Vocational Rehabilitation Administration and co-sponsored by the Division and the Tennessee Association for Retarded Children and Adults, Inc. The federal funds were matched by local county court funds and other public and private funds which were raised by local associations and/or local volunteer boards. The local boards of directors also assumed responsibility for the subcontract work and prime manufactory and maintained these operations in the same way that a private, nonprofit workshop would operate them. There were ten centers in nonmetropolitan areas which served the mentally ill, mentally retarded, and the physically handicapped (56).

By an act of the Tennessee legislature, these centers were placed under the administration of the Tennessee Division of Vocational Rehabilitation in 1965. The financing of the centers is by an appropriation from either a city or county or by both or by several cities or counties. The money provides matching for federal funds which in 1969 was at a ratio of 30 percent local funds to 70 percent federal funds. The average budget for the centers is 35,000 dollars per year. The local board of directors has been maintained as an advisory body consisting of twelve local citizens. Its role is to assist the manager of each center in securing contract work, local appropriation, placements, and giving general advice on local circumstances.

In 1969, the Division operated sixteen centers in nonmetropolitan areas. The objective of the centers is to provide evaluations and make placements in private employment in the community. However, those who cannot be placed in private employment are provided sheltered employment without a time limit. In 1969, about four hundred individuals were served at a given time in the centers and approximately twelve hundred persons were served during the year (57).

Two Vocational Adjustment Centers were started by the Vocational Rehabilitation Division of the Department of Education of Nevada in recent years. The first was established in Las Vegas in 1964, and the second in Reno in 1965. The majority of persons served are clients of the Division of Vocational Rehabilitation, although other community and financing agencies use the shops. The administration of the shops is the responsibility of the state agency. There is no community advisory board as in the South Carolina program. In the Reno shop, 305 persons were served from April 1965, to January 1967, for an average attendance of from three to five weeks.

The shops emphasize evaluation. Psychometric testing, production evaluation, and evaluation of work potential are the principal services. At Las Vegas, job areas are explored. Though assessment is emphasized, a person who cannot meet criteria of employment may remain in the shop if he is progressing towards such criteria.

However, extended employment is not provided. The work of the shop is of such a nature that it can be accomplished without an extended period of learning. It consists of direct mail advertising, making of highway stakes, designing and making name plates for casinos, sewing operations, and repair of state-owned vehicles (58).

Direct tax funds in considerable amounts support workshops in addition to those for the blind. Such shops are in publicly sponsored rehabilitation facilities or are jointly sponsored with private voluntary rehabilitation agencies. In the first category is a workshop in a vocational rehabilitation center in Oregon, operated by the state vocational rehabilitation agency. In Oregon, the workshop is in the Salem Rehabilitation facility which is located in a state hospital.

An outstanding example of a state where control is shared is Alabama. There the Alabama Society for Crippled Children and Adults sponsored eight workshops in 1966 which were cooperately operated with the Vocational Rehabilitation Services of the Division of Rehabilitation and Crippled Children of the Department of Education. The shops were started with money supplied by the voluntary agency which was used by the state to match federal funds and were expanded by subsequent federal grants. The shops provide evaluation, adjustment services, vocational training, workshop employment placement, and follow-up services (59).

Public Workshops in Local Jurisdictions

Publicly supported workshops in local jurisdictions are in county welfare organizations or in school systems. They have not flourished in great numbers in either sponsorship. Since public assistance organizations and school districts have large numbers of persons in their programs who can benefit from workshops, the relative absence of workshops in these jurisdictions is unexpected. Although many reasons may account for their small numbers, important inhibiting factors in the development of county assistance programs has been the sometimes unclear legal status of relief recipients as workers, and the identification of workshops with shameful work houses or county poor farms of the past. Also in some parts of the country, the tradition of private agencies as sponsors of workshops prevailed.

Scant material is available about local public workshops. It is estimated that there is a handful of public assistance workshops and a scattering of workshops in public school districts.

Public Assistance Workshops

The largest and probably the first public assistance workshop was started by the City of Chicago, Illinois, during World War II. The initial work was making bandages for the Red Cross. Only persons on general assistance were accepted. In 1958, Cook County took over the general assistance load and the operation of the workshop. Only persons on public assistance were served in the workshop. These included a wide range of persons with physical and mental disabilities and with social and financial problems. In the 1960's, the shop served from 400 to 450 persons at a time.

The principal object of the workshop was to place persons in employment and thus take them off public assistance. Towards this end vocational evaluation, personal and social adjustment, vocational training, and placement services were provided. The work done consisted primarily of subcontracts. The principal operations were in spray painting, machine shop, arc welding, electronics, power sewing, sorting, assembly, and packaging. Large numbers of work orders are received daily when the economy prospers, and workers are placed from the work floor when they are considered ready for competitive employment. In good times, as many as sixty to seventy persons a month were placed. Average stay was from six to eight months, and stay was limited to approximately one year. No wages are paid but workers are provided a small allowance for expenses in connection with going to work.

Other prominent local workshop programs are the two workshops operated by the Department of Public Health and Welfare of San Mateo County in California. The first was started in 1957, by the Social Service Division of the department. The program provided work evaluation, work habit training, and stimulation to remunerative employment. It was viewed as a supportive service to aid the social worker in helping the client to achieve the maximum physical, emotional and economic independence. Vocational training in electronics and vocational guidance and placement was also provided. The work consisted of power sewing on wine bottle jackets, electronic assembly, clerical work for county departments, and some packaging. Wages were not paid, but many placements were made especially in the electronics industry in which there was a large demand for workers in the area. From 1955 to 1962, the numbers served increased from ten to thirty at a given time. In some instances, the stay was short when vocational training was given, but in other instances the stay was varied according to need. A few stayed for long periods of time. The clients served were those with emotional problems, low educational level, lack of employment skills and those who were aged.

In 1962, a grant was received from the State Department of Social Welfare under Public Law 10606 to upgrade the program to serve larger numbers of Aid to Families with Dependent Children recipients. The staff was increased, the program industrialized, and from ten to one hundred persons were served. This emphasis prevailed until 1968, when the Work Incentive Program was initiated by the Department of Employment and those nondisabled on Aid to Families with Dependent Children were referred to that program and put to work on projects that paid them wages. The Workshop took physically and mentally handicapped persons and the aged. In 1969, from forty-five to sixty were served at a time. No wages were paid to the recipients.

In the period after 1962, when the workshop was serving principally those on Aid to Families with Dependent Children, the Division of Mental Health became dissatisfied with the inability of the workshop to serve sufficient numbers of persons from the mental hospital and outpatient services. Consequently, they established another workshop that worked primarily with the same contracts of the social service division workshop but served exclusively persons with psychiatric disorders who were served by county mental health facilities. The goals of the mental health workshop of the county were similar to those of the regional workshop, with the exception of more emphasis on personal and social adjustment.

Two county workshops in Los Angeles, California, took different forms of organization. The Toy Loan workshop developed as a result of the recognition on the part of judges and probation officers that if children were loaned the use of toys it would reduce the incidence of juveniles stealing them. First toys, principally dolls, were collected and loaned to children of relief recipients and other needy children. As the toys were used, they needed repair and a shop was set up to repair and repaint them. Later the toys were given to the children. Relief recipients were put to work in the shop. They received no wages in money but the hours they worked were recorded. When the numbers of hours they worked, multiplied by the regular wage per hour, reached the amount of their assistance budget, they could work no more. The shop grew with the population of Los Angeles and a large two-story building ultimately was assigned for the operation. The goal of the shop was to prepare toys for children. Unskilled persons and skilled craftsmen who were relief recipients worked voluntarily in the shop without pay. Such improvements in their condition as resulted were secondary. They worked in the shop because it provided them with acceptable activity.

Another type of local workshop was the two workshops at Rancho Los Amigos, the chronic care hospital of Los Angeles County. Here the shop was set up for evaluation and work adjustment and training. Placements outside the shop were made for those whose conditions made it possible. Here wages were paid to provide chronic care patients with incentive. Subcontracts of a simple nature were taken. The administration of the workshops was carried on by county employees.

A different development took place in Redding, California, where the public assistance program operates a shop. Here a work training center for mentally retarded only was started in 1962 by an association for the retarded. However, financing proved difficult, and appeals were made to the Department of Vocational Rehabilitation and the county public assistance program. To get such assistance, it was necessary to broaden the range of disability groups accepted. The county finally received state-federal funds under Public Law 10606 and county employees were placed in the workshops while the shop was still under the direction of the association for the retarded. However, as the financing became predominately county and state, the county public assistance program took over the operation of the shop. Because of the different origin of the shop, wages are paid, and all handicapped persons are accepted for service.

Summary

The public assistance shops suffer from a number of common problems. Often the income from work goes into the county treasury. The earnings are not readily available for equipment, materials, and other operating expenses. Equipment, therefore, must be supplied by the contractors, but there is usually no ready revolving fund to use for repair or maintenance. As a result, the operations of the shop are impeded and much work that could be obtained is lost.

Where wages are not paid or where attendance at the shop is mandatory, incentive suffers. Staff in these shops are usually of the opinion that wage payments would increase both incentive and the levels of accomplishment. While it is not maintained that money payments will provide universal incentives, it is usually believed that for many public assistance recipients' low incomes, money supplements to relief budgets for work done in the shop will provide added incentive.

The rationale for these obstacles to progress in public assistance workshops often arises from legal and administrative considerations. Informal legal opinions are given that question the right of recipients to receive pay for their work in workshops. It is not certain, however, that such opinions would be upheld in court tests. In any case, wages have been paid in public assistance workshops without challenge, and public assistance recipients in the national Work Incentive Programs are paid sums in excess of relief budgets while working on the job training programs similar to workshop training programs. Apparently, some administrators, in light of overwhelming problems of handling public assistance loads, are reluctant to undertake the burden of variable payments to relief recipients, which would be necessary if wage payments were made in public assistance workshops. As a result of the obstacles enumerated and the lack of understanding of the constructive nature of these workshops by some public assistance personnel, workshops have not thrived in public assistance programs in the United States. This may change, however, if concepts about work incentives discussed in the late 1960's are written into national laws governing public assistance programs.

Workshops in Public Schools

A recent development in workshop programs is the reappearance of the school as the operator of workshops for their students. Although workshops were initially established by schools in this country, mainly private schools for the blind, the school gradually gave up the operation of workshops. In 1960, it is doubtful if there were any workshops administered and operated by schools.

After 1960, a few public schools undertook the operation of workshops. These were often operated by special education programs. It is difficult to determine where such workshops existed because of the problems of definition and because some school programs started small workshops on an experimental basis and did not publicize their programs. Some schools operated vocational classes in which products were made and the money from their sales was given to the students that made them. Other schools had classes in which products were made but the students were not paid. Some school programs which began with nonpaid work took subcontracts and began paying the students. At present, some school programs are in transition from a class to a workshop. A scattering of school programs exist where work activity and work training is carried on but students are not paid for work. In the following account, only paid work programs will be discussed.

Probably the earliest workshops started by public schools after 1960 were found in California. In the early 1960's several workshops were started by special education programs. Prototypes were the Whittier shop for the cerebral palsied and the Santa Cruz shop for the mentally retarded. After 1968 a number of additional shops were started by special education programs and one by adult education in Barstow, California.

A number of school workshops and work activity programs were started in Illinois after 1968 for the mentally retarded. The first was probably at LaGrange, Illinois. The shop is operated by special education and serves the mentally retarded until they reach the age of twenty-one. The shop is staffed by certified teachers. A number of Illinois schools started similar programs for the mentally retarded. Examples are the programs at Leyden Township and at Wheaton. In 1970, several programs providing nonpaid work were planning to develop paid work programs.

The shops previously discussed were established or developed by school programs. In other instances, school systems took over existing workshops or developed existing programs into workshop programs. In Fargo, North Dakota, in 1969 the school district took over the operation of an existing privately operated workshop. In Salt Lake City in 1970 a number of school programs were consolidated into a work training program which included paid work programs.

The existence of few workshops sponsored by public schools prior to 1968 does not mean that handicapped students did not attend workshops. In many places in the country, public school students spent half the day in school and the other half in privately operated workshops. Usually the time spent in the workshop is considered time spent in school. Often, however, the private workshop does not provide services to students unless the school pays for them. The ability of school systems to pay for such services varies, primarily because of differences in availability of funds.

A SUMMARY OF WORKSHOP DEVELOPMENT

Workshops in the United States developed differently depending upon the time when they started, the antecedents they followed, and the philosophies they espoused. Some followed European precedents, others developed spontaneously in response to indigenous ideas, and still others combined these two sources into an institutional hybrid. The workshops that made progress, however, tended to lose the characteristics of their origins as they copied from other workshops or initiated changes in response to community needs. It is therefore difficult to find meaningful hallmarks for the progressive group of shops as a whole.

Although the history of workshops cannot be divided accurately into distinct periods, certain overlapping trends are discernible for some major groups of workshops. It may be useful to describe these trends, even though they represent but gross descriptions of workshop development and will not serve to describe the course of development of some individual shops. Where variability is the rule, classification by time and type is difficult. Probably the safest approach is to identify periods by growth rate.

The First Period

In the first or early period of workshops from 1838 until the first World War, workshops with a few exceptions developed following European precedents. The workshops for the blind duplicated British workshops, manufacturing and selling the same British products, attempting to train for occupations, but providing primarily sheltered employment. The workshops of religious origin or affiliation as a rule adopted the schemes of their European counterparts, renovating and selling household discards, and attempting usually to use work as a basis for the salvation or moral improvement of those who were spiritually derelict or morally deficient. A few workshops during this period departed somewhat from either mold. Workshops in Boston, Cleveland, and in Brooklyn, for example, undertook sewing and manufacturing operations different from the workshops for the blind. They, too, were interested in moral improvement but gave up this emphasis earlier than the shops of religious origin. This last group of shops will be labeled indigenous community workshops to distinguish them from the other two groups who maintained a fairly stable structure based on European influence.

Although most workshops during the first period were generally isolated from other community agencies and from the community generally, this was less true of the indigenous community shops. They sold their manufactured goods through charitable events and depended largely on private giving for financing. The workshops for the blind also sold their products at times on a noncommercial basis, but the household nature of their products tended towards the commercial approach. The shops of religious origin, on the other hand, found it possible to sell their products profitably on a more commercial basis. They did not have to appeal to community sources for funds. Their very independence kept them isolated from the rest of the community.

The workshops did not increase in large numbers during the first period. Their growth was possibly restricted by their isolation from the community, their dependence on a single source such as sales of products to generate work, and their moral emphasis which was becoming less acceptable to handicapped persons. In any case, though no accurate data is available, it is estimated there were less than one hundred workshops in the United States before World War I.

The Middle Period

In the middle period from World War I to the midcentury, new types of workshops arose based on indigenous concepts or European influences. The shops which were based on indigenous American concepts were started primarily in rehabilitation centers espousing the concept of comprehensive services. Workshops for the tubercular and curative workshops, both influenced by European precedents, were started during the period but soon changed to resemble workshops in rehabilitation centers or indigenous, freestanding community workshops. Also a few more indigenous community workshops were started, following precedents set by similar types of workshops in the earlier period.

During this middle period, the emphasis on serving the needy and morally deficient shifted to serving the physically handicapped, principally the orthopedically handicapped. This may have been influenced by the emphasis on orthopedic medicine and the growth of private agencies interested in children with orthopedic handicaps. In any case with the exception of the blind, the tubercular, the cardiacs, and some aged, persons with disabilities other than the orthopedic were not served by most workshops in large numbers. The mentally retarded and mentally ill were generally excluded.

During the middle period, the renovating workshops grew in numbers and size. They developed discard renovation into a generally lucrative operation which provided increasing work for handicapped persons. Probably for this reason, they did not change their basic operations except to engage more extensively in occupational training.

The indigenous community workshops also grew and expanded rapidly. Their growth was accompanied by a major shift of operations into subcontracting. Subcontracting was also adopted by the rehabilitation center workshops and transformed the workshops for the tubercular. Subcontracting became an established source of work in this period, although prime manufacturing played an important role. Subcontracting was not, however, adopted generally by the renovating workshops who were succeeding with the renovation of discards.

During this middle period, very little attention was given to specific workshop doctrine, theory, or rationale. The workshops were busy with the practical problems of getting footholds. Some attention was given, however, by some shops to rehabilitation philosophy and some workshop personnel speculated about the identity of workshops. The emphasis on rehabilitation philosophy and particularly on the comprehensive service concept and the team approach lead to more contracts with other agencies in the community. During this period, some of the shops began to lose their isolation from the community.

The numbers of workshops increased more rapidly during the middle period than in the early period. Though no survey data is available, it is estimated that over 400 workshops were in existence in 1950. In 1950, 15,572 persons were employed by 91 Goodwill Industries (59). During 1948, approximately 4,000 persons were served by more than 50 workshops in California. It is estimated that less than 35,000 handicapped persons were served by workshops in 1950, for an average of about 85 per shop.

The Latest Period

During the last period of workshop development after 1950,

two specialized types of new workshops were started. The first served only persons with a designated disability such as mental retardation or cerebral palsy or mental illness. The second group served persons with adjustment problems or similar functional problems. They served the psychologically maladjusted, or the chronically ill, and the aged. These shops provided either short-term services or long-term services but not both as a rule. Exceptions were the workshops for the mentally ill. Although the shops serving special disabilities grew rapidly in numbers, each shop's population generally was small.

Both groups of specialized shops developed new and radically different types of services and methodology. Both stressed the psychosocial factors in the work environment. The special disability shops used the psychosocial factors in long-term services to develop personal and social competence or to provide therapeutic or ameliorative services of lasting nature. The Jewish Vocational Services, on the other hand, stressed the importance of psychosocial services in short-term services to enable persons to work in competitive employment.

The new specialized shops influenced the older shops in two principal ways. The older shops, the renovating shops, and the indigenous community shops began accepting new types of disabilities previously rejected such as the retarded and mentally ill. They also added new techniques to their array of methods, adding principally work adjustment to their work habit training programs and expanding their psychosocial services. However, neither of the older groups abandoned their primary emphasis on work as the principal source of enablement. The rehabilitation center shops, however, who had anticipated the specialized shops in some measure in their psychosocial emphasis, now intensified their psychosocial services in the latest period.

During the middle period, some workshops, mainly those in the rehabilitation centers had moved towards closer integration in the community and better liaison with other private community agencies. They also sought private community funding. The shops which were started in the middle period continued their movement towards community integration and financing in the latest period. Some of the shops started in the latest period, however, did not seek large scale community integration and financing. They depended more on government support or on contract income for financing. They identified more exclusively with government agency objectives. Others identified more with industry and its objectives.

The new specialized shop started in the last period engaged primarily in subcontract work. During this period, the renovating shops also began engaging in subcontract work. Only some workshops for the blind and a few other major shops which manufactured proprietary items engaged in prime manufacturing exclusively. Many workshops which had started with prime manufacturing and renovating of discards adopted subcontracting as the principal work operation during this period.

Subcontract work was suitable as a basis for work evaluation and adjustment and for development of psychosocial services. The spread of these services was reinforced by the state vocational rehabilitation agencies who purchased them. The new psychosocial services were promoted through federal grants by the Social and Rehabilitation Services. The support of government agencies and the relatively small amounts of money required to start subcontract workshops led to the proliferation of hundreds of workshops. More workshops were started after 1950 than in the previous 122 years of workshop history.

Thus by 1970, a great variety of workshops existed in the country serving most handicapped groups of persons whose disabilities were subject to medical diagnosis. The workshops were short-term workshops moving persons into competitive employment, long-term workshops providing sheltered employment, and workshops providing both types of programs. There were workshops serving single disability groups and others serving persons with any type of disability. There were workshops doing renovating, prime manufacturing, subcontracting, and service work. There were workshops training in occupational skills, in work adjustment, in social and personal maturity, and those which provided long-term work for wages and for health and happiness.

It is not known how many workshops there are in the United States. No national survey has been conducted. From such data as exist, it is reasonable to assume that there are more than 1500.

The most complete count of workshops derives from the Department of Labor in the course of their certification of workshops permitted to pay handicapped workers less than the statutory minimum wage. That count is incomplete because the law applies only to shops whose products enter into interstate commerce. Furthermore, public workshops were not generally certified.

In the course of the previous narrative, estimates have been made of the numbers of workshops and of workers served in them. The estimates were made at various times in the last few years and are based on sources which vary in their accuracy. Nevertheless, since there are no available estimates other than the partial Department of Labor figures, it may be useful to summarize the estimates. No claim is made for accuracy.

The Wage and Hour and Public Contracts Division of the Department of Labor reported there were around 1,169 workshops certified to pay workers less than the minimum wage in 1969 (60). These would not include workshops which are publicly sponsored or workshops not selling their products in interstate commerce. In the course of the previous narrative, approximately 1,460 work places were identified which are considered workshops. Some new workshops are started each year. Estimates vary from 50 to 150 per year (61).

Since the estimate was made from figures during the last several years, some additional workshops were probably started since the various counts were taken. For these reasons it seems reasonable that there were more than 1500 workshops in the United States in the beginning of 1970.

It is even more difficult to estimate the number of handicapped persons in workshops. The figures are given in two ways: the number in workshops on any given day, and the number served during a given year. In mid-1968, the National Association of Sheltered Workshops estimated that about 60,000 handicapped workers were found in workshops on any one day. The Wage and Hour Division of the Department of Labor estimated that from 100,000 to 125,000 were served in workshops during 1968 (62). A summary of the workers in workshops indicated previously yields figures in excess of those given above. For example, the

National Goodwill Industries alone served 91,596 handicapped persons in 1968 (63). It is estimated that there were more than 65,000 persons in workshops on an average day in 1968, and that workshops served more than 175,000 in that year.

NOTES

1. Gellman, W.: Job Adjustments of "Apparent Unemployables" through a vocational Adjustment Shop. Workshops for the Disabled, Chouinard, E. L. and Garrett, J. F. (Eds.). Washington, U. S. Dept. of Health, Education and Welfare, 1956, pp. 113-128.
2. Gellman, W., Gendel, H., Glasser, N. M., Friedman, S. B., and Neff, W.: Adjusting People to Work. Chicago, Jewish Vocational Services Monograph No. 1, second ed., June, 1957, pp. 83-85.
3. Gellman, W., and Friedman, S. B.: The workshop as a clinical rehabilitation tool. Rehabilitation Literature, pp. 36-38, Feb. 1965.
4. Read, W. (Superintendent, U.C.P. of Kings County): Personal communication, August 13, 1965.
5. Nelson, N.: Workshops for the Disabled in California. V.R.S., 1958, p. 4.
6. McCavitt, F. M. (Executive Director, U.C.P.A. of New York): Personal communication, December 21, 1965.
7. Friedman, H. D.: The Challenge . . . and Some Solutions. Philadelphia, United Cerebral Palsy Association of Philadelphia. 1965, pp. 113-128.
8. Sheltered Workshops Certificated by the U. S. Department of Labor, June 30, 1964, and January 31, 1966. Washington, U. S. Department of Labor, 1966.
9. Directory of rehabilitation centers. Journal of Rehabilitation, pp. 65-70, May-June, 1964.
10. Davies, S. P. and Ecob, K. G.: The Mentally Retarded in Society. New York, Columbia University Press, 1959, pp. 20-22, 121-129, 196-198.
11. Nelson, op.cit., p. 30.
12. Katz, E. (Director Independent Living Program): Personal communication, October 7, 1965.
13. Wallin, J. E.: Sheltered Workshops for Older Adolescent and Adult Mental Retardates. In Stahlecker L. V. (Ed.): Occupational Information for the Mentally Retarded. Springfield, Charles C Thomas, 1967.
14. McCann, R. V.: Sheltered Workshops in Massachusetts: A Descriptive and Functional Study. Boston, Massachusetts Rehabilitation Commission on Vocational Rehabilitation Administration, 1963, p. 30.
15. Vocational Rehabilitation Administration Research and Demonstration Projects, An Annotated Listing, 1965. Washington, U. S. Department of Health, Education and Welfare, Vocational Rehabilitation Administration, 1965, pp. 27-42.
16. California Workshop Newsletter, Vol. IV, No. 4, pp. 1-2, 1965.

17. Ibid. Also Report of the Governmental Affairs Committee, State of Missouri, Jefferson City, Missouri Association for Retarded Children, 1966.
18. These estimates are based on the Department of Labor figure in Sheltered Workshops, June, 1964, and Sheltered Workshops, January, 1966.
19. Nelson, N. and Dibb, E. (Eds.): Census of Workshops for the Handicapped in California, 1964, Sacramento, California Vocational Rehabilitation Service.
20. Sheltered Workshop: A Study of Wage Payments to Handicapped Clients in Sheltered Workshops Certificated under the Fair Labor Standards Act (Washington, U. S. Department of Labor, Wage and Hour and Public Contracts Division, 1969, p. 13.
21. Statistical Abstract of U. S. 1965, 86th Annual Ad., U. S. Department of Commerce, Bureau of the Census, pp. 23, 217.
22. Meadow, L.: Vocational adjustment of the emotionally disturbed aged. Journal of the Jewish Communal Service. p. 396, Summer, 1957.
23. The San Francisco Utility Workshop for the Aged and Handicapped. Jewish Social Service Quarterly, p. 1-4, Winter, 1952.
24. A Survey of Sheltered Workshops. New York, Jewish Occupational Council, 1962, pp. 13-17.
25. Meadow, op.cit., p. 398.
26. Rusalem, H., Baxt, R., and Barshop, I. (Eds.): The Vocational Rehabilitation of Older Handicapped Workers. Washington, U. S. Department of Health, Education, and Welfare, 1963, pp. I-IX.
27. Vocational Rehabilitation Administration Research and Demonstration Projects, op.cit., pp. 100-101.
28. Sheltered Workshops Certified by Wage and Hour and Public Contracts Division, op.cit., Directory of Workshops for the Handicapped, op.cit. Nelson and Dibb, op.cit., p. 8.
29. Risch, F.: A Report of the Epilepsy Program Committee, Los Angeles Area. The Epilepsy Research Program, October 1949-October 1951. The account of the establishment of the workshop is taken from this report.
30. Risch, op.cit., p. 88.
31. Research and Demonstration Projects, An Annotated Listing, 1955, p. 7-9. Vocational Rehabilitation Administration, U. S. Dept. of H. E. W., Washington, D.C.
32. Black, B. J.: Industrial Therapy for the Mentally Ill-Observations on Developments in Western Europe and Significance for Programs in the U. S., Bronx, New York, Altro Work Shops, Inc., December, 1965; Dax, E. C., Industrial occupation in Dutch and English mental hospitals. Mental Hospitals, pp. 14-18, November, 1958.
33. Gladin, W. (Ed.): Directory of Sheltered Workshops Serving the Emotionally Disturbed. Altro Workshops and Health Services, Inc., 1966.
34. Black, B. J.: Rehabilitation of post-psychotic patients by industrial

workshop. Diseases of the Nervous System, Monogram Supplement, pp. 1-4, April., 1961; Black, B. J.: "The Protected Workshop," Rehabilitation of the Mentally Ill. Washington, American Association for the Advancement of Science, 1959, pp. 199-210.

35. Black, B. J., Meyer, H. J., and Borgatta, E. F.: Altro Health and Rehabilitation Services: case study of a protected workshop. The Journal of Social Issues. Vol. XVI, No. 2, pp. 44-46, 1960.

36. Toedter, A.: Survey of the Current Sheltered Workshop Programs within the Department of Mental Hygiene. Sacramento, Department of Mental Hygiene, 1963.

37. Brennan, J. J.: Modified community employment project in a hospital paid work program. Bedford Research, pp. 15-20, June, 1962. Brennan, J. J., and Ekdahl, A. G.,: Paid Work – An Essential Element in the Rehabilitation of Mental Patients. Bedford, Counseling Psychology Service. Brennan, J. J.: Modified community employment for the mentally ill. Journal of Rehabilitation, July-August, 1964.

38. Hubbs, R. S.: The sheltered workshop in psychiatric rehabilitation: therapeutic modality and socioeconomic resource, The American Journal of Orthopsychiatry, pp. 76-79, January, 1964. Hubbs, R. S.: Rehabilitation means restoration – the sheltered workshop. Mental Hospitals, pp. 7-9, April, 1960.

39. Frost, E. S.: Community Hospital Industry Rehabilitation Program, Workshops at the Crossroads, Procedings of the National Association of Sheltered Workshops and Homebound Programs. Washington, NASWHP, 1964, pp. 33-35. Winick, W., and Walsh, F. X.: Community hospital industrial rehabilitation program. Mental Hospitals, pp. 147-150, March, 1964.

40. Denber, H. C. B.: Personal Communication, August 8, 1966. Denber, C. B., and Rajotte, P.: Problems and theoretical considerations of work therapy for psychiatric patients. Canadian Psychiatric Association Journal, pp. 25-33, February, 1962. Denber, C. B.: Industrial workshop for psychiatric patients. Mental Hospitals, June, 1960. Denber, C. B.: Work therapy for psychiatric patients. Comprehensive Psychiatry, February, 1960.

41. Census of Clients. Unpublished data, Sacramento, California, Department of Rehabilitation. Compiled 1967.

42. Toedter, op.cit.

43. Mrs. Edna Steen's report to the National Staff Council of the National Association for Mental Health, June 28, 1965.

44. Hoffman, H. J.: Paid employment as a rehabilitative technique in a state mental hospital. Mental Hygiene, April, 1965.

45. Cohen, M. E., and LaFave, H. G.: Structured work program aids schizophrenics. Journal of Rehabilitation, p. 17, July-August, 1965.

46. The account of PROP is taken from Patients Rehabilitation Occupation Program, Inc.: A Structured Sheltered Workshop Program at Boston

State Hospital Sponsored by Volunteers. A manuscript sent the author by Nicholas H. Thiesse, December 15, 1965.

47. The narrative on the workshops in Mental Hospitals in Illinois is summarized from reports supplied by the staff of workshops in those workshops.

48. Dunn, S., and Dunn, E.: Soviet Attitudes and Achievements in Disability and Rehabilitation. Washington, Social and Rehabilitation Service, 1968, pp. 62-70.

49. Godlin, W. (Ed.): Directory of Sheltered Workshops Serving the Emotionally Disturbed, 1965. New York, Altro Workshops and Health Services, Inc., 1966.

50. Ibid., pp. 82-101.

51. Ibid., pp. 88-101. Nelson, N.: Workshops for the Disabled in California, Sacramento, Vocational Rehabilitation Service, 1958, p. 11.

52. Godlin, op.cit., p. 88.

53. Suazo, A. C. (Ed.): A Study of the Characteristics and Practices of Sheltered Workshops. Washington, NASWHP, undated.

54. Beckman, D.: Personal communication, June 10, 1969. Handbook Rehabilitation Workshop Facilities in South Carolina. Columbia, Vocational Rehabilitation Department, 1968. Operating Agreement and Budget. Rehabilitation Workshop Facility, South Carolina.

55. Dixon, A. J. (State-Department of Education): Personal communication, September 30, 1949. Johnston, C. L., Dixon, A. J., and Corbin, D. R., (Eds.): State Plan for Rehabilitation Facilities. Baton Rouge, State Department of Education, 1968.

56. Donaldson, H. C. (Supervisor of Vocational Training Centers): Personal communication, October 26, 1965. Also, VRA Grant RD 956-1D, Progress Report of Tennessee Association for Retarded Children and Adults, October 30, 1964.

57. Hawkins, R. F. (Supervisor, Tennessee Vocational Training Centers): Personal communications, November 13, 1969, and December 9, 1969.

58. McMillian, R.: Personal communication, January 26, 1967.

59. Jacobs, H. L.: Personal communication, October 25, 1965. Cowen, J. W.: Personal communication, July 3, 1969. Dees, L. O. (Administration of Huntsville Rehabilitation Center): Personal communication, October 5, 1966. They'll Never Walk Alone. Montgomery, Alabama Society for Crippled Children and Adults, undated.

60. Schloss, C. F.: Personal communication, April 16, 1969 (for Wage and Hour Division of Department of Labor).

61. Sheltered Workshops, A Study of Wage Payments to Handicapped Clients in Sheltered Workshops Certified Under the Fair Labor Standards Act. U. S. Department of Labor.

62. Ibid., p. 8.

63. Statistical Report for the Year 1968. Washington, Goodwill Industries of America, 1969.

Part Two

Workshops Today
Their Nature and Characteristics

"It is not enough that you should understand about applied science in order that your work may increase man's blessings .... Concern for man himself and his fate must always form the chief interest of all technical endeavors ...."

—*Albert Einstein*

V

THE NATURE OF WORKSHOPS

W ORKSHOPS for the handicapped in the United States have been developed in a variety of community settings by differing types of sponsors to meet many kinds of needs of different groups of handicapped, impoverished and disadvantaged persons. It is not surprising, therefore, that they have evolved without common purposes and methods. They do have in common the general aim of helping people they serve in a work setting. Most workshop organizations share the philosophy that the individual should be helped to reach his highest potential, but their applications of this principle vary. The workshop in the United States is a pluralistic institution. Nevertheless, workshops have common elements.

THE COMMON ELEMENTS IN WORKSHOPS

Perhaps the common elements in workshops can be stated in the following incomplete schematic description: The workshop is a place where a group of handicapped persons perform remunerative, productive tasks. Oversimplified, a workshop program is a productive group performance. It differs from group therapy or group discussion in that the group performs rather than talks; yet verbalization may take place and therapy may be a result. It differs from a class in a school in that there is production and more emphasis on learning through action and example than on verbal instruction. It differs from a game, since winning or excelling is not the principal objective; yet striving for levels of accomplishment is essential. It further differs from play in that play is for fun alone and work is for a purpose. It differs from socialization in that object-directed activity is required, as distinguished from the individual variation of behavior allowed in social intercourse; yet socialization is an important benefit of the

121

workshop program. In the group performance, each person participates, either positively or negatively, in the action. It is thus the most realistic substitute for work in industry yet devised to test the individual's ability to work, to prepare him for work, to provide nonprofit employment, and to assist in maintaining or improving his health and well being.

It is sometimes held that a workshop program need not be in a specific place but is a process which can take place anywhere. This view holds that the workshop can operate in many different types of programs such as schools, hospitals, and so on, and that its activities can be scattered in and about many programs. This view fails to take into account the importance of the work place as a milieu or environment in which the group action takes place. The worker can go from work area to work area, and these can be in buildings, in households, in forests and agricultural fields, and in other places; but at any given time the work area should be a controlled work environment that is not simultaneously used for another nonwork purpose. However, the work area can be used for many different purposes, and it can be surrounded with many complex and varied services of a rehabilitative, psychosocial, and recreational nature. Indeed, it is the variable uses of the workshop that have appealed to sponsoring groups who found in it ways to reach the numerous types of objectives they had in mind.

In addition to the common elements which have been described, there are other common practices which all workshops should observe if they are to be effective and justifiable socially. Among the latter are two which seem to be in conflict at first consideration. The workshop must put first the interest and benefit of the individual it serves. The workshop must also create a viable business enterprise if it is to provide the reality element which is essential to the accomplishment of constructive outcome for the individuals in it. Since the individuals who come to it are required by admission policy to be less effective than workers in industry, the workshop must conduct a successful business and a good program for the handicapped at the same time.

THE WORKSHOP DUALITY

In analyzing the dual types of activities in a workshop, it is important to distinguish the difficulties involved in performing dual types of functions from the basic nature of the process itself. Difficulties do exist, and they are severe. To create in a workshop the reality environment essential to human development, it is necessary to conduct an effective business enterprise. To use that environment effectively, it is necessary to understand and apply successfully the techniques and methods of helping persons with severe problems. When the ability to exercise the dual skills does not exist in a workshop program, it may easily appear that the workshop program involves an inevitable conflict. Unfortunately, often in workshops, the dual abilities do not exist. This should not, however, inhibit an analysis of the common workshop process.

A common workshop process consists of providing the individual opportunities to function suitably in keeping with graduated, progressively increasing requirements of reality. Throughout the individual's stay at the workshop, there must be a constant shifting of demands as the individual develops or deteriorates in his abilities to perform assigned tasks and to behave appropriately. If he cannot tolerate any demands, he must ultimately leave the workshop. If he can easily perform all work tasks and meet all behavioral requirements on an industrial level, he should be placed in industry. Most of the time, however, he will be in a situation in between these two states. The levels at which demands and accommodations are made from time to time will be somewhere between his need for accommodation and his need for exposure to demand in his own interest. The combination of the dual needs into a level of performance viable for the individual at any given time is the basic synthesis common to rehabilitation workshops.

THE WORKSHOP SYNTHESIS

The synthesis of accommodation for the individual and demand made of him results in movement to higher levels of functioning. If the synthesis were charted on a graph, it would show on the part of the workshop an increasing measure of demand and a decreasing amount of accommodation as the individual moves towards higher levels of functioning. Usually, the higher functioning would not move in a straight upward line but might level out in plateaus and sometimes even decline. The general trend, however, should go upward. In the long run, this process of synthesis, of accommodation and demand, is developmental, maturing, healthy, and increases the ability of the individual to function at higher levels of work and other aspects of his life.

The working out of the workshop synthesis has other problems which present challenges to the director. The philosophy of the agency and of rehabilitation generally emphasizes the individual approach as a means of solving problems. The workshop program, however, is basically a group process. There are usually a number of groups in it. If the individual is not assigned to a group, he loses the benefit of the group process. If he is assigned to a group, it may not meet his exact needs. The conflicts of an individual in a group may arise, and the shop may not be able to achieve the original synthesis desired for him. Thus, the desired workshop synthesis for the individual may have to give way to the demand of a larger reality, that of the group, and a new synthesis will be achieved. This is inevitable if the workshop attempts to provide a simulated reality experience.

THE NEED FOR ESTABLISHED DOCTRINE

The essence of the workshop synthesis has never been described definitely and comprehensively. The concepts and rationale which have been applied to workshops have been taken from other disciplines which emphasize the individual casework approach. Workshops do not have significant indigenous rationale and methodology of a comprehensive nature which encompasses the whole genre. Workshop personnel have no well-authenticated body of doctrine which has been recognized by the field as a whole. Thus the workshop is like a rough diamond that has inestimable value but needs to be cut and set before its value can be identified and defined.

The fact that extensive indigenous workshop principles and practices have not been written and agreed upon does not mean that workshops are poorly conducted. Most directors of workshops have spent many years in operating workshops and have learned their craft by experience. The more experienced of workshop directors probably have developed practices which they have found effective and which they use as a basis for the operation of their workshops. These directors could probably formulate statements of their practices. In all probability, however, their practices would have only broad similarities. They would differ as the objectives of their workshops differ. They have developed techniques on an empiric basis which are suitable to the individuals they serve, the purposes for which the shop was established, and the work of the shop. Those shops that serve varied groups of individuals, have a variety of types of work, and many objectives probably have working guidelines upon which workshop concepts and practices will ultimately be based.

In the sections which follow, some significant written ideology and oral traditions of workshops are summarized. The qualifying criteria for inclusion is that the content be developed by persons from the workshops or rehabilitation fields for application to workshops. From among these primarily have been selected the definitions, the philosophy, theories and practices and the standards applicable to workshops. To these few fundamental doctrines have been added interpretations of their significance and implications, their shortcomings or omissions.

VI

THE DEVELOPMENT OF DEFINITIONS
AND CLASSIFICATIONS OF WORKSHOPS

"BEAUTY is in the eye of the beholder." This old saying reminds us that a definition derives from the outlook of the definer. As makers of definitions differ in their outlook, so will their definitions.

Definitions of workshops have changed as workshop personnel developed the philosophy, purpose, and scope of their programs. In the first seventy-five years of workshop history, only gross descriptions are found. Next followed a period of general definition, and more recently, after 1960, a period of concrete definition and classification.

The definition and classification of workshops have been the concern of two principal groups: workshop operators, and government agencies which use or regulate workshops. The function of their definitions differs. Generally the workshop operators aim to upgrade and unify their facilities; the government seeks to create a useful screening phraseology for its purposes.

Definitions made by operators of workshops embraced generally their concepts, objectives, and aspirations. Those of government usually were framed by law or regulation to identify workshops eligible for use, funding, or certification. The workshop operators typically defined their goals. The government agencies most often enunciated gross, qualifying criteria.

In this chapter, the development of the schema of the workshop operators and of the government agencies will be taken up separately and then discussed in current relationship with each other.

WORKSHOP ORGANIZATIONS DEFINE THE WORKSHOP

In December, 1968, the National Association of Sheltered

Workshops and Homebound Programs adopted this definition of a sheltered workshop:

"A sheltered workshop is a non-profit rehabilitation facility utilizing individual goals, wages, supportive services, and a controlled work environment to help vocationally handicapped persons achieve or maintain their maximum potential as workers."

This identification of commonality and high purposes by the leadership of the workshop movement was the outcome of organizational and leadership efforts in the field spanning thirty-eight years. It came about 130 years after workshops had their beginning in this country.

Early Beginnings

The innovator in a new field, before he generalizes, must first attempt to describe his innovation. Thus in the beginning, there were descriptions by early workshop pioneers of their own programs, and these descriptions emphasized their desired goals.

In the early programs for the blind, the shops were originally conceived as schools that would train the blind in skills for jobs in industry. This fixed idea prevailed in writings about shops for the blind long after the shops had become places of employment for blind persons.

Some other nineteenth century shops, such as the ancestors of the Community Workshops, Inc., of Boston, were conducted by persons who were interested in social betterment. Their descriptions of their programs combined social objectives, such as the moral and physical amelioration of the condition of the poor, with work, the work being a means to the social objectives. As a result of this emphasis, they did not dwell extensively in their writings on the nature of the work program.

William Booth, in his blueprint for the Salvation Army's program, identified and described specifically the workshops that organization was establishing in the United States, England, and other parts of the world. In 1890 he wrote:

> These workshops are open for the relief of the unemployed and destitute, the object being to make it unnecessary for the homeless and worthless to be compelled to go to the Workhouse or Casual

Ward, food and shelter being provided for them in exchange for work done by them, until they can produce work for themselves, or can be found elsewhere (1).

Booth differentiated his workshops from the workhouse, the progenitor of workshops. He thus followed what has become accepted as a cardinal workshop concept: voluntary participation by the client. Also, he enunciated the expectation that the client would accept minimal remuneration in acknowledgment that his stay with the workshop was a stopgap measure and that his entry or return to the general labor market was anticipated.

The Middle Period

Just as the early innovators in the first period of workshops were responding to an expressed purpose or ambition of the society of their time, the leaders in the workshop movement of the early twentieth century responded to the expressed purpose or goal of the society of their time.

How workshops began to meet the enlarged expectations of society is detailed in a description of the services of Curative Workshop of New York made in 1926, not by the operator of the workshop, but by a third-party user, Frederick G. Elton, of the New York State Vocational Rehabilitation Agency. That agency, in the spirit of the recently passed workmen's compensation law, was using the Curative Workshop to prevent lack of confidence and growth of idleness by referring industrially injured workers to the workshop immediately after hospitalization. Elton indicated in his writing that the object of the shop was to enhance employability and that actual productive work should be conducted under actual employment conditions. He describes the conditions as follows:

1. Engaging in a regular industrial job.
2. In a regular work atmosphere.
3. Weekly wages for work based on actual market value.
4. A commercial product. In other words, a necessity, not arts and crafts.

Elton describes how it was necessary to find simple work so that workers could benefit who could not take extensive or complicated training. He goes on to give what is probably the first description of the modern rehabilitation approach in a workshop.

Owning to the curative features involved, all . . . had to be applied with due regard to the disability and characteristics of the individual. This then meant the application of practical psychology, a thorough understanding of the reaction of the patient, the gradual lengthening of the hours for the individual according to his strength, and proper consideration for the physical strength as regards rest periods (2).

Thus the Curative Workshop, first based on the techniques of occupational therapy, departed from them to find a greater reality in "a regular industrial job."

The description of the Curative Workshop of New York City in 1926, however, was not characteristic of the workshops of the country at the time. Sullivan and Snortium, in *Disabled Persons, Their Education and Rehabilitation,* described sheltered employment that year as follows:

Sheltered employment consists in the operation of an establishment primarily for a group of handicapped persons, assuring them of an income and making conditions favorable for them. It may be run on a strictly production basis, and differ from the commercial plant only in restricting employment to the handicapped and adjusting surroundings and regulations to them. It may, on the other hand, necessarily, deviate from a profit-making course and resign itself to a regular deficit made up by some subsidizing guarantors. Every gradation is represented by those now in the field (3).

Ten years later, in 1936, this first effort at definition was amplified. In the Purposes and Policies of the National Association of Goodwill Industries, the authors wrote:

Sheltered workshops are places where persons of limited employability or those who have lost their skill are given employment at tasks for which they are fitted, and compensated in accordance with their abilities, and through training are equipped for self-employment or placement in commercial industry (4).

The three major rehabilitation centers, which developed in New York, Cleveland, and Detroit, influenced the development of ideas about workshops. The director of one of these, Col. John M. Smith, of the Insitute for the Crippled and Disabled of New York City, in addressing the International Society of Crippled Children in Cleveland in 1938, said,

A comprehensive sheltered workshop, which I think should more aptly be called a Rehabilitation Center, is one which includes among its activities [1] Occupational therapy, [2] Provision of artificial limbs, prothetic devices and aids, [3] Homebound services, [4] Vocational or trade testing, [5] Vocational guidance, [6] Vocational or shop training, [7] Preindustrial employment, remunerative or otherwise, [8] Placement service, [9] Social case work and advisory services – for cases needing medical, surgical, psychiatric and psychological care, [10] Relief and family service, [11] Recreational and health educational services (5).

From the foregoing accounts it is apparent that the program definition of the Curative Workshop, the Goodwill Industries, and the Institute for the Crippled and Disabled vary as do the professional traditions, concepts, and environments of the organizations. The Curative Workshop language stems from occupational therapy modified for workshop purposes; the Goodwill emphasis is on training which arises from opportunities available in materials-reconditioning operations; and the Institute for the Crippled and Disabled presents a multidimensional approach available to a large, well-endowed institution in a metropolis with readily available professional staff. Each institution had similar general aims, that is, helping handicapped people to work; yet each differed from the others in how it achieved those aims. Quite naturally, spokesmen of each institution described the workshop in terms of their own organization.

Efforts of Workshop Operators to Define Workshops

The first group of workshop and rehabilitation personnel who came together in an attempt to define a workshop were brought together as an advisory committee by the Department of Labor after the passage of the Fair Labor Standards Act. In an effort to embrace the large variation among workshops in operation by that time and to unify the world of workshops, this group drafted and adopted a definition far more inclusive than the Department of Labor's official regulation issued shortly after the passage of the Fair Labor Standards Act. This advisory committee published the following definition of a workshop in 1944:

A charitable, religious, educational, or philanthropic organization or institution conducted not for profit but for the purpose of carrying out a recognized program of rehabilitation for physically, mentally, spiritually, and socially handicapped individuals and to provide such individuals with remunerative employment or other rehabilitating activity of an educational or therapeutic nature (6).

The advisory group's definition included among those served "the spiritually and socially handicapped" while the official regulations did not. As for types of services provided, the advisory group's definition terminated by including "other rehabilitation activity of an educational or therapeutic nature," thus ambiguously, albeit generously taking a much more general view than did the official regulations which went no further than to conclude with "other occupational rehabilitation activity."

Omission by the advisory group of the qualifyer "occupational" in the final catchall category of services to be provided left a large ambiguous area. Individuals were to be provided a program of rehabilitation activity of an educational or therapeutic nature, but these activities were not specifically identified.

In 1949 at the National Conference of Social Work held in Cleveland, the National Committee on Sheltered Workshops and Homebound Programs was formed. The following year it issued this definition of a workshop:

A sheltered workshop is a voluntary organization or institution conducted not for profit but for the purpose of carrying out a recognized program of rehabilitation for physically, mentally, and socially handicapped individuals with remunerative employment and one or more other rehabilitating activities of an educational psychosocial, therapeutic, or spiritual nature (7).

This definition, which resembled the previous definition of the Advisory Committee of the Department of Labor, eliminated the ambiguity of the former, but did not include all workshops. Workshops which provided only remunerative employment were not included in the definition. In 1950, numerous workshops provided only remunerative employment.

In 1961, the Advisory Committee of the Department of Labor revised its 1944 publication. It identified a sheltered workshop as follows:

A sheltered workshop is a facility maintained on a non-profit basis by either a public or private agency for the purpose of providing training and employment service to a defined population of handicapped persons. Employment service may comprise any one or a combination of the following: (a) to help develop employability for placement in competitive employment; (b) to utilize work for rehabilitation purposes other than employment; (c) to provide extended remunerative employment as needed (8).

Many operators of workshops were not satisfied with the Advisory Committee's definition. In 1958, at Bedford Springs, Pennsylvania, over two hundred experts from rehabilitation and related fields had met to discuss definitions and other concerns of the workshop movement. Many significant developments stem from this meeting, including the establishment of standards for workshops and the revision of the definition of workshops. In the meeting, philosophies, concepts and a large range of possible objectives were discussed and recorded in the publication *The Role of the Workshop in Rehabilitation.* The concept that the individual should be helped to reach his highest potential was spelled out, including the encouragement of positive moral behavior acceptable to the social order, the facilitation of "basic human experiences such as courtship and marriage and the development of Civic Responsibility." The report also recommended that functional classification of workshops be made (9).

The Bedford Springs Conference brought out the differences of emphasis and approach then existing among workshop authorities. One group emphasized broad social responsibilities for the workshop but another held that the evolving concept of the workshop was that of a center providing a work environment and work experience for evaluative, diagnostic, therapeutic and employment purposes, and relying upon other community rehabilitation resources for other specialized evaluative and supportive services (10). A new definition was needed to express emerging concepts. Following the Bedford Springs Conference, the following definition was worked out and approved by the National Association of Sheltered Workshops and Homebound Programs in 1962.

A sheltered workshop is a work-oriented rehabilitation facility with a controlled working environment and individual vocational goals which utilizes work experience and related services for assisting the handicapped person to progress toward normal living and a productive vocational status.

This definition was probably the best yet devised from the point of view of the workshop operators of the early 1960's. It reflected the rehabilitation philosophy in designating the workshop as a rehabilitation facility. It embraced the school of thought that sees the workshop as primarily a work center. It included the emphasis of the socially oriented professionals and the idea of assistance towards normal living. It seemed to have elements that enabled it to accommodate all the different groups of workshop personnel. Yet, in 1964, Jerome Bernstein, the project director of the National Institute of Workshop Standards, wrote, "There is no consensus of opinion among workshops themselves as to what specifically constitutes a sheltered workshop facility" (11). Many workshop directors had demurred when asked to agree upon standards based on the 1962 definition.

Finally in 1968, the National Association of Sheltered Workshops and Homebound Programs adopted the presently current definition:

> A sheltered workshop is a non-profit rehabilitation facility utilizing individual goals, wages, supportive services, and a controlled work environment to help vocationally handicapped persons achieve or maintain their maximum potential as workers (12).

Eliminated from the old definition was the phrase "to progress to normal living" and added was the phrase "*maintain* their maximum potential as workers." The focus was more clearly on work and the achievement or maintenance of the worker status. The workshop movement was finding its identity.

In the meanwhile, the Congress, government agencies, and their administrators were making definitions and classifications in laws and regulations. They now need to be considered.

GOVERNMENT DEFINES THE WORKSHOP

Statutory Definitions of Workshops

The first legal definition of workshops in the United States and of workers in workshops came about as the result of the passage by Congress of the Fair Labor Standards Act of 1938.

The objectives of the framers of the Fair Labor Standards Act encompassed more than the workshop field. The broad concern was to prevent exploitation of workers by employers. The major emphasis was upon workers employed in competitive profit-seeking firms. In the course of its passage, specific recognition was given to the special circumstances of workers whose capability to produce is impaired by handicap. An exemption was written into the law for those workers who may be producing as their limited capability permits.

Section 14 of the Fair Labor Standards Act gives the Administrator of the Wage and Hour Division of the Department of Labor authority to provide by regulations or by orders for the employment of individuals "whose earning capacity is impaired by age or physical or mental deficiency or injury" under special certificates at wages lower than the minimum wage. The regulations which followed the passage of the Act defined workshops as follows:

> Sheltered Workshops. A charitable organization or institution conducted not for profit, but for the purpose of carrying out a recognized program of rehabilitation for individuals whose earning capacity is impaired by age or physical or mental deficiency or injury, and to provide such individuals with remunerative employment or other occupational rehabilitating acitivity of an educational or therapeutic nature (13).

The statutory language of the exemption defining the handicapped worker is specific and has been unchanged since its passage in 1938. The language of the regulations, on the other hand, is broad in light of the law they implemented. The legal definition was probably a realistic description of the majority of handicapped persons in the workshops in the United States for many years following the promulgation of the regulations (14).

In the early 1960's, there was a movement by some organizations for the blind and others to eliminate the minimum wage exemption for handicapped persons in workshops. It was proposed that all individuals working in shops be paid the minimum wage. Opposition from rehabilitation organizations resulted in compromise, which was included in the Fair Labor Standards Act Amendments of 1966.

The Act divides workshops for wage certificate purposes into two major groups: those which paid wages at 50 percent of the minimum or more and those which paid less than 50 percent of the minimum wage. Those workshops which paid less than 50 percent of the minimum were divided into two classifications: a short-term group and a long-term group. The short-term group consisted of evaluation and training categories; the long-term group of those employing multiply handicapped workers with severe handicaps and of work activity centers.

Work activity centers were defined as centers planned and designed exclusively to provide therapeutic activities for handicapped clients whose physical or mental impairment is so severe as to make their productive capacity inconsequential. In the regulations which followed in July of 1968, the work activity center was further defined as a workshop or a physically separate department of a workshop where the average productivity per handicapped worker is less than 850 dollars per year working at an hourly rate or less than 600 dollars per year when piece rates are used (15).

Workshops could be judged to be classified into one or all of the above groups for wage purposes and certificates issued in several categories.

The State-Federal Vocational Rehabilitation Act Definitions

Another group of legal definitions of workshops is found in the state-federal vocational rehabilitation legislation. The Vocational Rehabilitation Acts of 1920 and 1943 made it possible to use workshops but did not define them. The first definition is found in the Vocational Rehabilitation Amendments of 1954 in Public Law 565. A workshop is defined as "a place where any manufacture or handiwork is carried on and which is operated for the primary purpose of providing remunerative employment to severely handicapped individuals who cannot be readily absorbed in the competitive labor market" (16). This was interpreted to mean the provision of remunerative employment to severely handicapped individuals [1] as an interim step in the rehabilitation process for those who cannot readily be absorbed in the labor market, or [2] during such time as employment opportunities for them in the labor market did not exist (17).

The Vocational Rehabilitation Act Amendments of 1965 did not change the definition or the twofold classification of workshops of the 1954 Act. However, the Vocational Rehabilitation Act Amendments of 1968 made a drastic change in the treatment of workshop definitions. They tried to delete use of the word *workshop* from its terminology entirely. The law calls for the word *workshop* to be deleted and the words *rehabilitation facility* to be used instead whenever workshop was formerly used. However, in one instance the phrase "rehabilitation facility which is primarily a workshop" is used and in another the phrase "for a rehabilitation facility which is a workshop" is used (18). Thus where necessary, the 1968 law considers that some rehabilitation facilities are workshops. But the definition of a workshop is deleted (19).

To compensate for the deletion of the workshop definition, the elements of a workshop which were not formerly part of the definition of a rehabilitation facility are incorporated into it. The new definition is given below with the workshop elements underlined.

> The term "rehabilitation facility" means a facility which is operated for the primary purpose of providing *vocational rehabilitation services to, or gainful employment for,* handicapped individuals, or for providing *evaluation and work adjustment services for disadvantaged individuals* and which provides singly or in combination one or more of the following services for handicapped individuals: [1] Comprehensive rehabilitation services which shall include, under one management, medical, psychological, social, and vocational services, [2] testing, fitting or training in the use of prosthetic and esthetic devices, [3] *prevocational conditioning* or recreational therapy, [4] physical and occupational therapy, [5] speech and hearing pathology, [6] psychological and social services, [7] *evaluation,* [8] *personal and work adjustment,* [9] *vocational training (in combination with other rehabilitation services),* [10] evaluation or control of special disabilities, and [11] *extended employment for severely handicapped who cannot readily be absorbed in the labor market;* but all medical and related health services must be prescribed by, or under the formal supervision of, persons licensed to practice medicine or surgery in the State (20).

The reasons for the combination of the two definitions into one were several. The previous definition of a workshop in the law and the provisions for the establishment of a workshop under the Amendments of 1954 and 1965 had been restrictive on funding for staffing in workshops. The national organizations of workshops and rehabilitation centers had recently decided to merge into one national organization. The image of one type of facility was organizationally useful. Also, the sheltered workshop connotation carried with it unfavorable public relations aspects. The change was advantageous to workshops. It was not based on analysis of the essential nature of the workshop.

In any case, the 1968 amendments gave the rehabilitation facilities any or all of three purposes: the provision of vocational rehabilitation services to handicapped individuals, the provision of gainful employment for handicapped individuals, or the provision of evaluation and work adjustment services to disadvantaged individuals. They also required that workshops provided one or more of the services listed in the definition of a rehabilitation facility. Under this definition, a workshop whose primary purpose is to provide gainful employment for handicapped people and provides extended employment for the severely handicapped who cannot be readily absorbed among competitive labor is a rehabilitation facility. In this definition, the traditional concept of rehabilitation as a process for developing higher levels of functioning for handicapped individuals is presumedly interpreted to mean increased functioning in extended employment. Sheltered employment is given a new name and the sheltered workshop is called a rehabilitation facility.

While the definers were making definitions, others were using their definitions to classify workshops. We will next describe their efforts.

THE CLASSIFICATION OF WORKSHOPS
BY OPERATORS AND REHABILITATION PERSONNEL

Informal classifications of workshops have been made by groups of workshop operators and rehabilitation personnel whenever they got together to discuss general rehabilitation problems. In 1938 in Cleveland at the annual convention of the International Society for Crippled Children, discussion centered on such topics as workshops as a testing field, workshops as a training center, workshops as a sheltered factory, and workshops in the home (21). Many groups of rehabilitation personnel made classifications in a number of ways in the following years. The principal ways were the following:

1. By general type or function.
2. By type of sponsorship.
3. By length of service, i.e. short-term or long-term.
4. By type of disability groups served.
5. By age groups served.
6. By type of work done in the shop.
7. By type of service in the shop.
8. By nature of objectives, i.e. transitional or terminal.

The first formal classification of workshops was made by the National Committee on Sheltered Workshops and Homebound Programs in 1950. The Committee divided workshops into three classifications: the Industrial Workshop for Sheltered Employment, Industrial Rehabilitation Workshop, and Institutional Rehabilitation Shop. The description of each of the three types can be summarized as follows:

> *The Industrial Workshop for Sheltered Employment* provides remunerative employment and other social and personal adjustment services for persons whose handicaps are so severe that they cannot be absorbed in the labor market.
>
> *The Industrial Rehabilitation Workshop* provides paid training or employment and other rehabilitation services including personal and social adjustment, vocational counseling and placement in order to prepare and place the handicapped person in competitive employment.
>
> *The Institutional Rehabilitation Shop* serves individuals with personality, emotional, and behavior problems who have for the most part been committed by court orders and attempts to train and educate them so that they might return to the community as emotionally and morally mature citizens qualified for competitive employment (22).

The above classifications covered the main types of workshops existing at the time with the exception of the physical therapy and occupational therapy types of workshop. They did not, of course, include workshops which rendered long-term services to persons for whom substantial remunerative employment in the workshop was impossible. Such workshops did not exist at the time.

A more analytical system of classifying workshops was suggested by Albert Feintuch in 1951 (23). He divided workshops into six groups and identified these six classifications as follows:

1. *Physical therapy workshop (industrial)* aims at preparing clients for entering or returning to regular industry or vocational training programs by improving the functioning of their muscles or by building up their physical conditions or work tolerance. They used paid industrial work experience to achieve this goal.

2. *Physical therapy workshop (nonindustrial)* has the same objective of Physical Therapy Workshops (Industrial) except that they did not have industrial work but made objects which were sold or kept by clients.

3. *Occupational therapy workshops (avocational – recreational)* provide avocational activity to persons so handicapped that they are unable to work in competitive industry or workshops maintaining a production schedule. The main values of this type of workshop are the psychological benefits of group activity, although some clients may graduate to a sheltered workshop with regular production schedules.

4. *Therapy workshops (social and moral rehabilitation)* have as their basic purpose the rehabilitation of wayward, delinquent, alcoholic clients through aquisition of regular work habits and a sense of responsibility. It is hoped these clients will take their place in regular industry.

5. *Vocational training workshops* aim to give handicapped clients necessary vocational training for entering the labor market.

6. *Terminal employment workshops* give employment to persons who because of advanced age or physical or mental disabilities are not expected to be able to work in regular industry. The majority can, however, earn enough to become partially self-supporting and a few graduate to regular employment.

Feintuch's classification was a perceptive analysis of the results which can come from using work to help people solve some of the problems of their major life activities. Since he wrote, the terminology of work programs has changed, and the emphasis on physical therapy has lessened, but the basic organization of work to achieve the objectives he names still goes on in categories similar to those he designated. A major change has been the combining of several of his categories into integrated programs.

The next classification of workshops of importance was made not for the country as a whole but for the state of Massachusetts. This classification is of importance because it was the first based on a detailed study of specific workshops. In 1963, the Massachusetts Rehabilitation Commission sponsored a study of thirty-eight workshops in Massachusetts. These were analyzed in depth. On the basis of the survey findings, the workshops were classified as follows:

Type I – General Services Workshops.
1. Clients representing a variety of disabilities.
2. A wide range of client services (evaluation, job training, personality adjustment, work conditioning, transitional and long-term employment, placement).
3. Production activities that provide a resource of income and payment of wages.
4. A work program used as a basis for rehabilitation services such as evaluation and conditioning.
5. Ties with the business and industrial community.

Type II – Training Centers for the Mentally Retarded.
1. Serve mentally retarded exclusively.
2. Training stress social skills rather than specific job training.
3. No paid work or employment.
4. Work activities on small and sporadic basis.
5. Tenuous ties with the professional, industrial, and business community.

Type III – Specialized Evaluation Centers.
1. Accept all clients regardless of disability.
2. Principal service is evaluation of employment potential.
3. Clients are not paid with one exception where clients are paid incentive wage one hour a day.
4. Not evaluated on business or industrial activities of the shop for wages but practice varies with use of work samples, work stations, and agency administrative jobs.

Type IV – The Mental Hospital Industrial Workshops.
1. Serves exclusive hospital inpatients.
2. Have paid work programs.

3. Adjunct and assistive to total treatment program.
4. Provide realistic norms to evaluate patient's capacity to leave hospital.
5. Provide adjustment period prior to release. (A bridge from hospital to community.)

Type V – Transitional Sheltered Workshops (Salvage and Repair).

1. Accepts wide variety of self-referred persons, many with alcoholic and geriatric conditions.
2. Principal service transitional employment.
3. Paid work or token gratuities.
4. Workers defensive against counseling, social service, medical and similar personnel and not responsive to their services.

Type VI – Extended Employment: Sheltered Workshops

1. Mostly for the blind but some take cerebral palsied.
2. Paid work at substantial wages often at self-support level.
3. Permanent employment with little movement (24).

It should not be assumed that the description of shops in each category of the Massachusetts survey describes workshops similarly categorized in the country as a whole. In fact, one of the many valuable contributions this survey made was to call attention to the fact that great differences exist among workshops across the country that use the same label. Many workshops in other parts of the country which bore the designation of work training centers were quite different than those formed in Massachusetts at the time. Certainly, large numbers of workshops that considered the word transitional as descriptive of their type of program did not believe their programs were like those called "transitional sheltered workshops, salvage and repair" in Massachusetts. The study also illustrates the difference that is encountered when specific research findings are compared with generalizations made from observation or group consensus.

The most recent classification of workshops made by rehabilitation personnel was that made by the National Institute on Workshop Standards. This organization had been established following the Bedford Springs Conference in 1958, for the purpose of developing standards for workshops. In the course of its deliberation, it attempted to set up categories of workshops and apply different standards to each classification. In 1961 and 1962, it drew up six classifications of workshops and asked 650 workshop directors to indicate which classification most nearly described their programs. Three hundred thirty-eight workshops identified their programs in one of the six categories (25).

As will be seen, the six classifications ended up as two: Extended Employment (Terminal) Workshop Program, and Transitional Workshop Program. The original six classifications and the percentage of responding shops in each are given below.

Classification A — 28 percent. Primary emphasis is upon remunerative employment of handicapped individuals for an indefinite period of time who appear to be unemployable in the competitive labor market. A few individuals may, however, develop sufficient productive skill which would enable them to move out of the workshop from time to time to the competitive labor market. *Any rehabilitation services within this setting would play a supportive role to the objective of achieving successful employment within the workshop.*

Classification B — 25 percent. Primary emphasis is upon remunerative employment of handicapped individuals for an indefinite period of time who appear to be unemployable in the competitive labor market. A few individuals develop sufficient productive skill that would enable them to move out of the workshop from time to time to the competitive labor market. *Within this setting there is an evaluation and/or rehabilitation unit which provides services for individuals who are employed in the workshop or individuals for whom services are being purchased by community organizations.*

Classification C — 13 percent. Primary emphasis is upon remunerative employment of handicapped individuals for various periods of time to prepare as many as possible for employment in the competitive labor market. *Substantial work orientation and/or rehabilitation services are available to every employee in the workshop.*

Classification D — 23 percent. Primary emphasis is upon remunerative employment of handicapped individuals for various periods of time to prepare as many as possible for employment in the competitive labor market. *A comprehensive work-oriented evaluation and/or rehabilitation unit provides services for individuals who are employed in the workshop, and individuals for whom services are purchased by community organizations.*

Classification E – 7 percent. Primary emphasis is upon comprehensive work-oriented evaluation and/or rehabilitation services to prepare handicapped individuals for employment in the competitive labor market, *with limits upon the time an individual may remain in the shop. Employment within this setting would be primarily for evaluation and therapeutic purposes.*

Classification F – 4 percent. Primary emphasis is upon employment which would enable an individual to meet an economic or personal crisis caused by psychological problems.

After the questionnaires were received, the classification A and B were combined into an Extended Employment category and classification C, D, and E were grouped together to form a Transitional category. Workshops in Classification F were excluded (26).

The two final classifications of workshops were identified as follows:

Extended employment (terminal) workshop program. Primary emphasis upon remunerative employment of handicapped individuals for an indefinite period of time who appear to be unemployable in the competitive labor market. A few individuals may, however, develop sufficient productive skills which would enable them to move out of the workshop to the competitive labor market. *Any rehabilitation services within this setting would play a supportive role to the objective of achieving successful employment within the workshop.*

Transitional workshop program. Primary emphasis upon comprehensive work oriented evaluation and/or rehabilitation to prepare handicapped individuals for employment in the competitive labor market, *with limits upon the time an individual may remain in the workshop. Employment within this setting would be primarily for evaluative and therapeutic purposes (27).*

Thus after more than twenty-five years of discussion, workshop personnel arrived at classifications of workshops which had the advantage of simplicity. They thereby achieved a unified description of their institutions and a suggested common terminology in a field which was characterized by variability and differences in the programs and had previously diverse nomenclature. Unfortunately, the classifications and terminology were based on 338 replies, or approximately one-half of the 650 workshop directors who were asked to respond; they probably constituted approximately one third of the workshop directors in the country at the time.

Informal Classification Schemes

Although the 1968 rehabilitation amendments included all workshops under the rehabilitation facility rubric, distinct categories of workshops can be discerned. In addition to the classifications discussed before as rehabilitative or sheltered, long-term or short-term, workshops can be classified by types of disabilities served, by age groups, by types of work done, and by sponsorship.

Often there is a connection between types of disabilities served and sponsors. Thus, societies for the mentally retarded established workshops for the mentally retarded, organizations for the cerebral palsied established workshops for the cerebral palsied, and epileptic sympathizers developed workshops for epileptics. Mental health societies established workshops for the emotionally disturbed and mentally ill. Blind groups and public agencies generally sponsor workshops for the blind. Multidisability workshops were developed by local organizations not affiliated with national health agencies. Multidisability workshops were also developed by the Goodwill Industries while the Salvation Army and the Volunteers of America emphasized services to single or homeless men with alcoholic or psychological problems.

The groups of workshops serving special disability groups, such as the mentally retarded and cerebral palsied, tended to serve the young, since parents often dominated the sponsoring organization. However, with the passage of time, the average age of those in special disability shops has increased. The aging are served in both special disability shops for the aging and in multiple disability shops such as Goodwill Industries and Jewish Vocational Services shops.

Workshops have also been classified by type of work done. Workshops started out by doing prime manufacturing, and some still do it. Workshops as a class have not been generally successful in prime manufacturing largely because of lack of adequate capital resources. The traditional work of the religious organizations shops, the Goodwill Industries, Salvation Army, Volunteers of America, and Deseret Industries has been the collection, reconditioning and resale of household discards. However, some other workshops such as the single disability shops have entered the field. With the falling off of the value of discards, some of the above-mentioned organizations, principally Goodwill Industries, have gone into subcontracting. Subcontracting constitutes the work of the largest number of workshops in the country. Closely related to contracting is service work, sometimes done by a subcontracting workshop and sometimes done by a shop that specializes in services such as household or industrial painting services, office work, mail outs, and the like. A last type of work is product development from industrial discards. Examples are surveyor's stake manufacture from scrap lumber, nursery cans from food containers, and the like. However, few workshops specialize in product development, often doing it to fill in slack periods in subcontracting programs.

SUMMARY

The definitions and classifications of workshops have changed as the workshops have responded to the unmet needs of society. In the tradition of American business, they have seen needs and organized their programs to meet them. As their programs evolved, their definitions and classifications changed accordingly.

The definitions of workshops were made by two groups: by workshop operators and rehabilitation personnel, and by Congress and government agencies making definitions for legal purposes. The definitions of the first group were expressions of the ideals and aspirations upon which they could agree. The definitions of the second were in the main statements of gross qualifying criteria for regulatory purposes, use by rehabilitation agencies, or funding under grant provisions of statutes.

The salient characteristic of the definitions was their

changeability. There is reason to believe they will continue to change as their makers develop new programs in response to social developments.

NOTES

1. Booth, W.: In Darkest England and the Way Out. New York and London, Funk & Wagnals, 1891, pp. 107-108.
2. Sullivan, O. M., and Snortium, K. O.: Disabled Persons, Their Education and Rehabilitation, New York, Century, 1926, pp. 361-362.
3. Ibid, p. 481.
4. Blair, D.: Sheltered Workshops, Their Role in Meeting the Needs of Handicapped Persons, University of Southern California, master's thesis, 1949.
5. Trapini, E. A.: General Description of What Workshops Are. In Chouinard, E. and Garrett, J. (Eds.): Workshops for the Disabled. Washington, U. S. Dept. of Health, Education, and Welfare, undated, pp. 14-15.
6. National Advisory Committee on Sheltered Workshops, Wage and Hour and Public Contracts Division: A Statement of Elementary Standards Respecting the Policies, Organizations, Operation, and Service Activities of Sheltered Workshops. Washington, U. S. Dept. of Labor, 1944. Stanpeck, P. (Ed.): Occupational Information for the Mentally Retarded. Springfield, Thomas, 1967, p. 547. See also Trapini, op.cit., p. 15.
7. Chouinard and Garrett, op.cit., p. 15.
8. Advisory Committee on Sheltered Workshops: A Statement of Principles Respecting the Policies, Organization, Operation, and Services Activities of Sheltered Workshops and Homebound Programs. Washington, Wage and Hour and Public Contracts Division, U. S. Dept. of Labor, 1961.
9. National Institute on Workshops Standards: Standards for Sheltered Workshops. Washington, 1964, p. 5. See also Thompson, N. Z. (Ed.): The Role of the Workshop in Rehabilitation. Washington, NASWHP, 1958, pp. 38-40, 46-47.
10. Ibid, p. 34.
11. Bernstein, J. S.: Compare Standards for Sheltered Workshops previously cited with an Experimental Evaluative Instrument Based on Potential Standards for Sheltered Workshops. Washington, National Institute on Workshop Standards, 1962.
12. Resolution passed at Annual Meeting of NASWHP, San Francisco, California, December, 1968, from Report of the NASWHP Sheltered Workshop Policy Committee to the Board of Directors, October, 1968.
13. Public Law 718, 75th Congress, Chapter 676, 3rd Session [S2475], Section 14; Title 29, Chapter V Code of Federal Regulations, Part 525. Regulations applicable to the Employment of Handicapped Clients in

Sheltered Workshops, December, 1964, U. S. Dept. of Labor, Wages and Hour Division, p. 1.

14. Hall, F. P.: The Fair Labor Standards Act and Sheltered Workshops. Master's thesis, Counseling and Behavioral Studies, Madison, University of Wisconsin, 1965.

15. Public Law 89-601, 89th Congress, H. R. 13712, September 23, 1966, Title V, Section 14(d) (1), (2), (3), pp. 13-14, Federal Register, Vol. 32, No. 14, January 21, 1967, part 525, pp. 716-717; and Federal Register, July 23, 1968, Title 29, Part 525 2C.

16. Public Law 565, 83rd Congress Chapter 655, Second Session, [S 2759], Section 11, [d].

17. Chouinard and Garrett, op.cit., pp. 3-4.

18. Public Law 90-391, 90th Congress, H. R. 16819, Section 11 (a), (2) (c), Section 12(e).

19. Public Law 90-391, op.cit., Section 10 (d).

20. Public Law 90-31, Vocational Rehabilitation Amendments of 1968, Section 10 [b].

21. Chouinard and Garrett, op.cit., p. 14.

22. Trapini, op.cit., pp. 15-16.

23. Feintuch, A.: Classification of Sheltered Workshops. In Occupations. Washington, National Vocational Guidance Association, 1951.

24. McCann, R. V. (Ed.): Sheltered Workshops in Massachusetts: A Descriptive and Functional Study. Boston, Massachusetts Rehabilitation Commission, 1963, pp. 1-16, 17, 30, 40, 41, 47, 57-61, 72-79.

25. Bernstein, op.cit.

26. Ibid, pp. 16-17.

27. Ibid, Section 11, Evaluation Instrument.

VII

PURPOSES AND OBJECTIVES
OF WORKSHOPS

THE workshops in the United States are operated by voluntary private associations or public agencies which try to achieve various goals for differing groups of handicapped or disadvantaged persons. Their objectives are determined by the nature and magnitude of the handicap of those who are served. One sponsoring group serving persons with potential to work in industry will have objectives directed towards competitive employment. A second group serving persons who cannot be employed in industry but who can work in workshops will have objectives different from the first sponsoring group. Quite different from either group may be the objectives of a third group which had in mind primarily the alleviation of the trauma of persons whose functioning is declining. The problem of analysis is complicated because the intended objectives which workshops hope to achieve may not be realized for some persons. Groups with one set of objectives add others as their original objectives are not met and the needs of the handicapped remain. As a consequence the objectives of workshop organizations often become mixed.

In spite of the different and mixed objectives of workshop sponsors, their programs nearly always have in common the purpose of helping handicapped and disadvantaged individuals improve their ability to work. To the extent that they aim to help people improve their functioning, they participate in achieving the goals of rehabilitation. Thus workshop programs are usually, but not always, parts of the rehabilitation process. The parts they play may be many or few, depending upon the scope of the workshop program. In the description of the purposes and objectives of workshops which follows, an attempt will be made to summarize the principal objectives of workshops briefly in concrete terms. However, the primary goals of some shops may be achieved as the secondary objectives or incidental results of others.

When the purposes of workshops have in common the goals of rehabilitation, they are often quite different specifically. At other times, the purposes of workshops are different from the goals of rehabilitation. They may seek to maintain the individual and prevent further decline. The most useful division can be made by the length of time it takes to achieve the goals. They may be divided into two categories: objectives which can be achieved in a relatively short period of time, and those which take a long or indefinite period of time. An individual shop may have both short-term and long-term objectives.

The fact that an objective is either short-term or long-term gives no indication of the quality of the services necessary to achieve the objective. Neither is there any necessary relationship between the length of the time used to achieve the objective and the inherent value or importance of the objective to the individuals served. The kinds of purposes and objectives chosen by workshops do not necessarily determine the excellence of their programs. The value of their programs depends upon the skill and effectiveness with which the workshops achieve the purposes and objectives which they set for themselves.

SHORT-TERM OBJECTIVES OF WORKSHOPS

Under short-term objectives are those which may be achieved in a foreseeable period. When the period is over, characteristically, the person leaves the workshop. The objective may or may not have been achieved. In long-term objectives, by contrast, the expectation is that the period of time required in the workshop to achieve the objectives will be very long or indefinite. The objectives may vary: they may involve movement to higher levels of functioning and thus may be rehabilitative. They may involve maintenance of the individual through work. The short-term objective may be employment in industry, the long-term objective increased employability in a workshop. Society may value the first goal more highly than the second. The person served or his family may value the objectives quite differently.

Assessment of Work Potential

Although all workshops do assessment either superficially or in depth as part of their programs, some workshops do assessment exclusively as their primary purpose. In general, workshop programs having assessment as a primary purpose most often evaluate ability to work in competitive industry or in a sheltered environment, or determine the services needed to enable the person to work in either.

The specific objectives of assessment may vary greatly, but in practice assessment addresses itself mainly to the concerns of the person evaluated, the conjectures of the evaluator, or the questions asked by a third party such as the referring agency or the family. The person served is enabled to determine what he can or cannot do, to find out if he likes to do that which he thinks interests him, or to determine if he can meet the requirements of work. The evaluators discover the prospective worker's areas of strength and weakness and make evaluation of work potential or needed services. In the process the evaluators are able to answer the specific questions of third parties. Thus the objectives of assessment are to enable the person served and his helpers to arrive at an understanding of his current capabilities and potential, his desires or preferences, and make joint decisions for future action.

Few workshops in the United States have assessment as their primary purpose. In most workshops, assessment is a necessary pre-requisite for the accomplishment of their primary purposes. In many workshops, assessment goes on continually as long as the person served is in the workshop. There is general agreement that continuing assessment is necessary if the individual is to be well served. Often assessment is not valid except in combination with other services which are of an educative or adjustive nature and given over a long period of time. Thus assessment programs may develop other rehabilitative services which are secondary but necessary to the principal purpose of assessment.

Demonstration to Industry and Workshops

There are a small number of workshops in the United States

whose primary purpose is demonstration. Demonstrations are made to two principal groups: to business and industry, or to other rehabilitation or social welfare programs. Some workshops which make demonstrations have many other program objectives. Demonstration is incidental to their primary purposes. Many other workshops which do not make formal demonstrations make individual demonstrations when they show a prospective employer the good work that the workshop workers are doing. Only those who make formal demonstrations as their primary purpose are discussed here.

Demonstration to industry is usually made to show that workers with certain disabilities can be valuable employees. Often these shops serve persons whose unemployment arises not because of genuine inability to work but out of the prejudice or fears of some employer groups. A striking example is the epileptic. Experts in the rehabilitation of the epileptic believe that many epileptics are quite capable of becoming acceptable employees. The demonstrating shop proves that epileptics are capable of acceptable production, that seizures at work are negligible, that work is not disrupted by the employment of epileptics. Similar demonstrations have been made for the mentally retarded, public assistance clients, and school dropouts.

The demonstration shop eliminates or reduces the third consequence of the handicapping condition. The first is the handicap resulting from the disability itself. The second is the added handicap arising from secondary psychological results of the disability. The third consequence is that arising from external factors or the unfavorable effect the disability has on others. To the extent that the unfavorable external response is reduced the severity of the handicapping condition is reduced.

The second group of demonstration workshops are those which usually develop new programs, services, techniques, or methods for the guidance of other workshop programs. These demonstrations have been made in numerous disability group programs and in many areas of development of methodology. As a rule, these programs have been financed by government grants which have been limited in time. When the grants expired, the programs were sometimes terminated but more often were converted to an on-going service program of a somewhat different nature.

There is a need for permanent demonstration workshops in the United States to make demonstrations in a variety of program areas and to develop techniques for providing services. Such demonstration and research centers which do exist in the field do not operate workshops and thus do not have the benefit of empirical experience.

Preparation for Employment

The preparation of handicapped and disadvantaged persons for employment is a major goal of medical, rehabilitation, educational and social welfare programs. Workshops most often become involved in the process at the following stages:

1. The individual's condition is static or it is chronic, and it has been stabilized to the extent that there is no expectation that it will change substantially as a result of the intervention of other treatment, adjustive or educative measures in the foreseeable future.

2. The individual's condition has been temporarily or substantially stabilized, but other procedures will need to continue in order to maintain the existing level of stabilization of the condition.

3. The individual's condition has not been stabilized, but it has been determined or conjectured that exposure to a work environment may assist the individual to benefit from other procedures and progress to employability.

Workshops have not as a rule become involved with the preparation for employment when an individual's condition is acute and intensive care and treatment are necessary, but when exposure to a work environment is indicated to enable him to function more capably in the light of his relatively stabilized condition.

Among the workshops in the United States whose objectives are short term, the primary purpose of the greatest number is preparation for employment. The majority of these workshops usually aim to prepare for employment in competitive industry. However, some place their graduates in selected jobs in protected environments in industry or public institutions, or in sheltered employment in other workshops. Of those whose primary purpose is employment, the principal objectives are the development of work readiness, work adjustment and occupational skills. Some of these workshops may have two of these objectives, or all three.

The Development of Work Readiness

One reason why individuals cannot work is that they are not ready to meet work requirements of competitive employment. Their unsatisfactory levels of performance result from a variety of factors including impairment of physical functions, reduced functioning as a result of long hospitalization or idleness, inadequate motivation, erratic productivity due to inability to concentrate or tolerate work requirements, and others of a similar nature. Often if the individual is given the opportunity to work under favorable conditions, he is able to mobilize his physical and emotional resources and develop the required physiological work efficiency. The process of developing work readiness takes place through work experience.

The development of work readiness through work experience is probably the most frequent objective in short-term workshops. This objective can be most economically achieved in workshops because it requires no extensive professional superstructure. If the individual who has no overwhelming psychosocial problems in his work behavior is given opportunities to do work he can master progressively, good results occur. The successful accomplishment develops a sense of achievement and self-confidence. Continued work success brings recognition from staff, fellow workers, family, and friends. Increased motivation and better performance results.

Development of Work Adjustment

There are large numbers of individuals who are potentially capable of working at standard norms of productivity but who are not acceptable employees because of aberrations of performance or behavior. For them, exposure to work and the encouragement of the staff is not usually sufficient to enable them to meet the requirements of employment. The staff must make an analysis of the specific deficiencies in work behavior or performance and carry on a program designed to deal with them. The objective is not necessarily to eliminate the defects entirely but to reduce the intensity and incidence of them to a level acceptable in employment. This can be done only when there is understanding of the reasons for unacceptable work behavior and the individual is helped to unlearn unsatisfactory behavior and relearn satisfactory work behavior.

It is not always easy to distinguish between individuals who can achieve a productive and acceptable work capability through work experience alone and those who need the more analytical approach of work adjustment. Consequently, careful assessment is necessary so that the proper service is made available. When severe problems exist in the work personality, work experience alone will not be successful. In such instances, it will be necessary to modify behavior to enable the individual to become an acceptable worker.

Competence in Vocational Skills

Some workshops prepare individuals for employment by training in vocational skills. The kind of training undertaken depends upon the interest and ability of the individual and the resources of the workshop. In general, however, training takes place at three general levels: in skilled occupations such as upholstery repair or television repair; in production skills such as electronic assembly, machine operation, or drill sharpening; or in service occupations such as janitorial and maid service or gardening.

As a rule skill training given in workshops is of an on-the-job or short apprenticeship type. Formal courses in occupational skills are given in some workshops, but they do not usually include the background theory given in trade schools. Many individuals receiving skill training need other services, and the training on the job lends itself to the provision of them. In the lower skill levels in particular, the adjustment component is crucial to work success. Many individuals need medical or psychosocial services concurrent with their training program, and the training on the job allows for such services. The skill training objective is not achieved in a predetermined time sequence as in training schools but is paced to suit the individual's needs. Thus, skill training in workshops can be more flexible than training in schools and has the advantage of the earned income.

Improvement of the Handicapping Condition

There are some workshops whose primary purpose is to participate with other health or rehabilitation programs in the improvement of the individual's mental health or physical functioning. Such workshops are usually in hospitals or rehabilitation centers. Other freestanding workshops undertake these similar objectives without direct involvement with such health or rehabilitation programs. In either case, the individual may or may not work following the completion of services depending upon his desires, needs, or ability. Even though employment does not result, the workshop considers its program successful if the therapeutic objective has been achieved. As parts of hospitals or rehabilitation centers, workshops usually undertake their objectives after initial medical care has been completed. However, they often previously participate as an adjustive or enabling agent to a concurrent therapeutic process.

Improvement of Physical Function

A few workshops have as their primary purpose the improvement of physical function. Indeed, this was the original purpose of the curative workshops. Now the workshops which emphasize physical restoration are usually in rehabilitation centers or hospitals. Their objectives are similar to those of occupational therapy programs. They differ from occupational therapy programs in that they provide paid work in a production-oriented group setting while occupational therapy programs usually involve the patient in medically prescribed individual projects which do not provide payment of wages. Thus such workshop programs may prove more effective with individuals who do not respond to the individual, nonpaid creative project. Conversely, they may not be effective for those who do not respond to the more realistic paid-work group activity. A determining element seems to be the meaning which work has had for the individual.

Restoration of Mental Health

There are a growing number of workshops whose primary purpose is to improve mental health or reduce emotional disturbance. Many of these workshops are parts of mental hospitals or psychiatric clinics but a few are freestanding facilities. The objective may be to restore constructive patterns of functioning directly or to make the patient more responsive to other therapies. In the first instance the realistic work program, which is more demanding than other therapies, may enable the patient to adapt to the demands of reality. In the latter case, the work program may serve as an adjunctive aid to psychotherapy. For example, as a result of work a depressed patient may begin to externalize his feelings and thus benefit from psychotherapy. Or the money received as wages may aid the recovery program by enhancing the dignity and social status of the patient.

Prevention of Mental Breakdown

As a result of the growing belief that the mentally ill should be kept in their home communities whenever possible, a few workshops have been started in the seventh decade of the twentieth century whose purpose is to help an individual avoid impending mental breakdown. Since work ability and work behavior often hold up the longest in cases of impending breakdown, work and the work setting can be used as a base or underpinning around which the patient may mobilize his psychological resources. The preventative workshop programs are new, but it is their assumption that work can be used as a stabilizing influence and that together with other services it can aid the patient to avoid mental collapse.

Provision of Related Services

Some workshops in the United States are, in the main, holding operations or "launching pads" from which other services may be started. Their purpose is not primarily to use work in the shop to effect change but to use employment as an attraction to get persons into the shop where they may become interested in or more responsive to services which will benefit them. The other services may be of a medical, social, psychologic or educational nature. For example, a person with severe personal and family problems who would not seek social or psychological services may come to the workshops for employment. Once in the shop the individual may become interested in other kinds of help and benefit from them greatly. Or persons whose medical regimes which are not well observed may come to workshops for work, and once there, may be helped to respond more faithfully to medical prescription with favorable results. Again, individuals in a workshop may be better prepared to make a job application when the teaching is related to a real job prospect as it comes up. Thus, the counseling process is enhanced. The "holding" workshops serve a unique purpose for social welfare programs whose range of objectives cover the entire spectrum of human problems.

The short-term purposes of workshops have been described separately because they exist separately as the principal emphasis in some workshops. In others several or many of the objectives described above are combined in an integrated program based on work and the work environment. For example, a workshop which has as its principal purpose preparation for employment may also stress improvement of mental health and may uncover and deal with a variety of human problems which are encountered as a result of the close, full-time relationship developed at work.

Workshops which have as their purpose preparation for work often call themselves "transitional workshops" to stress their goal of movement from the workshop to competitive employment. Workshops which have integrated programs consisting of a number of short-term objectives designate themselves as "rehabilitation workshops" to describe their aim of improving the function of the individual. In either case, the goals may or may not be reached for some individuals. When the individual fails to meet the goals set for him in a short period of time, some workshops terminate the program and refer him elsewhere when indicated. In other cases, if further workshop services are needed, the sponsoring organizations, which are dedicated to serving the continuing needs of individuals, often find it necessary to provide that further service themselves. This is usually done in two ways: the short-term shop continues to serve the individual or another long-term workshop is established. In either case, a long-term workshop develops, either with a short-term shop or by the establishment of a separate long-term shop.

LONG-TERM PURPOSES OF WORKSHOPS

Under long-term objectives are those which it is anticipated will be achieved only after an extended stay. At times, this may mean a long stay in the shop, after which the individual moves out of the shop to outside employment. At other times, it may mean an indefinite stay in the shop. Because the long-term shop can pursue objectives for individuals indefinitely, it can have purposes and objectives that differ from short-term shops. The principal long-term purposes are these: the provision of long-term employment, the sustaining or maintenance of physical and mental health or social adjustment, and the reduction of personal dependence.

The most common purpose of workshops prior to 1950 was the provision of employment for handicapped persons in workshops. In the second half of the twentieth century, the provision of employment assumed a less prominent role. However, the level of employment in workshops changed after 1950, and probably its nature. Before that date, the majority of individuals employed in shops were capable of substantial productivity and were paid substantial wages. After 1950, many individauls came into workshops whose productivity was low and consequently their wages were low. While it is not possible to define the point at which a wage is substantial and when it is minimal, it is true that many persons worked in shops after 1950 for reasons other than the amount of money they received. This does not mean that minimal earnings were not significant, but that other reasons were more important to the individual. Employment in workshops can therefore be considered as falling in two categories: employment where the amount earned is a principal consideration, and employment where earning money is meaningful but other considerations predominate as the reason the individual desires to stay in the workshop.

Employment for Wages

Historically, more people came to workshops to earn money than for any other reason. Since these persons could not get jobs in competitive industry, the places where they worked were called "sheltered workshops" and their employment was called "sheltered employment." The implication of the use of the word *sheltered* was that few demands were made of them in such workshops, that they were sheltered from the demands of real work. There are, of course, workshops which probably should be appropriately labeled sheltered workshops. However, progressive workshops do not think that they provide a "shelter." They regard employment in their shop as not being sheltered because individuals are encouraged to work at their maximum productivity and are paid in accordance with what they produce. The payment for each unit of work is comparable with that paid in industry. The number of units produced is basically smaller. Thus the long-term shop provides employment for producers whose output is less than that of workers in competitive industry. Their productivity, however, enables them to earn money sufficient for their total or partial support.

Although the long-term workshop makes demands on its workers, these are generally not as rigid or inflexible as those made in competitive industry. When there is failure to meet requirements, the individual is not necessarily dismissed from employment. In rehabilitation workshops, the failures in performance or defects in behavior are not overlooked or condoned but are evaluated, and a plan is made for their elimination, modification, or reduction. If initial efforts to reduce deficits are not successful, others are tried. Because these workshops continue to try to improve performance, they consider themselves to be rehabilitation workshops. Thus, there are two kinds of long-term objectives where employment is the major emphasis: sheltered employment, where the worker continues indefinitely at his existing level of performance; and extended rehabilitation employment, where the worker is accepted at his existing level of performance and continuing attempts are made to improve his performance.

Employment for Supplementary Income

Another long-term objective is to provide supplementary income for persons who are capable of producing but not in substantial amounts, often at less than half the industrial production standard. These persons are supported by their families or are receiving assistance from public or private sources. They are usually severely handicapped, and their prospects for leaving the shop for private industry are not great. Although they are attracted by the need for supplementary income, their workshop often provides other advantages which add up to a better life for them. Their employment in the shop gives them prestige or respectability in the eyes of their families and of the community. Their work provides a more rewarding existence than idleness at home. They make friends in the shop and develop social and recreational outlets. The shop provides for them as great a level of rehabilitation as they can achieve.

Maintenance of Health and Social Adjustment

Another objective of long-term workshops is to help individuals in the shop preserve their mental or physical health or their social adjustment. The individuals who are served in shops for such reasons may or may not earn wages, but their wages when paid are often minimal, due primarily to their variable productivity or irregular attendance. The reason they are kept in workshops is that upon termination they get into trouble physically, mentally, or socially. They return to chronic care or mental hospitals, are imprisoned, or become alcoholics or beggars. As long as they remain in workshops, they maintain a precarious stability. The objective is to prevent further disintegration of health or personality. This objective is usually carried out by workshops sponsored by public assistance, social welfare, or mental health agencies and by religious organizations.

More stable and socially acceptable groups whose health and personal happiness are enhanced in workshops are the aged and chronically ill. The elderly and those with chronic disabilities are served in workshops, both in homes for the aged, and in freestanding workshops which they attend from their homes. The elderly work short hours and do not make much money in workshops. However, what little they make enables them to buy extra comforts they want without appealing to their children for money. In workshops serving the aged, they find friends and escape from the terrors of loneliness. While they are in workshops, their health remains better than would be the case if they remained at home in idleness. For those among the elderly for whom work has a significant meaning, the workshop can make the difference between a miserable life and a happy one.

Reduction of Personal Dependence

All the long-term objectives discussed before involved substantial employment and substantial wages. A great many new shops in the country which started after 1950 have activities which involve work only minimally and where wages are unsubstantial. There is question on the part of some if such shops should be called workshops at all. However, they do provide work for wages, even though the work is intermittent or part-time and the wages are exceedingly small. The fact that several hundreds of such shops arose in a few years warrants a close look at their objectives. They include the development of social maturity, the increase in personal independence, and the release from parental or family care. Occasionally, and especially when the work program is well developed, the individual is enabled to work in another long-term workshop at more substantial wages or in a protected environment in public or private employment. These shops usually include training programs in household skills and comprehensive recreational programs. Altogether, their objectives add up to an increase in the personal happiness of the mentally retarded and cerebral palsied, who are their principal beneficiaries, and of their families, who are partially released from the burdens of their care.

The objectives of long-term shops — employment, the

maintenance of personal well-being, and the reduction of personal dependency — tend to be commingled in many shops. The emphasis which is placed on each objective usually depends upon the nature and severity of the handicapping condition of the workshop population and the philosophy of the sponsoring group. Where the total rehabilitation of the individual is attempted, several of these objectives are combined. Where the provision of income through sheltered employment is the single objective, other problems of the workers may be neglected.

COMBINATION OF SHORT- AND LONG-TERM OBJECTIVES

The majority of workshops in the United States probably have both short- and long-term objectives. This combination comes about naturally when workshops are devoted to the needs of handicapped persons. Handicapped persons are brought into workshops to achieve the best that is possible for them, usually employment in the open labor market. Some move into open employment; others cannot. The reasons why some cannot are many. The handicap may be so severe competitive employment is impossible. The handicap may not be great, but work capability does not come about for a number of reasons. Or work capability may be adequate, but jobs are not available at the time they are needed. In other instances, jobs may be available, but employers will not accept some individuals because of fears or prejudices associated with certain disabilities. For these and other reasons, the workshop is faced with the problem of the future of those they serve. A few workshops terminate services at the point when the handicapped individual is ready for work or refer the handicapped to other long-term workshops. Many keep the handicapped on as long-term workers whenever possible because other long-term shops are usually not available.

SUMMARY

The purpose and objectives of workshops fall into two groups: short-term and long-term. Among short-term purposes are found assessment, demonstration, preparation for employment, the improvement of the handicapping conditions, the prevention of mental deterioration, and the provision of related services. Long-term purposes include the provision of employment, the maintenance of health and social adjustment, and the reduction of personal dependency. The short-term purposes are often integrated in shops having limited stay programs. So also are the long-term purposes in shops that help individuals indefinitely. Both short-term and long-term purposes are found in many shops, probably in the majority of workshops in the country.

Though the shops with short-term and long-term purposes are probably in the majority, they are not alike in emphasis, operations, or service patterns. In addition, there are many shops that have only short-term or long-term purposes, not both. The selection of objectives and emphasis is dependent upon a number of factors. These include the orientation and concepts of the sponsoring organizations and the nature of the handicaps of individuals they wish to serve; the needs and influence of local public and private health, educational and rehabilitation organizations; the finances available from local, state and national sources; and the economic and social organization of the community.

VIII

THE DEVELOPMENT OF STANDARDS
AND ACCREDITATION OF WORKSHOPS

T HE growing cooperation between workshops, first evidenced by exchange of ideas and later by formation of workshop associations, reached its most concrete results in the formulation of standards. From 1944 to 1967, and more intensively between 1959 and 1967, state and national groups developed criteria which served as elementary tests of workshop excellence. Though standards have been twenty-three years in the making, they constitute only beginnings of a measuring system of acceptable practice. They are, however, the basis upon which a more complete system of standards must be built. In the process of their development, much was learned about the nature and the problems of workshops. The lessons of the standard and accreditation process were perhaps as important as the establishment of the standards. The record of that development will be traced here.

STANDARDS

Standards for workshops were developed in the United States by two groups: the government agencies who purchase services from or give grants to workshops, and the private associations of workshops and rehabilitation facilities and accreditation bodies. Before associations and accreditation bodies set national standards for workshops, the government agencies had no alternative but to set standards themselves. First state vocational rehabilitation agencies and later the federal agency did so. Since the national federal standards have been issued, some state agencies have used them as a basis for purchase of service, but many have not as yet done so. The standards of the federal rehabilitation agency, moreover, are similar to those of private accreditation bodies. Whether the state vocational rehabilitation agencies will adopt the national standards of the federal agency or the private groups will probably depend upon their experience with the standards as a measure of quality of services. Jerome S. Bernstein (1), writing at the conclusion of a six-year study of workshop standards, concludes:

> The effectiveness of any accreditation program will depend largely on the standards and criteria employed to evaluate workshop programs. To the extent that sheltered workshops exist to service and rehabilitate the handicapped individual, evaluative standards and criteria should reflect this "reason d'etre." To the extent that the standards and criteria are employed, to evaluate this function, such standards are functional.

While there is general acceptance of the value of standards, there are different approaches to the use of standards in the United States generally. Standards may be used by those to whom they apply for purposes of self-measurement and improvement, or for the purpose of self-improvement through measurement by an organizationally chosen accreditation group. Standards may be used to improve efficiency of operation or quality of services or both. However, administrative efficiency may be accomplished without improvement of quality of services, and quality of services may sometimes be improved with improving efficiency of operation.

The nature of standards depends upon the objectives of the standard setters. Standards have been used at times to discourage growth of suppliers of services and to restrict entry in professional fields. When standards are used, they tend to define accepted practices as a base line for legal concepts of malpractice, in which case they provide some protection to the consumer of services to the extent that the standards are adequate.

A question which must be asked is in whose interest the standards are set. Too often standards are set to do the following:

1. Protect the interests of organizations providing service.
2. Enhance prerogatives of administrators or professional staff.
3. Provide a minimal level of standards to preclude the growth of more adequate standards.

Standards should be set in the interest of the individuals who receive services from workshops. In evaluating standards, these questions must always be kept in mind: To what extent do the standards assure or encourage the establishment of high levels of service to the individuals receiving the services? Who sets them and who determines how they are applied?

Early Discussion and Formulation of Standards

Consideration of desirable practices in workshops began with their inception. William Booth of the Salvation Army and Edgar Helms of Goodwill Industries discussed the ways in which workshops should be operated. In the first half of the twentieth century, the publications of the Institute for the Crippled and Disabled of New York City and of other comprehensive rehabilitation centers described program principles which had the force of standards. But these early discussions presented the points of view of individuals or individual organizations. No written standards presented by a group of workshop operators or users appeared until 1944, more than a hundred years after the first workshop was started in the United States.

In 1944, the National Advisory Committee on Sheltered Workshops, appointed to advise the Wage and Hours Division of the Department of Labor, found that no generally accepted standards for workshops existed. They therefore proceeded to write a set of standards "in the thought that they might be helpful to others who might be called upon to appraise and evaluate the programs of sheltered workshops . . . ." They called their brochure *A Statement of Elementary Standards Respecting Policies, Organization, and Service Activities of Sheltered Workshops* (2).

The standards set by the committee were fundamental and clear. The workshop should be incorporated; it should have a representative citizen board and a qualified staff. It should keep adequate service records and should make quarterly operating and balance statements which are to be audited annually. It should have on balance an amount equal to one month's operations requirement and should keep special restricted reserve funds for replacement of equipment and care of facilities based on recognized depreciation tables. Earned income from operations should not be set aside for initial capital expenditures until the shop pays the minimum wage. The shop should conform with state and federal wage and hour laws and maintain wage standards comparable with those of private industry. Building and equipment should be located and maintained so as to be conducive to the health, safety, and well-being of the clients. The workshop should observe fair trade practice in the sale of products and good business practice in payment of obligations.

The standards of the National Advisory Committee were general in nature and did not specify the criteria required for adequate qualification or good practice. However, they outlined the fundamental precepts which were to be made more specific in future years. Unfortunately, they did not attract much attention. Seventeen years went by before standards were given further attention at a national level. There are a number of reasons for this delay. Workshops did not have national organizations at the time and were often isolated from other rehabilitation agencies. Workshops were not used much by state rehabilitation agencies during this period. Their numbers were small and they served relatively small numbers of physically handicapped persons. The workshops had not yet come of age.

In the 1950's, with the establishment of many hundreds of new workshops serving additional types of handicaps, state vocational rehabilitation agencies became more interested in workshops and the quality of their services. Some state agencies had become accustomed to the use of standards in connection with the provision of medical services following their authorization to provide such services in the Barden-LaFollette Amendments of the Vocational Rehabilitation Act in 1943. However, workshops were considered to provide training services, not medical services, and the state agencies varied greatly in their application of standards to training programs. As a rule, there was greater local autonomy in the choice and use of training services than was the case for medical services. As state vocational rehabilitation agencies developed state office units concerned with the development of workshops, they began developing standards for the purchase of services from workshops.

In addition, with the passage of the Vocational Rehabilitation Act Amendments of 1954, 1965, and 1968, state vocational rehabilitation agencies acquired responsibilities for approving grants of federal funds to workshops. Some states passed appropriations for provision of state funds to workshops. In some of these states, agencies set standards for the programs which received the funds. Thus, both for the purpose of purchasing services and of awarding public money to workshops, state agencies developed standards for workshops.

The Standards of State Rehabilitation Agencies

In 1959, the state of California passed legislation providing funds for the creation of a state consultation service to workshops, the first of its kind in the country. The service was part of the state vocational rehabilitation agency. The writer was appointed to head this program. One of the first things done under the new program in 1960 was to set standards for the selection of workshops from whom the agency purchased services. It was, however, impossible at the time to set detailed and thoroughly adequate standards for all aspects of workshop operations. Many new shops were struggling for existence and were not able to meet comprehensive standards. They needed to be used until they could develop the resources to meet more adequate standards. As a result, a simple set of standards was adopted in 1960, emphasizing qualifications for personnel employed in workshops. These standards were revised in 1963.

The first standards set provided as follows:

1. The workshops should be incorporated as a nonprofit organization.
2. The board of directors should be representative of the community.
3. The workshop should observe state and federal laws relating to wages and hours.
4. The workshops should observe all state and local laws relating to the health and safety of its handicapped workers.

Services to be purchased by the state agency were divided into four categories: evaluation, work adjustment, vocational training, and work experience. In order for a workshop to be paid for one of these services, the staff of that workshop had to be qualified to render that service. The qualifications of staff for each of the services were spelled out. However, a number of disciplines were listed as eligible to render services in the various categories. The rationale of this system of use of workshops was that the quality of service would be best where the staff was qualified by training and experience to render the service. The importance of this concept was that it placed the principal emphasis on the quality of services based on the qualifications of the personnel (4).

In 1962, the State of New York passed legislation providing for money payment to private workshops for salaries of professional staff in workshops. In connection with this program, the state agency developed standards which were probably the most comprehensive state standards for workshops developed at the time. The standards consisted of two parts: standards for personnel, and standards for the rehabilitation program.

The standards for rehabilitation programs were divided into three parts: standards for program services, standards for organization and administration, and standards for community relations. The provisions of the latter two topics were similar in many respects to those later set by national accreditation bodies, but some of the provisions of the standards for services, although basic to good practice, were new at the time.

The following are excerpts from the New York standards:

> The workshop shall have a clearly identified program of services . . . to develop the client's maximum potential for employment . . . wherever the client's needs are best served. The programming of workshop services for the clients will be based on professional evaluations of rehabilitation needs, progress, and vocational goals.
>
> The workshop shall periodically evaluate its total program, its coordination with related rehabilitation programs in the community, and the capacity of each client for movement to competitive industry, and the adequacy of its program.

In its standards for rehabilitation personnel, the New York State agency indicated the qualifications for the following positions which had to be met if the positions were to be funded:

> Doctor of medicine, social worker, psychologist, vocational rehabilitation counselors, evaluator, physical or occupational therapist, employment counselor, executive director, vocation teacher, psychometrist, and registered nurse.

The importance of the New York State standards was that they were the most comprehensive standards yet developed whose objective was to assure quality of service through exacting requirements for qualified staff (5).

The Development of National Standards

The first large-scale attempt to develop national standards came as a result of the National Conference on Workshops held at Bedford Springs, Pennsylvania, in April, 1958. This conference recommended a study be made to formulate workshop standards. Subsequently, the National Institute on Workshop Standards was established by the National Rehabilitation Association and the National Association of Sheltered Workshops and Homebound Programs. The Institute studied workshop standards from 1958 through 1964, issued several interim reports, and a final report in 1964. These publications contain the most comprehensive information about workshop standards available in the United States (6).

The rationale of the National Institute on workshop Standards was based on the principle that,

> ... self-regulation would be better than government regulation by forfeit; that the workshop movement itself was better equipped to develop evaluative standards and criteria; that the workshop movement could best formulate a basis for ongoing development of future standards for evaluation of workshop programs and could best implement such standards and criteria via a national accreditation program or by some other means (7).

This reasoning is important in understanding the work done by the study group. The tests which were applied to the standards were related to existing practices and the validity of the standards was decided primarily by consensus of the directors of workshops.

The staff of the Institute gathered much information. This was used in an Experimental Evaluative Instrument, which consisted of sixty standards and 719 criteria. The intent was to test the evaluative instrument by determining if it would distinguish between workshops designated as "good" or "bad" by experts.

The instrument was sent to 650 workshop directors in June, 1961. Three hundred and fifty-eight workshops replied. Thirty-six standards were rated as significant by the respondents. Two advisory committees from the eastern part of the United States reviewed the standards and reduced them to thirty. The initial 719 criteria were reduced to 198.

Workshops had originally been divided into six classifications. They were combined into two classifications — extended employment workshops, and transitional workshops. These shops were again divided into "good" and "bad" shops and compared with evaluations of experts. Jerome Bernstein, the project director of the Institute, pointed out that the standards instrument appeared to be more predictive for workshops in the extended employment category than in the transitional category. However, he concluded that "if the results of the study are accepted at face value then it can be stated that the resulting two Standards Instruments (Extended Employment and Transitional) contain experimentally tested and statistically valid items" (8).

The standards statements which were finally published left out about eighty standards and criteria which had been judged as important by workshop experts. The workshop directors and the review committees had not been willing to accept them. As other standard-setting groups later developed standards, most of them were included in their requirements for accreditation.

Thus the standards that workshop directors were willing to accept at the time were less demanding than those workshop experts thought were necessary.

The National Institute on Workshop Standards divided its standards and criteria under five heads as follows:
1. Organization and Administration
2. Program of Services
3. Facilities
4. Staff
5. Community Relations (9)
Subsequent standard setting groups used similar heads and expanded them.

The Emergence of Standard-Setting Bodies

Four other groups have provided national standards for workshops. The first was the Goodwill Industries of America. It first set standards in 1961, and revised them in 1962 and 1966. The Commission on Standards and Accreditation of Services for the Blind issued *The Comstac Report: Standards for Strengthened Services* in 1966. The Commission on Accreditation of Rehabilitation Facilities published standards in 1967. The National Policy and Performance Council of the Social and Rehabilitation Services of the Federal Department of Health, Education, and Welfare published standards in the same year.

All the above groups except the Policy and Performance Council developed their standards as a basis for accreditation. The Policy and Performance Council established its standards as a basis for eligibility for federal training services and workshop improvement grants under the provisions of the Vocational Rehabilitation Act amendments of 1965.

The Goodwill standards were created by directors of Goodwill Industries to improve the functions and prestige of the members of the organization. The Comstac standards were developed by educators, representatives of organizations for the blind, rehabilitation officials, social welfare officials, workshop operators, industrialists, librarians, rehabilitation center operators, professional organization representatives, and others. The groups are listed above in descending order of their numbers. The Social and Rehabilitation Services standards were developed by the National Advisory and Performance Council which consisted of rehabilitation center and workshop operators, rehabilitation officials, and public representatives. The Commission on Accreditation of Rehabilitation Facilities standards was created by representatives of the Association of Rehabilitation Centers and the National Association of Sheltered Workshops and Homebound Programs. The Comstac group was the only accreditation group that included representatives of associations for the persons served in the programs that were accredited.

The Goodwill Standards

The majority of the Goodwill Industries standards are in the content area designated as Organization and Administration by the National Institute for Workshop Standards. The Goodwill standards subdivide this classification under the following headings:

Goodwill Categories	Standards
Organization and Administration	77
Staff Organization	14
Corporate Organization	10
Business Administration	18
Performance	20
Production	5
Insurance	10

The rest of the standards are grouped as follows:

Physical Facilities, Housekeeping, and Safety	21
Services to Clients	16
Public Relations	11

In addition, the document has a grading schedule for sales and merchandising, induction and orientation of workers, and a check list of minimum equipment needs.

The Goodwill standards are usually specific or concrete. Their meaning is clear and the intent of the statements obvious. When a phase of workshop operations is covered in detail, as in Business Organization or Performance, the standards reflect a combination of good business theory and the wisdom born of long experience. The Goodwill standards provide an excellent basis for the efficient operation of their workshops (10).

The Comstac Standards

The standards of the Commission on Standards and Accreditation of Services for the Blind, published in 1966, were established for all types of services for the blind. General standards were grouped in Agency Function and Structure, Financial Accounting and Service Reporting, Personnel Administration and Volunteer Service, Physical Facilities, and Public Relations and Fund Raising.

Special standards were set for seven service programs: Education, Library Service, Orientation and Mobility Services, Rehabilitation Centers, Sheltered Workshops, Social Services, and Vocational Services.

The standards for workshops were divided under the following headings:

Commission Categories	*Standards*
Purpose and Policies	13
Organization and Administration	25
Business, Financing, and Insurance	15
Production	5
Physical Facilities	14
Health and Safety	11
Worker Benefits	10
Staff Qualification	3
Records and Reports	13

The Comstac standards are probably the most comprehensive guidelines available in the several fields they cover. They not only emphasize the requirements for an efficient operation but also provide some standards for quality programs. The Comstac standards were the first to state the specific mandatory qualifications for staff. They first emphasized the importance of specific policy statements as requirements for accreditation. Thus they first required a policy statement that the worker who left the shop for private employment and is let go through no fault of his own is guaranteed his previous job in the workshop for a limited time. They also required that there must be a policy that the client is paid for his work while undergoing evaluation and related services.

Although the Comstac standards were developed for services to the blind, the section on workshops for the blind is usually applicable to workshops serving other disability groups (11).

The Commission on Accreditation of Rehabilitation Facilities

The Commission on Accreditation of Rehabilitation Facilities was created in 1966 by the Association of Rehabilitation Centers and the National Association of Sheltered Workshops and Homebound Programs to serve as an accrediting organization for both rehabilitation centers and workshops. The Commission issued its standards in 1967. They were based on the Standards for Sheltered Workshops published by the National Institute on Workshop Standards and the Standards for Rehabilitation Centers of the Association of Rehabilitation Centers in 1965. The standards were intended to apply to medical and vocational rehabilitation centers as well as workshop facilities. A significant augmentation of significance to workshops was made in 1969.

The *Standards Manual* published by the Commission classifies service programs into four categories: physical restoration, social adjustment, vocational adjustment, and sheltered remunerative employment. Many of the standards are applicable to facilities in all of the above four categories, and some are applicable only to facilities in specific categories. On May 1, 1970, thirty-four facilities had been accredited as having a vocational adjustment emphasis and twelve as having a sheltered remunerative employment emphasis. The twelve facilities accredited for sheltered employment were among those accredited as having acceptable vocational adjustment programs. Of the thirty-four with acceptable vocational adjustment programs, thriteen were accredited for social adjustment programs (11).

The standards and the requirements in the subheadings were grouped under eight categories (12). The numbers of items relevant to workshops follows:

Commission Categories	*Standards and Requirements*
Purposes	14
Organization and Administration	59
Fiscal Management	48
Physical Facilities	42
Services	65
Personnel	42
Records	49
Community Relations	18

The National Policy and Performance Council Standards

In the Vocational Rehabilitation Act Amendments of 1965, the

National Policy and Performance Council was created to advise the Commissioner of Vocational Rehabilitation on standards for training services and workshop improvement grants. In 1967, the Council recommended a set of standards which were accepted by the Commissioner, Mary E. Switzer. By the same law, the Secretary of Labor was given responsibility for setting safety standards. In 1968, the Rehabilitation Services Administration published the *Safety Manual for Rehabilitation Facilities.* These two documents provide the basis for the standards the federal government uses in its grant programs for workshops (13).

The principle standards used by the federal rehabilitation services agency is found in its *Standard Manual.* The *Safety Manual* spells out the criteria for general standards for safety. The *Standards Manual* has the following categories and statements in each:

Performance Council Categories	Standards
Organization and Administration	49
Services	27
Staff	20
Client	6
Record and Reports	16
Community Relations	5
Safety	5

The National Policy and Performance Council was the last to issue standards and had the advantage of the work of its predecessors. Its standards are less detailed in some respects than those of its predecessors, but the major standards are well covered. Its standards for the staff of the facility, on the other hand, however are probably originally more precise than those of its predecessors. The emphasis is primarily vocational. Its standards represent a good brief summary of good practices in a workshop.

The Combined Standards

If the contents of all four standards manuals are combined and compared with the original standards of the National Institute on Workshop Standards, a greater coverage results. Of the seventy-odd significant standards and criteria deleted by the National

Institute of Standards from its final report, most are found in the standards of the various accreditation groups.

The few standards and criteria identified as important during the early work of the National Institute of Workshop Standards and which are still not included in any of the four standards manuals deserve some attention. They deal with significant requirements.

The missing standards deal with administration and planning. The Institute standards required that written policies and regulations spell out the way in which the workshop would achieve its objectives. This requires an administrative and policy manual. While accreditation standards require written admission, personnel coordination, and discharge statements, a requirement for formal administrative and policy manuals still is absent. Also missing is a requirement for inventory records of supplies in storage, work in process, and finished work awaiting disposal. Though evaluations of the program by the staff are required, there is no requirement of a written plan for the long range development of the shop.

SUMMARY

Workshop standards have been more than twenty-five years in the making. The National Institute on Workshop Standards made a great sustained effort to produce standards from 1958 to 1964, and came up with a great deal of information about desired practices in workshops. The standards it published were less exacting than its studies indicated were desirable. However, some of its standards were accepted by the practitioners in the field and so provided a base line for future progress.

Four standard-setting groups then followed by laying down a set of standards, each approaching the problem from its own point of view. None of the standards, however, is as complete as all four put together. A summary of the standards of all four groups present what is probably the best approximation of desirable workshop practice which is generally acceptable to workshop operators at the present time (14). This summary may be found in the Appendix on pages 419-443.

The standards which have been developed can be of great value to the governing body, the administrator, and the staff of the workshop when a desire exists to improve the program. They can help as a guide to building a more efficient workshop through self-analysis. The standards can serve the purchasers of services from workshops who can use them as a basis for selecting workshops for their use. The standards can also serve funding agencies and community funds. The providers of funds can be more secure in knowing that the money will be more efficiently spent when standards exist.

How do the standards affect the consumers of workshop services, the handicapped individuals who come to the workshops? They do afford them some protection in wages and working conditions, in health and safety protection, and in the indirect advantages that result from an efficient organization. They do not, however, assure that they will be well served. Well-qualified personnel working in ideal physical surroundings with the best of equipment can serve well or not so well, depending upon how thoroughly and consistently they apply best available techniques and methods and how appropriate the concepts are they apply to the problems of the handicapped person in light of his philosophic and cultural aspirations.

The first priority in improving standards should be to develop more criteria for effective service. Such criteria should test the adequacy and scope of service and the extent of participation of the individual in the selection of objectives and the initiation of services. A random sample of cases can then be checked against the criteria to determine if the action taken is appropriate in light of the goals desired by the individual.

Secondly, criteria can be developed to test the effectiveness of industrial operations. These can be stated as specific principles of work set-up, work flow, and production practices. Specific criteria can be developed for determination of direct labor time for pricing and adequacy of quality control systems.

Finally, attention needs to be given to standards for public responsibility. Most of the attention given to community relations by accreditation bodies relates to involving the community groups which are influential and can support the programs. Additional standards are needed for responsibility to the public interest. Ways should be found to test whether the workshop does what it says it does when it appeals for public support. Should an organization claim that it serves all types of handicapped persons when 95 percent of those served are of one disability group? Is there a reasonable relationship between its publicized objectives and its accomplishments? Should an organization state publicly that it is a transitional workshop placing persons in industry when more than half of its population has been in the shop more than five years? Are its contributions to the handicapped population appropriate in light of its expenditures? If an organization not doing research spends nearly a half-million dollars a year serving thirty handicapped persons, is it expending the money fruitfully for handicapped persons? How many should it serve as a minimum? If it serves more persons, are the results it produces reasonable in light of the benefits received by the handicapped persons and by the community?

Though standards have come a long way since the first were written in 1944, they have yet some distance to go. Undoubtedly, they will grow and develop as the workshops achieve greater maturity and sophistication. The direction of their growth will depend upon the changing nature of workshop patterns of organization and financing, the changes in the kinds of persons in the shops and the services they need, the way in which society may see fit to assume responsibility for their functions, and for the changing scope and objectives of their programs. Finally, an important influence on standards will come from the philosophy of workshops about the individual and his role in their programs.

NOTES

1. National Institute on Workshop Standards: Sheltered Workshop Standards. Washington, 1964.
2. National Advisory Committee on Sheltered Workshops: A Statement of Elementary Standards respecting the Policies, Organization, Operation, and Service Activities of Sheltered Workshops. New York, U. S. Department of Labor, Wage and Hour and Public Contracts Division, 1944.
3. Massie, W. A.: The evolution of standards for sheltered workshops. Journal of Rehabilitation, pp. 32-33, May-June, 1968.
4. Workshops for the Disabled, Vocational Rehabilitation Handbook, 2.9c.

Sacramento, Department of Education, 1960.
5. Division of Vocational Rehabilitation: The Rehabilitation Workshop Support Program. Albany, State Department of Education, 1963.
6. National Institute on Workshop Standards: Experimental Evaluation Instrument based on Potential Standards for Sheltered Workshops. Washington, first ed., March, 1962; second ed., October 16, 1962. National Institute on Workshop Standards: Sheltered Workshop Standards. Washington, 1964. National Institute on Workshop Standards: Standards for Sheltered Workshops. Washington, 1964.
7. Bernstein, J.: Sheltered Workshop Standards. Washington, D.C., The National Institute on Workshop Standards, 1964, p. 4. op. cit., p. 4.
8. Ibid, pp. 11-27.
9. Bernstein, J. (Ed.): Standards for Sheltered Workshops. Washington, D.C., The National Institute on Workshop Standards, November, 1964, pp. 7-9.
10. Goodwill Industries of America, Inc.: Standards for Accreditation. Washington, 1966, pp. 3-26.
11. Koestler, F. A. (Ed.): The Comstac Report: Standards for Strengthened Services. New York, Commission on Standards and Accreditation of Services for the Blind, 1966, pp. 33-165, 286-304.
12. Commission on Accreditation of Rehabilitation Facilities: Standards Manual for Rehabilitation Facilities. Chicago, 1967. Overs, R. P.: Standards manual for rehabilitation facilities. Rehabilitation Literature, pp. 139-141, May, 1968.
13. Vocational Rehabilitation Administration: Standards for Rehabilitation Facilities and Sheltered Workshops. Washington, Department of Health, Education, and Welfare, 1967. Social and Rehabilitation Services: Safety Manual for Rehabilitation Facilities. U. S. Department of Health, Education, and Welfare.
14. See Appendix, Summary of Standards.

IX

PHILOSOPHIES OF WORKSHOPS

THROUGHOUT the history of workshops, their administrators have said much about the reasons why they established and operated workshops. Usually the reasons given are based upon social and ethical philosophies.

A basic reason for the existence of workshops is to enable handicapped persons to achieve their work-related goals in life. This presupposes that an individual should be enabled to pursue his socially acceptable aims and that it is important that he do so. Such reasoning is part of the ethical belief that each human being is unique and important, and that he has the right and should have the opportunity to pursue his goals in his own interests. A further expression of this belief is that the individual should be able to maintain his integrity while seeking his objectives. This concept may be called the primacy of the individual in society.

The concept of the primacy of the individual is part of the common legacy of western society. While it stems from the Judeo-Christian tradition, it had little practical economic and social meaning for handicapped and troubled people until late in modern times. In medieval times, the respect and dignity church fathers proclaimed to be due the individual did not enable him to better his economic condition. Nor did the early modern social system provide a mechanism to enable the handicapped person to seek his destiny with dignity. When Vives in 1520, accepting the social beliefs of the time, wrote a plan for the work houses, he made participation compulsory so that society would save money by the forced labor of its unfortunate members. Apparently the first attempt to apply the philosophy of Christianity for the relief of the poor and aged in workshops was made by St. Vincent de Paul in the last part of the sixteenth and the beginning of the seventeenth century.

St. Vincent de Paul stands between medieval and modern times in his social philosophy. He accepted the social and economic conditions of his day but tried to ameliorate their more unfortunate consequences for the poor and handicapped. Believing in the primacy of the individual, he set up social mechanisms which provided for the relief of the distressed with dignity and respect. Among the institutions he created for this purpose were his workshops. He had provided for lay participation in the religious and social organizations he founded, and he may have done the same in the operation of his workshops. If so, he set the precedent of the modern workshop as a private voluntary organization. In any case, his workshops were the first of record dedicated to the welfare of the individual and based on the philosophy of the primacy of the individual.

The next man who influenced workshop philosophy was Valentine Haüy in the eighteenth century in France. A believer in the rights of man as expressed during the French Revolution, he sought to enable the blind persons he saw about him in Paris to enjoy equal status as workers by training them to work in regular occupations in the community. Although he failed in some of his plans, his beliefs have survived among workers for the blind to the present day. Some of the ideas expressed by Samuel Girdley Howe of the Perkins Institute near Boston, Massachusetts, in the nineteenth century were similar to those of Haüy.

In the middle of the nineteenth century in the United States, there were two different approaches to providing care for the blind — keeping them in homes for the blind, or enabling them to live in the community. In espousing the second approach, Howe (1) wrote in 1849:

> ... It should be a cardinal principle of the education of the blind to keep ever in view the fact that they are to become members of general society, and not a society of blind persons. ... the blind youth needs, as much as any other, ... to go out and buffet the world; to wrestle with difficulties; and to get strength and courage by long and varied exercise of his faculties .... I do most earnestly hope ... that, in enlarging our work department and putting it on a permanent basis, that we may adopt the system which will give them the greatest possible personal independence consistent with their true interest.

Howe's ideas received considerable theoretical acceptance. In the last half of the nineteenth century in the United States, there was a growing belief in the desirability and justice of having free and universal education to give the individual a more equal start in the competitive race. Since the workshops for the blind were viewed as part of educational institutions, they were accepted and grew rapidly. However, they often did not maintain their educational character, but became employment institutions. Thus Howe's theories were not carried out. It was left to persons interested in disadvantaged groups other than the blind to pursue the ideas enunciated by him, St. Vincent de Paul, and Valentine Haüy. Nevertheless, while Howe did not see his ideas put into practice generally, he did state for the first time in the United States the basic goal of the rehabilitation movement: the achievement of independence and self-respect for the individual handicapped person.

In the second half of the nineteenth century, organizations with religious or moral purposes espoused the cause of the poor, the disabled, and the disadvantaged. The philosophy of the Cooperative Society of Visitors Among the Poor of Boston, founded in 1887, and the sponsor of the predecessor of the Boston Community Workshops, Inc., was typical of one of them. The Cooperative Society opposed giving money to needy as being degrading. They proposed instead to give them work and to understand their condition, so that the causes of poverty could be corrected. In the Society's report of 1879, the following explanation of their activities appears:

> The constant endeavor of our faithful visitors has not been to alleviate distress and destitution, but to investigate and correct some of the causes of pauperism, such as improvidence, intemperance, and idleness. Our task would be an easy one if we had to contend with want alone, and not with the vice and ignorance that often be at its root (2).

Modern workshop personnel respect the Society's desire to understand the lives, character, and work habits of their clients. While the Society did not specify a technique to find that understanding, they and other like agencies at the time stressed the importance of understanding those they served, a tenet which has become essential to the workshop philosophy.

Among the leaders of the religious groups that started work

programs, the most eloquent was William Booth of the Salvation Army. He went a step further than the Boston Society in his emphasis on the need for a rapid movement into competitive employment. In *Darkest England and the Way Out,* he stated his philosophy and objectives as follows:

> Any person who comes to a shelter, destitute and starving, will be supplied with sufficient work to enable him to earn . . . his bed and board. This is a fundamental feature of the scheme, and one which will commend it to all those who are anxious to benefit the poor by enabling them to help themselves without the demoralizing intervention of charitable relief.
>
> There is no pretense of charity beyond the charity which gives a man remunerative labor. It is not our business to pay men wages. What we propose is to enable those who are destitute to earn their rations and do enough work to pay for their lodging until they are able to go out into the world and earn wages for themselves (3).

By the end of the nineteenth century, workshop philosophy had progressed from the idea of beneficence with dignity to that of independence through work. The providing of work was conceived as not being a charity but as a means of creating independence. An early slogan of the Goodwill Industries of America first publicized this concept – Not Charity, but a Chance.

During the first half of the twentieth century, a number of concurrent developments took place which put workshop philosophy in a broader social framework. At first, private voluntary agencies and later state and federal government agencies developed programs for the rehabilitation of physically handicapped persons. From these programs emerged the philosophy of rehabilitation. Since both the rehabilitation programs and the workshops served disabled persons, it was natural that the workshops were influenced by the beliefs of the larger groups of rehabilitation agencies. Workshop personnel adopted rehabilitation philosophy, modified it or amplified it at times, and applied it to their programs.

The philosophy of rehabilitation was also based upon the principle of the primacy of the individual, a principle which first influenced the development of workshops. However, rehabilitation philosophy made several specific amplifications. The principal additional concepts were that the handicapped individual had the right to expect to achieve his highest potential, and that society had the obligation to enable him to do so. These concepts were developed as a result of two principal influences: the experience and precepts of voluntary rehabilitation agencies, and the experience of government programs in attempting to help handicapped persons under existing legislative mandates.

The philosophy of voluntary agencies arose from their experience in providing services to handicapped persons in the early years of the twentieth century. One such agency was the Federation of Associations for Cripples in New York City, organized by Douglas C. McMurtrie in 1912. The Associations began by providing restorative medical services but found that services of other kinds were needed. McMurtrie was able to publicize such multiple needs in his *American Journal of the Care of Cripples.* His educational efforts and the return of disabled soldiers from World War I brought to the attention of sensitive citizens the need to organize more comprehensive services for the care of the disabled.

One such citizen was Jeremiah Milbank of New York City. Milbank, a wealthy man, employed several trained persons — an occupational therapist, a social worker, and vocational teachers — to study the problems of the disabled and to make recommendations for their care in an institute which he planned to support. Milbank's contribution to rehabilitation consisted not only in his gifts to the Institute for the Crippled and Disabled of New York but to the realization that the Institute program should be more comprehensive than the specialized recommendations his consultants suggested. He conceived of rehabilitation as a composite service which combined other elements with physical restoration and vocational training in a total program (4).

Milbank's concept influenced the program of the Institute for the Crippled and Disabled and its directors. The staff conducted research programs, publicized their findings, and did much to spread the concept of rehabilitation as a composite service. At the same time, the Association for the Crippled and Disabled in Cleveland and a similar group in Detroit were espousing similar ideas. Colonel John M. Smith, Jr., who was appointed director of the Institute in New York in 1933, secured the interest of Walter Bingham, Chief Psychologist of the United States Army, and the

Surgeon General, Norman T. Kirk. Military personnel were sent to the Institute to be trained in the new concept. The Veterans Administration also sent personnel to the Institute for training (5).

As a result of the influence of the Institute, Milbank, and of writers and leaders in the field, such as Mary Richmond, Frederick M. Thiese, and Kenneth Hamilton, the concept of a comprehensive service as the basis of rehabilitation became well accepted among rehabilitation agencies in the first half of the twentieth century (6).

The concept of composite or comprehensive services was later given theoretical underpinning. The complex services were needed because the handicapped person must be conceived as a "whole person." As a whole person, his needs are interrelated. Treating one aspect of his problems does not achieve his rehabilitation. To assure his rehabilitation, it is necessary to deal with a constellation of problems in the medical, psychosocial, and vocational phases of his disability. This version of the principle of comprehensive services is known as the "holistic" approach to rehabilitation. Its advocates regard it as the keystone to the philosophy of rehabilitation (7).

The view of rehabilitation as a composite service was in decided contrast to the assumptions which were made by the initiators of the early federal legislation in the field of vocational rehabilitation. Although the Institute for Crippled and Disabled of New York had devised a model law in 1917 suggesting composite services, the recommendations were ignored in the first federal vocational rehabilitation act of 1920. The provisions of the law limited services primarily to vocational training. In the 1943 amendments to the law, medical services were added (8). Subsequently, other services were added in the amendments of 1954, 1965, and 1968. However, the vocational rehabilitation law of 1920 and its amendments were based on the principle that rehabilitation is a process of providing specified services to specifically identified groups of handicapped persons to enable them to engage in remunerative employment. As the number of services permitted in the law increased, the differences between the nature of public and private rehabilitation programs decreased, but the difference in principle remained. The philosophy of the private voluntary agencies called for the provision of any service or combination of services necessary for any goal or combination of goals for those they served. In contrast, the mandate of the vocational rehabilitation legislation was generally that only specified kinds of services could be given for the purpose of enabling specified groups of handicapped persons to engage in remunerative activity.

The early limitations and restrictions of the federal law led the practitioners in public vocational rehabilitation programs to adopt a working philosophy which was different from the holistic approach to rehabilitation. From their experience and their observation of workers in industry, they found that it was often possible to enable many handicapped persons to work successfully without resolving all their psychosocial problems. They observed that a person does not act invariably as the same whole person in all situations, but that he often functions at different levels of acceptability in different situations or in different kinds of functioning. More specifically, they found that the handicapped individual can often function suitably in the worker part of his life without functioning acceptably in other psychosocial aspects. This observation had its influence on vocational rehabilitation programs before it was conceptualized as the segmented or elemental approach to rehabilitation as distinguished from the holistic approach. Later, Walter S. Neff was to explain theoretically what the counselor found empirically — that it is possible for some persons to have severe disturbances in one area of their lives yet function well at work (9).

It is important to note that those who practiced the segmented or elemental approach to rehabilitation in public agencies did not depreciate the value of services geared to objectives other than work. The difference between the segmented and holistic advocates was that the latter believed that composite services were essential to achieve the objective of employment. Neither view prevailed, and practitioners often respected both points of view. Many began to conclude that neither approach was appropriate in all cases. Sometimes comprehensive services were necessary for the employment objective but not always. Sometimes the handicapped person had a number of goals other than employment, and the services needed were predominately of a psychosocial nature. A third view, the *eclectic* approach, then gained acceptance. The concept was an adaptation of Frederick C. Thorne's approach to counseling and psychotherapy. It holds that the services to be rendered should depend upon the assessment of the handicapped person's condition and his desires (10). Thus the individual should receive the services he needs and wants. The services the individual needs and wants might be partial or total.

Thus, three varying views are held by workshop personnel about the services that are required by handicapped persons in workshops: the *holistic* approach, which holds that the handicapped person needs a system of interrelated, comprehensive services which attempt to achieve simultaneously various interrelated goals one of which is employment; the *segmented* or *elemental* view, which holds that work goals may be achieved without necessarily achieving other basic psychosocial goals and that specific work-related services alone may very usefully serve some handicapped persons; and the *eclectic* view, which holds that the individual's condition and wishes must determine the services he should be given and that they may be either comprehensive or segmented depending upon the individual.

All three views, however, emphasize the importance of assessment of the individual's condition. They probably agree that assessment should be comprehensive. They differ primarily about what services must be given to achieve work objectives. They agree that the individual should be given the services he wants.

The different approaches to serving handicapped persons were influential in the development of workshop organizational philosophy. At the Bedford Springs conference in 1959, there was a division of opinion between those who advocated the holistic approach and those who advocated the segmented, or work-centered, approach. This difference among workshop personnel exists to the present day.

Philosophy of Workshops

At the time of the Bedford Springs Meeting amplifications of existing rehabilitation philosophy were developed. The notion was stressed that handicapped persons not only had the right to try to reach their highest potential and that society should help them, but that almost all handicapped persons could do so if they were given appropriate opportunities. The belief was widely publicized that handicapped persons previously thought to be incapable of improvement were able to enhance their situations in life if proper treatment was available. To the rational components of right and responsibility was added positive belief in the potentiality for improvement of all handicapped persons regardless of disability. This belief resulted in the influx into workshops of large numbers of severely handicapped persons, such as the mentally retarded or the mentally ill, who had not been admitted to most workshops previously (11).

Another concept closely related to the belief in the improvement of the handicapped person's condition was the notion that every handicapped person should assume as much initiative and responsibility for his future activity as possible. A logical extension of this idea was that the individual should participate as much as possible in all aspects of his program including decision making. Rehabilitation personnel had long before expounded the principle that the person's program should be "client centered." Often, however, this was interpreted to mean that the professional person suggested a program which was in the individual's best interest. The idea that the individual should determine his goals and control the course of his activities became more prevalent. Care was taken to make sure the individual understood the means necessary to the achievement of his goals. Thus, programs of the individual should be "client initiated" and "client controlled" to the extent possible under this concept.

In many workshops, this concept resulted in a new role for the handicapped person. In some workshops, the individual participated in staff meetings when matters of concern to him were discussed. In other workshops, handicapped persons were given positions of responsibility for output, quality, and teaching. These new concepts stood the workshops in good stead, as they began providing services to disadvantaged, ethnic groups who were challenging the traditional attitudes of our industrial society.

THE WORKSHOP DUALITY

There is general agreement by critics of the workshop and by its advocates of varying schools of thought that a workshop program is dual in nature. On the one hand, the workshop accepts people into its program who are not acceptable in competitive industry because they do not meet the requirements of industry. On the other hand, the workshop must produce products or services with results which are acceptable to industry or it cannot maintain the reality environment which enables the individual to become acceptable to industry or productive in workshops. The workshop must expose the individual to some of the demands of industrial reality while shielding him from its full demands. How does the workshop meet the demands of its industrial customer and at the same time the needs of the handicapped individuals it serves?

The answer to this question is usually made by workshop personnel in three ways. One view is that this workshop problem is best understood as a conflicting dichotomy — that the needs of the individual and the demands of industrial reality are in conflict. Therefore, the needs of the individual must be given priority. Another belief is that there is no conflict. The individual's primary need is to meet the demands of industrial reality and he should be exposed to it. A third precept takes an intermediate position. The individual's need is indeed to meet the demands of reality, but since he is unable to do so he must be exposed to such demands gradually. Both the second and third views see no conflict in the workshop duality. The third emphasizes the concept that the workshop process is a synthesis between the individual's need to meet the demands of reality and his need for acceptance of his inability to do so until he becomes able to function more adequately.

Three Views of the Workshop Duality

The school of thought that considers the workshop as a conflicting dichotomy emphasizes the philosophy that the needs of the individual must predominate. This philosophy is stated in several aspects. Rehabilitation or training or treatment comes first.

The workshop's objective should not be production. The shop should be client centered and the inability of the individual to work should be respected fully.

Opponents of this emphasis point out that it often leads to an environment lacking in industrial reality: respecting the individual's inability completely leads to the perpetuation of the inability and the increase of dependency. They allege that workshops with this emphasis fail to use quantitative measures of functioning and mislead the individual to feel he is able to function acceptably when in fact he is far from it. When the individual leaves the shop, his inability to function shows up with traumatic results. If he stays in the shop under such conditions, he becomes a custodial charge without the possibility of growth and development.

The second school of thought holds that the individual should be exposed to reality thoroughly and realistically. It is futile, in this view, to acquiesce to behavior or productive norms that do not approach industrial expectancy if employment is the goal. The industrial world and indeed society in general will not accept the standards of the permissive workshop. The individual should be given an opportunity to respond to reality with support and understanding, but he should not be deceived into believing that he is doing what he is not, or that he will be rewarded in life because he is trying. If it is impossible for the individual to meet expected norms, it is important to him that this be known so that realistic planning may take place.

Opponents of this view point out that its advocates are missing the main purpose of a workshop, which is to accept substandard performance until the individual is able to increase his level of performance. If performance or behavior approximating general expectancy is insisted upon immediately, the workshop must either terminate those who cannot meet general requirements or reject such individuals upon admission screening. Individuals should be judged not only by their level of performance and behavior but by their improvement in performance and behavior. The workshop requiring high standards of performance and behavior are denying the benefits of the workshops to those who need their services most. They are adding to the discrimination against those who are rejected by industry.

The third school of thought believes that neither of the first two views is correct. If a workshop is overly permissive it creates dependency regardless of how virtuous its rationalization might sound. If a workshop makes demands clearly beyond the ability of the individual to respond, it deprives him of a chance to improve and meet increased demands. The requirements made of the individual should be somewhat in relationship to his ability to meet requirements from time to time, but they should often be at a higher level than he has been able to accomplish previously. Such requirements should be objective, in relation to established norms of performance, and the individual should in most circumstances understand how he is doing in relation to such norms. This may be accomplished through wages in accordance with performance and other objective means of recognition. He should understand the difference between reward for accomplishment and encouragement for effort. Only thus will he be prepared to live satisfactorily in the world of work.

Critics of the third school point out that emphasis on objective criteria of performance and rational rewards fails to recognize the essentially emotional and subjective nature of human personality. Handicapped individuals need to relate to staff whose response to them is not based on objective evaluation of performance success but on understanding of their failures and their personal needs. The individual is too complex and varied in his makeup to be judged by quantitative standards. Responses based on subjective clinic judgments are more significant than objective norms. Only by subjective identification with the individual's problem will the workshop staff be able to help the individual grow and develop.

The Synthesis of Workshop Duality

The various philosophies resulting from the workshop duality are really not as dramatically opposed in their implementation as they are in theory. To some extent, their differences are those of degree. Workshop personnel want handicapped persons to be as effective as possible, in all respects, including their productivity. They recognize that handicapped individuals have contrasting needs — the need for stress on effective functioning and the need for toleration of ineffective level of functioning. The major differences in theory relate to the emphasis put on the first need or the second, and the relative importance which is placed on the drive for effectiveness versus acceptance of ineffectiveness in the workshop process. However, at any given time, in most shops, some demand is made on the individual. At the same time, some allowance is made for inefficiency and inadequate behavior. The relationship between the two — the demand for increased performance or adequate behavior and acceptance of less than adequate performance and behavior — nearly always exists. Thus the workshop process is a continuous synthesis between demand for functioning and acceptance of malfunctioning at varying levels. Depending upon the philosophy of the workshop, more emphasis is put on one factor of the synthesis than the other. Also depending on the philosophy of the workshop, the criteria used to measure functioning and malfunctioning is either objective or subjective.

It would be difficult to make comparative studies on a large scale to test the validity of the different philosophies, and this has not been done. However, perceptive observers point out that different types of workshops are successful with some individuals and not with others. Individuals who fail to improve in workshops of the first school which make few demands on individuals succeed in workshops of the second school which make great and immediate demands on individuals. The reverse is also true. Thus, lacking definitive evidence, workshop personnel choose their philosophies in keeping with their training, experience, and personal predilections. In practice, however, they often strike a balance somewhat different from their precepts to meet the demands of reality and the degree of vocational handicap.

The writer believes that workshop personnel should use objective criteria as a basis for identifying the status and progress of individuals in workshops. He believes a workshop should state its assessment of individuals in quantitative norms. For example, an individual who is considered ready for competitive employment should be able to produce within a predetermined range of an industrial norm. If the objective is employment in the shop, then another range of productive norms should be determined. The workshop should set quantitative criteria for all its objectives. Such objectives should be stated in quantitative norms for behavior as well as production. Only when objectives are stated in specific and identifiable terms can the workshop have assurance that it is achieving its objectives for individuals.

For example, assume a workshop has as its objective the adjustment of the work behavior of a group of individuals. It has norms which the staff hopes they will meet. But faulty or subnormal behavior slows the work. If it is not accomplished, the work will be lost and there will be no work upon which to meet the adjustment norms. The shop, therefore, acquires a well-adjusted core of workers, handicapped or nonhandicapped, who can supplement the work of the unadjusted group, thus assuring completion of the work and setting an example of good adjustment. The staff is now free to effect the synthesis of accommodation and demand necessary to reach the adjustment norms.

Assume the workshop has as its objective the increase of the average productivity of a group of low producers from 40 percent to 70 percent of the standard norm. At 40 percent of the norm, not enough work can be accomplished to meet deadlines and there is no substantial flow of work upon which to practice to increase productivity. A core of workers capable of producing at 80 percent of standard is obtained. The accomplishment of the work is assured. The staff can concentrate on bringing the productivity of the nonproductive group up to the desired norms.

The achievement of quantitative goals and the synthesis takes much effort and perseverance and costs much money. The way in which money may be secured to operate workshops is not only an administrative problem but is also a part of workshop philosophy. Such philosophies are based in turn on general social philosophies in the United States.

THE FINANCIAL RESPONSIBILITY
FOR WORKSHOP SERVICE

Workshops early in their history held the philosophy that

handicapped individuals should be given employment in shops if work in industry was not available to them. During the first half of the twentieth century, they adopted the rehabilitation philosophy that the individual should be given a chance to function at his highest potential. During the same period and more extensively during the second half of the twentieth century, some workshops accepted the philosophy that the chronically ill or aged person should be maintained at work even if his ability to function is deteriorating. These services in both categories had to be financed. Which social or political units in the nation should assume organizational and financial responsibility for these services? What portion of the cost should come from the work done in the shop and what portion from other sources? What should these other sources be? These were some of the questions that faced workshops in the twentieth century.

The large majority of workshops were started by private voluntary organizations. Only a very few claimed they could support their programs from income from work. From what source then would come the money for services to handicapped people in workshops? The logic of the situation seemed to be that since the voluntary agencies took responsibility for the programs, they should raise the money for their support. In only a few large cities in the United States were voluntary agencies willing or able to raise sums remotely approximating the needs of workshops if substantial numbers of handicapped individuals were to be served in accordance with the philosophy and goals of workshop organizations.

The reasons for the failure in general of voluntary agencies in the United States to support workshops adequately even when they sponsored them are somewhat obscure. Their general failure cannot be attributed to their inability to raise money for charitable causes. Many voluntary health agencies raised substantial sums for education, research, social welfare, and occasionally for medical care. Others, however, such as the societies for the mentally retarded and the cerebral palsied, found it difficult to raise money continuously for workshops. In the first half of the twentieth century, few central community charitable funds contributed substantially to workshops, and only a minority have done so subsequently. Typically, the voluntary charitable institutions of the United States did not provide the workshops with abundant means for their support. Their greatest failure, however, has been in their lack of support for long-term services.

The answer to the question of why private voluntary agencies sponsored workshops without supporting them adequately must be sought in the social philosophy of the United States. The basic philosophy of the United States is that each individual is to seek his own interest in his own way. The public provides him with a free education but after that he is on his own. If he fails to succeed, that is his own affair. If he runs into difficulties and needs public help he may get it on a minimal basis, but he suffers public condemnation by so doing. He is expected to see to it that he does not need public help if he wishes to be a respected member of society.

The handicapped individual is in some respects an exception to the general rule. He is unable to succeed for reasons beyond his control. Therefore, it is recognized that he needs help to overcome his handicap — to equalize his opportunity in the competitive race. Thus the public — the national government and the voluntary agency — should help him to become employable. The national social philosophy stops there. It does not contemplate the possibility that he may not be able to become employable and self-supporting. There is no concept of "social employment," as conceived in the Netherlands where the national government provides funds to create jobs in workshops for its citizens who cannot work in industry, or any program comparable to Remploy in England where the national government operates industries for its handicapped citizens. American social philosophy provides the handicapped individual with an opportunity to prepare for employment in industry, but it leaves him without an honorable work alternative if he does not make it. He must take the disreputable course of seeking public assistance. Or he may work in the few sheltered workshops which exist under circumstances which the American public does not understand and therefore regards as questionable — possibly a disguised form of the disreputable public assistance.

In light of this analysis, the lack of enthusiasm of many

voluntary agencies to raise huge sums for long-term services in workshops becomes somewhat easier to understand. The exceptions are the parent organizations whose members have a close personal involvement in the problem and by a few voluntary agencies who from eleemosynary zeal add a small addendum to American social philosophy.

The effect of the American philosophy puts the workshop organization in the position of providing opportunities for the handicapped individuals to prepare for employment, but it does not indicate a way to find enough money to provide employment for the many handicapped individuals who cannot make it in industry. Since the workshop does not usually make enough from work projects to support total workshop costs, it often limits its operations to short-term services for which it is easier to get money from public agencies and from charitable sources. When it does provide long-term employment, it seldom meets the need. There are, of course, a few exceptions.

The workshop organization is in a philosophic dilemma. On the one hand, it proclaims that the handicapped individual should reach his highest potential. On the other hand, if that highest potential is not high enough to work in industry, the workshop must most often forsake the handicapped individual since it lacks the money to take care of his long-term needs. The best it can do is make clear that it is not prepared to carry out the philosophy in which it believes, and that it will terminate services to most of those who may not prove able to work in industry.

In practice, workshop organizations have gotten money wherever they were able to acquire it: from work income, from charitable sources, and from grants or fees for services from government agencies. In general, there is almost unanimous agreement that a workshop needs sources of support other than from work income, but no common philosophy of where it should come from has been reached. If the practices of workshops were conceptualized, the resulting generalization would be that the workshop should seek funding from whatever sources were available from time to time. Actually, however, large numbers of workshops receive a major share of their funds from work income. Generally, workshops believe that a major share of financing should come from sources other than work income.

The instability created by the difference between philosophy and practice is often traumatic. As a result, many private voluntary workshop organizations, to find stability, took to state and federal governments as a source of financing. Since present government philosophy limits its funds to short-term purposes and the amounts of its budget vary, this approach has its limits. If workshop organizations are to carry out the philosophy of enabling the handicapped individual to function at his highest potential, they will need to develop a philosophy of financial responsibility for the process.

The instability of financing inhibits the development of another principle necessary for good workshop administration and for the encouragement of the receipt of funds. When workshops receive funds from a number of sources, some are under pressure to use such funds for all or a number of necessary purposes. Such indiscriminate use of funds incurs the displeasure of the sources of funding. In the long run, workshops will need to expend funds for purposes for which they are intended.

In summary, it may be said that although workshops have developed admirable goals and philosophies, they have not developed a unified philosophy of social responsibility for the financing of their programs. Large groups of workshops look to government agencies for funds. Other groups look to private charitable sources for financing. Many workshops approach both of these sources for support and are in fact aided by various sources, public and private. To the extent that a generalization can be made, workshops are supported by public tax money and by private charitable contributions, depending upon the availability of funds from either source from time to time.

Regardless of which sources give funds to workshops, few make permanent or stable commitments to workshop programs. Thus, the basis of financial support has been and is uncertain. It is uncertain because the American public generally does not understand the role of the workshop in preparing handicapped persons for employment in industry and has not been asked to finance employment in workshops nationally or in many parts of the country. Furthermore, financing employment in workshops on a large scale without a great deal more understanding of the problems of handicapped persons than it has had is unlikely. The development of a sense of social responsibility for institutional mechanisms to provide work opportunities for persons unable to work in competitive industry is a basic problem facing workshops.

TOWARDS A PHILOSOPHY OF RESPONSIBILITY FOR WORKSHOP PROGRAMS

As workshop sponsors seek a philosophy of social responsibility for workshops, they find themselves caught between the utilitarian and philanthropic conceptions of social welfare and rehabilitation. They inherit tenets which do not reflect the unique potentials of workshops to combine the two. Thus some existing parts of rehabilitation philosophy limit workshop ideology. An example is the utilitarian concept that rehabilitation pays; because the handicapped person is changed from a burden to society to a taxpayer, every dollar spent is returned many-fold to the public coffers. No matter how one evaluates this ethos, it clearly limits services to those who can repay society for its investment in them. It is doubtful if a single dollar-counting rationale can justify programs for large segments of the severely handicapped and disadvantaged population who need recurrent, extended, or permanent assistance. Workshop philosophy must consider the needs of those who cannot return completely in dollars society's investment in them. It should be based primarily on human need. Such financial benefits which accrue to society from workshops should be considered a welcome but secondary windfall.

The workshop philosophy must, however, be considered in light of the overall social philosophy of the country. That philosophy assumes that those who cannot work and earn sufficient for their support must be provided for by society. In the past, those who needed assistance were divided into two general groups, those who could not support themselves for reasons arising out of disability, and those who could not support themselves for a variety of reasons considered not to arise out of disability. In either case, however, the group was given money, not work. Since the money provided was usually inadequate for a decent standard of living, and its receipt was generally considered prejudicial to personal dignity, the outcome was unfortunate in all respects. Both groups remain unproductive. The handicapped person remains debilitated and frustrated. The nonhandicapped person tends to become hostile and resorts to deceit or antisocial activity to improve his condition.

In the 1960's, the dividing line between these two groups has been somewhat obliterated. It became clear that many of those considered not to be in the handicapped group often are found there. It is also recognized that in any case, the provision of work is preferable to the giving of public assistance from all points of view. Such work must be voluntary under acceptable conditions if it is to be an adequate substitute for public assistance. If the workshops could base their philosophy on what they are now doing, they would provide a social mechanism beneficial to both society and the handicapped and disadvantaged.

Such a philosophy would provide for a workshop system which does basically two things — prepare persons for work outside the workshop, and provide work for them in the workshop if they cannot work outside it. For those who chose to remain as workers in workshops, their wages would serve in lieu of public assistance payments. Such wages should be at a standard above relief payments and at least equal to the national minimum wage. Through working, the person would produce what he were able and receive a wage large enough for an adequate life. Thus the workshop would perform both a utilitarian and a humanitarian function simultaneously. It would contribute to the productive capacity of the economy and provide a constructive substitute for public assistance.

Such a workshop system would require considerable amounts of public support. Probably the excess of wage payments over earnings would have to come in the main from money raised from public taxation. More important, however, is the fact that the workshop institution as a dual means of moving men into industry and providing jobs in workshops would be presented as a solution to social problems for which society should assume financial responsibility. The overall justification for such a system, however, cannot depend upon the concept of saving money for society. It should frankly rest upon the ethical philosophy that society should be willing to pay the cost of providing the handicapped person the opportunity to work in industry or in the workshop as he can or as he wishes. A further justification might be that such a solution to problems of people is worth the price in the personal happiness it creates for the handicapped person and the social stability it creates for the community. Such a philosophy depends in a great measure upon public understanding of the importance and value of work to the human being as distinguished from its economic or social value.

From the point of view of the individual, work takes on a vastly different meaning for him than it does to society. The work a person does in a workshop or in an outside job may have tremendous significance to him even if it is low in the social value system. Since workshop philosophy is geared to the individual and his needs, the meaning and value of work should be conceived in terms of the individual. Thus, society and the workshop personnel are often not communicating well when the importance of work is the subject. Society considers work important to the individual as it enables him to gain a position of value in its eyes. The person considers work important when it meets his needs. Though there is a relationship between the two — the value society places on a man's work and the satisfaction he gets from it — his work may have value and meaning to him even when society downgrades it.

THE MEANING AND VALUE OF WORK

One of the difficulties in determining the meaning and value of work results from the great variety of interpretations of what the word means and encompasses. If the word means manual labor, it will have one set of meanings and values. If it includes intellectual and artistic endeavors, it will have others. If it includes managing a fortune or an estate or wielding influence at court or in a capitol or a community, it will have still other meanings and values. Thus, one can show that work was of little value in some historical periods or is of little value presently if one defines work narrowly. Before the role of work can be evaluated, the word must be defined.

Here we are faced with other difficulties. The definitions of work are many. Even when work is used in connection with human activities, the definitions are numerous. When work is defined broadly as a human activity the purpose of which is to maintain life through affecting the environment, it does not cover many aspects of working which influence handicapped persons. Such a definition does not include the persons who work to pass the time pleasurably, who work for the joys of creativity, or who work for the pleasure of the company of others. When a man works, he restricts his freedom of activity in exchange for returns he must have or desires. This is just as true of the criminal and the artist as it is for the banker or the laborer. The key to understanding the social contract called work is the returns for which the worker works.

A primary reason why man works is to make money for the things he needs or wants. This is a very important reason why many handicapped persons work. Some handicapped persons will work for very small sums of money, and the small sums are very important to them. Others will not work for money unless other circumstances or rewards are also present. Some will not work for money under any circumstances if the work is not of the right nature, that is, if they do not see themselves doing the work with dignity. Thus, while money is a necessary reason to make persons work in shops or elsewhere, it is by no means the only reason and sometimes not a sufficient reason. Man works for a variety of other reasons. One important reason is probably what Thorstein Veblen called the instinct of workmanship and Ives Hendrick labels the "mastery instinct." It may be that the mentally retarded youth who wants to work at the shop "to pass the time" is responding to the same need. That need is to perform in a purposeful manner with desired utilitarian or creative results.

Since the need to perform in a purposeful manner must often be carried out in groups, work often provides secondary social benefits. It provides at times friends, colleagues, or fellow workers, banded together in common purpose who recognize individual achievement. This, in turn, engenders respect and results in self-esteem. Even when the worker works alone, he may achieve recognition and respect. The successful performance of purposeful valued activity engenders self-esteem.

Finally, the need to work is reinforced by social ideals. American society values a man in accordance with the work he does. If he does not work at all, he is looked down upon, even if he has great wealth and social position. Thus, the unemployed severely handicapped person and the wealthy person both need work in American society. Money, though it is necessary for some, is not always the sufficient return from working.

Some workshop personnel or researchers have specific reservations about the attractiveness of work to some individuals. Walter Neff, for example, believes that some people find work onerous and will not work if they can avoid it (11).

Olshansky and Unterberger list some groups of people who do not wish to work and who work sporadically or not at all (12). They believe that if one accepts the concept of the right of an individual to choose his own course of action, he must be accorded the right to refuse work. While granting the right of an individual to choose his course of action, it might be useful to inquire if the refusal to work arises out of the work which is available or the inherent disinclination to work.

Granting that some persons do not respond to work opportunities which are available, it is probable that a great majority of handicapped persons wish to work within the scope of the work which is available. It is also probably true that they wish to work for other reasons as well as the making of money. The additional reasons may be combined in a general wish to engage in work activity which will give their lives worth and purpose in their own eyes and in the judgments of others they respect. Thus, workshop philosophy should be based on the premise that work is generally beneficial and necessary to the happiness of man. This basic philosophy should be kept in view as the alternatives to workshops are considered.

THE SUGGESTED ALTERNATIVES TO WORKSHOPS

The philosophies which have been explained have common beliefs about the value of workshops. They all assume that workshops as now constituted are generally socially commendable, that they are beneficial to handicapped persons. Those who hold such views generally believe that workshops should expand their programs and that their numbers should increase. There are others who do not share such views. They do not approve of workshop programs as they are now constituted. The critics fall into two groups: those who think the idea of work programs for the handicapped is good but would like to see them in a different setting, and those who think workshops are not desirable and would like to see them restricted or abolished in their present forms. Of those, the second group has the longest history and presents the most fundamental challenge to workshops.

The Criticism of Jacobus ten Broek

Many energetic critics of workshops are found among the organizations for the blind. Their most eloquent leader was Jacobus ten Broek, and many of their concepts stem from his thinking. His formulations are probably the most systematic criticisms of workshop philosophy and theory made in recent times (13).

Ten Broek's analysis combines historic analysis with existing evaluation. He describes workshops as maintaining the undesirable features of the medieval church, the hospital or asylum, the workhouse, and the school. The workshops of religious origin "view their workers not as free citizens and responsible adults merely handicapped by physical limitations, but as helpless sinners and proper subjects for moral uplift." He describes workshops of medical origin as the lineal descendent of the medieval hospital and the county poor farm, who seek to "fulfill the 'double function' of healing the sick and employing the handicapped." This double function is a "dubious dualism" and a revival of the "medieval practice of combining medical services with the almshouse conditions of sheltered employment." The workshops providing employment stem from the old workhouses and "still preserve, albeit in a more kindly way, the essential characteristics of the old style workhouse, a system of public aid to the idle in which public cost is minimized through the work contribution of the beneficiaries." A recurrent criticism is directed against workshops which attempt vocational training programs. Such attempts, he states, were discredited in the nineteenth century. He is also critical of attempts to use work for purposes of rehabilitation (14).

Ten Broek concludes that there is no place for the "sheltered workshop" in vocational rehabilitation. Whether the workshop as a place of terminal employment is justified depends upon its wages, hours, perquisites, and labor management relations. But wages in workshops, he said, cover only a small part of the cost of living. When based on individual productivity, "the wage must indeed be a pittance." He finally finishes as follows:

> It is difficult to escape the conclusion that the only real justification for such an institution is a psychology of human nature derived from the 17th century Puritan ethic; namely, that idleness is a sin, and that work — however routinized or demeaning, unproductive or unrequited — is a virtue sufficient unto itself (15).

Throughout his vivid descriptions of the evils in workshops, ten Broek builds a framework of value judgments which go to the heart of workshop philosophy. He points out that in each of the types of workshops he describes, there is a questionable duality. He ignores the rationale that work in a workshop can be used justifiably for psychological purposes, for treatment, for training, and for work experience. He rejects the idea that work can have any justification in a workshop unless it can produce wages high enough for an adequate standard of living. If all his assumptions are granted, there is indeed little justification for workshops in their present form.

If ten Broek's critical statements about workshops seem exaggerated, it is well to remember that he wrote in the 1950's and based his writings primarily on conditions in workshops for the blind in the first half of the twentieth century. He shows not much awareness of the development of other workshop programs except those in reconditioning of discards and of a few work adjustment programs. His importance lies in two areas. First, many of his disciples still preach his philosophy. Secondly, he attacked workshops as unworthy institutions whose fundamental philosophy and premises were not tenable. In the process, he identified fundamental propositions upon which workshops are based.

In order to attack the use of work as a beneficial process for training or rehabilitation, he labeled it a "dubious duality" and analyzed the duality to prove it was not useful. As a result, he made what is probably the earliest systematic study and analysis of the dual nature of a workshop process. Few will deny that the duality exists. Ten Broek found in it essential conflicts which are irreconcilable. Most workshop personnel believe it to be a beneficial and enabling duality.

What are ten Broek's alternatives? Although he does not spell them out in his writing on workshops, his alternatives are given in other places (16). Ideally, blind and handicapped persons should work in competitive industry. In attempting to reach this goal, the stereotyped attitude of society towards the blind is the principal handicap. This stereotyped attitude should be changed. Regular employment opportunities of many varieties should be made available to the blind. Training is important, but it should be provided in specialized vocational training schools, not in workshops (17). If the blind cannot find work in industry, they should have available adequate sums to take care of their needs under circumstances which enable them to manage their own affairs. They should not work in workshops where work in and of itself is considered the goal. If they must work in workshops, they should work under favorable conditions and be paid wages adequate for an adequate standard of living.

Few will disagree with ten Broek's goals. Most will agree that competitive employment should be the goal, that prejudice against the handicapped should be eliminated and that all should enjoy a high standard of living, whether they can work or not. Two problems exist with his philosophy. The first is practical or realistic. There is no immediate prospect that all handicapped persons who want to work in industry will be able to do so or that all will have a fine standard of living whether they will work or not. Something must be done for the handicapped until that time comes. Secondly, ten Broek seems to assume that no special adjustment training in workshops needs to be given to enable handicapped persons to work, that counseling and training in skills are sufficient. Workshop personnel believe that the work adjustment and work experience are often necessary to enable them to do so. Thus they consider ten Broek's alternatives impractical or inadequate.

But if ten Broek's basic ideas are often premature or inadequate, some of his criticisms have merit. When he stresses the need for desirable wages, perquisites, and good labor management relations in long-term employment workshops, he states goals that are shared by many workshop personnel. His insistence that work not be "routinized or demeaning, unproductive or unrequited" is now also shared by progressive workshop operators. Finally, his emphasis on good labor management relations in workshops is shared by farsighted managers who believe that the handicapped should participate in the operations of the workshop.

Workshops in Industry

Another set of alternatives to workshops is based on the philosophy that industry should do what workshops are doing. These alternatives have one thought in common: If work reality is the goal, why not have industry itself conduct the workshop programs. These suggestions take various forms. One is that industry be paid to take handicapped persons into their regular programs and enable them to become acceptable employees. Another is that industry be paid to set up special programs or divisions which will do the same things that workshops do. Still another is that charitable or nonprofit agencies buy and take over industrial firms and hire handicapped persons as employees. A variation of the latter is that handicapped persons organize companies and operate businesses which will provide employment for themselves. These proposals appeal to some handicapped persons and to some theorists because they are closer to the regular work process or do not have the appearance of seeking "help" from a charitable agency.

There is no extensive experience in the United States with the proposals for workshops in industry. The possibilities must therefore be considered theoretically. In theory, the main differences between a workshop and a business enterprise are found in their respective objectives. A business enterprise has among its objectives making a profit. The workshop has as its objective providing services to people. To the extent that the charitable agency or an association of handicapped persons has employment as the objective, there should be no reason why they could not operate an industrial firm and provide employment. They should be able to compete with industry where the only bar to the employment of the handicapped is an unfounded prejudice. The real question is whether they can compete and still provide work for persons who have genuine handicaps in employment without financing from nonwork income. The same problem will confront regular industry.

Thus those who wish to provide handicapped persons with workshop-like processes in industry without the appearance of seeking "help" will find themselves in a dilemma. Competitive industry will be reluctant to participate in work services to handicapped persons without the assurance of profit. To the extent that it is widely subsidized, it will become identified as a "helping" process. Actually, competitive industry may be already providing "sheltered" employment in government contracts where the demands made on employees are less severe than those made in competitive projects. But the present arrangements disguise the process. In the workshops, the procedure and often the rationale emphasize the "helping" aspects. The difference is in the terminology and extent of the handicap. In industry, the person is "working." In the workshop, often the "client" is being "provided" with work or being helped. In industry there is the appearance of independence — in the workshop, often the reverse. Society may be willing to pay industry a profit for creating the appearance of independence. If so, industry could participate increasingly in workshop-like programs, particularly for the disadvantaged groups whose handicaps are not as great as the physically and mentally handicapped, and whose unemployment stems from employer and employee prejudice.

The possible introduction of work-service processes in industrial operations will not change the essential philosophy or rationale of the workshop programs. There may merely be a shift to a new habitat. Both the industrial plant and the workshop will have the same problems. Both will encounter the same duality in work and improvement processes, or of work and substandard operations requiring special procedures. And both will have to justify the program on a similar philosophy.

That philosophy will be based on the importance of the individual and the importance of work to him as an individual. That philosophy will hold that the work environment will need to reduce its demands upon him until he can meet greater demands, or it will need to reduce those demands indefinitely. The philosophy will stress that whatever contribution the handicapped person can achieve is important to society because it is important to him.

NOTES

1. Howe, S. G.: Report of 1948. Outlook for the Blind, pp. 43-44, April, 1908.
2. McCann, R. V. (Ed.): Sheltered Workshops in Massachusetts, A Descriptive and Functional Study. Boston, Massachusetts Rehabilitation Commission, Vocational Rehabilitation Administration, 1963, pp. 161-162.
3. Booth, W.: In Darkest England and the Way Out. London, Funk and Wagnalls, 1890, p. 75, 120.
4. Hinshaw, D.: Take Up Thy Bed and Walk. New York, G. P. Putnam's Sons, 1948, pp. 32-41, 48-49.
5. Ibid., p. 53.
6. Richmond, M. E.: Federal Grants for Vocational Rehabilitation. Chicago, University of Chicago Press, 1944.
7. Block, W. B.: Operational Principles for Counseling the Disabled. In Patterson, C. H. (Ed.): Readings in Rehabilitation Counseling. Champaign, Stern, 1960, pp. 100-101.
8. Krantz, J. A.: Vocational Rehabilitation, Past, Present, and Future in the United States. Ibid., pp. 25-26.
9. Neff, W. S.: Presidential Address Division 22 of American Psychological Association, San Francisco, California, September 1, 1968. Neff, W. S.: Work and Human Behavior. New York, Atherton Press, 1968.
10. McGowan, J. F. and Porter, T. A.: An Introduction to the Vocational Rehabilitation Process. U. S. Dept. of Health, Education, and Welfare, 1967, pp. 121-122. Thorne, F. C.: Clinical Judgement. New York, Henry Hall, 1958.
11. Neff, op.cit.
12. Olshansky, S., and Unterberger, H.: The meaning of work and its implications for the ex-mental patient. Mental Hygiene, Vol. 47, 1963.
13. ten Broek, J., and Matson, F. W.: Hope Deferred, Public Welfare and the

Blind. Berkeley and Los Angeles, University of California, 1959.
14. Ibid., pp. 258-265.
15. Ibid., pp. 266-268.
16. Ibid., pp. 2-9.
17. Ibid., p. 252.

X

THE THEORIES AND PRACTICES
OF WORKSHOPS

W HAT is it in a workshop that enables the handicapped individual to achieve his goals? Why does the achievement take place?

The discussion in this chapter will deal with theories of the workshop process which bring about the desired results and with examples of techniques required to bring them about.

The definitions of workshops, dealt with in an earlier chapter, provide descriptive boundaries sufficiently wide to encompass all kinds in the field. They cannot deal with the dynamics of the workshop schema. They also are silent on the relationship of the workshop to the culture of which it is a part.

Workshops, in the present state of their diverse development in the United States, do not have a common theoretical foundation. They have a variety of theoretical bases depending upon their objectives, their historical development, the orientation of their sponsors, and the training of their staff.

James F. Garrett has pointed out that there is a "very vague rationale for the workshop" (1). The vagueness of which Garrett complains is particularly true when workshops are conceptualized generally, as for example cultural, social, special, rehabilitation, or welfare institutions.

A workshop can of course be conceived as a cultural, social, or welfare institution in the same sense that a business firm or a transportation system is. The categories are so general, however, that using them only points to the need to identify what kind of a cultural or social institution is intended. The general designation does not connote specific purpose, dynamics, or rationale.

Neither does the conception of the workshop as a special facility provide a basis for theory. Salmon and Spar use the word to mean a number of different kinds of facilities with different ranges of service, either as units in a larger facility or as a freestanding unit using other community facilities (2). Edward Chouinard, who earlier used the "special" designation, hastens to add that it does not sum up the direction of the workshop (3). The "special" designation has not been used in recent years to identify workshops, primarily because it does not specify what is special about them.

The most popular general term used to signify the nature of the workshop process in recent years has been the word *rehabilitation*. This has had the effect of identifying workshops with the rehabilitation movement. The concept often has relevance, but is too vague to use as a basis for a theoretical framework in all circumstances. Unfortunately, this conception does not always describe what there is within the workshop which results in achieving its objectives.

At the heart of the matter is the meaning of rehabilitation. If rehabilitation is the restoration of the handicapped person to the fullest physical, mental, emotional, social, vocational, and economic usefulness of which he was formerly capable, then the workshop always has done more than rehabilitation implies; it increases functioning to levels higher than those the individual has ever exercised. Some rehabilitation personnel hold that the improvement to levels higher than those formerly exercised are implied in *rehabilitation;* others call this *habilitation*. However, some workshops enable handicapped individuals to maintain their level of functioning without improving it. This is preventative insofar as it prevents deterioration. This, too, is now implied by some but is not generally inferred. Finally, workshops relieve or allay the psychologic trauma associated with diminishing functioning when the individual's condition is deteriorating. This analgesic function accomplishes the maximum well-being possible during declining functioning. There are basic differences in theory in improving functioning, maintaining functioning, and alleviating the discomforts of declining functioning.

Finally, there is a controversy about the usefulness of the term *rehabilitation* as a general basis for theory. There is a school of thought which maintains that rehabilitation is not a specific process or a specific vocational or social program, but rather a philosophy that describes attitudes used in helping people in whatever field the assistance is given. These fields are education, public assistance, religion, recreation, and the like (4). All of them accept the philosophy of rehabilitation as a fundamental requirement of constructive programs which help people. That rehabilitation is a specific process and has a specific theoretical foundation is challenged by some.

As a philosophy of achieving constructive results for individuals, rehabilitation is generally accepted by workshop organizations and personnel. As a process, rehabilitation has been limited in the past to steps directed towards improving functions. For this reason, and because workshop objectives are varied, the rehabilitation concept is at present not the most useful for an analysis of all aspects of workshop theories. Nevertheless, the rehabilitation concept and process are important to the understanding of those workshops which limit their programs to improving functioning.

Thus it may be said in summary that workshops are social institutions, since they participate in the organization of society to assist handicapped persons. Workshops are rehabilitation facilities in the sense that they follow rehabilitation philosophy. But these designations do not express specifically how all workshop sponsors and personnel see their organizations functioning to achieve their objectives. A review of the specific operating theories of different groups of workshops will be used to arrive at a clearer understanding of the theoretical foundations of workshops. These may be conceived as economic, industrial or vocational institutions; as public health or long-term chronic or self-care facilities; as clinical, therapeutic, or spiritual modalities; as educational or training programs; or as social service or socialization centers.

THE SPECIFIC THEORIES OF WORKSHOPS

Perhaps it will be useful to review each specific orientation of the different types of workshops classified by theoretical framework before describing each in detail. The first, the economic type, is conceived as related to the industrial and commercial life of the nation and is based on the reality principle and the practices of business. The second, the health service type, is based on or related to medical treatment and public health principles and practices. The third, the clinical or therapeutic model, is based on the theories of the phenomenological psychologists. The fourth, the educational or training type, is based on the principles of special education. The fifth, the social service type, is based on Freudian concepts, the theories of sociologists or anthropologists (5) and the approaches of philanthropists.

THE WORKSHOP AS AN ECONOMIC ORGANIZATION

Historically, the majority of workshops in the United States have functioned as if they were economic organizations. In 1969, the largest numbers of handicapped persons certificated by the Department of Labor worked as regular employees in such workshops, although individuals in work training centers were nearly as numerous (6). These workshops perform work in a manner similar to other business organizations. They differ from competitive, profit-making organizations in their objectives, and to some extent, in their methods. They are more flexible in applying standards upon workers than profit-making firms, but not necessarily in the nature of such demands. Furthermore, they use business-like requirements for the purpose of enabling individuals to meet the demands of reality. They consider themselves more reality oriented than workshops with other types of orientation. Thus they believe they are effective in providing for the enablement or reenablement and employment of handicapped individuals. They are similar to the group of workshops formerly labeled industrial rehabilitation workshops.

The rationale of workshops of economic orientation has not been formulated in a complete theoretical framework. The idealogy is based on oral tradition and on a shared common experience. It finds expression incidentally in presentations or group discussions taped at conferences and rarely finds its way into print in the proceedings of such meetings (7). It will therefore be necessary to organize the essential elements of the empirical wisdom of this group into theory.

An analysis of the thinking of workshop leaders from Samuel Gridley Howe and Edgar Helms to present-day directors of the freestanding industry-oriented community workshops in the United States reveals that a common idea is basic to their understanding of the reasons for the effectiveness of their workshop programs. The prevailing concept is that exposure to work reality creates the enablement or reablement of the handicapped individual. Their rationale is based on the principle that a person will often learn to do real work if he is given the opportunity to do it. Thus these economic workshops are distinguished from other groups of workshops by their greater emphasis on the influence of work reality and expectancy on the progress of the individual.

The reality principle is not of course held exclusively by this group of workshops or indeed by workshops generally. It is discernable in many phases of life and has applications in many other fields such as education and therapy (8). It arose in workshops out of the common observation that when individuals are exposed to real, challenging, and meaningful work, they often respond positively. On the other hand, when individuals are exposed to contrived, synthetic, or unchallenging work, they often react negatively, sometimes with hostility, more often with passivity or perfunctory, *pro forma* performance. Exposure to contrived situations involving the form but not the essence of reality creates either rejection or dependence upon the artificial conditions.

It may appear that the workshop itself is fundamentally an ersatz or simulated environment. It may be asked what is meant by reality. Reality is of course a relative matter. In a workshop, reality exists when there is a quantitative relationship with work in industry. Economic workshops set a system of specific requirements or norms for performance and behavior which measure the achievement of the workers in the shop. The norms or requirements may not be as demanding as those of industry, they may be higher in some shops than in others, they may be more flexible in some shops that others, but where they exist the shop is reality oriented.

Many types of workshops claiming to be reality oriented would not be included in the group labeled as economic organizations here. They would not be included because they believe that exposure to work reality alone is not sufficient to enable handicapped individuals to work. They believe the handicapped require substantial intervention in depth by the psychologist, counselor, or social worker either in the role of the foreman or as caseworker to complete the enablement. In the economic organization, the above professionals would be used only in a supportive or consulting capacity. The main thrust of the program centers around expecting the individual to learn to work and giving him a viable opportunity to do so. The main development takes place as does apprenticeship or on the job training, by teaching work competence and meeting requirements. This workshop develops capability, not verbal insight. However, this is possible only if the individual has no major problems in his work personality.

In order to draw the distinction between the individual whose level of handicap is such that he can benefit principally from exposure to work and one whose handicap is more severe so that he needs intervention of other services or of integrated services, it is necessary to understand what we will call the theory of participation. One of the major problems of severely handicapped persons is that they are not offered the opportunity to participate in some or many aspects of life. Their inability to participate may be inherent in their condition or may result from the prejudices or cultural patterns of society. Nonparticipation may in turn lead to isolation, alienation, or withdrawal (9). When participation is impossible because of the handicapping condition or its consequences, these must be reckoned with before participation can be effected. When the inability to participate has been removed through the intervention of medical or other procedures, the opportunity to participate may be the principal service the individual needs. Such participation is possible under certain circumstances. The principal circumstances often are the following:

1. The individual has the desire and the potential ability to work.
2. The individual has no other overwhelming problems in his work personality.
3. The individual cannot immediately meet the high requirements of industry but can become productive if allowed a

grace period of participation during which he can develop vocational competence.

4. Sometimes social and economic prejudice and attitudes without an objective basis may have impeded the development of employability and its absence produces the opportunity required to learn to work.

The economic workshop provides a concrete work experience. The work experience provides primarily an opportunity to learn how to work at acceptable standards. The learning takes place primarily as a result of exposure to the work setting. The work environment provides its own kinds of learning. By exposure to work, the individual can see how he functions, what it feels like to work, and how he compares with others. He gets a feeling for the nature of work and how it differs from school or other social situations. He is enabled to have this experience without as much anxiety as that which would confront him if he were to attempt a similar experience in industry. He can test himself without the fear of being fired. He is helped to learn by the basic assumption that he may need instruction in the mechanics and rules of working but that he is basically competent to function as a worker. What he wants and gets is opportunity to learn to work under favorable circumstances. He does not want or need help in changing or modifying his personality.

In summary, the nonparticipating handicapped person who has potential competence needs exposure to work reality in an environment where the emphasis is on work and on his own ability to cope with work in his own way. This individual is not a "client." He is a worker who may have personal problems but they usually do not interfere greatly with his ability to work. If they do interfere minimally, he works them out with an assist from other workers, from his leadman, or from foremen close to the work process. If this assist is not enough, the probabilities that he will benefit from the intervention of a professional in this setting are not great. He is probably in the wrong kind of a workshop. The assessment of his condition was probably overly optimistic. The chances are, however, that many an individual admitted to this kind of workshop will benefit if the assumption is made that he is potentially competent and that he can benefit from exposure to work. He can use some help in learning to work, but mostly he needs an opportunity to succeed in an environment which gives him a feeling of confidence and self-respect.

The economic workshop bases its theory on a number of assumptions. The first is that the individual will benefit from exposure to work without alteration or modification of his basic personality. If he has problems in his life when he comes to the shop, he will probably have them when he leaves to go to work. He will be able to succeed only if he is able to learn to work in spite of his problems. Another way to say this is that he will be able to contain or encapsulate his problems and work successfully. The workshop is able to provide an opportunity to learn to work successfully, even if it does not produce basic benefits in other aspects of the individual's life.

There are of course some individuals who are so maladjusted, emotionally disturbed, or mentally retarded that they fail to learn to work. There seems to be no way to predict this outcome in all instances before these individuals are tried out in the shop. When it becomes clear that the individual will not learn to work successfully without other types of services, the workshop determines what action to take based on the condition of the individual and his desires.

Workshop personnel have long been aware of the phenomenon that some individuals with severe psychosocial problems are able to work successfully and others with equally severe or lesser problems are not, that there is something about their work personalities which determines their ability to work. William Gellman made an early statement of this theory (10). Workshop personnel have accepted its implications. Recently, however, Walter Neff has provided a more comprehensive theory which corresponds to their observations (11).

Neff has developed a "two-factor" theory of work, which views work behavior as a relationship between the characteristics of the individual and the features of his surroundings. In analyzing the characteristics of the individual, he finds that he has various components in his personality, and that there is the component which Gellman called the "work personality." This factor seems to Neff to function somewhat independently from the other factors of the personality. This he calls the "semiautonomous operation of the work personality" (12). Thus a man may be deficient as a father, lover, or friend, mentally ill or emotionally disturbed, and still be a good worker. The concept explains much that workshop personnel have observed about some individuals they serve. When the individual's work personality is stable, he may be able to work in spite of personal problems. When he has problems in his work personality, he may not be able to work even though he has few disturbances in the other aspects of his personality. The economic workshop does not usually try to work with individuals who have severe problems in their work personalities.

Another assumption the economic workshop emphasizes is also discussed by Neff (13). It is that the workshop is primarily a place for nonverbal communication — for learning by example and for learning by doing. The workshop foreman does better to show the individual than to tell him. The individual learns by observing what others are doing that is acceptable or admired. A smile communicates "well done" better than a flowery phrase. If the workshop worker could benefit from "talking," he probably would have benefited before he came to the shop. Many who come to the shop cannot benefit much from "talking therapy."

From what has been said about the workshop as an economic organization, it will be surmised that it assumes that comprehensive services are not necessary in all instances, that some individuals can acquire work competence without the substantial involvement of integrated services of a psychosocial nature. Since the experience of this type of workshop has shown that exposure to work under realistic conditions has produced competence for employment in industry and in the workshop for many handicapped persons, it is unlikely that this kind of shop will change its theory. However, since such shops often need to improve their evaluations, they are increasing their use of professional teams for assessment and consultation. It is likely that they will give more consideration to an eclectic approach to improve their assessment processes. However, at present, their rationale is based primarily on the principle of the segmented approach, i.e., that the work problems of some people can be solved without dealing with all their other life problems.

Having described the theory of the workshop as an economic organization, perhaps a description of a few characteristics which result from it will be in order. The workshop emphasizes the importance of its work and its work process, its equipment and its plant. The relationships of its workers to its staff center around the foreman. The foreman acts like his counterpart in industry and "the foreman is the boss" if anyone is (14). Actually, however, the handicapped individual is allowed to assume as much independent responsibility as possible. He has no overseer from the "helping" professions because he does not usually need "help" in any special or exceptional sense. The foreman relates closely to the handicapped person as a fellow worker in the industrial process who is more experienced and knowledgeable than the workers on the line but is not of a superior class with esoteric training.

Although the reality principle and the principle of participation which form the basis of the economic workshop have not been expressed completely, it has been anticipated in an embryonic form. Howard Lytle, the former director of Goodwill Industries of Indianapolis, has made this observation:

> The development of an employable personality and a marketable skill is accomplished primarily in a workshop to which raw material is brought, in which the material is processed into salable products and from which these products are sold for sums of money with which the worker is paid a wage. Productivity itself is a rehabilitation tool and the work process is at the very core of the workshop (15).

Ted Pezman, formerly director of Community Rehabilitation Industries of Long Beach, California, has described the importance of performance and reality in the economic workshop as follows:

> I have referred to the workshop as a confidence operation because it is in the area of confidence, of self-esteem, of measurable self-worth that a workshop is frequently able to do the most good . . . . It is the confidence that comes from performance that establishes the base line for proving to others what you can do . . . .
>
> There is no more logical and practical focal point for combining the resources of industry, the community, and rehabilitation agencies than in a workshop. Here the fullest kind of implementation from these three essential influences can be incorporated into a joint rehabilitation effort. This is rehabilitation not in a specialized vacuum – but in a very real life, three dimensional way (16).

The theories of the economic workshop do not provide for the needs of handicapped persons who have difficulty in their work personality, who need work primarily as a means of improving their physical functioning, who need special educational training in order to work, or whose problems in their social and personal lives affect their ability to work. The needs of these persons are given attention in the theories of other types of workshops which will follow.

A number of reservations have been expressed about the economic workshop. Some question the justification of using workshops for potentially competent individuals who do not need to modify their behavior significantly in order to work. "These persons do not belong in workshops. They should go directly to work in industry," it has been said. The fact is, however, that industry often will not take them unless the labor market requires it and that they often fail at jobs when they are hired by industry without the confidence-and competence-building experience of the workshop.

Another criticism of this kind of a shop is that it is limited in its goals. Does it help the individual accept his condition more comfortably and function like a nonhandicapped person? Does it help him reach his greatest potential in other respects than work? Does it help him make a better social adjustment generally? Does it also develop the uniqueness in each individual and help him in his right to fulfill his nature (17)? Some workshop personnel answer that it is difficult to be all things to all persons, and that work is a sufficiently important part of man's life to warrant emphasizing it. Others answer that if one believes in the integrity of the individual, one should respect his right to choose his own goals. Large numbers of persons who come to these workshops wish to become able to work or to obtain work, but often they have little desire to change their general personality. Neither do they often wish to modify their uniqueness. Often they consider their uniqueness precious, are satisfied with it, and some are even fearful that help might even diminish it.

THE WORKSHOP AS A HEALTH AGENCY

In contrast to the economically oriented workshop which uses work to enable people to work, the health-oriented workshops use work to help individuals improve their condition and their functioning, to maintain their improved condition and functioning, and to achieve the maximum well-being possible when their condition or functioning is deteriorating. The second named use of work may be preventative in nature. These shops try to enable handicapped individuals to get work in industry, but they do it primarily by improving his physical or mental condition. Often, however, employment in industry is not possible for those individuals with the more severe types of chronic conditions. The health-oriented workshop performs an improvement or enabling function, a maintenance or preventative function, and an alleviating function of an analgesic or comforting nature (18).

The workshops which are health-oriented may be divided in two general classifications, those which emphasize short-term physical or mental therapy for the improvement of the individual's condition, and those which provide long-term care that enables the individual to improve his general well-being without improving his functioning to a point of no longer needing continuous care. The first group serves the physically handicapped who reach a point of maximum improvement after a given period of treatment, and those emotionally disturbed who can improve dramatically at times but may need recurrent short-term services. The second group consists of long-term programs which serve the young who are permanently and severely handicapped and the chronically ill or the aged.

THE THEORIES OF WORKSHOPS
PROVIDING FUNCTIONAL IMPROVEMENT

The theories of the first group of workshops providing functional improvement or work conditioning were applied to the tubercular. The theory was relatively simple. The ex-patients were having relapses after returning to work. Workshops were therefore established to expose tubercular ex-patients to harden them for employment. By gradual increase of work pressures, the workers were accustomed to the requirements of work. From 1915, when Altro Workshops was established, to the late 1950's, when tuberculosis was diminishing as a health problem, workshops in many parts of the country provided work hardening or work conditioning as a major service in their programs. As the incidence of tuberculosis diminished, the workshop took in cardiacs, then the mentally ill and mentally retarded, at first applying the principles of work conditioning and later changing to a variety of services in which evaluation and work conditioning were prominent.

The first workshops to use work as a basis for work conditioning of the orthopedically handicapped were the curative workshops. At the close of World War I, Frank H. Albee established vocational reconditioning services in the United States, General Hospital No. 3 at Colonia, New Jersey. Subsequently, other such services were established in other Army hospitals. The workshop where the reconditioning was done was called the curative workshop. As stated above, this label was adopted by community workshops which began with similar or related objectives. The purpose of the original Army program was to stimulate physical recovery and emotional stability, and to prepare for recovery after discharge (19). The purpose of the curative workshops which adopted the name of the Army workshop was in the beginning to increase the functioning of the disabled individual, to provide "curative" services.

Frederick Elton, then District Director of State Vocational Rehabilitation in New York City, became interested in Albee's ideas and supported the development of the Curative Workshop of New York City. This workshop was first involved primarily with the rehabilitation of injured workmen. He described the methodology of the shop as follows: "It was determined that since employability was the goal, the method employed must be economic and the work done an actual productive experience under actual employment conditions" (20). This work orientation influenced the development of some of the curative workshops until later in the century, when a large number became rehabilitation centers.

It will be seen that the theory Elton describes implies departure from traditional occupational therapy practice and is closely related to the reality principle of the economically oriented workshop. The history of the curative workshops is an account primarily of how these shops fluctuated between the occupational therapy principle, the reality principle, and a compromise between the two.

The difference between the occupational therapy principle and the reality principle turned on the way work was used. In occupational therapy at the time, the work itself was not important. The article was a by-product. The relationship of the patient to the therapist and to other patients and his physical or mental gains from the activity were stressed. In the reality setting, the product is the center of focus. The product has commercial value, and the accomplishment of the requirements for its production communicates recognition by the real world that the worker has worth and value.

Elton describes how the Curative Workshop of New York gave up the reality principle as follows:

> After several years of experimentation with a workshop operating on a production basis, the method was changed in 1933, and the name of the local operating unit [The Curative Workshop] was changed to the Rehabilitation Clinic for the Disabled. It had been found that limitations were placed upon the purpose of its service by manufacture of goods and the meeting of production. It was decided to devote its full attention to apply its methods to the making of workers rather than merchandise (21).

It is interesting that this statement or others like it will appear again and again whenever the reality principle is rejected for other methods. The theory that the demands of production can be utilized to develop employability was to come later.

In making its changes, the Curative Workshop of New York was influenced by the theories of Harold D. Storms, founder of the Rehabilitation Clinic of the Workmen's Compensation Board at Ontario, Canada. Storms used physical therapy to get his injured workers back to employment. The physical therapy was on "heavy forms of therapeutic work related to the former occupation to rebuild more quickly or directly" (22). Thus was introduced simulated work as a substitute for real work. More specifically, the handicapped person was put to work on tasks like those he did on his former or other jobs. Thus, if a man was a laborer, he was put in a pit to shovel sand or rock for given periods of time depending on his ability to tolerate the work (23). This kind of simulated work has been used occasionally in United States workshops, although not necessarily on the work done by the handicapped person in his former occupation.

Though Elton rejected the use of real work in favor of made work, the program did use some real work in its printing division. It also had elements of occupational training, on-the-job training, and occupational therapy. In 1948, he describes the rationale of the program of the American Rehabilitation Committee as consisting of the performance of prescribed exercises on work based on the anticipated occupational objectives for the improvement of physical impairment and emotional disturbances. This has the advantage of stimulating the interest of the handicapped person and increasing the therapeutic value of the service (24).

Elton clearly designates work therapy as a short-term enabling service and distinguishes it from extended employment. He states: "Sheltered workshops operated to provide sheltered employment for the disabled may include, under certain conditions, the basic purposes and philosophies of Work Therapy, reconditioning, or the rebuilding of human beings. It depends on the purpose of the particular service being rendered . . . ." (25)

Since Elton wrote in 1948, workshop practice has substituted job families for the specific job he indicated must be the goal. However, with this exception, some workshops in rehabilitation centers, in hospitals, and some freestanding workshops with medical orientation accept his basic rationale. That theory would be, in summary, that real work and/or made work may be used to accomplish the following:

1. Assess employability.
2. Rebuild work tolerance and emotional stability.
3. Promote interest, motivation, and confidence.
4. Improve physical functioning.
5. Stimulate recovery from disability and foster work readiness.

The theory developed by Elton and the Curative Workshop is similar to that developed by the workshops serving the tubercular. However, when those workshops began serving other disabilities, they adopted other working principles. The remaining shops serving the tubercular exclusively tended to serve the few remaining chronic patients in hospitals. Their theory is similar to that of shops serving the chronically ill.

WORK FOR THE CHRONICALLY DISABLED AND AGED

The rationale of the curative workshops and their successors justified their activities in terms of movement of their handicapped persons to higher work efficiency through improvement of physical and emotional functioning. Other groups of shops which use work for chronically disabled persons did not use this rationale. Some of the chronically disabled, ill, or aged they serve cannot hope to improve their functioning. At times, and in the long run, their functioning will diminish. These shops justify their programs by the sense of well-being and happiness they make possible for the chronically ill and aged.

The programs for the chronically ill or aged are usually in hospitals for the chronically disabled or in homes for the aged, but a few exist as freestanding facilities. Their rationale is similar. The main difference is that among the young chronically disabled, some improve and go onto competitive employment, while among those over sixty-five years of age, the justification of the service is usually found in therapeutic value of work.

For the chronically disabled who are not expected to work in competitive employment, long-term work in shops having realistic contract jobs provides benefits other than money which are important to the patients' well-being. For those who equate inactivity with worthlessness, work provides a better self-image, reduces anxiety and depression, and improves morale. The work setting establishes social relationships naturally which enhance personal happiness. If a person must spend a long or indefinite period in a hospital or chronic care home, work makes the stay more congenial and satisfying (26). It also makes the disabling or diseased condition more tolerable to bear.

For the aged, many of the same benefits accrue from long-term employment, whether in a freestanding workshop for the aged or a chronic care hospital or a home for the aged. For those with fixed incomes which decline in value, the additional money from working is particularly welcome, especially when it makes it unnecessary to appeal to family for minor essentials of life. But the major appeal lies in work itself. In the home for the aged in particular, work is crucial for some persons. Jacob Rheingold summarizes the value of the workshop in the home for the aged succintly:

> .... for the person whose most central perception of self came from his role as a worker and breadwinner, life in a home for the aged can be particularly demoralizing. He is the resident who can derive no sense of self from discussion groups, from the arts, from recreation ... even from work as a volunteer. For this kind of person, the work environment, fashioned by the rules and regulations of the market place, is the only place where he feels complete as a person, sure he knows the name of the game and how to play it (27).

The effectiveness of a workshop in aiding older persons with psychological problems was studied in a five-year project by the Jewish Vocational Service of Chicago. The report of its findings, made in 1965, indicated that the workshop was able to reduce the psychological problems of the aging. It was found that the aged studied fell into three groups. These were [1] the work-motivated dependent aged, [2] the employment-minded floundering aged, and [3] the troubled aged seeking therapeutic activity. Those in the first group were described as "unemployables," past retirement age, long out of work, generally in poor health and desiring work. This was the group that benefited from long-term employment in the workshop.

The rationale of the project was that remunerative employment in a therapeutic workshop would enhance ego strength, relieve and reduce stresses arising from enforced inactivity and reduced incomes, and foster aging in developmental terms. For the first group described above, it was found that they evidenced great satisfaction during their stay in the shop and had difficulties when they left it. Other forms of participation including counseling were minimal. The long-term sheltered workshop per se was the need, and produced the hypothesized benefits (28).

THE WORKSHOP AS AN AID
TOWARDS PERSONAL INTEGRATION

The workshops whose theories have been presented have several features in common. In general, they become involved with individuals after treatment for the acute phases of their illness has been terminated. The shops accept those who have some work potential either in industry or in a long-term employment shop. Another group of shops, primarily in mental hospitals, starts earlier in the history of the illness and sometimes accepts the individual whether he has potential to work or not. Their reason for providing service is to aid in the integration of the individual's functioning. This may lead to a number of outcomes: work in industry, work in workshops, or neither. In any case, it is intended that the service be useful to the improvement of the individual's mental health.

Workshops for the mentally ill in mental hospitals or in the communities are of recent origin. Their theories and practices are in embryonic stages. What happens in such shops stems from theories which their operators have learned and accepted in previous employment or from principles learned in their education and training. Thus they may be applying such varied concepts as that of the therapeutic community, of Freud or later psychoanalysts, or of behavior modification or operant conditioning. As a result, there is no common theory, nor is there likely to be one as long as the workshops are operating such varied programs. At this point, several other theories will be described which are pertinent to workshops for the mentally ill. They have to do with the use of the workshop in the acute or active phases of the mental illness.

One theory of the workshop as an aid to treatment is based on the preliminary assumption that the key to work benefits may be found not in the description of the diagnostic or categorical classification of the individual, but in analysis of his functioning. Common observation of the mentally ill individual has led to the belief that his ability to function as a worker is sometimes unrelated to his functioning in other aspects of his life. In such instances, he can work relatively well when he is seriously ill (29). This is another version of what Neff has called the semiautonomous nature of the work personality (30). In this event, work may contribute to the improvement of his mental condition.

Another theory which seems useful in understanding the mentally ill person's work functioning is the belief that human functioning can be understood in terms of object relations, or more specifically, the various relationships of the individual to the objects in his environment. The objects may be inanimate things, conditions in the environment such as noise or temperature, or most importantly, people. If the objects affect him abnormally, his relationship with them becomes disorganized and his functioning where they are concerned disintegrates. He can, however, retain integrated relationships with some objects and not with others, or restore integrated relationship with some class of objects and not easily with others.

The basic concept of object relations comes from psychoanalytical theories. However, the terminology is sometimes used to label theories which do not follow the implications of psychoanalysis. These more simple interpretations have been applied to occupational and industrial therapy. Nevertheless, to understand the relationship, it will be well to review the application of object relations theory to the psychiatric work environment. This was accomplished in a comprehensive manner by the Azimas in the late 1950's.

THE THEORY OF OBJECT RELATIONS
IN OCCUPATIONAL THEORY

In 1959, the Azimas, finding the existing theories of occupational therapy inadequate to explain therapeutic dynamics in psychiatric occupational therapy, completed a theoretical foundation for occupational therapy based on the central position of object relations. Although the Azimas did not apply their theories to workshops, their formulations have considerable relevance to workshops, especially those in psychiatric settings, as will be seen later. For these reasons, their "Outline of a Dynamic Theory of Occupational Therapy" will be discussed in some detail here (31).

The Azimas first outlined the diagnostic and therapeutic functions of occupational therapy. The diagnostic process is compared to a projective technique. The patient's mode of approach to objects, attitudes to staff and others, production and completion of work, and association and interpretation are analyzed. The therapeutic functions are designated primarily as exploration, gratification, and the defense formation. The process is distinguished from individual or group psychotherapy. In psychotherapy the individual is in a situation where he can verbalize, but not *do* anything, and there is no unstructured object to which he can relate in its entirety. In occupational therapy he can verbalize and *do* things to objects.

The importance of this concept to workshops lies in its emphasis on the work object as distinguised from the activity or verbalization. It takes issue with the frequent assumptions which were being made by workshop theorists that the work itself is of small consequence and that the benefits of a work environment comes primarily from the social relationships or from the psychotherapeutic intervention of the professional staff.

The Azimas go on to develop definitions of objects, the object hierarchy, object needs, the various defense mechanisms related to objects, and symbolic meaning of objects. These concepts apparently were influential in very few workshops except those in psychiatric facilities. What is important about the Azimas' presentation is their emphasis on the meaning and significance of the work object as a source of influence on those who apply themselves to it. Here is an area of work concepts which have been recognized intuitively by workshop personnel for many years but which have never been given substantial theoretical or research consideration.

If the theory of objects relationships and of the independent nature of the work personality are considered together, a rationale of the workshop for aiding in treating mental illness may result. In the acute or chronic mental illness, an individual may retain the ability to relate to inanimate objects when he cannot relate to people. If he can be exposed to inanimate objects or nonpersons in a work setting with a minimum of intervention by people, he may be able to function successfully. If the successful functioning provides satisfaction to him, he may accept the gradual intervention of people when such intervention is minimal and is work connected. If disturbing human relationships are partially avoided temporarily, the individual may gain stability and integration with the more positive relationships of a nonpersonal work task.

The dynamics of the process are these. By engaging in

nonpersonal object-related activity, the individual reduces anxiety and depression and gains confidence and pleasure. To retain the desirable results of the work relationship, he may be willing to establish other relationships to the work environment. He may observe time schedules, follow ground rules, and cooperate with work-flow requirements. In the process of developing these coping behaviors, he may establish relationships with people associated with them. This new kind of object relationship, namely, with people in the shop, may then be extended to other people in the environment who can help him in other areas of functioning. Thus he may become more responsive to other therapies. In this sense, the workshop is a start-up operation or a staging area from which other therapeutic programs may be launched. The ability to relate to nonpersonal work tasks is thus used as interim aid to recovery.

Virgil Vogt, Rehabilitation Workshop Manager, Chicago State Hospital, Chicago, Illinois, describes this process well in a memorandum on workshops to the mental hospital workshop staffs.

> Workshops have been useful in getting some of the most regressed patients mobilized and involved in treatment. We have numerous cases in which very chronic patients, completely non-verbal and unresponsive to other programs, have with proper encouragement become interested in some very simple task in a workshop. This requires no verbal response, the patient works with 'things.' The task itself is simple in the extreme. Yet if he does it successfully, he becomes part of a total program, which is obviously a productive and significant enterprise. He gets approval from the staff and other patients, plus wages, either in cash or in kind. The success experienced in such simple beginnings has been a kind of catalyst, leading to improvement in other behavior, and in many cases to discharge (32).

It may be suggested that there are the same object relationships existing in occupational therapy which preceded workshops in mental hospitals. Is there any difference? The answer given is found in the reality theory. The disturbed or retarded individual, the theory holds, recognizes reality, even when he cannot cope with it. Thus an object which is part of a useful life process is more meaningful than an object which is contrived to make work. To the extent that the work has elements of real relationships, the individual recognizes those elements and responds to them.

H. Leopold, Rehabilitation Officer at Littlemore Hospital,

Oxford, England, writing on the therapeutic effect of repetitive industrial work in workshops in psychiatric hospitals points out: "The awareness that this work is contracted from industry, paid according to output, and performed under near realistic industrial conditions, and the fact that the criteria of success are clear and recognized, may enhance the restorative power of this type of repetition in relation to the accumulation of new, well differentiated ego sets" (33).

Leopold points out that while he cannot prove with data that industrial work is more therapeutic than creative work, "the fact, however, that industrial contract work has been accepted in almost all psychiatric hospitals in this country (Great Britain) and that the more 'creative,' work, frequently referred to as occupational therapy, reduced to a minimum would at least give some general support to our assumption."

Leopold develops the theory that repetitive work on work objects has therapeutic value and may deal successfully with two symptoms resistant to other forms of treatment, namely, psychomotor retardation and attentive disorders. He quotes assertions from existentialist and phenomenological thoughts that perception is an act of selecting a certain set of facts, an act of choice in accordance with one's mood. Thus in many schizophrenic patients, "the ego is overwhelmed by a mass of external stimuli, its function impaired and disorganized. It would seem likely that repetition as in the form of industrial work, i.e. repetition of the same stimuli, and the same (encouraged and expected) response, would introduce a nucleus of structure and stability into an ego unable to discriminate between relevant and irrelevant information."

In summary it may be said that the theories discussed hold that the mentally ill individual may retain the ability to work when other aspects of his functioning are disorganized or disintegrated. He is often able to maintain better relations with inanimate objects than with the people in his environment. The relationship with work objects provides stability. In a workshop, he recognizes the reality elements in work and responds to them. This response to nonpersonal work-task relationships and the reality elements in work may result in a therapeutic gain and provides aid for entry to other therapies. Whether he will benefit from the object relationship depends upon many other factors (34). However, the work process may contribute to the integration of the disordered personality whether or not the individual may learn to work substantially or whether or not the other components of personality disturbances are reduced.

To provide a comprehensive guide for work therapy in a controlled work setting, Leonard Oseas has outlined a seven-dimensional treatment model. Its purpose is to describe the work conditions and concepts appropriate in each dimension. Thus, for each dimension, he gives the orienting concept, the therapy and work objectives, and the supervision, production, and task factors. The dimensions are the [1] ameliorative, [2] modulational-expressive, [3] modulational-suppressive, [4] redirective, [5] reeducative, [6] self-restorative, and [7] the role restorative. For the ameliorative dimension, for example, the following are given:

> Orienting concept — Work stresses kept well within the patients ability to tolerate them.
> Therapy objective — Reduction of anxiety increased tolerance of stress.
> Work objective — Willingness to remain in work setting.
> Supervision factor — Supportive-permissive; reassurance freely given; dependence tolerated.
> Production factors — Generally deemphasized; patient permitted to set his own standards.
> Task factors — Minimally demanding, noncompetitive; difficulty within range of ability.

Each of the dimensions is analyzed in a similarly thorough manner (35).

Until Oseas wrote this schema, there apparently had appeared no theoretical framework as comprehensive. It assumes that a work setting has available variable conditions or the ability to create them. Since many workshops in psychiatric settings have limited, routine work, they are not able to implement such a complex model. Probably for this reason, the schema has not received as extensive application as might be expected.

THE WORKSHOP AS A BRIDGE TO THE WORLD OF WORK

Some workshops have a rationale which is intermediate between those of the short-term and chronic types of health programs. They are usually found in health institutions, most frequently in mental hospitals. For this reason, the mental hospital workshop of the bridge type is used for illustrative purposes, but a similar theoretical framework may exist in other health institutions.

In most health institutions, and more clearly in mental hospitals, one basic situation exists regardless of the theoretical assumptions: the institution is different from the world to which the patient will return when released. Whether the theoretical framework is custodial, psychotherapeutic in the classical Freudian sense, or is that of the therapeutic community, the environment is usually less demanding than that of the community to which the patient will return. In one sense, the more therapeutic the hospital, the greater the difference between the hospital and the outside world. The released patient who returns to a metropolitan community from the therapeutic community in the hospital will be subject to the continuing shock and abrasiveness of a hostile world. It may be more than he can take. If he returns to a less hostile environment in a rural area, the shock may be less, but a difference usually exists to a significant degree. Something needs to be done to help him bridge this psychological and social chasm. If he can be prepared for the industrial part of that world, the transition is made easier.

In some hospitals, the workshops attempt to narrow the difference between the hospital environment and that of the outside world. This is done by duplicating as nearly as possible in the workshop the conditions of work in competitive employment. The shop is able to affect only the part of the patient's time that is spent in the workshop, but if the conditions of work are realistic, the patient may be better prepared for work when he leaves the hospital. In theory, the patient should not be released until he is able to meet the work demands of the workshop. Actually, the workshop is not always able to keep the patient until he can meet work demands, but to the extent that the patient has been exposed to real working conditions, the chances of his meeting the demands of outside work are enhanced.

The theory of the bridge workshop in an institution is that demands as nearly equivalent to those found in industry as possible should ultimately be made of the patient. This will give him an optimum chance to succeed in the work-related parts of his life when he leaves the hospital (36). This workshop resembles in theory the workshop which builds work tolerance of a recovered patient. The difference is that the hospital workshop sometimes attempts to reinforce mature behavior in other than work situations in the workshop. The bridge workshop is often hindered when general hospital standards of behavior are used by hospital personnel. The bridge shop often works best when it is located on or near the hospital grounds but not in hospital buildings. Its value lies in its ability to increase the level of pressure on the patients over those of the hospital to prepare them for the pressures of work in their communities.

WORKSHOP THEORIES OF PERSONAL CHANGE

The workshop theories reviewed previously dealt principally with approaches to persons whose physical capability to function at work needed improvement, who needed to learn to work, or who needed to work for purposes related to their physical or mental health. Another set of workshops developed psychological and social theories which considered the means of effecting change in the person's work behavior or in other aspects of the individual behavior in life.

These theories may be divided into two types: one type which emphasizes change in work behavior, and a second, more amorphous in scope, which deals with change in work behavior but also considers means of effecting change in other aspects of the individual's behavior. The second type of theory emphasizes general or specific changes in behavior. The first will be called the theories of work adjustment. This second type will be designated as the theories of behavior change.

The Theories of Work Adjustment

Among the work adjustment shops in this country, those most given to research and development of theory were the workshops of the Jewish Vocational Services. Although not the first in the country, the most persistent in analysis and comprehensive research is the Vocational Adjustment Center of the Jewish Vocational Service of Chicago. Beginning in 1951, under William Gellman's leadership, Walter Neff, Simon Friedman, Nathan Glaser, and others pioneered in the development of theories of work adjustment. These provide the most comprehensive body of theoretic information available in any aspect of workshop theories today. Subsequently, Walter Neff has expanded and extended these theories to include other aspects of work (37). For this reason, the work of Gellman and his colleagues will be summarized as illustrative of the rationale of work adjustment shops.

The Identification and Improvement of the Work Personality

The establishment of the Work Adjustment Center of Chicago in 1951 followed the experience of many Jewish Vocational Services in large cities in serving immigrants from Europe who had had previous work experience in Europe but who had not worked for many years after their appearance in this country. Despite a great need for workers, they were unable to find or keep jobs. They were described by Gellman as being industrially inept, unable to adapt to work or to assume the role of workers. Their vocational handicap appeared to reside in a negative attitude toward work, an inappropriate vocational pattern rather than in the disabilities themselves. The Chicago Jewish Vocational Service employed available techniques such as counseling, on-the-job training, group guidance, role playing, job solicitations, work trials, and others, without sufficiently satisfactory results. Consequently, the theories of the Work Adjustment Center were developed. They outlined situational techniques which used the workshop as a therapeutic tool to influence change in client attitudes and work behavior.

The theory of the Vocational Adjustment Center of Chicago was first stated in 1951 and has been refined and extended with subsequent experience. At the inception of the program, the rationale was stated as follows:

First, the majority of unskilled and semiskilled positions require a "work personality" rather than specific experience, and job turnover is more often due to inadequate vocational adjustment than lack of skill.

Second, each individual reacts in a characteristic manner to the entire range of vocational situations, and when work acquires a positive value for an individual, his job seeking efforts, job performance, and job satisfaction will increase.

Third, a successful work experience which generates job satisfaction will help an individual to identify with and strive to attain the "work personality" stressed in our culture (38).

Following the first two years of experience, Gellman restated the rationale of the Work Adjustment Center more comprehensively and specifically. More attention was given the vocational pattern generally and its relationship to the personality structure. The significant aspects of the vocational pattern were described as follows:

1. The meaning of work to the individual.
2. The ability to derive satisfaction from work motivation.
3. Mobilization of energy in a work situation.
4. Capacity to adjust to interpersonal relations on the job.
5. Positive and negative work identifications.
6. Ability to adjust to work pressures.

Although the vocational pattern reflects the personality structure, vocational adjustment is not a direct function of the total personal adjustment, and total personal adjustment need not lead to vocational adjustment. The correlation is determined by underlying personality dynamics and ego dynamics.

Vocational patterns result from cultural goals and individual life experiences. The ability to work is a learned process and can be taught and developed. Job performance is dependent upon an adequate vocational pattern and sufficient ability to meet job requirements (39).

In the analysis made by Gellman in 1953, the lack of correlation between the total personal structure and vocational adjustment is recognized, but the focal element in the relationship between personality and work adjustment is not specifically described. He developed such a description, the beginnings of a definition, in 1960, when he stated that the work personality is an integrated constellation of behavior and attitudes which permits an individual to function in an accepted work role or to exhibit an adequate vocational pattern. It determines the nature of adjustment on the job by relating personal needs to job satisfaction and interpersonal relations. The two axes of the work personality are the meaning of work and job satisfaction. The latter is intrinsic — the activity itself, the environment, feeling productive; or extrinsic — economic self-sufficiency, being like other people, having a place to go (40).

The Gellman concept of the work personality as a principal determinant in work adjustment, together with his interpretation of it as a psychosocial constellation distinct from other aspects of the personality, laid the theoretic foundation for the vocational adjustment workshop. As more specifically delineated by Walter Neff, it represents a most carefully conceived body of doctrine in the workshop field (41).

In the early fifties, Gellman's focus was on the "apparently unemployable" and the ways in which they might become employable. The major emphasis was on work acculturation (42), designed to enable the individual to see himself and act as a good worker through role playing and reality testing as principal modalities. As the program progressed and the case load became more varied, Gellman found by 1960 that the vocationally handicapped could be divided into three groups — the nonproductive, the unplaceable, and the unadjustable; and each required a different type of program.

The Nonproductive

The nonproductive group consists of persons who are unmotivated for work, do not see themselves as workers, and are unable to function at work. Usually they have never had a meaningful work history. For this group, it is necessary to reproduce the stages of development that persons go through to become good workers. Simple tasks are used to assure success and praise to foster motivation. Reassuring supervisory attitudes help the individual to function more effectively at work. Wages are used to induce a feeling of independence, and the work is meaningful and satisfying so that the person begins to see himself as a worker.

The Unplaceable

The unplaceables are persons who, because of lack of confidence, a feeling of uselessness, a sense of failure, and for other reasons, give the impression that they are not good workers. Since the individual is capable of working, the program for him emphasizes work acculturation. Appropriate dress and demeanor and the development of self-confidence are initial objectives. Varied supervision, role playing, and reality testing are used to develop ability to handle frustration.

The Unadjustable

The unadjustables are persons with poor interpersonal relations and unacceptable modes of work behavior. They seek and cannot find satisfactions they should not expect to find at work and are therefore frustrated. For this group, the workshop provides group activity which stresses cooperation and collaboration. The patterning of the work group and choice of tasks encourage working towards common goals — a decrease of frustration with fellow workers. Then they are given opportunities to work as a group leader and to experience monetary and other rewards which lead them to accept the requirements of work (43).

By 1961, Gellman had developed his theory of vocational adjustment. It held that an individual learns to adjust to the gamut of productive situations including work. The work adjustment workshop is preparing an individual to work in a wide variety of different settings and occupations. The specifics of the job modify the level of vocational adjustment without altering the components of adjustments.

Closely related was Gellman's theory of the therapeutic situational technique. This was based on the assumption that the workshop modifies or alters the work personality and that the changes induced by the workshop result in an enhanced ability to function in industry. Such behavioral or personality modifications are brought about by essentially nonverbal, social interactions of work. The workshop serves as a situational constellation with provision for varying psychosocial and demand factors of tasks to influence change in client attitudes and behavior (44).

In Gellman's initial approach to the problems of vocationally maladjusted persons, with the possible exception of his analysis of the problems of the immigrants and his theory of acculturation, he saw their problems arising principally from inadequate or inappropriate reaction to work or interactions in the work setting. More recently he has viewed their problems historically and sociologically as well. In 1966, he broadened his description of those he had called the unplaceables to include the socially disadvantaged and the culturally deprived and labeled the broadened category the disemployed. He defined the disemployed as the long-term hard-core unemployed who are employable but are not acceptable because of disability, social disadvantage, crime, cultural deprivation, age, or underprivileged status.

The inclusion of new groups of underprivileged persons in the definition of the disemployed necessarily affected theory. Individual programs had to be based on culturally oriented and acceptable goals. Groups must be used more extensively to produce social learning (45).

As a result of his expanded concept of the disemployed and later experience with underprivileged and with severely disabled and chronically ill, Gellman expanded and revised his theoretical framework by placing more emphasis on social learning. For the expanded group of unplaceables and the disemployed, Gellman visualized two general programs — the acculturation program, as originally conceived, and a social learning program. For the nonproductive, he outlined a vocational development program and a work identity program. These programs are used as needed or may be modified to develop an individual plan for the individuals.

Gellman has also expanded on his concept of vocational development. It is defined as the process of evolving and shaping a work personality eventuating in adulthood. The ability to work is a learned ability which is acquired during the process of vocational development. Knowledge of work rules, the achievement drive, and motivation are incorporated during the developmental stages. The theory explains the how and what of the work personality and the part played by cultural components, how vocationally immature individuals or those with retarded or underdeveloped work personalities may be developed vocationally (46).

Gellman's theories have been widely discussed in the United States. In the main, his theories have been well received. Only one concept has been questioned. That is the concept of the need for a highly skilled practitioner as a counselor-foreman. Gellman holds:

> To use work as a therapeutic tool, it is necessary to utilize foremen who understand the dynamics of the work personality and can control and vary the psycho-social aspects of the work situation. The tool for modifying the work personality is a constellation of the counselor-foreman modifiable work situation. The use of personnel who can measure, modify, and evaluate forces influencing change permits visualization of the workshop as a therapeutic tool capable of changing the work personality (47).

The theories and conceptualizations of the Chicago Work Adjustment Center have been developed over a period of twenty years by a group of researchers, theorists; and practitioners under the direction of William Gellman. Their rationale has been expanded, modified, and revised from time to time. Their work has generally been well documented and researched. No substantial refutation of their theoretical framework has yet appeared in print. Their doctrine represents the most significant body of theory in the area of work adjustment in workshops. As such, it has laid the groundwork for serious study of workshop programs in the United States.

Phase and System Theories

The Gellman approach to work adjustment was generally typological; a syndrome was identified which explained the individual's behavior and attitudes, and a treatment program followed in accordance with the assessment. If necessary the assessment could be changed, but the basic approach was that of a differential diagnosis and treatment. In 1966, Phyliss Hallenbeck and John Campbell proposed a conceptual framework for work adjustment involving a phase-task approach to work adjustment.

Four phases are described as settling in, learning, growth, and job readiness. In each phase, the individual has problems, is assigned tasks to be mastered, and environmental factors are manipulated to enable the individual to solve the problems and make the critical role transitions which are necessary from phase to phase. Thus the workshop process is a series of phases which can be identified by the individual's ability to accomplish the tasks and solve the problems identified with each phase. It is assumed that in general all go through all four phases, except possibly the fourth when the individual does not become ready for work (48).

In 1969, additional elements in the theory of work behavior were proposed by a group of researchers headed by William H. Button at the Rehabilitation Research Institute at Cornell University. This group based its assumptions on research findings in the field of management and proposed a model in systems terms. The three principal components of the model are behavioral activity, social ecology, and technology. Through a Work Behavior Observation Scheme it is hoped that the significance of different variables relating to client behavior and rates of client change may be isolated (49). The Work Behavior Observation Scheme measures aspects of behavior and work contexts by observation of work delay and contact sequences. The conceptualization appears to parallel in some respects the clinical analysis of Paul Lustig stated in systems terminology (50).

Since the Work Behavior Observation Scheme had not been used extensively at the time of the publication of the theory, and the systems approach has not been applied in workshops elsewhere, it is not possible to predict the validity of the theory. However, the prominence given to technology is a new element in behavioral theory in workshops, and the injection of quantitative elements in the scheme may add a firmer basis for work behavior rationale.

The Theories of Behavior Change in Workshops

Unlike the theories of work adjustment, which are usually well-defined and unified, the theories of general behavior change are varied. Some ascribe change to general conditions in the environment without identifying specific determinents which effect change. Others indicate specific stimuli or reinforcements which purport to result in planned results. A variety of names are given to these theories, the most general being *behavior modification.* A large number of different or overlapping theories have been suggested by psychologists, and workshop personnel have sometimes selected some of them as a framework for the processes in their workshops (51). In general, these theories assume that behavior is learned and that it may therefore be changed by learning or relearning.

Some of those theories which are used by workshop personnel in their shops will be described here under two general heads: first, those that explain change as resulting from a total environment and second, those dealing with specific approaches which affect discrete aspects of behavior. Since the general terminology used does not always differentiate theories, the two groups of theories will be designated as *general environmental* theories or *specific conditioning* theories. This may be a distinction of emphasis rather than definition, since it may be difficult to separate the two at times. However, it is made because some workshop personnel reject specific conditioning theories such as those of operant conditioning as being narrow and in conflict with the philosophy of the dignity of the individual. These objectors prefer to influence behavior through a "therapeutic milieu." The latter emphasize the effect of the environment itself but also include at times the intervention of staff in dealing with the internal problems of the individual (52).

THEORIES OF THE THERAPEUTIC ENVIRONMENT

An early statement of the way in which the workshop environment modifies behavior was made in 1958, by Alfred Feintuch, Director of the Jewish Vocational Service of Montreal, Canada. He indicated that the components of the workshop which influenced behavior were work experience, which reduced social isolation, social interaction which enhanced communication, supportive group experiences resulting in reeducation, and the opportunities to meet successfully graduated work standards which result in confidence and satisfaction. The emphasis is on the group processes in a supportive environment, although he stressed the importance of counseling when integrated with the workshop findings. Together they enable the individual to effect improved behavior (53).

A somewhat analogous but more extensive analysis of the use of the workshop environment is made by David Hershenson. He suggests that the workshop environment can be used in a life stage approach to effect desired change. These stages are described as adapting to the milieu, recognition of problems by individuals, reaching of set goals, and experiencing the satisfactions involved in interaction with people and with work. Through these stages the individual moves to improved vocational behavior (54).

Another example of the use of the total workshop to effect change may be found at the Community Workshops of Boston. Simon Olshansky, its director, has applied the theories of the therapeutic milieu to his program (55). To effect change, the attempt is made to involve all staff members in creating an atmosphere which gives every person an increased sense of his worth. This is done by communicating a variety of messages, the least important of which is the verbal message. The nature of the plant and the kind of work done conveys an initial message. The expectancies of the staff give signals which influence behavior. Each person is given the maximum opportunity to make his own decisions, even when they are wrong, so that he may gain increased self-respect. He is provided a variety of opportunities to learn from successful experience so that he may gain confidence that acceptable performance and behavior result in desirable outcomes. Through developing self-esteem, maintaining expectancies, and providing varied and viable opportunities, the individual is influenced to improve performance and behavior.

The characteristics of the workshop program are viewed as important in effecting change. The person is viewed as a worker, not as a client. The role of the worker and client are different, and the person who is asked to play both roles may become confused. If he needs clinical services he gets them outside of the workshop. The emphasis on the worker role signals the expectancy of competence. The major focus is on behavior, not attitudes. While attitudes may influence behavior, the worker may perform badly with good attitudes, and well with unacceptable attitudes.

There is no assumption that what is done specifically produces certain outcomes. The numbers of variables both inside and outside the shop preclude such a possibility. These variables are the available work tasks, the changing tension levels in the shop, the "fit of supervision," the influence of the family, of professionals and friends, and of the referring agencies. It is not assumed that all these factors can be controlled. The shop provides an environment generally conducive to desirable changes and some of the persons who come to it benefit from it (56).

The theories of the therapeutic milieu as practiced by Olshansky resemble those of the therapeutic community developed by Maxwell Jones in England in 1948. Some workshop personnel, many in mental hospitals, have adopted Jones' theories directly. His approach was to emphasize the influence of the total environment and all persons in that environment in effecting outcome as contrasted with specific procedures under medical prescription emphasized in similar hospital programs. In his program each person in the hospital including each patient becomes an integral part of the therapeutic process. His theories were not directed to workshop programs exclusively, since his plan was to cover a wider range of hospital objectives. However, his program included workshops, and they applied the theory of the therapeutic community (57).

SOME SPECIFIC THEORIES OF BEHAVIOR MODIFICATION

Of the specific theories of behavior modification, two groups in particular have received emphasis in workshops. The first, which propose to initiate, control, or manipulate stimuli, components, or determinants in the external workshop environment to modify behavior, will be labeled the *control of environmental determinants.* The second, which plan to effect change by associating behavior with desirable or undesirable consequences, will be discussed under their commonly used name of the theories of *operant conditioning.* Other theories of behavior modification exist of course; those which are most pertinent are the theories of education and of counseling or psychotherapy. Educational theories tend to be emphasized in workshops which supplement special education programs. The verbal methods of counseling and psychotherapy seem less useful in workshops as principal modalities than the more direct methods of environmental manipulation and conditioning and are often conceptualized as secondary or ancillary procedures. The workshop personnel who have written on theory usually have emphasized situational manipulation as their major emphasis, or operant conditioning as their major emphasis.

The Control of Environmental Determinants

In the therapeutic milieu a generally beneficial situation is structured, but the alternatives open to the individual are somewhat limited. In the workshop which controls environmental determinants, the alternatives are more extensive. The basic theory is that if the determinants are well controlled, the desired ends will be achieved. Thus the stimuli or components are arranged so that the person will increase his production or modify his behavior. The desired change will be effected if there is the predicted interreaction between the characteristics of the worker, the internal factors, and the determinants in the environment, or the external factors.

Workshop personnel have probably informally experimented with the manipulation of environmental determinants to effect change since workshops began. A comprehensive theory has not been developed, however, which is based on comprehensive scientific experiments in workshops. Paul Lustig has applied interaction behavior theory to the workshop setting and has outlined rationale which explains how workshop stimuli or determinants may effect change. Part of his clinical analysis is presented in reviewing his theory for behavior modification in the workshop by means of controlling the external stimuli in the workshop, here labeled the determinants in the workshop environment (58).

Lustig begins with the assumption that the model of behavior consists of a stimulus, a person, an act, and a response to the act. The stimulus is processed by a person who performs the act, which is followed by a response to the act. Any change in any part of the model affects the other parts of the model. A workshop implies a situation in which the stimulus, the act which follows it, and the response to the act can be controlled. Some of the stimuli or determinants of the workshop which may be controlled are [1] the time of activities, [2] the position of workers, [3] the rate of work, [4] the type of interpersonal relationships and the work flow relationships, [5] the organizational structure, and [6] the physical environment.

Each of these determinants may be controlled to affect individual behavior. The duration of activity, the speed of production, and position or location of the individual may effect communication and participation. By locating a person in an isolated or crowded area, he may be shielded from or pushed into contacts with objects or people to produce desired results. By controlling the rate of speed of an assembly line or a conveyor belt, the production of a worker may be increased. The people with whom he works or the tools and materials with which he works may be controlled to effect desired changes. By controlling the organizational structure and changing the nature of relationships with professional staff, foremen, leadmen, and co-workers, the role of the worker may be changed with favorable results.

A most important set of determinants which may be influential is the work flow relationships. They may be used to illustrate the rationale of environment manipulation. Lustig classifies these relationships as [1] parallel or coincidal, [2] additive or sequential, [3] subtractive or antagonistic, and [4] unrelated. The nature and use are described as follows:

Parallel or Coincidal. In this relationship two or more workers performing the same task independently contribute to the total work flow. This relationship may stimulate a moderate degree of competition and thus may improve production gradually.

Additive or Sequential. Each worker receives a partially completed item, adds to its completion, and moves it on to another for more work on it. This push-pull interaction may be used to modify ascendency or submission in peer relationships and produce more integrated behavior.

Subtractive or Antagonistic. Every worker performs the same task and takes his material from a common limited pool, after which he is out of work. This involves a piecework rate, so that the wage is affected. The situation provides an intensified stimulus. It may be used for some high-ability, low-esteem individuals to improve esteem and productivity.

Unrelated. The work done by each worker is removed or separate from other operations. The emphasis is less on co-workers relations and more on work and the supervisorial relationship. This allows the worker to become acquainted with work and supervision without coping with co-workers.

An example of control of determinants may be found in the following history. A mentally retarded young man of twenty-four who had a WAIS IQ score of 70 is slow in his work and talks incessantly with co-workers. Separated from co-workers and working on individually produced work, he is slow and tries to talk to his supervisor whenever possible. Assigned to an assembly line where his task is routine and predetermined, and the work flow is dependent on his production, he responds to the pressures of his situation and his co-workers to produce work in the required amounts. In some of the above situations, reinforcement exists automatically through responses of co-workers or is introduced additionally by design. Reinforcement may exist, however, without an initial change in stimulus.

Operant Conditioning Theory in Workshops

The theories of operant conditioning have received considerable attention and some use by workshops. The theories state that the probability of the increase or decrease of an act of behavior depends upon what follows that act. What follows is called reinforcement. It can be positive or negative. If the act of a person is followed by something he wants (positive reinforcement), the chances that he will intensify that act are enhanced. If it is followed by something he dislikes (negative reinforcement), he will tend to desist from that act. The kinds of positive reinforcement are many different rewards – money, social approval, or tokens or status representing prestige or privileges. Negative reinforcement may be withdrawal of privileges or punishment.

The principle of generally following an accomplishment by reward or approval has probably always existed to some extent in workshops. The payment of wages or general social approval are such rewards. The difference between such general responses and the theory of operant conditioning which became prominent after

1960 in workshops lies in following a specific act soon afterwards by a specific reinforcement instead of providing wages or approval at some later time for general or vaguely defined sets of behavior.

The concept of a more specific reward had also been used by workshops previously. Piece rates had been substituted for hourly rates to increase productivity. This had resulted in increased general production and in increased productivity in many workers. It did not, however, result in increased productivity for all workers. The money reward simply does not appeal to some workers. In operant conditioning, the nature of the reward is crucial. The reward or reinforcement must appeal to each person whose behavior is to be affected. Thus it becomes necessary to find reinforcement which will contain attractive elements to all whose behavior is to be modified.

In some rehabilitation facilities where operant conditioning is used, the reinforcement is tailored to each individual. In some large workshops this approach is impractical on a large scale. Reinforcement must be found which is effective with a large percentage of the workshop population on common activities. This is often accomplished by the use of tokens which represent a variety of rewards. Another related problem in large institutions is that the behavior of individuals is at different levels of maturity. Reinforcement in progressive steps must be contrived. Reinforcement thus takes place in a number of ways. The principal ones are by individual reinforcement, by tokens for groups, and by progressive steps of reinforcement components.

Operant conditioning has been used principally in workshops in mental hospitals where the hospital uses this technique as a means of behavior therapy. In such case, the workshop uses the same system as the hospital. The best known of these is the step system, as practiced at Medfield State Hospital. This procedure provides progressive higher rewards for designated packages of behavior which increase in complexity.

The effectiveness of the token system was demonstrated in a research project conducted by Joseph Zimmerman at Indianapolis Goodwill Industries in 1968 (59). The experiment consisted of making available rewards to individuals in excess of those usually received in the workshop for increased production. Point cards were used which could be exchanged for opportunities to work overtime, tours to industrial plants, social hours and recreation, conversations with staff members chosen by the worker, and purchases at the canteen. The results showed that token reinforcement increased productivity significantly in multiply handicapped persons in the workshop. Reinforcement which provided a reward immediately after the action was more effective than that which involved promise of later reward. When reinforcement was withdrawn production was reduced.

An important question about operant conditioning relates to the durability of the results in another environment. It is not likely that a business establishment will provide tokens or other specific rewards which will coincide with those used during operant conditioning. Will increased productivity or accepted behavior learned in operant conditioning be maintained in an industrial environment? The workshop personnel who have proceeded on the principle that their operations should duplicate industry as nearly as possible will probably not accept operant conditioning principles until it is shown more clearly how its results in workshops will carry over in an industrial environment for extended periods of time. Until such demonstrations are made, it will probably be regarded by some workshop personnel as an experimental laboratory procedure.

In spite of the objections and reservations about operant conditioning, there are some advantages that should be considered. Though they are not usually stressed, the assessment possibilities of operant conditioning are important. The nature of the reinforcement which affects the individual may tell a great deal about his vocational choices and the kind of environment which will influence motivation. Since this data is based on quantitative results, another objective, reality measure, is added to the assessment. The use of objective, quantitative measures of behavior and the application of such measures to workshops are greatly needed (60). Also, there is the possibility that it may be demonstrated that the increased activity generated in some projects initiated by operant conditioning may carry over to other projects in the workshop without similar conditioning when confidence has been generated in the person and he can respond to more general or different types of reinforcement in a constructive environment.

THE WORKSHOP THEORIES OF PERSONAL AND SOCIAL DEVELOPMENT

The rationale of workshops previously described explains how experience in the work environment together with related supportive services enable the person to function better as a worker. There are some who hold that the workshop may be used to mount crucial services not indigenous to workshops but which may benefit the person in other aspects of his life not related to his role as a worker. This will be labeled the *holding operation* rationale. Another view is that the work environment may be used as a basis to achieve social objectives with or without achieving employment objectives. This use of work to move the person into social improvement will be called the *launching gun* theory. Finally, there are those who hold the theory that behavior change is influenced by ego development; therefore, all behavior modification is inseparable from the treatment of the ego. Thus, the work environment must be modified to meet ego demands until the therapy in depth can alter the basic personality structure. The last will be called the psychoanalytical theory.

The Holding Operation Rationale

One initial question quickly appears to need answering. If individuals need basic services and therapies which are not related to the work setting, why cannot they be provided just as well in other rehabilitation or health programs. Bertram Black provides one answer to this question. He says:

> I am also convinced that we have only just begun to realize the usefulness of the workshops as a "holding operation" to allow for other forms of medical, psychological, and educational therapies to function.... We have found that tuberculous patients take their drugs while coming to our workshop even though nothing else of a satisfactory rehabilitation nature seems to be taking place. Cardiac patients stabilize their balance between work and symptoms and let the cardiologist test the limits in a way he never would were the

patient home . . . . For the newer case loads of the aged, school drop outs, and others, the "captive caseload," for which the work setting becomes in part a lure, can receive education, social attention, and medical services that they would not be, or are not even now, motivated to seek out (61).

Work is often the lure that brings persons into the workshop. Individuals sometimes come to the workshops who would not come to a social service agency to discuss family problems or to a vocational guidance agency to discuss their vocational problems. Once they come to the shop to work, they may not seem motivated to do anything else, even to adjust adequately to work. Nevertheless, they often may later do something else. When the things they can be induced to do — to take medication, to accept social services — are not resulting in work progress in the shop, the staff may consider that a "holding operation" is taking place. Nothing is happening to forward the planned work objectives, but movement may be taking place towards other social or personal objectives. Something is happening as far as the person is concerned — he is working, so he remains and may be induced to do many necessary things. Thus there exists a "captive case load," persons who come to work and are induced to engage in other activities.

The "holding operation" may have real benefits to the handicapped person. He may be induced to take his medication more regularly. He may be involved in social and recreation activities he would not seek out. He may consult the social worker for simple housing or transportation problems and find himself discussing distressing family problems, or the social worker may routinely discuss his family problems. He may find himself discussing with the counselor many problems he did not expect to solve in the workshop. Finally, he may find himself receiving psychological or psychiatric service of a type he never contemplated. During all this time, he may not be making much progress in the shop. In fact, he may not finally end up achieving the objectives he came to the shop for — to prepare himself for a job in industry or in the shop. The shop has performed a "holding operation" which has enabled him to achieve personal objectives.

The Launching Gun Theory

In the "holding operation" the work environment has been a lure, but it has not served as a basis for movement of the person towards personal or social goals. Other supplementary services have done the job. In the "launching gun" theory the work environment itself provides the push that brings about personal and social objectives. In both cases, the objectives may not be those of work or employment. In the "holding operation" services such as counseling or psychotherapy do the job. In the "launching gun" framework the work and the work environment do the job. In the latter case, the following illustrate the theory. A school dropout identifies with an adult masculine role through the work of the shop and returns to school to complete his education. The male head of a family becomes a worker and provider as a result of his employment in the shop and assumes a greater role as the father in the family and in other social relationships. In both instances, work has played an active part in reaching social objectives.

An example of the way the "launching gun" approach is used to achieve nonwork objectives is shown by the work therapy project for adolescent delinquent boys conducted by the Jewish Vocational Service of Milwaukee from 1962 to 1968. The youths in the programs had been in correctional institutions, had police records, were on probation, or had other severe delinquency histories. They were to go to school half-days and spend half-days in the workshop. The objective was not to place them in jobs necessarily at their ages but to modify their behavior.

It was believed that if the youths could be "captured" in the work environment, it would bolster self-confidence and remove in part the failure experience in school and in crime. Work in this rationale became the common denominator when applied in a therapeutic atmosphere where acceptance was different from school, home, or the community. Through work, the delinquent youth is motivated to change as he begins to realize that work carries with it discipline and authority and that it has rewards.

In reporting on the project, it was noted that many youths

remained only one semester and returned to school on a full-time basis. While there was no dramatic adjustment of their previous behavior, there were no requests for them to return to the project. The school authorities felt that their adjustment was better so that they could be retained in the normal school setting (62). Thus work was used not to produce an acceptable worker but to produce a more acceptable adolescent student.

The Psychoanalytical Theories

In the same general category yet quite different from the "holding operation" and the "launching gun" approaches are the ways in which the followers of psychoanalytical theories apply them in workshops. These applications take a number of forms, but since there appears no published description of them in workshops, they are described generally from observation. Most often, apparently workshop personnel attempt to superimpose psychoanalytic theories upon the workshop structure. Assuming the validity of such theories, they modify the workshop arrangements in accordance with the postulates. More rarely they attempt to apply ego therapy or psychoanalytic theories of work.

Psychoanalytic Modifications of the Work Environment

A principal tenet of psychoanalysis is that adult behavior may be understood by the analysis of the early relationships of the child to his parents. If this is so, then the way the individual relates to others in the workshop depends upon his relationships with his parents in the first few years of his life. His response to authority figures — to the foreman, instructor, or quality controller — will then be predetermined and not subject to modification by training or adjustment formulas. In this situation, it is necessary to change the environment to accommodate to the individual's emotional response system which has been fixed in childhood until therapy in depth can be successful. Since analysis is not readily available or effective immediately, the believer in psychoanalytic concepts seeks to change the workshop environment to accommodate the individual.

The accommodations which need to be made are those relating primarily to the supervisor or foreman. If the individual has difficulty with authority figures, those figures must be changed to provide a less threatening situation for the individual in light of his childhood traumas. Thus the foreman must cease to be a demanding and thus threatening figure and must minimize his authority role by giving it a warmer, more permissive character. Or perhaps no man will do — he still reminds the individual of his threatening father — and a woman should be substituted as the foreman. A number of variations can be developed on the theme of the residuals of the early familial drama.

From Freudian or most neoclassical points of view, however, the environmental modification has only temporary value. It may enable the person to work in the modified setting for the time being, but the person's essential reaction to authority figures has not changed, and the change remains to be made if he is to work in the community. But the work environment alone cannot enable him to deal adequately with authority figures. Only a change in his ego structure can do that. Thus the followers of this school of thought must logically seek or give treatment for the person or depart from psychoanalytical assumptions. From a logical point of view, such manipulations of the workshop environment can only be a holding action as prelude to the psychotherapy which is needed.

Although modification of the influence of early childhood on adult behavior has been suggested by neopsychoanalysts such as Erik H. Erikson, the body of theory still points to a verbal and psychotherapeutic approach to the problems of the person who cannot relate well on the workshop floor. Those belonging to this school will therefore tend to emphasize psychotherapeutic rather than situational solutions to workshop problems. The workshop then becomes a "holding operation" to keep the person "captive" until the effects of psychotherapy take over, and a place to test the results in work behavior.

Walter Neff points out that even with the recent modifications and amendments to psychoanalytical theories, questions still remain about the appropriateness of such theories in relation to work (63). Until more information becomes available or research is carried out, it would seem inappropriate to draw conclusions about such oriented intervention in workshops. If the restructuring of the basic personality is indicated, it appears that it may be accomplished primarily and more effectively elsewhere. The workshop could, of course, still remain a "holding operation" in those instances where the person feels the need to work while undergoing psychotherapy.

THE WORKSHOPS AND THEORIES OF SPECIAL EDUCATION

Until 1950, most workshops provided services principally to those physically handicapped persons who had become disabled in their adult life as a result of injury or disease. The workshop offered them opportunities to restore their functioning to the extent possible to enable them to work in industry or in workshops. Persons with massive congenital conditions which had retarded their normal development were either rejected or provided with sheltered employment under permissive work conditions in workshops. When they were accepted for service, the residuals of their arrested development were often neglected. In the 1950's, many workshops, and particularly those sponsored by parent groups, began serving larger numbers of minors and young adults whose arrested development as a result of their handicapping condition was an initial obstacle to their employability.

The disabilities of these young adults had made it difficult for them to benefit from education, or to develop mature social relationships during their childhood and adolescence. They had never learned the primary skills of working and living. The workshops which accepted them had to teach them elementary productive and social skills if they were to perform substantive work. They needed services which recapitulated normal human development at a pace suitable to their ability to learn if they were to be brought to their highest functional potential (64).

Often the arrested development resulted from multiple disabilities. In such cases, the services of many health, welfare, and educational modalities were needed, and some needs fell in between these services (65). Although some workshop organizations attempted to supply the in between services, in the main, the workshop environment was best suited to meet the entry or initial work-related needs of young adults. These services resembled, for the most part the services of special education programs. Thus, some workshops found themselves augmenting special education programs by applying different types of treatment theories developed by educators, psychologists, and sociologists.

The principal areas in which workshops had to supplement the educational system were in teaching the rudiments of the three R's, especially the literary skills of communication, the development of personal adequacy and social competence, and the acquisition of work competence. Since the largest number of professional workshop personnel came from the fields of counseling, psychology, or social work, they often attacked the problems of personal adequacy and social competency more thoroughly than those of elementary academic learning and work competence (66).

Some workshops, finding no ready-made comprehensive theoretical guidelines, simplified Leonard Oseas' conceptual framework and used it for work and social development training. To do so, they had to restate Oseas' theoretical terminology into theory-free language. For example, his reeducative dimension (the concept of clarification of external work realities to reinforce reality-fantasy discrimination) and its operating conditions are restated as follows:

> If you want to develop activity or task comprehension and judgment, make the realities of the activity clear and understandable. Do this by clarifying the nature of the activities and call attention to objectives and standards of performance. Emphasize actual achievement and real-life activity goals. Be sure the activity is clearly defined, its duties delineated, and its purpose useful (67).

The fact that this translation does violence to the original is less important than the fact that it can be more readily followed by floor personnel.

To the development of personal and social adjustment, they often also applied the familiar theories of counseling, of situational techniques, and sometimes of conditioning and social learning. A few teachers who joined workshop staffs applied educational theories to workshop problems, but these were not the majority, and they usually were not in positions to influence program rationale. Very often they applied such theories to the teaching of work-related educational rudiments without applying theory to the development of work competence. Thus not much attention was paid by any group of professionals in workshops to theories for developing work competence as differentiated from work adjustment.

It may be useful to describe what is meant by work competence and to distinguish it from occupational skill competence. Work competence does not necessarily involve the ability to perform skilled tasks independently in connection with an occupation. It consists rather of the ability to apply oneself to work, to learn and accomplish tasks for jobs, and to perform such tasks productively and acceptably. The tasks may be simple or complex. Since many workshop personnel were not familiar with theories of developing work competence, they emphasized work habits and personal adjustment, often skirting the problem by assuming that the employer would train their workers in work competence.

The problems of developing work competency were often left to personnel at the floor level of workshop supervision. The few supervisors at this level who had previous experience in developing work proficiency usually came from industry or teaching. The supervisors from industry understood useful practice methods but seldom applied identifiable concepts. The teachers usually were most knowledgeable in academic or vocational teaching theories. Thus, workshop personnel of special education shops did not apply as specific a theory for developing work competence as they did for work adjustment.

In addition to the emphasis on personal and social adjustment, the new areas in which the most careful consideration was given to theory were in the teaching of rudimentary useable skills of communication, independent living, and recreation. Of great importance to developing employability was the teaching of communication signs and symbols, counting, time-telling, street signs, and signatures. Self-care and simple household skills were taught. Socialization through parties and games was arranged. Simple skills in gardening and janitorial services were taught. Very simple routinized job tasks requiring little learning were undertaken.

As in other types of shops, general teaching principles were involved. The jobs were broken down into the simplest possible components, and a progression of the simple to the more complex was attempted. Repeated demonstrations were made by instructors and foremen. Cooperative group activities were arranged in jobs, and projects were set up in games and social affairs. When incentives were involved, it sometimes became necessary to teach the meaning or value of money and other rewards through symbol recognition. Thus the floor persons in these workshops applied the theories of progression, of imitation, and of learning through projects sometimes without awareness of theory.

There were, of course, available after 1950 learning theories which were relevant to work processes. In the main, however, these had been developed under experimental laboratory conditions or in connections with classroom settings. More recently, there have been a few demonstrations in workshop settings which are important to workshop practice. Unfortunately, their theoretical framework is couched in highly technical terminology so that they are difficult for floor personnel to apply. Nevertheless, the basic approaches are useful and top level staff can translate them into workable rationale.

Among the groups of handicapped persons whose development has been arrested, considerable research attention has been devoted to the mentally retarded in the 1960's. It has been shown that mentally retarded persons respond to incentives and determinants in the work environment, that they can be taught complex tasks, and a difference between the retarded and the nonretarded lies mostly in length of time of training and not in level of performance. Furthermore, when properly motivated, mentally retarded persons can work with minimal supervision. Procedures for them can be standardized (68).

Most findings of learning theory emphasized the importance of training strategies and the techniques used. The importance of goal setting, of associating goals with prestige and other reinforcements, and the great value of creating an expectancy that goals can be achieved have been demonstrated; also that discrimination and associated learning can take place on a complex task unless a verbal process is involved. Thus the ability to accomplish a work task depends upon the technique involved in the training process and the goals, incentives, and expectancies set for the workers (69).

A recent study of interest to workshops in the field of learning discrimination was made by Marc Gold in a workshop for the mentally retarded. Using principles of discrimination learning, sixty-four moderately and severely retarded people with a mean IQ of approximately forty-seven were taught to assemble a fifteen piece and a twenty-four piece bicycle brake. Using experimenters not experienced in working with the mentally retarded, Gold and the experimenters demonstrated how the assembly was done and then followed up by notifying the individual in subsequent trials when errors occurred and asking him to try another way. Verbal and monetary reinforcement was used. In two groups, color was added to the parts to help the worker learn the task, and the addition of color made the task easier to learn. This suggests that the retarded may be able to assemble color-coded parts in electric current boards.

Gold points out that the lowest performing groups exceeded the expectancies of the workshop staff and that manipulation of the training procedures increased performance. Procedures such as those described above should be instituted when expectancies are elevated. Such procedures can improve the capability of the retarded and the skill level and profitability of subcontracts in workshops (70).

THE LACUNAE IN WORKSHOP THEORY

Workshop theorists have in the main concerned themselves more with objectives of various programs and less with their structure. They have been much concerned with the individual and how he interacts but less concerned with groups of individuals and how the group interacts. They have been much concerned about the meaning of work in our culture but have been less concerned about the nature of the work itself. Often they have discounted the importance of the work object or the nature of the work as being unimportant. They have, in fact, kept the work simple and routine, even minimizing it in keeping with their assumption that its nature is unimportant. A workshop, however, whatever its type, includes two basic structural elements — groups of people and kind of work. What is done with these is important of course, but also important is the nature and structure of the elements themselves.

It may be that the failure of workshop theorists to emphasize these structural elements has left serious lacunae in workshop theory. These lacunae may then have weakened the validity of theoretical formulations.

Workshop theorists have neglected the group primarily because of their interest in the individuals. As a result, workshop analysis of the individual may have been narrow and limited. Too often the analysis has consisted of categorizing and describing functioning in terms of the category of the individual or of the individual himself rather than his group. Thus a mentally ill person functions in such a manner, or a cardiac or tuberculous person functions in such a manner, or an individual relates in such a manner to his supervisor, counselors, or co-workers. It is common observation, however, that a given individual may function quite differently in one group than in another, and that the members of one group will function quite differently in juxtaposition to one group than to another. Functioning then cannot be interpreted solely in terms of the individual. It is composed of what the individual brings to the situation, the group in which he functions, and the immediate and general social environment in which he functions. Of these, the group has been relatively neglected in workshop theory, even though much consideration has been given the group in other fields.

The nature of the work done has been equally neglected except in a negative sense. Broad assumptions are made that the nature of the work object is unimportant, even though the worker should engage in work on an object if any purpose is to be served in the workshop. The extent of satisfaction or dissatisfaction in that engagement, the fit of the specifics of the work object and the needs of the worker, its implications to him, and the status of the work object have not been seriously considered except in general terms. What is needed is analysis of the specifics of work and specific work objects and their influence on individuals. Research is needed on the relationship of kinds of work to the responses of types of workers.

Insufficiently considered in workshops is the effect that a specific job will have in motivating the worker to accomplish it. Infrequently considered is the status of the job in the value judgments of the workers. The fact that a task may signal a low estimate of the worker is too often ignored. Yet it is known that jobs are rejected or resented because they are "dummy work" or "baby work" or "factory work." In shops which bring in more complex or more meaningful work where simple work existed before, the former is often more highly regarded and those who work on it are regarded as having higher status.

The Azimas have studied the meaning of work objects to emotionally disturbed individuals in hospitals and have suggested numerous ways in which patients interpret them. Their work has been in occupational therapy settings. A similar approach to the meaning of specific work objects in workshops may be useful. What does putting nuts and bolts in a plastic bag mean to various groups of handicapped persons? Completing a cable harness assembly? Making hospital garments on a sewing machine? Machining a part for an aircraft assembly? Typing a manual of specifications for defense suppliers? Making a Kennedy memorial candle? Filling a bag with gravel?

It is commonly observed that troublesome, nonproductive individuals often become productive and well behaved when put on new tasks that seem to engage them happily. It is often assumed that the individual makes the change because he is better able to do the new task. But often the difference in ability required is not appreciably different. Perhaps there is something about the job object or the nature of the task itself that makes the difference. Simon Olshansky points out that the type of work made available is important and that work should be varied (71). Until more study is given to the meaning to handicapped persons of work objects and work tasks, perhaps the assumption may be made that the workshop which best enables the individual to respond positively to work is that which has both simple, routine tasks and a variety of job objects and tasks at different levels of complexity and in varying industrial, business, and service fields in the economy. Thus the individual may experience simple, uniform tasks or a variety of complex tasks as his needs dictate.

SUMMARY

A review of the various theories presented seems to indicate that these different theories arise out of the different treatment needed by different groups of handicapped persons. These different groups of individuals can best be identified by a dynamic formulation of their prognosis for functioning, not by a medical, psychological, or social label or classification or by combinations of them. Thus the economic workshop has a formula for individuals who can become employable through realistic work experience; the work adjustment shop — a theory for using the work situation to deal with persons who need to develop acceptable work behavior and attitudes; and the workshop for the aged and chronically ill — a way of making the person's life more livable in his later years. Thus workshops lead different kinds of persons down different paths to reach various destinations.

Common to workshops is the concept of the central role of real work. This concept holds that real work is beneficial in helping individuals. However, workshops have different theories explaining how they see themselves helping individuals in the work setting.

One theory considers real work as the principal ingredient necessary to bring about work enablement. Another emphasizes the importance of selectively applying the many forces in the work situation as needed to improve the work personality in order to develop acceptable work behavior. Another holds that work serves very usefully as a holding or launching operation while other psychosocial interventions are being employed to develop a higher level of total functioning of the individual. Still another theory holds that the general therapeutic nature of the work environment may bring about work enablement. Others hold that phased approaches are needed to develop work capacity, and yet others maintain that specialized approaches are needed to diminish work deficit and to develop work capabilities.

All in all, the benefits of real work are recognized in each theory; the emphasis placed on it varies.

NOTES

1. Garrett, J. F.: Sheltered Workshops — Whither Goest Thou. In Stubbins,

J. (Ed.): Horizons for the Handicapped. Los Angeles, Los Angeles State College, 1960, p. 6.

2. Salmon, P. J. and Spar, H. J.: Historical Development of the Special Workshop. In Chouinard, E. L. and Garrett, J. F. (Eds.): Workshops for the Handicapped. Washington, Office of Vocational Rehabilitation, 1956, pp. 135-144.

3. Chouinard, E.: Sheltered Workshops – Past and Present. In The New Outlook for the Blind. New York, American Foundation for the Blind, 1957, p. 283.

4. Straus, R.: Social Change and the Rehabilitation Concept. In Sussman, M. B.: Sociology and Rehabilitation. Cleveland, American Sociological Association, 1965, p. 21.

5. Overs, R. P.: Sociologic Aspects of Rehabilitation. An address presented to the Wisconsin Rehabilitation Association, November 17, 1965, Milwaukee, Wisconsin. The above presentation uses some of Over's terminology in a different frame of reference. However, his rubrics suggested the treatment.

6. Sheltered Workshops, A Study of Wage Payments to Handicapped Clients in Sheltered Workshops Certified under the Fair Labor Standards Act, Washington D.C., 1969, p. 13.

7. Kimball, H. W.: This is Goodwill Industries. New York, The Newcomen Society in North America, 1962, p. 6 and throughout. Workshops in the 1970's. National Meeting of Board Members from N.I.B. Affiliated Agencies, Washington, D. C., 1968. Proceedings of the Third Annual Meeting. California Conference of Workshops for the Handicapped, Los Angeles State College, Los Angeles, California, 1962. Lytle, H. G.: The Role of the Workshop in Community Planning. The Role of the Workshop in the Community, California Conference of Workshops for the Handicapped, San Mateo, California, 1961. Proceedings of the First Institute on Sheltered Workshops in New York State. New York, State Commission for Public Health, 1957, pp. 10-15.

8. Glasser, W.: Reality Therapy. New York, Harper & Row, 1965.

9. Feintuch, A.: Sheltered workshops – a conceptual framework. Journal of Rehabilitation, p. 9, January-February, 1958.

10. Gellman, W.: Vocational Adjustment and Personality. Chicago, Jewish Vocational Service, 1953, pp. 6-8. Gellman, W.: Components of vocational adjustment. Personnel and Guidance Journal, p. 537, May, 1953.

11. Neff, W.: Work and Human Behavior, New York, Atherton Press, 1968, pp. 150-154, 254-255.

12. Ibid., pp. 151-154.

13. Ibid., pp. 194-197.

14. Lytle, H. G.: Staff Requirements in a Sheltered Workshop. At DePaul University Institute on The Role of the Executive in a Workshop Administration. Chicago, Illinois, October 9, 1967, p. 9.

15. Ibid., p. 2.
16. Address delivered to Southern California Chapter, National Rehabilitation Association, January 24, 1962, Los Angeles, California.
17. Lustig, P.: Current Objectives of Sheltered Workshop Programs. Madison, University of Wisconsin, mimeographed, 1965.
18. Black, B.J.: The workshop in a changing world — the three faces of the sheltered workshop. Rehabilitation Literature, August, 1965.
19. Elton, F.: Work Therapy. New York, American Rehabilitation Committee, Inc., 1948.
20. Sullivan, O. M. and Snortium, K. O.: Disabled Persons, Their Education and Rehabilitation. New York, Century, 1926, pp. 362-363.
21. Elton, op.cit., p. 4
22. Ibid., p. 4.
23. Ibid., pp. 20-21.
24. Ibid., p. 15.
25. Ibid., p. 21-22.
26. Ayers, G. E. and Mahan, S. P.: A sheltered workshop meets authentic needs of the chronically disabled. Hospitals, pp. 103-105, 107, October, 1967. Black, B. (Ed.): Creative Use of Sheltered Workshops in Rehabilitation. New York, Altro Health and Rehabilitation Services, 1957.
27. Rheingold, J.: The establishment of a sheltered workshop in a home for the aged. Journal of Jewish Communal Services, p. 271, 1966.
28. Levy, J. H.: Psychological Gains, Engagement, and Disengagement of Older Persons Employed in a Therapeutic Workshop. Chicago, JVS, 1965.
29. Walker, R.: Mistreatment of the mentally ill. The American Journal of Psychiatry, pp. 219-220, September, 1964.
30. Neff, W.: Work and Human Behavior. New York, Atherton Press, 1968, p. 153.
31. Azima, H. and Azima, F. J.: Outlines of a dynamic theory of occupational therapy. American Journal of Occupational Therapy, pp. 215-220, 1959.
32. Vogt, V.: Memorandum Re. Workshop Program, to Track Directors, Illinois Department of Mental Health, June 28, 1968.
33. Leopold, H.: Repetition. Rehabilitation Journal of the British Council for Rehabilitation of the Disabled, p. 14, April-June, 1968.
34. Oseas, L.: Work requirements and ego defects, work dilemmas of the recovering psychotics. Psychiatric Quarterly, 37:106-117, 1963.
35. Oseas, L.: A model for establishing therapeutic work conditions. Journal for Counseling Psychology, pp. 369-370, Winter, 1963.
36. Hubs, R. S.: The sheltered workshop in psychiatric rehabilitation: a therapeutic modality and socioeconomic resource. The American Journal Orthopsychiatry. pp. 76-79, January, 1964.
37. Neff, op.cit., pp. 184-201.

38. Gellman, W. and Friedman, S. B.: A Workshop for Overcoming Barriers to Employment. Chicago, Jewish Vocational Service, 1953. Vocational Guidance Quarterly, Winter, 1953. Gellman, W., Gendel, H., Glaser, N. M., Friedman, S., and Neff, W.: Adjusting People to Work. Chicago, Jewish Vocational Service, 1957, pp. 135-136.

39. Gellman, W.: Components of vocational adjustment. The Personnel and Guidance Journal, pp. 537-538, 1953. Gellman, W.: Vocational Adjustment and Personality. Chicago, Jewish Vocational Service, 1953, pp. 2-5.

40. Gellman, W.: The Vocational Adjustment Shop. Philadelphia, American Personnel and Guidance Association, 1960, p. 3.

41. Neff, op.cit., pp. 150-164.

42. Gellman, W., Gendel, H., Glaser, N., Friedman, S. and Neff, W., op.cit., p. 13.

43. Gellman, W.: The vocational adjustment shop. Personnel and Guidance Journal, pp. 632-633, April, 1961. Gellman, W., op.cit., pp. 8-9, 11.

44. Gellman, W.: Personal communication, September 25, 1969.

45. Gellman, W.: New Perspectives in Rehabilitation. Chicago, Jewish Vocational Service, 1966, pp. 5-6. Also, in Bulletin, Division 22, Psychological Association, November 1966, Vol. 13, No. 3.

46. Gellman, W.: Achieving productivity for the cerebral palsied. Journal of Rehabilitation, May-June, 1961. Also, Gellman, W.: Counseling Persons with Cerebral Palsy Toward Productive Living. New York, Eighth World Congress of the International Society for the Welfare of Cripples, 1960.

47. Gellman, W.: Influencing Vocational Bias and Vocational Development through Work Experience and Clinical Workshop Programs. Sydney, Australia, The Australian Council for the Rehabilitation of Disabled, 1969.

48. Hallenbeck, P. N. and Campbell, J. L.: A conceptual framework for work adjustment. Journal of Counseling Psychology, pp. 409-415, 1966.

49. Button, W. H., and Kimberly, J. R., Lubow, B. K. and Kimberly, R. P.: A Conceptual Framework for the Analysis of Work Behavior in Sheltered Workshops. Ithaca, Cornell University, undated.

50. Lustig, P.: Differential Use of the Work Situation. Paper delivered at the American Psychological Association, Los Angeles, September, 1964. Also, Lustig, P.: The Clinical Use of Various Work-Flow Relationship in the Sheltered Workshop. Madison, University of Wisconsin, 1966.

51. For a brief summary of these theories, see Pigott, R. A.: Behavior modification and control in rehabilitation, and Durfee, R. A.: Another look at conditioning therapy. Journal of Rehabilitation, July-August, 1969. Also, Leslie, R. G. (Ed.): Behavior Modification in Rehabilitation Facilities. Hot Springs, Arkansas, Research and Training Centers and Association of Rehabilitation Centers, Inc., 1968.

52. Ibid., p. 6-15.

53. Feintuch, A.: Sheltered workshops – a conceptual framework. Journal of Rehabilitation, January-February, 1958.

54. Hershenson, D. B.: A vocational life-stage approach to sheltered

workshop practice. Journal of Rehabilitation, pp. 26-27, November-December, 1968.

55. Olshansky, S.: Behavior Modification in a Workshop. Paper delivered at the National Rehabilitation Association, October 21, 1968, New Orleans, p. 2.
56. Ibid., pp. 1-15.
57. Jones, M.: The Therapeutic Community. New York, Basic Books, 1948.
58. Lustig, op.cit., Also, Lustig, P.: The Clinical Use of Work Flow Relationships. Madison, University of Wisconsin, 1965 (mimeographed). Also, Lustig, P.: An Overview of Training Techniques in the Workshop. Madison, University of Wisconsin, 1965 (mimeographed).
59. Zimmerman, J., Stuckey, T. E., Garlich, B. J. and Miller, M.: The effects of token reinforcement on productivity in multiply handicapped clients in a sheltered workshop. Rehabilitation Literature, pp. 34-40, February, 1969.
60. Ibid., p. 41.
61. Black, B. J.: The workshop in a changing world. Rehabilitation Literature, August, 1965.
62. Porter, H. M.: Work Therapy Program for Adolescent Delinquents. Milwaukee, Jewish Vocational Service, 1967, pp. 8, 38, 40.
63. Neff, W., op.cit., pp. 95-100.
64. Ibid., pp. 157-158. Also, Gellman, W.: Achieving production for the cerebral palsied. Journal of Rehabilitation, May-June, 1961.
65. Reynolds, M. C.: A framework for considering some issues in special education. Exceptional Children, pp. 368-369, March, 1962.
66. Kimberly, J. R.: Professional Staffing in Sheltered Workshops. Ithaca, Cornell University, 1969.
67. Oseas, op.cit., pp. 369-370.
68. Hudle, D. D.: Work performance of the trainable adults as influenced by competition, cooperation, and monetary reward. American Journal of Mental Deficiency, pp. 198-215, 1967-1968. Also, Gold, M. W.: The Acquisition of a Complex Assembly Task by Retarded Adolescents. Urbana, University of Illinois, 1969.
69. Klibhan, Sister J. M.: Effects of goal setting and modeling on job performance of retarded adolescents. American Journal of Mental Deficiency, pp. 220-225, 1967-1968. Also, Miller, L. K., Hale, G., and Stevenson, N. W.: Learning and problem solving in retarded and normals. American Journal of Mental Deficiency, p. 681, 1967-1968. Also, Rolter, J.: Social Learning Theory and Clinical Psychology. New York, Prentice Hall, Inc., 1954.
70. Gold, op.cit., pp. 30-31.
71. Esser, A. H., Chamberlain, A. S., Chapple, E. D., and Kline, N. S.: Productivity of chronic schizophrenics in a sheltered workshop. Comprehensive Psychiatry, Vol. 6, no. 1, pp. 49, 1965. Chapple, E. D. and Esser, A. H.: Workshops in state hospitals. The Psychiatric Quarterly Supplement, part 2, Utica, State Hospital Press, 1964, pp. 4-5.

XI

THE PROGRAMS AND SERVICES
OF WORKSHOPS

By 1968 persons with many kinds of physical and mental handicaps were found in the workshops of the country. They were the mentally retarded, the mentally ill, the blind, the orthopedically handicapped, the cardiacs, the cerebral palsied, the epileptics, the deaf, the aged and those with respiratory conditions, alcoholism and drug addiction. In addition, there were small numbers of socially and culturally disadvantaged in workshops (1).

The persons with the above-named conditions need a variety of different services in workshops. However, the services they need do not depend exclusively on the nature of their conditions; they also depend on the severity of the handicaps which their disabilities impose. The programs they need are influenced too by the attitudes of industry and of society towards their disabilities. Their conditions, the severity of their handicaps, and society's attitudes towards their disabilities determine the objectives that can be projected for them. Workshops develop programs designed to achieve the objectives possible for the kinds of handicapped persons they are committed to serve.

The kinds of handicapped persons which workshops are committed to serve are determined by the workshops' philosophy and goals and by the external support they can get for their programs. Among their external supporters are suppliers of funds, purchasers of service, and referral agencies. As a rule, handicapped persons come to workshops by referral from public or private agencies which are committed to the service of different kinds of handicapped persons capable of reaching different objectives. The self-referred person is the exception in most groups of workshops.

Why do handicapped persons come to workshops? Apparently there are no comprehensive studies in which prospective applicants or enrollees have been asked this question. It is assumed by rehabilitation personnel that they come to workshops because they wish to work in industry and the workshop will help them get work there. The reasons why handicapped persons want to work indefinitely in workshops have been considered more extensively by rehabilitation personnel, and there are numerous points of view regarding permanent sheltered employment (2). The reasons why handicapped persons work in sheltered employment are complex and deserve some attention.

Sheltered employment is an effort to solve a human problem, the roots of which are found in our economy and culture. There are, for example, substantial numbers of handicapped workers in workshops earning twice the minimum wage and approximately the community going rate. Why are they in workshops and not in industry? Why are others with considerable competence making less than the minimum rate? Why do large numbers of handicapped persons work for wages who are receiving the public assistance payment (3)? Why do handicapped persons work for an hourly wage of less than 25 cents (4)?

We do not have specific answers to all these questions. In a culture where working is equated with human worth, the answers should be sought. We know of course that sheltered employment provides different benefits for different persons. In general, sheltered employment provides the person with work when work is denied him for reasons beyond his control. The exclusion may result from forces in our economic and psychosocial structure or it may result from conditions of the handicapped person. The epileptic or cardiac may be denied employment in industry irrationally and may earn high wages in workshops. The mentally retarded person may not be able to compete in industry as it is now organized and so is willing to work in workshops at menial work at low wages when he may be able to do more meaningful and more skilled work. And finally, the aged and chronically ill may be glad to work at low wages if the work gives them a happier way to spend their declining years. Sheltered work is a method of fulfilling human needs, or as the Dutch call it, social employment.

Until more research is done on the reasons why clients come to workshops, it will be assumed that they come to workshops because they need the services and programs that are found in them. This will become more apparent as these programs and services are reviewed and analyzed.

THE NATURE OF SERVICES AND PROGRAMS

Because workshops serve different kinds of handicapped persons and have different objectives or combination of objectives, they carry on a variety of different activities designed to achieve these various objectives. Such activities, which differ both in their nature and duration, may be divided into two groups: [1] those that are mainly floor activities, and [2] those that are mainly off the floor. One group consists of a constellation of activities which are connected with the work on the floor of the shop. Another group is that which relates separately to the handicapped person. The first named group of activities is usually carried on primarily by the handicapped person on the floor of the shop. The second named group of activities is carried on primarily by the staff off the floor. For example, in extended employment, the individual applies himself to work, and primarily by that action achieves an objective. On the other hand, when social casework takes place, the individual may be helped to solve social problems which have inhibited his ability to work. The second group of off floor activities are usually supportive of the basic programs. Thus, the activities of the shop may be grouped under basic programs and supportive services. There is usually an interrelationship between the two. In the above example, extended employment is a basic program and social casework is a supportive service.

Of course, some activities cannot be fitted as neatly into these two categories. In on-the-job training or vocational skill training, the trainer is immediately involved with the work done as well as with the trainee. And it can be held that the same relationship exists in some forms of work adjustment training. Nevertheless, the distinction is useful for analysis. Usually one or the other function predominates — a group of activities is basic or supportive. On the other hand, usually but not always both types of activity are necessary in varying degrees. Since many workshops serve severely handicapped individuals with many different kinds of problems, both basic programs and supportive services usually need to be combined to reach objectives. It is this typical combination that gives most workshops their distinctive characteristics.

Before identifying specific programs and services, it is useful to analyze the nature of their duration. Basic programs are usually continuous, while supportive services are usually intermittent in varying degrees. A basic program requires a continuous and substantial exposure of the individual to the activity. The individual usually participates in the activity a full day every day of the week for a substantial number of weeks. In supportive services, the individual is seen from time to time irregularly for short periods of time, usually less than an hour at a time. This time distinction is important because in some institutions whose programs consist of a number of intermittent services, the staffs often consider the workshop another intermittent service. A fundamental requirement of basic programs in workshops is that the individual be given a sustained and substantial exposure to its realities.

Statement of definitions or descriptions of the various programs and services in workshops entail difficulties. Since workshops need to get income from the provision of their activities for referrals from other agencies, they often vary their major customers. They may also find it necessary to use the terminology of their customers. Basically, however, the problems arise because there is no standard identification of terminology with accepted practice within a classification of a program or service. As a consequence, the activities carried on under a given rubric vary greatly. Thus, under "prevocational training" may be carried on training in activities of daily living, or social and personal adjustment, or remedial education, or other categories of activities which do not fall into other rubrics in the shop. Under the work adjustment or personal adjustment training rubric may be carried on such varied activities as teaching a worker to comply with the routine demands of an industrial setting or the development of tolerance for a full day's work or the modification of an individual's attitudes towards work or the development of a satisfactory work personality.

In light of the diversity of nomenclature and practice, programs and services can best be described by identifying services by subgroups of workshops. However, the specific information which exists about various workshop programs and services would have to be found in numerous research and demonstration reports of the Social and Rehabilitation Services of the Department of Health, Education, and Welfare, which are not easily available and would require a major research effort. Furthermore, there is no generally accepted typology for workshops (5). The best that can be done probably is to describe their development generally and to relate programs and services to objectives (6). In this account an attempt will be made to avoid general rubrics and use concrete designations whenever possible, showing alternate nomenclature for terms used. Before discussing the specific programs and services, we will summarize them under basic programs by objectives, and by supportive services.

PROGRAMS IN WORKSHOPS BY OBJECTIVES

Programs in workshops are classified under five headings as follows: [1] personal development programs, [2] physical and mental conditioning programs, [3] employment preparation programs, [4] vocational skill development programs, and [5] employment programs. There is some overlapping, as shall be seen.

Personal Development Programs

Personal development programs include a group of activities which try to overcome arrested development deficits due to disability, usually among young persons. They are given such names as [1] habilitation, [2] work experience, [3] work activities, [4] prevocational training, [5] activities of daily living and, [6] independent living services.

The individuals in such programs are usually not ready for preparation for work or employment.

Physical and Mental Conditioning

The persons in the above programs are not ready for

preparation for employment because of physical or emotional deficits which exclude them from employment. They usually have reached maximum benefits from medically oriented therapies but may be able to benefit from activities in a work setting. These programs are labeled [1] physical therapy, [2] occupational therapy, [3] work therapy, [4] work tolerance, [5] physical conditioning, and [6] work conditioning.

Employment Preparation Programs

Preparation for employment takes place at various levels of deficit. Vocational training, which is sometimes included under this heading, will be shown under the next heading separately. The two levels are shown under work training or work readiness and work adjustment or personal adjustment training.

Work readiness preparation covers exposure to work for the purpose of conforming to industrial routines and developing work competences. It is called [1] Work habit training, [2] work conditioning, [3] work competence training, [4] work tolerance, [5] work hardening, and [6] work training.

Work adjustment or personal adjustment training reaches a level at greater depth than work readiness preparation. It aids individuals to adjust to the psychological and social demands of work. It is called [1] work adjustment, [2] personal adjustment training, or [3] work adjustment training, and [4] personal and work adjustment.

Vocational Skill Development Programs

Vocational Training in this program has as its objective the creation of occupation or trade competence. The purpose is to develop, not general work competence, but specific skills. This program is labeled [1] vocational training, [2] occupational training, [3] trade training, [4] on-the-job training.

Sheltered Employment Programs

Under this heading are included relatively long-term

employment programs. General types of employment are carried on to achieve three objectives:

Transitional Employment. Long-term employment geared to upgrade the individual's productivity and possibly have him leave for outside employment. This is called [1] transitional employment, [2] rehabilitation employment, [3] work experience.

Extended Employment for Wages. This involves sheltered employment for substantial wages. It is called [1] extended employment, [2] terminal employment, [3] long-term employment, [4] homebound employment, [5] sheltered employment.

Sheltered Employment. In this type of employment, wages are small and the objective is the increased well being. This is called [1] extended work therapy, [2] sheltered employment, [3] homebound employment, [4] respite employment, [5] work acitivity.

Recapitulating, personal development programs may be synonymous with *rehabilitation;* physical and mental conditioning programs may be labeled either *habilitation* or *rehabilitation* or both; employment preparation programs are *rehabilitation;* vocational skill training are usually *rehabilitation;* and employment programs are *rehabilitation* or *maintenance* or *alleviation.*

Furthermore, each program is a constellation or group of specific services in different combinations from time to time as required. In this sense, the programs are a cluster of services. The label *programs* is maintained because it distinguishes these clusters of services from the more individualized services which are called supportive services.

Supportive services are divided into two categories, assessment services and assistive services. Assessment services are of course also assistive, but they sometimes help the staff help the individual and at other times help him more directly. The second category is assistive because regardless of whether they deal with a vocational or a psychosocial problem such services assist the individual to reach an objective.

ASSESSMENT

Assessment procedures may be divided into categories by

content areas, such as medical and psychological, or by their nature, such as verbal or cognitive and manual or performance. In either case, there is such considerable overlapping that either classification is not definitive. Because the content areas classifications are probably more familiar, they will be used here, beginning with the most used assessments in workshops. Before doing so, it is necessary to indicate that some workshops use the term *rehabilitation evaluation* or *rehabilitation potential determination,* which cuts across all content areas. As a rule, the rehabilitation assessment tends to stress vocational determinations. This discussion will be confined to the assessment of the individual primarily and will not include primary analysis of jobs or work.

Vocational Assessment

The major emphasis in workshops is on vocational assessment. Some of the designations used for general vocational evaluations are as follows [1] rehabilitation evaluation, [2] vocational evaluation, [3] occupational evaluation, [4] work evaluation, [5] prevocational evaluation, and [6] vocational exploration.

Some specific designations are as follows: [1] work tryout, [2] on-the-job tryout, [3] job-site tryout, [4] job sample, [5] work sample, [6] real work sample, [7] simulated work sample.

Psychosocial Assessment

Psychological and social assessments are often combined in workshop packages.

Psychological assessment usually comes under the following: [1] Psychological examination, [2] psychological evaluation, and [3] psychometric examination.

Social Evaluation. These are usually combined with psychological examinations. However, they are also indicated as [1] social evaluation, [2] cultural evaluation, and [3] personal and family evaluation.

To a lesser extent, workshops supply medical, educational, and speech-hearing assessments. These are most often secured elsewhere. Of the assessment services shown above, by far the largest percent are for vocational or work assessment (85%) and for psychological evaluation (54%) (7).

SUPPORTIVE SERVICES

In the supportive field there appears to be much less diversity in nomenclature. For this reason, services may be listed under one heading in order of prevalence.
1. Vocational counseling.
2. Placement and placement training.
3. Psychological or psychiatric counseling.
4. Social casework and family counseling.
5. Recreation.
6. Medical management.
7. Mobility training.

Having enumerated the programs and services in workshops, we will trace their development and relative predominance. As we do so, we will consider their nature and some of their relationships to workshops. Because of paucity of information about the early periods, it will be necessary to emphasize the more recent period after mid-century. With the exception of vocational training and employment programs, the more sophisticated services were developed principally in the last forty years. In these forty years, most of the information was published after 1950.

We will review first assessment methods, then the programs indicated previously, and finally the assistive phases of supportive services which we call "people services."

ASSESSMENT IN WORKSHOPS

An important characteristic of American workshops is their major emphasis on assessment. The reasons for this emphasis may be found in historic antecedents, financial necessity, and professional integrity. Throughout the history of vocational rehabilitation, there has been a continuous dissatisfaction with the considerable percent of predictive errors in planning for individuals. There has been a parallel effort to improve the accuracy of predictive methods and to develop new and different types of assessment techniques. This pervasive desire for better assessment has led to considerable allotment of public vocational rehabilitation funds for evaluation purposes and has enabled research-minded professions in workshops to pursue their inclinations to perfect their prediction of outcomes for individuals (8).

When assessment procedures began in workshops, they were probably made by staff observation of work performance and social behavior. Observation of the individual has probably been the most persistent form of assessment. After World War I at the Portvillez School in Belgium, observation was made of the individual as he worked in trade classes. The Belgium experience influenced the emphasis on vocational training in the public vocational rehabilitation program, and in the beginning in the 1920's and later in the 1950's, the Institute for the Crippled and Disabled stressed trade training and observation in trade classes from which the Tower System of Job Samples descended.

Three other components in vocational rehabilitation programs, however, influenced assessment during the first half of the twentieth century. They were [1] a medical basis for determining the functioning of the handicapped individual, [2] the use of intelligence and manual dexterity tests, and [3] the use of histories based on interviews with the individual giving facts connected with social, personal, and vocational factors. Thus, during the first half of the twentieth century, assessment in vocational rehabilitation generally was based primarily on medical evaluation, psychometrics, and interviews and histories by vocational counselors.

Although workshop personnel, especially those in rehabilitation centers and curative workshops, were influenced by the classical assessment triad, workshop personnel generally continued to depend upon an observation of the individual on the job and the reports of his performance for their assessments. By the middle of the century, it was becoming apparent that the medical-psychometric-interview approach alone was not predicting the assets of severely handicapped and uneducated individuals, but was denigrating them because they could not respond effectively to the verbal, abstract, symbolic, or physical criteria applied. It was also apparent that many who were rated highly by these means alone failed at work because of characteristics not tested by these methods. It was believed by many that the techniques were not accurate predictors of general feasibility for work when used without tests of performance and social behavior.

During the 1950's and 1960's, vocational counselors were thus ready for and seeking additional assessment methods to use, especially for marginal, uneducated clients in the case loads. When in these years workshops developed personal and social assessment through situational techniques, observation of performance, work samples, and measurement of productivity, they were able to make available to vocational counselors the kinds of data they sought to fill the gaps in the traditional assessment triad. When it was believed by state vocational rehabilitation agencies that the workshop could deliver comprehensive work-feasibility evaluations in written reports more conveniently and more reliably than they could be gotten from business firms, the state agencies became large purchasers of assessment from the workshops. Their purchase of evaluations changed the focus of workshop evaluation from tryout for jobs in the shop to assessment for jobs in industry. Whereas formerly vocational rehabilitation agencies had sent clients for evaluation to workshops so that they might be placed there permanently, after mid-century they began sending clients in large numbers for evaluation exclusively. Furthermore, once the referring agency began sending clients to workshops for work evaluation, they found it convenient to purchase other types of assessment for workshops, such as psychological evaluations, intelligence tests, and even medical evaluations. Thus in some places the workshop provided general assessments of the individual's potential.

The techniques used by the workshops to provide the added assessment components did not develop overnight. In 1935, the New York Institute for the Crippled and Disabled developed a "guidance test class" which was used to predict vocational potential. By 1956, this class approach had resulted in the development and publication of the Tower System of work samples, which used parts of jobs to predict potential for such jobs (9).

The initial introduction of the Tower System in the 1950's was not entirely successful. The job sample is a test that tries out an individual on a job or an important sampling of the essential operations of a job. A problem with the original Tower System was that it did not have tests on some jobs which existed in major industries in some parts of the country. For this and other technical reasons many workshops developed their own system of work samples in the 1950's and 1960's.

In the early 1950's, numbers of Goodwill Industries began developing work samples suited to their localities. For many years previously, Goodwills had been moving individuals from one job to another until an optimum placement was reached. After 1950, they began systematizing the evaluations, somewhat along the lines of the Tower System. In 1958, a committee of Goodwill personnel developed a publication, *Manual for Establishing of a Work Evaluation Program,* which contained a collection of job samples that could be easily constructed by a Goodwill Industries. Six Goodwill Industries received federal grants on projects studying evaluation services. In 1968, the original job sample manual was revised and reissued as *Work Evaluation Manual for Goodwill Industries.* In 1967, sixty Goodwill Industries were selling evaluation services (10).

In 1959, May T. Morrison Center in San Francisco developed a work sample system. At that time, the San Francisco Community Rehabilitation Workshop was a unit of the center. The system was related to *Worker Trait Requirements for 400 Jobs* published by the United States Department of Labor. Jobs are organized according to major job families according to the *Dictionary of Occupational Titles.* Of the eighty-three tasks, twenty-three are most commonly used. They fall into four groups: clinical and sales, service work, skilled and mechanical work, semiskilled and unskilled work (11).

The San Francisco project was followed by a Research and Demonstration Project carried on from 1959 to 1964 on *Obtaining and Using Actual Job Samples in a Work Evaluation Program* at the Cleveland Vocational Guidance and Rehabilitation Service. Its goal was to secure more and better work samples from industry, to measure performance quantitatively, and to demonstrate a method of job samples (12). The project also used job samples related to an occupational field rather than a job. It is interesting that this system which was one of the best of the work samples was not used as much as the better known systems.

In 1967, a more comprehensive version of the Tower System was issued. Over one hundred work tasks are tested in thirteen broad occupational areas in job families. Abilities, skills, aptitudes, and interests are tested. Rating of attitudes and behavior are made as well.

The Tower System was followed in 1968 by the Philadelphia Jewish Employment and Vocational Service with an experimental demonstration project directed towards disadvantaged persons residing in economically and socially depressed areas. Previous work sample systems had been directed towards physically and mentally handicapped individuals. The Philadelphia system was directed to develop work samples acceptable to disadvantaged individuals. It stresses sustained and structured observation of work behavior that reveals how the individual can change, thus offering a measure of adjustability. For socially maladjusted or alienated persons, the emotionally disturbed, and mentally re- tarded who may not be responsive to verbal communication, it presents a means of eliciting and modifying behavior where verbal and symbolic techniques fail. The sponsoring agency sees it as supporting the counseling function by isolating particular client traits which need correction or development. It provides a vehicle for reality testing and acquisition of a larger repertory of work related behaviors. It offers a means of engaging the resistant and reluctant client in an initial counseling relationship through making immediately available for discussion his experiences in the work sample program (13).

The objective of the work sample systems described, whether they used work in the shop or got work samples from industry, was to make predictions for work in industry. Another use of samples was developed in large workshops. The shop developed norms for elements of work continuously done in the shop and used the job sample for screening purposes for placement in the shop. Thus if a shop had electronic assembly, it might try an individual on soldering or color recognition to determine if he should be placed in the electronic department. Job sampling of this kind speeded the process of assigning an individual to his placement in the shop.

In spite of the activity in connection with work samples, not all workshops used them and some preferred to emphasize the work on the real job as the best indicator of the individual's ability. If work samples are shortcuts to the total job as is believed, they would be useful because it is not possible to have large enough numbers of jobs in a shop. However, if an individual could be put to work on an actual job under actual working conditions, a better assessment would probably result. The nonusers of work samples either assumed that the skills tested by work samples were not valid, or they sought better evaluations for jobs they did not have in their shops in business job sites in the field. Those that did not use work samples used situational techniques, job site tryouts, productivity norms in shop jobs, and finally a combination of some of these latter elements in a workshop evaluation outline which was usually presented to the purchaser of services.

The standard workshop evaluation or rating sheet became quite ubiquitous in workshops after 1954. In many states, it was required by the state vocational agency before it would pay the bill. In some states, the purchasing agency prescribed the form. In others, the workshop developed it. In spite of the heterogeneity of forms, the general content areas were similar, including the following elements:

Performance. Here were given quantitative measures of productive ability in comparison with shop norms, minimum wage, or industrial norms — usually in percentages of norm. Usually a grading of the quality of work followed in gradation from excellent to poor.

Work Skills. Here were evaluated in graduation such components as ability to learn, ability to work without close supervision, capacity to work under pressure, and the like.

Psychosocial Factors and Attitudes. Here were evaluated relationships with co-workers, passive or aggressive attitudes, ability to handle supervision or need for it, attitudes towards work, and other aspects of personal adjustment.

Workshop evaluations may thus be divided into two general types: general rehabilitation evaluations and specific work evaluations. In the first instance, the workshop might provide a complete psychometric work-up with extensive personal, social and employment history, with medical histories sometimes added. When special work evaluations were made, the components varied in nature and depth. Workshops emphasized one or more of the following:

1. Work tryout in shop or industry of work skills and productivity.
2. Job or work samples (where used).
3. Situational assessment of work behavior and attitudes.

The majority of workshops do not provide work samples, and although most make evaluation of work behavior the nature of such assessment varies greatly. Common to most workshops, however, is the assessment of the individual's work skills and productivity, although this evaluation is not always made on a quantitative basis or in comparison with industrial norms. Added to this is some evaluation of behavior, but this varies from a description of work habits to assessment in depth of components of social behavior and attitudes.

THE PROGRAMS OF WORKSHOPS

During most of the history of workshops in the United States, especially before mid-century, the majority of the persons who attended them came for employment. After mid-century, a number of political and professional developments took place which shifted the focus of workshops from employment to a variety of other objectives. Because of the lack of comprehensive information for the country as a whole, it is not possible to state definitively the extent of employment programs in workshops today. However, it is apparent that the predominance of sheltered employment has given way to a broader emphasis on a variety of programs which have been indicated (14).

Several trends which developed simultaneously after 1950 effected the predominance of extended employment programs in workshops. The major influence was that of the public state-federal vocational rehabilitation program which stressed movement through workshops into private employment. This kind of program emphasized the transitional approach. It received increased state and federal funds after 1954. At the same time, however, workshops were influenced by private voluntary groups to accept people with new and severe types of disability, such as mental retardation and cerebral palsy, many of whom could not readily move into private employment. Workshop organizations responded variously to these conflicting pressures. Some accepted only those who could move into competitive employment. Other groups of workshops accepted more severely handicapped persons with the intent to move them into private employment, but were not always able to do so. In the latter circumstances they had the choice of terminating services or providing long-term or sheltered employment. Some terminated services but others kept those they could not place in private employment. Finally, other groups accepted numbers of individuals for whom extended sheltered employment was the initial objective. Unfortunately, "sheltered employment" has pejorative overtones in the United States. The President of the United States stated in 1966:

> For thousands of mentally and physically handicapped Americans, employment has too long been considered the exclusive concern of "charity." Yet, we know that many handicapped citizens can learn important skills, and can become effective workers (15).

Sheltered Employment in Workshops

There is at present no study in depth of the nature, meaning, and psychodynamics of sheltered employment in all types of workshops in the United States. The research that has been done concerns wages or earnings (16). The principal studies have been done by the United States Department of Labor, starting with the Sheltered Workshop Report of the Secretary of Labor in 1967. These reports indicate that the average hourly wage of workers in workshops from 1967 to 1968 has approximated half of the minimum wage (70 cents an hour), and that approximately half of the workers earned less than half of the minimum wage in 1967 (17). These would be the wages of workers covered under the provision of the Fair Labor Standards Act. The Secretary of Labor concluded in his 1967 report that "while there are many handicapped workers who do perform competitively and others who can be trained to do so, there are some who need help after they have reached their full potential" (18).

Before discussing problems in sheltered employment, we must analyze the typology of the workers in the various sheltered workshop programs. What types of workers engage in what kinds of sheltered work and for what reasons? The following rubrics are suggested for consideration and study. They are the [1] stigmatized or alienated high producers, [2] transitional employees or the marginal producers, [3] the low producers, [4] the inconsequential producers, and [5] the producers in decline.

The Stigmatized or Alienated High Producer

The stigmatized high producer is able to work relatively as productively as the nonstigmatized worker in industry. He is not given work in industry because industry is afraid of or does not understand his condition. The blind, epileptic, cardiac, the cosmetically disfigured, and paraplegic are examples. In some workshops they make wages equal to those paid in industry. The stigmatized high producer is handicapped not by his disability but by the discriminating requirements of industry.

Industry discriminates against another group because of their social attitudes, manners, dress, life style, race, color, and for a variety of social or ethnic reasons not directly connected to the demands of productivity. Here categorization is difficult but many of these can be described as the alienated. Some are both stigmatized and alienated. The requirements of industry are repugnant to the latter. These persons do not wish to or cannot modify their life styles. The workshop may provide them with opportunity to work without the repugnant restraints of industry or the requirement that they "modify" their natural characteristics. The alienated may also be high producers and earn big wages in workshops.

There are, of course, stigmatized or alienated individuals among low producers, but they may be multiply handicapped as well. And of course there are workshops which do not accept the stigmatized or alienated.

Cadre and Labor Core

The stigmatized or alienated worker should not be confused with those in workshop cadre or labor core. Workshops sometimes have superior workers as permanent lead men or key hourly workers who assume an important role in providing informal supervision to those with whom they work or in getting out the work. The "cadre" usually provides informal supervision while working. The labor core, on the other hand, is a temporary or permanent labor force whose role is to get out the work. The individuals in both groups make better wages than the rest of the workers and prefer to remain in the shop for a variety of personal reasons. They are allowed to do so because they enable the shop to provide work for rehabilitation purposes or to provide sheltered employment for the less productive. The role of the supervisor-worker in each of these groups needs study.

The Transitional or Marginal Producer

The transitional worker, who is considered to be in rehabilitation employment, is producing close to the industrial norm but cannot find a job in industry because of employment conditions or because he is not an attractive candidate for employment. He is kept in the shop to maintain his skills until a job can be found.

The marginal worker is not uncertain he can make it in industry. His experience has taught him that his level of performance is sometimes good enough and sometimes not good enough depending on labor demand. He prefers the security of the workshop. He will often try to remain in the workshop as long as possible and will accept a lesser wage than the stigmatized high producer. His productivity is marginal and he may also exhibit an inadequate behavior pattern which is not subject to modification. He is also handicapped by the changing requirements of industry. His wage range is from 50 to 80 percent of the minimum wage in the writer's estimate.

The Low Producer

For the low producer there is no possibility of leaving the

workshop. He will work there or no place. His choice is to work there or be supported from some other source. Often he may require both. He has to accept a low wage because he has no alternative. If he wishes to work, he will work in almost any kind of workshop. Among the individuals in this category are the multiply handicapped, neurologically impaired, mentally ill and mentally retarded. The low producer is estimated to make between 50 to 25 percent of the minimum wage.

The Inconsequential Producer

The inconsequential producer works in the workshop because it provides him with a package of gratifications he can find nowhere else. Among the principal gratifications is work. This is meaningful to him even if the pay is inconsequential by Wage and Hour Division standards because it has great significance to him. He will usually work at any kind of work. In the workshop which gives him constant opportunities, he sometimes "blossoms" and becomes a more productive worker in the low producer or marginal producer category. Among the persons in this category are the severely mentally retarded and the brain-injured. The wage for this group is estimated as less than 25 percent of the minimum wage.

The Declining Producer

The declining producer is one whose physical and mental faculties are failing and whose possibilities of producing are diminishing. His wages are usually less than the minimum wage. Often he has some means of support, and although he usually wants to make additional money, he will come to the workshop only if other conditions are satisfactory to him. He comes for a combination of work, socialization, and recreation. Among this group are the aged and those with retrogressive conditions.

Disability, Functional Level and Productivity

Two threads run through the above descriptions. First, it was not necessary to discuss disability to make the classifications though medical designations were given to illustrate. Secondly, though productivity and therefore money play a role in each category, it plays a somewhat different role in each category. Thus, two elements need further discussion — functional level and its relationship to money earned. It is often assumed that productivity and therefore money making depends upon functional level. Button has suggested that other factors are involved as well (19). More specifically, wages are a result of the resources and capability of the workshop as well as the condition of the individual. Although Button finds a strong correlation between disability categories and hourly wage rates, he also finds that wage rates are a function of skill requirements of work. He states that workshops which pay wages equal to or in excess of the minimum wage have [1] older clients with relatively longer service, [2] clients with physical disabilities or chronic disease, [3] jobs requiring higher skill levels, and [4] income generated primarily by sales.

Workshop capability is thus an important factor in shop wage levels. An important element is the existence of experienced and capable workers. One way to engender capability is through vocational training.

Vocational Training

The first programs initiated by workshops in the nineteenth century were in vocational training. Vocational training has usually figured prominently in workshops either as a means of placing persons in industry or a means of training workers for workshop jobs. After 1950, the idea was current among workshop personnel that vocational training was not as important as work adjustment training. The rationale was that if the individual could adjust to the job, the employer would train him in the necessary skills. Although this notion is still widely current, its predominance in the workshop field was challenged after 1965 with the public clamor for vocational training. The Manpower Development and Training Program of the Department of Labor and the various grants for manpower training focused workshop sights once again on training. A scattering of workshops across the country received vocational training grants from the Department of Labor.

The principal impetus toward a resurgence of vocational training in workshops came from the Vocational Rehabilitation Amendments of 1965, Public Law 89-333. In Section 13(a), grants were authorized to public and private nonprofit agencies to pay 90 percent of the cost of projects for training services and allowances to handicapped persons in public and private nonprofit workshop and rehabilitation facilities (20). The financing was favorable and administrative costs were allowed in determining matching ratios so that many workshops applied for grants. By 1970, thirty-nine grants had been made and the initial results as judged by placement of graduates of training courses in placement in industry was favorable. From July 1, 1967, to September 30, 1969, 6,235 persons were referred, of which 1,794 were placed in competitive employment, and 220 were placed in sheltered employment (21).

The importance of the training services grants program becomes clear when reviewing the nature of previous vocational training in workshops. Previously vocational training had been principally of an on-the-job or apprenticeship type of training. Training had often taken place on work being done in shops and was therefore limited to the kind of work available. To qualify for the training services grants, training objectives had to be chosen in occupations or job families for which there was a demand in the community. Training curricula had to be in written form. Thus workshops began training on a large scale for work not in the shops and under formal and planned curricula. The workshop had to meet the standards of the Policy and Performance Council (22). In addition, skilled instructors were often hired with specific training in the occupations they taught. Training was given in many levels of occupations such as janitors, data processors, and electronic assemblers.

Training on Job Sites

The practice of placing handicapped persons in training in industrial plants had been carried on by the public vocational rehabilitation programs since their inception in 1920. This type of training was called on-the-job training. Workshops, however, did not engage in the practice on a large scale until the middle of the century. In the late 1950's, the Milwaukee Jewish Vocational Service was using on-the-job training on a substantial scale. After 1959, this type of training was used in connection with the prototype project, *An Evaluation Study and Demonstration Work Experience for the Mentally Retarded During Their Last Year of School, 1959-1964.* This prototype was repeated by the Jewish Employment and Vocational Service of St. Louis, Missouri, which was completed in 1967. Extensive experimentation with job site training was undertaken in twenty-three types of sites in culinary trades, maintenance occupations, beauty operators, and other services occupations. The Milwaukee Jewish Vocational Service also increased its use of job site training until a large percentage of its total of handicapped persons are found outside its shops (23).

Another type of job site training was developed in the western part of the United States. In 1966, Orion Industries of Seattle, Washington, in cooperation with the Division of Vocational Rehabilitation, sent crews of mentally retarded into forests to train as forestry workers. Subsequently, arrangements were made with lumber companies for the employment of crews of mentally retarded. Also in Bellevue, Washington, in 1960, Services, Inc., developed a program in which crews of mentally retarded persons were trained in maintenance work on job sites. In this program, there was no central work site and all the training was done in job sites.

The basic value of "job site" training is that it provides realistic training media. When the workshop maintains a supervisorial relationship, the industrial plant becomes an extension of the workshop. As shall be seen, it also becomes an invaluable aid to assessment (24).

Preparation for Employment

Since 1950, a major development in workshops has been the emphasis on preparing handicapped persons for work in industry.

As has been indicated, the goal often was not to train in occupational skills but to enable individuals to meet requirements of work other than those of specific occupational skills. The activities undertaken in various types of shops differed greatly not only in nature but in depth. In general these activities were labeled personal adjustment training or work adjustment. However, these labels did not necessarily indicate the nature of the program, since one program doing work adjustment might carry on a variety of activities quite different from another using the same name. Because of the variations among programs, it is not possible to describe generic programs precisely. However, it is possible to describe grossly identified activity groups which have overlapping functions.

In theory the activities in programs preparing individuals for work are developed to meet the individual needs of all types of persons unable to meet work requirements. If work deficiency can be said to stem from the individual's lacks, then the objective is to deal with the various deficits that may be remedied. The deficits are interrelated and exist in varying degrees of significance. In practice some programs emphasize the typical needs of the kinds of individuals that the shop serves. Other shops tend to deal with those lacks which it is best able to handle. If those it deals with successfully are the major deficits, the lesser deficits may sometimes be nondecisive. For this reason, a shop may be successful with one type of individual and not with another. What one workshop calls personal adjustment training or work adjustment training may be different from that of another because they emphasize different major deficits.

There are some shops which can deal with the needs of those individuals who are unfamilar with the requirements of work and who are unaccustomed to working. These individuals want to work and can get along fairly well with supervisors and co-workers when they learn what is expected of them. However, they are slow at work, unable to make independent decisions, have poor concentration or perseverence, exhibit poor work habits, and lack confidence. Thus they lack work skills and work competence. If they can be exposed to meaningful work, taught good work habits, encouraged to work effectively, and experience success, they may become satisfactory workers. The workshop may call what it does work adjustment training. What happens primarily is that a foreman may help the individual to learn to work adequately because he has the work and work environment in which to gain the needed work abilities and tolerances. What is provided is work training and work experience for work readiness.

The individuals who benefit from work experience and work training are not grossly deficient in their attitudes towards work and their ability to relate to co-workers and supervisors. Many individuals in work adjustment or personal adjustment are deficient in these respects as well as the other components such as work habits and work efficiency. Different workshops organize their activites differently to deal with such combined deficits. However, for ease of presentation, the programs of these shops will be divided into two groups: the first into a training model, and the second into a clinical or medical model. In the first, the deficits and assets of the individual are evaluated against training level steps, and the individual is placed in a training sequence related to his estimated level of development. In the second, a diagnosis is made of his condition and a treatment program is prescribed to deal with deficits. In both instances the analysis of the condition is usually made by a professional person, usually a counselor, who is usually not positioned on the floor of the workshop.

In the first program framework described, the deficits and assets of the individual are roughly approximated and estimated to correspond with a level, stage, or step of development where the major deficits can be given attention. For example, if the individual is functioning at a low functional speed level, he is started at a low step in the porgress, while if his work competence is adequate but his behavior with co-workers and supervisors is deficient, he is started at a higher level focusing on behavior. When improvement takes place in one or both of these levels, the individual may be moved to a higher integrated level for more improvement of both work competence and behavior and finally to an exit or bridge level where the individual is prepared to leave for competitive employment. These levels or steps may be achieved in separate units or in separate workshops. This structure moves the individual from floor personnel to floor personnel in various units and requires considerable supervision by the counselor or case manager (25). It is difficult to effect in a small organization.

In the clinical approach to work adjustment, a diagnosis is made and a treatment program indicated. In some workshops, the assets and deficits of the individual are assessed and attempts to deal with them are planned. In other shops, dynamics of the personality structure are formulated or the typology determined and a strategy is devised to deal with the configuration. In both cases, the individual is usually put to work in one workshop setting and he usually does not leave it. The modifications in treatment or in the environment are made for him by the staff.

Whether the asset and deficit enumeration or the typology or configuration analysis is made, where the clinical orientation exists, the emphasis tends to be on the social and psychological demands of the work setting and the attitudes of the individual. However, the asset-deficit approach tends to include more often the demands of the industrial environment, work competence, and productivity. In practice different degrees of emphasis are given to various problems of the individual and those get most emphasis that seem the most important to staff. Thus the emphasis often depends on the kinds of staff that are used and the different roles in which they function.

Usually two staff members function at the heart of the treatment process in the work adjustment shop — the case manager and the foreman. The case manager is usually a professionally trained individual practitioner, a rehabilitation counselor, psychologist, social worker, or occupational therapist who serves in a counseling role. The foreman may be one of the above-named professionals, a teacher, an industrially experienced foreman, or a person with no relevant experience. In some shops, however, persons with little training in counseling are used as foremen. In the latter instances the counseling case manager often assumes a major role in directing the development of satisfactory work behavior. The industrially oriented foreman tends to emphasize the development of productivity, work skills, and work competence. This division of emphasis is coordinated by having frequent staffings or discussions by the immediately involved staff members. When such meetings give equal consideration to the observations of the foremen and the counselors, the individual is helped to achieve both the interpersonal relations and the productive competencies necessary to work in industry: to get along with people, and to get along with the work.

Placement and Placement Training

Closely related to personal adjustment training are the efforts made in workshops to prepare the individual for placement and to find him a job. Here the activities vary greatly from intensive programs with full-time personnel to routine referral to other agencies for placement. Regardless of the nature of the placement program, workshop personnel seldom indicate that they have no placement program. In practice, workshops have substantial placement programs or they have unsubstantial placement programs.

Workshops which have unsubstantial programs usually depend upon another agency or upon the individual to make the placement. The placement potential then depends upon the effectiveness of the placing agency or of the individual. There are apparently differing points of view about the ways in which placements should be made. Some hold that the individual should secure his own job. Others believe that handicapped individuals should be placed in employment by the sponsoring agency. Some believe assistance should be given by the counselor; others believe it should be given by a placement officer. Perhaps the nature and severity of the individual's condition should influence the choice of the method used. In any case, in practice placement is made in a variety of ways depending upon the individual and the economic conditions of the times. Thus a workshop producing individuals with high level skills and efficiency in communities where such skills are in demand may not make as much placement effort as workshops working with individuals with marginal productivity and behavior.

Probably the majority of workshops allot some staff time to placement. The amount varies because most often the placement duty is assigned to a counselor. Where the counselor has a large counseling load, his placement activities are limited. In a minority of workshops, usually large ones, full-time placement men are employed. Until the 1960's, the placement responsibility rested with individual staff members, most often the counselor. After 1960, some workshops began using contract procurement men or salesmen as part-time placement officers. Because of their knowledge of industrial and business needs, they proved successful in making placements.

The principal development in placement activities, however, took place in placement training. Extensive training programs were developed whose purpose was to train handicapped applicants to secure jobs effectively. They were trained to make effective applications, to appear appropriately dressed for interviews, and to make the most favorable presentation of their qualifications in interviews. Role playing is used, and at times motion picture tapes are made to demonstrate effective and faulty techniques to prospective job applicants.

Personal Development Habilitation Programs

Many of the individuals in work adjustment programs had work experiences and failed during their employment. Another group of individuals that come into workshops have never had work experience. Nor have they had adequate life experiences necessary to enable them to work. Whitehouse described the program that the latter need as being "habilitation" (26), as contrasted with rehabilitation. The individuals need education in fundamental capabilities, knowledge, experiences, and attitudes. This type of program may require a program of long duration (27).

The individuals who need habilitation or a long-term developmental program may be enabled to work in industry after a long training period, or they may never be able to work in industry. In spite of the vast array of predictive instruments which are available, it is still not possible to determine with precision the potential of individuals whose development has been seriously arrested. Therefore, such individuals are placed in long-term habilitation programs. The program treats deficit areas in the life of the individual on the assumption that improvement in these areas may create employability, but it will in any case develop independent and mature living and will enable the individual to work more meaningfully and productively in sheltered employment (28).

Because the treatment given those with higher potential resembles with some additions the components described previously in the training model of personal adjustment, the habilitation outline will deal exclusively with those who are less able and who are not expected to work in industry. The programs for them may be classified in the following areas:

Personal and social maturity. Development of mature relationships with peers, staff, family and friends, and acceptable social attitudes.

Use of leisure time. Development of recreational programs during free time when work tolerance is limited in paid day work programs. Development of ability to handle free time with maturity and good social relations.

Development of personal independence and maturity. Development of regular living patterns with proper eating habits, cleanliness, and grooming. Development of household skills and activities of daily living.

Vocational competence. Development of awareness of work requirements and discipline:

1. Proper attendance, work consistency, and work rhythms.
2. Acceptance and tolerance of criticism.
3. Acceptance of authority figures and peer relationships.
4. Development of full-day work tolerance.
5. Work-pay relationships and use of money.
6. Development of work speed and accuracy.

Remedial education. Teaching of needed communication symbols as counting, reading signs, understanding production requirements.

Not many individuals needing the programs indicated above are likely to become productive workers in industry. Therefore, some hold these programs do not come under the rubric of workshops. Experience has shown, however, that some needing services described above can perform acceptably in industry. Furthermore, others unable to perform in industry can work at a productive level in a long-term workshop. The less able handicapped individuals will need workshops for longer periods than those who can more rapidly move to industry.

The Improvement of Physical and Mental Functioning Programs

Since the 1920's, when the curative workshops were established, formal programs in physical and occupational therapy have probably diminished as a percent of programs in workshops. There remain occupational therapy programs in 16 percent of workshops and physical therapy programs in 9 percent of workshops (29). However, the physical improvement function has sometimes moved onto the production floor of the workshop and the occupational therapist has often changed his habitat. In general, physical improvement programs occur most often in workshops in rehabilitation centers, chronic care facilities, and homes for the aged.

More difficult to enumerate are the programs dealing with improvement in mental illness. In the 1960's, there was an increase in workshop programs in mental hospitals, but because of diverse terminology and rationale, it is difficult to identify workshop programs in this category. Often hospital workshops combine a variety of objectives in one program. Also, there is no comprehensive enumeration or description of community workshop programs serving the mentally ill exclusively. However, by the time this book goes to press, Bertram J. Black will have published his book *Principles of Industry Therapy,* a work which deals with the major developments in this field (30).

Behavior Modification and Operant Conditioning Programs in Workshops

In a few workshops in the country, conditioning programs using specific reinforcement techniques have been used. Apparently no general study of these programs in workshops exists. Experimental programs have been conducted and theories have been advanced as has been indicated previously. It is conjectured from oral responses at a National Rehabilitation Association conference meeting in New York in 1969, that there were at least a scattering of workshops using such programs or planning to use them. Because of the recent origin of these programs in workshops, it is probably premature to describe them in detail.

However, from observation in field visits, we can report that two general types of conditioning programs are being tried in workshops. They are the token economy system and the step system. Presumably, operant conditioning programs exist in workshops which are individualized in application, but we are aware of few accounts of them (31).

The token economy system consists of a series of tokens, usually material objects, which are given to individuals in workshops upon the performance of desired behavior. Conversely, tokens are taken away for unacceptable behavior. The tokens are convertable into a variety of desired rewards including money, creature comforts, privileges, and whatever may be highly desired by the individuals. These token are available more immediately than wages and thus provide a more spontaneous reward (32).

The second system which has been observed is the step system. This as observed is a combination of a pay system and a reinforcement system. A schedule of pay and privilege is set up based on a series of steps. The requirements for the pay rate and privilege at each step are sometimes published. Thus at the lowest rate of pay and privilege the requirements are minimal and few, at the highest rate of pay exacting and many. In this system, pay is not determined directly by productivity although rates of productivity may be required in the steps. Other kinds of performance can also determine the step levels and rewards. The system seems to be found in workshops in mental hospitals and in workshops for the retarded.

It is quite possible to combine the step system and the token economy system, paying wages in accordance with step requirements, and tokens for other types of required behavior. A merit of either system is the attempt to quantify performance and behavior.

SUPPORTIVE SERVICES IN WORKSHOPS

Regardless of the nature of a workshop, whether it is a long-term or short-term shop, it usually has some activities other than assessment services which are not related to activities on the floor of the shop in the production of work. These supportive services relate to various life problems of persons served, which may or may not directly affect the work on the floor. These services are labeled "people services" rather than rehabilitative services because workshops sometimes maintain people at a constant level or alleviate their distress when their functions are declining. Workshops organize and extend people services in a variety of ways and in varying amounts. Some render them incidentally and superficially, and others, in carefully developed, well-staffed supportive programs. Thus the services may be rendered incidentally by industrial foremen or personnel officers, or more substantially by professionally trained persons in rehabilitation counseling, social work, psychology, or occupational therapy. In the account which follows, these services will be labeled by the nature of the function and not by the training of the incumbent in the job. Thus he who counsels will be called a counselor whether he has been trained as a rehabilitation counselor, social worker, psychologist, teacher, or occupational therapist.

Existing descriptions of the nature of people services in workshops generally are vague. They are usually statements of philosophy, goals, and needs of individuals rather than specific outlines of technique and methods (33). The many descriptions of individual programs are highly individualized and are usually of large, well-financed programs which are atypical. In general, supportive services take these courses:

Support counseling for work floor. Direct intervention with the individual around his behavior and attitudes as shown on the floor, elicited by floor supervision, recorded by observers, and related by co-workers.

Consultative service. Supportive staff advises, guides, and directs floor staff in handling of immediate problems, development of approaches to on-going problems in relationships.

Assistance to the individual. Supportive staff undertakes to help with personal problems such as housing, transportation, recreation and social events, purchasing, and credit.

Social intervention. Involvement of the family, friends, employer, social and recreational organization, social welfare agencies, health agencies, and other groups associated with or needed by the individual in the solution of his problems or fulfillment of needs.

Direct therapeutic intervention. Verbal intervention with the individual to change attitudes or modify behavior in one or several aspects of his life. The rationale here is the holistic approach which assumes that all aspects of life are interrelated and that improvement in general behavior and attitudes will influence favorably accomplishment of workshop objectives. In some instances, the staff member will engage in psychotherapy.

Although many of these activities take place in some workshops, the amount of them which takes place is probably not as great as is assumed. The Cornell Regional Rehabilitation Research Institute has found that professional personnel have relatively infrequent contact with handicapped individuals in the workshops they studied (34). This corresponds with our observation that professional staff spend much time in off floor activities in intake, staffing, consultation, report writing, and involvement of referral agency personnel. An exception to this statement is usually the counselor in a workshop providing short-term services.

The Role of the Counselor

Perhaps the individual supportive staff member closest to the individual in the workshop is the counselor. Where the counselor is the case manager, i.e. the staff member who follows the individual throughout his stay in the shop and coordinates services for him, he is the staff member the individual sees regularly throughout his stay in the shop. Where the individual goes from unit to unit without a case manager, the counselor may still have continuity of relationship with the individual. Of the five supportive services enumerated before, the counselor may participate in all except perhaps therapeutic intervention, but in some places he may even engage in an attempt to modify the worker's general behavior in life. As a rule, the counselor is most likely to work with the individual's attitudes and behavior as related to his activities in the workshop.

Although the counselor may relate his counseling to the day-to-day performance of the individual on the floor, his major interest is in the individual's attitudes towards himself, towards work, towards supervision and co-workers. In the course of the individual's work in the shop, he may experience frustration, confrontation, failure, and criticism, and he may react aggressively, immaturely, or defensively or by withdrawal and passivity. The job of the counselor is to interpret what has happened to the individual and to explain to him the necessities of the work situation so that he may attempt to learn to respond appropriately in his relationship in the work setting. In doing so, the counselor indicates his expectations that the individual will be able to make the required responses and develop the confidence and self-respect which is an essential contribution of the workshop to the individual. If the individual is unable to meet requirements initially, the counselor arranges to alter the situation so that he may have a grace period in which to do so. If he cannot meet work requirements ultimately, the counselor tries to work out another type of program for him.

The counselor may often be the individual's friend at court and advocate when the floor supervisor or foreman is making demands on him. However, ultimately the counselor, too, attempts to get the individual to make efforts at improvement in behavior and attitudes in his own interest. As a rule, however, the counselor in a workshop engages in overt manifestations of behavior. If intervention in depth in subconscious factors is undertaken in the workshop, it is usually undertaken by the psychologist or social worker usually with the consultation of a psychiatrist.

In addition to counseling the individual, in workshops where the organization receives a large volume of referrals from the state vocational rehabilitation agency, the counselor may serve as coordinator of relationships with the state agency for the individuals in his caseload. He may also write assessment and progress reports.

The Role of the Social Worker

The function of social services in workshops varies greatly depending upon the type of workshop. In workshops in rehabilitation centers, there is usually a social service unit which renders considerable services. In medium size or large freestanding community workshops, the social service worker often coordinates intake services and provides the personal assistance services described previously. Often the social worker provides social intervention, handling relationships with the families of individuals served and with social and health agencies serving the individual or his family. In some workshops, social workers provide personal and social counseling and less often engage in therapeutic intervention in depth, usually with psychiatric consultation.

The Role of the Psychologist

Staff members trained in the discipline of psychology perform many functions in workshops other than those of the formal practicing psychologist. They are foremen, counselors, shop supervisors, and often workshop directors. When the psychologist is not an administrator, counselor or foreman, he often has a number of roles. When the workshop provides a complete psychological work-up to the state vocational agency, he is responsible for writing it. He also serves as a consultant to floor staff and participates in staffing. At times he provides personal counseling and conducts group discussion or group therapy sessions. He often develops new programs for shops and is usually found in research and development units in large shops when they have such programs. In general, the psychologist, whether in the role of psychologist or workshop director, contributes to the theoretical or conceptual basis of the workshop's operations.

Medical Services in Workshops

Few workshops have comprehensive medical services, although many use part-time physicians who either make general examinations or serve as consultants or both. The exceptions are workshops in rehabilitation centers or chronic care hospitals where medical staffs and physical restoration services are available or where workshops are serving individuals with chronic diseases such as tuberculosis or cardiac conditions. The workshop ordinarily gets medical reports from previous medical care facilities, and if treatment is going on elsewhere, the individual is encouraged to continue this service. The staff then develops communication with the medical facility serving the individual. Often the workshop staff discovers that the individual has symptoms that need medical investigation, and referral is made for appropriate medical services with the advice of the medical consultant when one is available.

SUMMARY

Workshops serve a variety of different kinds of handicapped persons. The objectives they have for them depend not as much on the nature of their disabilities as on the severity of their handicaps or their potential level of functioning. Depending upon the kinds of people they serve and their objectives, workshops engage in various activities to reach the results possible for them in light of their potential.

The activities of workshops can be divided into two categories — basic programs and supportive services. These may also be designated as continuous or intermittent activities. The intermittent supportive services are assistive in nature. They consist of assessment and services to people. They generally support the programs which achieve the objectives for the persons in the shops.

The programs in the shops provide the following:

1. Personal development for persons with arrested development.
2. Physical and mental conditioning for those who need such conditioning.
3. Preparation for employment for those who are not ready or able to work satisfactorily.
4. Vocational training for those who can be trained in skilled occupations.
5. Sheltered employment for the stigmatized or alienated, for

marginal and low producers, and those with declining functioning.

Workshops may engage in one or in any combination of the above programs. They also engage in assessment and in various kinds of supportive services such as counseling, social work, and psychological services. Typical workshops combine one or more of the above programs with one or several of the supportive services.

NOTES

1. Button, W. H.: Sheltered Workshops in the United States — an Institutional Overview. Ithaca, Regional Rehabilitation Institute, Cornell University, 1969.
2. Johnson, J. A.: The Pros and Cons of Terminal Employment in Sheltered Workshops. In Chouinard, E. and Garrett, J. F. (Eds.): Workshops for the Disabled. Washington, Department of Health, Education, and Welfare, Office of Vocational Rehabilitation, 1956, pp. 147-152.
3. Button, W. H., op.cit., 1970, p. 25. Nelson, N.: Census of Workshop Clients, 1964. Sacramento, California Vocational Rehabilitation Service.
4. Button, W. H.: Wage Levels in Sheltered Employment, Table 3. Ithaca, Regional Rehabilitation Research Institute, Cornell University, 1967.
5. A study by Kimberly, J. R. (A Systems Approach to Typology Construction. Ithaca, Rehabilitation Research Institute, Cornell University, undated, suggests a typology based on organizational models. However, his work had not been published at the time this was written.
6. There is some general information in Button, W. H.: Sheltered Workshops in the United States — an Institutional Overview, Rehabilitation, Sheltered Workshops, and the Disadvantaged, 1970, pp. 28-34.
7. Button, W. H., Ibid, Table 8. p. 29.
8. For a more detailed discussion of the impact of assessment see Button, W. H., Sheltered Workshops in the United States — an Institutional Overview, 1969, pp. 32-33. Overs, Robert B.: Vocational evaluation: research implications. Journal of Rehabilitation, pp. 19-20, January-February, 1970.
9. Tower: Testing, Organization, and Work Evaluation. New York, Institute for Crippled and Disabled, 1967, p. 25.
10. Miller, M.: Work Evaluation Manual for Goodwill Industries. Washington, Goodwill Industries of America, 1968, pp. 1-4.
11. Crouse, P. B.: The Development of Work Sampling at Morrison Center. San Francisco, Institute on Work Evaluation, May T. Morrison Center for Rehabilitation and San Francisco State College, 1959, pp. 29-51. Work Samples, Sign Posts on the Road to Occupational Choice. Philadelphia, Jewish Employment and Vocational Service.

12. Bannister, Mrs. H. F. and Overs, R. P.: Obtaining and Using Actual Job Samples in a Work Evaluation Program. Cleveland, Vocational Guidance and Rehabilitation Services, 1964.

13. Work Samples, Sign Posts on the Road to Occupational Choice, op.cit., pp. 1-23.

14. Button, W. H.: Sheltered Workshops in the United States, An Institutional Overview, Rehabilitation, Sheltered Workshops, and the Disadvantaged, 1970, table 8, p. 29.

15. Sheltered Workshop Report of the Secretary of Labor. Washington, Department of Wage and Hour and Public Contracts Division, 1967, p. 2.

16. Sheltered Workshop Report, op.cit. Sheltered Workshops: A Study of Wage Payments to Handicapped Clients in Sheltered Workshops Certificated Under the Fair Labor Standard Act. Washington, Department of Labor, Wage and Hours and Public Contracts, 1969. Button, W. H.: Wage Levels in Sheltered Workshops. Ithaca, Rehabilitaion Research Institute, Cornell University, 1967.

17. Sheltered Workshop Report, op.cit., p. 13.

18. Ibid., p. 8.

19. Button, W. H. Wage Levels in Sheltered Employment, 1967. See summary, op.cit.

20. Public Law 89-333, 89th Congress, H.R. 8310, November 8, 1965, Section 13(a) (1).

21. Massie, W.: Personal communication on training services grants, March 13, 1970.

22. Instructions for Applicants for Training Services Grants. Washington, Department of Health, Education, and Welfare, Vocational Rehabilitation Administration, 1967, pp. 2-9.

23. An Evaluation Study and Demonstration Work Experience for the Mentally Retarded During Their Last Year in Public School. Milwaukee, Jewish Vocational Service and Department of Health, Education, and Welfare, 1964. Work Experience Center, Habilitation of the Retarded. St. Louis, Jewish Employment and Vocational Service, 1967.

24. For a description of job site training, see Bitter, J. A.: Work Experience Center. St. Louis, Jewish Vocational Service, 1967, pp. 3-4, 7-8, 14, 16.

25. The above model is idealized. However, an analogous structure may be found in Linde, T. F.: A Manual of Work adjustment of the Jewish Vocational Service. Milwaukee, Wisconsin, undated.

26. Whitehouse, F. A.: Habilitation concept and process. Journal of Rehabilitation, (19) (2), pp. 3-7, 1953.

27. Bitter, J. A.: Training Guide for Vocational Habilitation. St. Louis, Jewish Employment and Vocational Service, 1966.

28. Katz, E.: The Retarded Adult in the Community. Springfield, Charles C Thomas, 1968, pp. 136-149.

29. Button, W. H. Sheltered Workshops in the U. S. A. An Institution Overview, 1970, table 8, p. 29.

30. Black, B. J.: Principles of Industrial Therapy for the Mentally Ill. New York and London, Grune and Stratton, 1970.
31. Zimmerman, J., Overpeck, C., Essenberg, H. and Garlich, B.: Operant conditioning in a sheltered workshop, further data in support of an objective and systematic approach to rehabilitation. Rehabilitation Literature, pp. 326-333, November, 1969. Johnson, R. F., Haughton, E. and Lafave, H. G.: Behavior therapy — use in a sheltered workshop. Diseases of the Nervous System, pp. 350-354, June, 1965. Crosson, J. E.: A technique for programming sheltered workshop environments for training severely retarded adults. American Journal of Mental Deficiency, March, 1969.
32. Zimmerman, J., Stuckey, J. E., Garlich, B. T., and Miller, M.: Rehabilitation Literature. February, 1969. Moriarity, F. M.: A Token Economy Program for Chronic Schizophrenic Patients. Topeka, V. A. Hospital, mimeographed. Moriarity, F. M., and McAllister, L. W.: The Efficacy of Social vs. Token Reinforcement on an Operant Conditioning Hospital Ward. Paper read at the Thirteenth Annual Conference, V. A. Cooperative Studies in Psychiatry, Denver, Colorado, April 1968. Roberts, C. L. and Perry, R. M.: A total token economy. Mental Retardation, pp. 15-18, February 1970.
33. Devereaux, J.: The Nature of Rehabilitation Services in a Workshop. Chouinard, E. L. and Garrett, J. F. (Eds.): Workshops for the Disabled — A Vocational Rehabilitation Resource. Washington, Department of Health, Education, and Welfare, Office of Vocational Rehabilitation, 1956, pp. 34-46. Sheltered Workshops, A Handbook. Washington, National Association of Sheltered Workshops and Homebound Programs, Inc., 1966, pp. 9-10, 30-31.
34, Lubow, B. K., Kimberly R. P., Button, W. H. and Kimberly, J. R.: Client Behavior in Sheltered Workshops: Two Case Studies. Ithaca, Rehabilitation Research Institute, Cornell University, 1969, pp. 30, 45, 52.

XII

THE ORGANIZATION OF WORKSHOPS

As one approaches a review of workshop organization it readily becomes apparent that the subject has scarcely been studied in any formal sense by workshop personnel. There has been much talk about administrative problems at organizational meetings and institutes for workshop personnel. It is therefore necessary to describe the total organizational universe so that what is not covered may be understood.

By the term *organization* is meant the arrangement of the various parts of the workshop as they function in an interrelation to each other and to the whole. Included would be the total population of the workshop regardless of status or activity and the technology and ecology of the workshop, whatever the nature or function. At this point, it is not intended to be precise about the requirement of objectives. Although workshops often have vague, general goals and purposes rather than precise objectives, these apparently satisfy most legal requirements for incorporation, so they will serve for present descriptive purposes. Neither will the question of formal organization be raised (1). Some workshops' formal structures provide vague indications of meaningful interrelationships, which are influenced as well by changing informal structures.

From the previous statement that little formal analysis has been made of workshops' organization and from the general scope and nature of the above description of organization, it will be apparent that the purpose of this chapter is to search for the edges of the surface, rather than to scratch it.

In the past, the major preoccupation of sponsors and administrators of workshops has been the needs of handicapped persons. When they thought about how these needs could best be met, they considered goals and philosophies, theories and methodology, and more lately the roles and functions of respective personnel. It was

306

not until the decade of the 1960's that workshop directors began giving systematic attention to their total organizations as a means of effecting their goals, and even then their efforts, with some exceptions (2), were minimal.

An important force in directing the attention of workshop personnel to organizational problems was the study and publication of standards in the period from 1958 to 1967. However, the major emphasis of the standards set by the accreditation groups prescribed administrative criteria. The problems connected with the implementation of the standards called attention to the need for broad scale study and analysis of existing and potential workshop structure. More recently, university programs in workshop administration have undertaken such studies. Initial publications suggest that these investigations have considerable potential (3).

Since there is little literature or extensive doctrine specific to workshop organization, what can be achieved by a discussion? Perhaps an analysis of the reasons why workshop personnel neglect organizational analysis may suggest clues to what is needed in developing organizational concepts. Also a comparative historical analysis of organizational development provides a helpful background for the understanding of workshop structure. In the historic and current analysis, the application of knowledge from other fields such as management, sociology, and anthropology will prove relevant. However, since none of the above analyses can be presently based on extensive research, any generalizations are conjectures based on historical development or observation of present day structure. Thus, the general statements which follow are somewhat in the nature of tentative assumptions to be used until they can be established or replaced. It is hoped that what is conjectured proves helpful in suggesting the areas of workshop organization that need study and definitive conceptualization.

THE REASONS FOR PAUCITY OF CONCEPTS

Since workshop personnel are generally conscientious and dedicated individuals usually given to rational thinking, it may be necessary to explain the absence of organization conceptualization by them. One reason may be that workshops were established and operated by professional practitioners: physicians, clergymen, teachers, social workers, occupational therapists, psychologists, rehabilitation counselors, and other individual practitioners. Their general orientation supports the belief that success with people results from an individual practitioner or a series of individual practitioners focusing on the problems of one person. It is commonly held that the clients will be well served if each member of the staff has the right philosophy and goals and is well trained. This orientation diverts attention from the whole organization and its subparts. It results in the assumption that freedom of action of the staff members best achieves client goals. Minimized in this orientation is the concept that organization structure other than the interrelationships between individual practitioners and their clients influences program outcomes.

This orientation has been reinforced by customary ways of thinking in the field of rehabilitation from which many workshop personnel come. Albert F. Wessen notes that there is relatively little analysis of rehabilitation services, that "rehabilitation has not yet been crystallized in a typical organizational format" (4). Those whose training was in rehabilitation had not usually been alerted to the importance of organizational structure to program results. They often did not commit time and thought to new organizational concepts because they had little awareness of their importance.

As a result of their orientation, workshop personnel did not develop a concept of workshop organization consistent with both the ideology of service to the individual and the nature of the workshop's basic components. They assumed the workshop was a professional organization, usually of the type with which they were familiar (5). Workshop organizations developed a number of definitions of workshops which varied from time to time but whose main thrust was to emphasize goals and philosophy. These definitions ignored organizational components. Workshop personnel studied and developed many classifications of workshops but finally settled on two which were statements of goals — transitional and extended employment workshops. Discussion of workshop organization was usually limited to informal considerations of specific administrative problems. Basic concepts dealing with the nature of workshops were ultimately stated by those who were on the periphery of workshops when they developed their ideas — users of workshops, men with business orientation, and personnel of schools of workshop administration. Until these basic concepts of the nature of workshops were developed, organizational concepts were not possible.

THE DUALITY OF THE WORKSHOP

An early statement of the basic nature of the workshops was made by the writer in 1964: "If a workshop uses real work and has rehabilitation objectives, it may be described as a business enterprise whose objective is the rehabilitation of its enrollees. Thus it has two types of activities: work or business activities, and training or rehabilitation activities .... The art of the workshop director consists of skillfully combining the business half and the rehabilitation half into a harmonious whole" (6).

Daniel Wolinsky, a certified public accountant working with Altro Workshop of New York City, suggested that existing definitions (1968) could be more clearly expressed if the duality of the workshop was recognized. He defined a workshop as a "socio-economic institution that deals with two products: the items it makes, packages, or distributes, and the handicapped people it serves." In describing administrative structure he indicated, "I have in mind . . . a blending of business practice as it exists in industry with the vocational and rehabilitation goals of the workshop" (7).

John W. Christensen, Chairman of the National Policy and Performance Council which sets standards for workshops, stated a similar concept: "A workshop is a business enterprise. There is no excuse from a social agency standpoint for a poor business operation and from the business side for a poor social operation. These twin goals are not mutually exclusive. They work together. The communication between these two divisions is an important factor in the success of the organization" (8).

The Cornell Rehabilitation Institute group of researchers, using a systems approach, described the workshop in more comprehensive, technical terminology as consisting of two sub-systems.

> What became apparent to us as we became more familiar with the operation of sheltered workshops was the fact that there were at least two subsystems of activity which could be abstracted from the concrete systems of behavior in any workshop. The first of these, the production sub-system, includes the activities, materials, processes, and people involved in the production of goods and services. The second of these, the rehabilitation sub-system, includes the activities, materials, processes and people involved in the modification of client behavior (9).

TOWARDS AN ORGANIZATIONAL DEFINITION

Though these concepts recognized the dual nature of workshop organization, they did not constitute formal definitions useful from an organizational point of view. A definition consistent with organizational concept is essential. Such a tentative definition is suggested now by the writer as a basis for future study.

> A workshop for the handicapped is a private nonprofit corporation or public organization which coordinates and utilizes sociology and technology of business operations and the services to people in a controlled work setting to enable handicapped and disadvantaged individuals to achieve defined work and work-related objectives.

The above definition contains elements new to workshop personnel. Previous definitions emphasized the content or nature of goals. In this definition, the nature of objectives is not defined. The objectives of workshops vary. The definition merely indicates that objectives should exist without indicating what they should be. The word technology may also be new to workshop personnel as it is applied to services to people. Perhaps it should be understood as being similar to systematic professional methodologies and techniques and may also include such instruments as teaching machines and the computer as they are used in processes of rendering services to people.

THE CHARACTERISTICS OF
ORGANIZATIONAL STRUCTURE

Having suggested that workshop personnel have not given major theoretical attention to organizational concepts, there follows the responsibility to find out how workshops developed organizational structure. It has been indicated previously that workshops often assumed functions that other social institutions were not providing. Often when a workshop supplemented certain institutional services, it took on the organizational pattern or an analogous pattern of the institution it was augmenting. Thus when a workshop augmented an institution with social functions, it followed at first the social agency format, or when it supplemented school functions, it assumed the organizational pattern of the school. However, almost immediately some basic variations had to be made to accommodate the work setting. Often changes continued to be made but they continued in different ways and influenced different organizational components. A frequent modification was towards an industrial model. But different industrial and people-service characteristics from different models were assumed from time to time in keeping with organizational perceptions, philosophy and goals, and historical, legal, technical, political, and social developments.

As the organizational development of workshops is traced, it may be well to keep in mind some of the characteristics to look for. In this process, a great handicap will be the difficulty in going back in time and studying characteristics when facts are not available. Clues will be used from characteristics about which there is little information. One source of information is the professional training of the directors and the administrative elite of workshops. Since workshop models have a heavy people-service component, the training of their personnel signals a significant ideological orientation.

Another topic in a schedule for organizational review will be the analysis of possible similarity between the workshop structure and other well-developed institutional structures such as the school, the hospital, the charitable or social work agency, and the industrial firm.

A third organizational characteristic to be observed will be the relationship and status of the various groups in the workshop population, the board, staff groups, and workers. Important here will be the class structure or integrative apparatus – the possibility of vertical movement. Closely related is another characteristic to be followed — the specific administration apparatus of the workshop.

As the organizational development is followed, two growth concepts can be tested. Albert F. Wessen has suggested an organizational perception model based on the ideas of James A. Wilson, which seeks to explain organization growth on two contrasting conceptions — a scarcity-fear approach and an abundance-innovation concept. The first is a "politics of scarcity," the second a "politics of abundance." The former perception, one arising out of insecurity of resources, devalues opportunity and reacts to challenge defensively. The latter arising out of adequate resources, reacts to opportunity with commitment and to challenge with adaptiveness or cooperation (10).

A different hypothesis is suggested by Arthur Stinchcombe. He suggests that organizational structure is determined by the time in history when the organization is started. He believes that the circumstance at the time when the organization is started makes a certain structure viable. The success of the structure tends to influence the organization to maintain that structure without subsequent change (11).

Although Stinchcombe's and Wesson's theories will be tested to explain development, another explanation of development of structure will also be kept in mind. That has to do with the influence of external and internal forces on organization (12). In workshop organizations, the influence of organizations of handicapped persons, of societies for special disability groups, of parent organizations, of the state-federal programs of vocational rehabilitation, of Federal Wage and Hour laws, and other social and political external forces may have influenced organization from time to time. So also may ideologies of staff be derived from professional philosophy. These external and internal factors may influence selection of goals and create goal displacement (13).

Another approach has been suggested by John R. Kimberly. He indicates that in general there are relationships between organizational environment, organizational orientation, and organizational structure. He believes that by knowing organizational orientation, one may predict organizational characteristics. His approach differs from previous concepts discussed, however, in requiring that the analysis be made at a recent point in time so that characteristics of many workshops may be adequately analyzed simultaneously (14).

Finally, some consideration needs to be given to the influence of technology — the development of new work or work methods or in use of machine tools on the production side, and of techniques or methods on the people-services side. These developments also affect organization in that they change the importance and status of personnel and of need to redefine people relationships.

THE DEVELOPMENT OF ORGANIZATIONAL STRUCTURE

The Workshops for the Blind

The first workshops in the United States, the workshops for the blind, were started after 1838 in residential schools and homes for the blind. The shops followed British precedent. The original objective of the workshop was to train the blind for occupations in industry. Consequently, the staff were often teachers of the blind. Since these teachers were not industrially trained, they continued instruction in the tasks they knew — principally the making of brooms, mops, brushes, mattresses, and chair caning. In the beginning these workshops adopted organizational forms similar to schools, although an occasional industrial man was hired to merchandize the manufactured products. However, the blind did not usually get jobs as a result of their training and returned to the school shops to work permanently. Thus, the shops early became places of employment for the blind. In this instance, the goal changed because of the failure of the original goal. With this change, they assumed a structure more industrial in nature. However, they usually maintained their teachers as instructors and continued the manufacture of their same old products.

An important difference in structure developed, however, between the public and private workshops for the blind during the twentieth century. The private workshop maintained more flexibility in promotion of workers to supervisorial positions than the public shops when the latter came under the influence of civil service procedures or were influenced by political considerations. Thus the private shops usually had more vertical upward movement than the public shops.

In the first decades of the twentieth century, both types of shop clung rigidly to the manufacture of the few same products, which they usually sold door to door sometimes on a sympathy basis. The result of the limited work tasks and small wages led to dissatisfaction among the workers. Both types of shops received the disparagement of the organizations for the blind, but little change took place until outside organizations were able to secure the passage of the Wagner O'Day Act in 1938. This added new products sold to the government and made it necessary for the shops to respond to volume and delivery schedules posed by outside forces, and required the development of new capability and the use of new machine tools. This combination made industrial personnel and organization essential. The shops which had already been moving to the industrial format now assumed a more comprehensive industrial-type organization. This was developed in a more specialized and technical sense when the National Industries for the Blind developed a more comprehensive system of merchandising, including rack selling and expansion of products in the 1960's. However, not all workshops for the blind were members of the National Industries for the Blind. Some workshops for the blind continued with the old products and operated at a lower level of technology.

Thus workshops for the blind changed slowly from a school structure with teachers as key personnel in the beginning in the nineteenth century to a more industrially oriented organization with industrial personnel, especially after the passage of the Wagner O'Day Act in 1938. One group of workshops for the blind developed as one goal a greater variety of products. Another group continued with the old technology. The changes in this organizational development took place slowly as a result of external pressures which resulted in a more varied technology in the first group of shops which required even more knowledgeable industrial personnel. This personnel ultimately emphasized the necessity of more varied products and modern sales methods. The success of this industrially oriented program resulted in turn in better wages.

It did not, however, satisfy all blind workers, especially in public shops where in some places workers organized and struck not only for increased wages and fringe benefits but also for more status and a more participatory labor union role in the organization (15). Also it had little influence on the organizations who maintained their old technology and traditional products.

In general, the structure of the workshops for the blind may be understood by how they responded to external pressures. These external pressures came from organizations for the blind, technology, and public policy. Their organizational perception has varied. Some organizations developed flexible work programs and included supportive specialized services. It has been principally one of a defensive posture until possibly the last decade, when larger numbers developed a less defensive stance. It is not clear that their organizational structure was based on characteristics of its time of birth, since its personnel, products, services, and organizational structure did change at given times due to external pressures, even though such changes were relatively infrequent historically. The goals they have maintained since shortly after their birth were continued because of constant pressure from organizations for the blind primarily, who insisted that they provide as a minimum an adequate place of sheltered employment for those blind who desired to work and were unable to find work in industry (16).

The Renovating Workshops

The renovating workshops founded by religious organizations brought new kinds of organizational structure into the workshop field, although all began originally with the same product — the discard. Their differences, however, were considerable.

The Society of St. Vincent de Paul was influenced organizationally by two men — St. Vincent de Paul and Frederick Ozanam. St. Vincent de Paul had organized lay groups of men and women to carry on social assistance activities. Ozanam carried out the lay concept of St. Vincent and added the admonition that the receiver of the gift of help be treated with respect. This led to the creation of an organization based on the lay social worker as the key member of the organization. These served either as volunteers or paid staff. In this respect the organization was unique among early organizational forms. This then led readily to a change to an industrial format. The lay, untrained social worker was as well equipped to function commercially as socially. He was probably responsible also for the organization's lack of categorical emphasis on disability or poverty as a basis for help and may explain the broad basis of the agency's acceptance of people with many kinds of problems.

The Salvation Army, on the other hand, is a highly structured organization based on a military format. The clergyman-officer is the key personnel both as administrator or practitioner. His mission is essentially spiritual or social service. The recipient of services, the beneficiary, has a status distinct from the officer staff — he is the receiver of benefits and as such plays a reactive role. He may, however, be given a permanent job in the industrial or commercial phases of the operations, in which case limited advancement is possible.

The stability of the Salvation Army is an important characteristic. In many essentials, it still operates in the spirit of the blueprint of William Booth, though there have been exceptions, such as the use of professional personnel. To achieve its early objectives, it often fought the establishment, and it has resisted external pressures. Thus, its goals, technology, and administrative structure, with the exception of use of professional personnel as consultants, has remained relatively constant. In this respect, it follows Stinchcombe's principle that an organization maintains the characteristics current at the time of its founding. It has also maintained a consistent aggressive posture. What has probably influenced stability most was Booth's comprehensive plan and its military structure, seconded by his charisma, and whose influence has lasted nearly a hundred years. Goodwill Industries, by contrast, had local autonomy and no required plan; its growth was consequently more varied. It is interesting to note that the Salvation Army has retained the discard as its principal product while some Goodwills have developed subcontracting.

The success of the Salvation Army format was so impressive that when Ballington Booth, the son of William Booth, broke away to form a new organization, the Volunteers of America, he maintained the essential organizational characteristics of the Salvation Army. The principal difference administratively is that the Volunteers of America do not follow the directions of an international office.

The Goodwill Industries of America also started with the clergyman as the administrator and caseworker, but its organization was originally more church oriented than military in structure. It began with the clergyman in charge of a small paid lay staff and unpaid volunteers. Often, the clergyman sought the help of a businessman to create a "business with a heart." Over the years, however, the clergyman disappeared as the chief executive and the organization took on a more industrially oriented model. The executive came up from the administrative staff or was recruited from industry or commerce. In recent years, a professionally trained person was often recruited to coordinate services to people. The volunteer was given supplementary functions – not those in the industrial operations. The trainee could progress from trainee to worker status and could be promoted to supervisor status and on without limit. Thus the Goodwill Industries developed relatively more upward mobility than other renovating organizations.

The Goodwill Industries in their early history were relatively isolated from external pressures. About the middle of the twentieth century, they showed signs of influence from the public and private vocational rehabilitation movement and from the local community organizations. This change took place slowly and affected different units at different times. One result of this influence was that new types of personnel, at first mainly occupational therapists and later mainly vocational rehabilitation counselors, became part of the staff structure. Often there was substitution of a person trained in rehabilitation instead of industrial personnel for the personnel officer job. This trend was reinforced by the necessity of serving new groups – the retarded and the mentally ill.

A change, however, in Goodwill Industries came about as a result of technological progress. With the change in textiles towards synthetics and the mass production of household products in plastics at cheaper rates, the profitability and utility of the renovated discard were reduced. Some Goodwill Industries responded to this change and others did not. Those that did often enthusiastically embraced subcontracting. Where sophisticated subcontract operations were initiated, more industrially competent personnel and additional equipment were required. Thus the Goodwill that accepted both the influence of vocational rehabilitation and the desirability of the subcontracting found itself acquiring expertise in two directions — industry and rehabilitation. In the main, however, the balance remained in the industrial direction and employment competence was developed principally through exposure to work and not as much through verbal modalities. At the same time, upward mobility was generally maintained to develop a sociology of the workshop which was closer to industry than in many other workshop settings.

From the above account it can be surmised that no single growth theory explains the development of the Goodwill Industries. Goodwills generally maintained similar general goals since their inception. Local Goodwill Industries responded variously at different times in their history to the major changes discussed — the introduction of rehabilitation personnel, the initiation of services to new disability groups, and the adoption of subcontracting on a large scale. Some Goodwills responded defensively and others with commitment to opportunities from time to time.

The Early Community Workshops

About the same time that the workshops for the blind and the renovating workshops were developing their characteristic structures, another group of shops was starting which can be compared as a group organizationally, although they differed in many respects. This will include the workshops for the tubercular because some of them changed into multidisability shops enjoying community-wide support. This group started either with a social welfare orientation, a medical orientation, or an indigenous industrial organization. Most of them are labeled freestanding community workshops.

The first community workshop was the Community Workshops

of Boston, formed in 1884, to induce moral virtue through the intervention of visitors. Although work, under the supervision of a sewing instructress, was central to the program, the objectives were to be achieved by lay social workers who volunteered for the task. In 1915, both the Altro Workshop of New York City and the workshop of the Social Service Society of Brooklyn were established with a heavy component of social workers who were from the emerging profession at the time. Later the shops for the tubercular such as Lanikila Crafts in Honolulu started with occupational therapists as key personnel. A significant development took place when in 1935 the Federation for the Handicapped of New York and in 1942 the Sheltered Workshop for the Disabled, Inc., of Binghamton were founded on indigenous industrial principles. Both of the latter started with an industrial structure. It is uncertain how this group of shops developed their organizational concept, but by 1935 the Community Workshops of Boston had changed its social work orientation to become a more industrially oriented shop. It may be that some of the other shops used the Boston shop as a model.

Two other workshops whose administration was highly industrially oriented need mention. The first was the Disabled Employees Inc., of San Francisco, started in 1936 by employees of the State Bureau of Vocational Rehabilitation. Since the State employees worked full time, they left management of the shop at first to the handicapped employees, and some of them assumed managerial roles. This shop has existed since that time, with its original personnel in charge of the shop and with no professionally trained staff. It is operated as an industrial shop and provides principally employment for severely handicapped individuals. Much larger but originally developed by handicapped persons is Abilities, Inc., in Long Island, New York. This is a large establishment which does not call itself a workshop. It has been directed and operated by handicapped workers. Henry Viscardi has been the director since its inception. It also operates like an industrial organization, although it has professional staff in varying roles.

Several programs of this group have special structural characteristics. The Federation for the Handicapped of New York was started by handicapped persons and the Binghamton shop was started to duplicate industry as precisely as possible. The Community Workshops of Boston had a junior staff or cadre, usually selected from workers. More recently this nomenclature has been discontinued to make no distinctions between people in the shop. Thus it had a vertical movement of workers and a more industrial, social setting. At Abilities, Inc., handicapped persons are the administrators and board members.

After mid-century, the movement of the freestanding shops towards an industrial model was influenced in a reverse direction by the availability of money from state and federal vocational rehabilitation agencies and of some state subsidizing programs which made the money contingent on the existence of professionally trained rehabilitation personnel. Also influential was emphasis of the state-federal vocational agencies supporting short-term training services and requiring reporting in professional rehabilitation terminology rather than in industrial terminology. Most of the freestanding community shops which had started with people-service staff moved towards industrial staff, and then moved again to people-service staff of a rehabilitation coloration as a result of external forces.

The Influence of Work and Beliefs About Types of Work

One of the components common to most freestanding shops, and indeed to many shops prior to the middle of the twentieth century, was the emphasis on prime manufacturing or renovation and resale. This emphasis, as has been seen, made an initial trend towards an industrial model necessary. In light of the shift to subcontracting in the latter part of the twentieth century, one may conjecture that this initial manufacturing and renovation approach was made necessary by the nonexistence of the subcontracting industries that were the principal customers of latter workshops. These were the packaging industry, the electronics industry, and the aerospace and aircraft industries.

It is customary to assume that in the early stages of workshop development, the physically handicapped and blind were served because they were capable of doing the relatively skilled work required in prime manufacturing and that the mentally retarded and mentally ill were excluded because they could not do the work. That they were excluded is clear. That they could not do the work is uncertain. In any case, it is clear that it was believed that the mentally retarded and mentally ill could not do relatively skilled industrial work and that they were thus excluded. The workers of early workshops and the type of work may have been selected in accordance with early beliefs which were faulty. The ideas of program planners about disabilities and capabilities in relation to work determined workshop policies. Ideology, true or false, influenced the nature of work and workers.

Finally, a comment may be made on organizational growth and development. For all the groups of workshops discussed to this point, no general growth theory such as Wessen's or Stinchcombe's seems to explain the development of all workshop organizations. To the extent that the development can be explained in any general way, it seems that external factors influenced development most, although other theories do explain the development of some groups of workshops. The external factors that influenced development of organization were: the states of industrial technology (manufacturing vs. subcontracting), the cultural ideology — the social, political, and philosophic ideas from time to time as they expressed themselves in sponsoring groups and in public support and legislation (the vocational rehabilitation program), and the influence of organizations of disabled and their supporters (the organizations for special disability groups). These in turn influenced the ideas of workshop administrators who developed or accepted philosophy and theories as a basis for program concepts. Goals were generally influenced by disability groups served and existing beliefs about their potential.

THE ORGANIZATION OF WORKSHOPS IN REHABILITATION CENTERS

In the middle period of workshop development, a new organizational structure influenced workshops. This came about when other types of rehabilitation facilities included workshops in their organization as units. From 1920 to the middle of the century, vocational and medical rehabilitation centers included workshops in their programs. These workshops, as a unit of the larger whole, were a part of rehabilitation center organization.

The rehabilitation center, whether medically or vocationally oriented, may have developed because of the failure of the hospital system to provide appropriate environment in which to handle the residuals of disability after the active phases of illness were terminated. The hospital system, with its doctor-administrator or lay administrator who was divorced from medical programming, placed authority and medical direction in the hands of physicians and surgeons who gave orders to staff who executed them obediently for passive bed patients. Whatever may be the virtues of such a system in treating acute illness, it was not suited to handle the social, psychological, and vocational problems of persons who were no longer acutely ill. For the prescription a substitute had to be developed. During this period, the holistic or comprehensive service approach was developing which considered the findings of professionals from various disciplines necessary for service excellence. Except in physical restoration settings where the physician still held sway, the rehabilitation center often replaced the order of the physician with the concensus of a professional committee.

This shift in emphasis made a new structure necessary. Since decision making and authority were now multidisciplinary, considerable new autonomy was given to the disciplines. In large organizations, this meant a number of highly autonomous departments; in small organizations, highly autonomous professions. Management and housekeeping functions usually remained highly concentrated in the administrator, who sometimes also exercised program direction, depending on his training and inclinations. To coordinate the decisions affecting people served, the staffing or meeting of the professionals took place frequently. Often the chairman was the physician, or the program director, or the administrator. Formally he was usually first among equals, while informally the professionals vied for prestige and decision-making power.

When the workshop became part of the rehabilitation center, it was usually treated as another unit or department, with similar status and functional privileges of the others. This had potential both for good and bad as will be seen. Some of the workshop staff, the professionals, became eligible to join the prestigious and professionally satisfying staffing committee. However, sometimes the industrial staff were excluded, since they were not professionals. Administratively, the workshop unit often did not have the autonomy it needed to conduct its business operations, since there were the tradition of central management of nonprofessional activities and a scant recognition of the dual nature of the workshop unit. This difficulty was particularly acute in public agencies where expenditure control units were loath to relinquish prerogatives. Most important, however, was the fact that the center staffing, which provided a medium of communication, often did not include the industrial personnel of the workshop.

The introduction of the staffing principle was important not only to the rehabilitation center workshop but to the freestanding workshop and other workshops which adopted it. Primarily, its utility in general is that it provides communication across hierarchial lines. This was essential both in workshops in rehabilitation centers and elsewhere, but it made viable the rehabilitation center plan with highly autonomous departments or staff. Its utility was greatest where the staffing included foremen and leadmen and least effective where it was limited to personnel with learned pedigree.

But if the staffing technique aided communication, the reliance on professional staff often had a less salutary effect on the workshop. There seemed to be no need to apply any special techniques or organizational restructuring in the workshop in the rehabilitation center. It was another unit in the center staffed by professionals from other disciplines. Since the professionals often stressed verbal techniques, they did not emphasize the situational techniques necessary in a workshop and consequently did not respond organizationally to the demands of the situational or environmental approach of the workshop. It is conjectured that this is one of the reasons why the major growth in workshops after 1950 did not take place in rehabilitation centers but in workshops in separate environments. Another reason was the short term rehabilitative concept of the rehabilitation center which with some exceptions could not accommodate the individual whose needs were for gradual development or continuous services for long periods of time. The rehabilitation center was structured for a relatively high-cost, short-term program and could not easily accommodate a low-cost, long-term program.

The use of professionals in rehabilitation centers and in their workshops had another influence on workshop structure. The holistic approach and the professional team were widely accepted after 1950. Purchasers of services and later accrediting bodies required that the workshop have professionals but not usually skilled industrial personnel in key coordinating positions. As a result, the trend from professional to industrial staff in upper echelons which has been seen in the early period of workshop development was revised considerably in many workshop groups, and professionals were brought in even when the major numbers of the staff performed industrial functions. This had a tendency to develop a more stratified class orientation between professional and industrial workers and between the professional and "client." As a rule, the professional assumed a "client-centered" approach, which often meant that professionals chose a program for the individual with his involvement (17). Industrial personnel were typically more flexible in the extent of participation of the individual in the choice of his program. Although the rehabilitation center departed from the hospital model, its professionals retained residuals of the doctor-patient relationship.

In general, the rehabilitation center and its workshop operated under a relatively rigid ideological system. Its workshop was accordingly unable in general to respond to technical change nor did it respond to external pressures to the same extent that other workshops did. The sociology of its setting remained as a residual from its ancestral origins in the hospital, with professionals superceding the doctor while modifying his role considerably. Thus, many workshops in rehabilitation centers grew slowly, if at all, while a few broke away to form separate organizations. It may be said, however, that most workshops in rehabilitation centers maintain the structural characteristics of the time of their establishment and that their organizational perception as a rehabilitation unit was relatively rigid.

THE STRUCTURE OF THE WORK ADJUSTMENT SHOP

The work adjustment shop structure was originally evolved by Jewish Vocational Services, which had previously been exclusively vocational guidance and placement services in private voluntary agencies. Their administrative structure centered around the counselor and his supervisor, responsible to the director of the agency. When counselors proved unable to place or keep clients working, the workshop was set up to prepare them for employment. The problem was to decide how to develop a structure that would perform a different function, i.e. a work function, and at the same time keep the counselor or the counseling psychologist very much in the picture. One solution to this problem was to make the foreman and the counselor or counseling psychologist one and the same.

In light of the organizational strains which we have seen existed in other workshops between professional and industrial staff, the placement of the professional in the foreman's role was an ingenious conception. Since the professionally trained person could hardly be expected to have training or experience in industry, the work which he supervised had to be kept simple. This did not appear to be a handicap in the rationale, since the purpose of the shop was the development of adjustment to work, not occupational skills, and adjustment emphasizing social relationship in a work setting could be developed in simple work. The counselor-foreman could concentrate on the psychosocial components of work and produce a well-adjusted worker. The employer was considered willing to train his employee in the required occupational skills. It should be pointed out, however, that not all work adjustment shops used trained professional foremen.

The decision of many of these workshops to engage in simple work has had far-reaching consequences. The workshops have not been able to take advantage of the technological progress of the country to get more and more varied work. Furthermore, the simple work is often least lucrative, providing less wages for workers and less income for the organization. It has made some workshops more dependent on purchasers of services and charitable funds, which have proven at times unstable sources of financing. Workshops which have developed capability to do complex work have been able to secure a much larger portion of their revenue from contract income (18).

While work adjustment shops did not always place the professionals on the floor as foremen, they did, as a rule, use professionals in other roles such as counselors, psychologists, and social workers. In general, they adopted a communication structure similar to the rehabilitation center with the use of staffing. This added to the pressure for academic requirements for staff. Similar, too, was the relationship of the professional to the individual services, which required the maintenance of a professional-client relationship.

The work adjustment shop used a simple technology, maintained a sociology consisting of the professional-client relationship, and operated on a predetermined philosophy. They were somewhat subject to external pressures. In some cases, the Jewish Vocational Service adopted the long-term objectives of serving the aged in addition to their transitional objectives. It is surmised they were influenced by community desires in this respect. Generally, the work adjustment shops were influenced by the public vocational rehabilitation agency. The structure was influenced by the need to accept agency clients for income purposes. They conformed to agency standards for personnel and reporting. With these exceptions, their goals were relatively consistent and their perception one of commitment within their self-prescribed limits.

THE STRUCTURE OF WORKSHOPS
SPONSORED BY PARENT GROUPS

In the forties and fifties, parent groups developed first schools and then workshops to meet the needs of their children whom other social institutions neglected. The workshops developed differently in different places. In metropolitan areas, the workshops were larger and usually encompassed a number of programs or sections of the workshop with varying objectives. In very small communities, a number of programs were combined into a school-workshop-recreation organization. In most communities, however, a structure intermediate between the above two developed which had recognizable characteristics. This organization served either severely mentally retarded or cerebral-palsied young adults whose development had been hindered by their condition. They needed the benefits of work, but they also needed to develop educational and social skills which they had not acquired at school or at home. The structure that the parent groups set up in these types of workshops resembled most nearly that of a school. The Department of Labor classified many of these workshops as work activity centers.

These workshops for the young adults with arrested development were often sponsored by parent membership organizations which influenced greatly the policies and objectives of the workshop through the selection of their officers as members in key positions on the governing boards. Individual members often viewed the shops as schools, and they visited them much as they did schools. The personnel, especially those in floor positions, were at first volunteers and then teachers, often teachers of the mentally retarded in shops for the retarded or often manual arts or arts and crafts teachers in other kinds of shops. Though the directors varied in training, they were almost never industrially experienced personnel. The work of the shop was considered unimportant so there was no reason to hire industrial personnel. It was often believed both by staff and parents that the workers were incapable of doing complex work. The purpose of the work was to develop social skills, to provide recreation, or to occupy enrollees when they were not being taught needed living skills. In time these shops found the work they brought in provided far-reaching benefits, but the structure of the shops was usually crystallized before this awareness took place.

The work activity center structure developed around a highly involved membership organization which reviewed carefully the decisions of the board and allowed very little discretion as a rule to be delegated to the director of the shop. The volunteer or teacher on the floor received as much residual minimal authority as was necessary from a director who was given not only detailed policy direction but detailed instruction about the activities of the shop. Relationships in the shops were highly informal, and lines between director and staff were at times disturbed by intervention by officers and members of the organization, sometimes in behalf of their own children or in support of personal predilections. When these circumstances prevailed, the result was a failure to develop substantial or complex work programs or to develop an efficient formal organization. These organizations were often less subject to external pressures either from the community or from public agencies but sometimes made demands for support on both. Both public agencies and political bodies often acquiesced in these demands for many reasons, mainly political and psychological, and the informal structures were thus perpetuated until recent times.

Lately these organizations have been progressively becoming more related to the community, adopting more comprehensive admission policies and recognizing their value, and have been developing more structured organizations which enable their personnel to reach predetermined objectives. This original type of structure arose basically because the parent groups had experienced years of unjustifiable neglect from the community and guarded very zealously the resources they could acquire and the policies and activities they considered essential. Other sponsoring groups who started workshops for young adults needing development services were less fearful in their organization constraints and developed structure similar to workshops in rehabilitation centers and work adjustment workshops.

THE PARTICIPATION OF THE WORKER
IN THE WORKSHOP STRUCTURE

The American workshop has generally been characterized by a hierarchial structure which delegated authority in varying degrees to professional or industrial staff in the development of institutional and individual programs for handicapped individuals. It is conjectured that where the industrial types of workshops predominated or where industrial personnel were dominant, the individuals served participated more in the workshop structure. It is believed that this took place not by design as a rule but because industrial personnel were accustomed to expecting more self-generated activity on the part of the individual while the professionals customarily initiated programs in which the individual was "involved." In the exposition which follows, consideration will be given to organizations in which attempts were made to include the worker as a participating member of the administration of the workshops, separate from or in addition to this role as a worker on the line. As far as can be ascertained, no studies have been made in this field, and the conjectures made are based on brief historical data reviewed previously.

Very few workshops in the United States were created by handicapped persons or are operated by handicapped people. Of those mentioned, the New York Federation for the Handicapped of New York, the Utility Workshop of San Francisco and the Disabled Employees, Inc., of San Francisco were operated by handicapped persons. The Utility Workshop was not operated by professional staff. Abilities, Inc., of Long Island is the only program known to the writer where the program was initiated and is still controlled by the handicapped persons. However, there are some workshops, principally long-term shops, where efforts are made by design to give handicapped workers executive participation in the administration of the workshop. It is towards these that the discussion will be directed.

Efforts to involve the worker in a more participatory role will be summarized for convenience into two categories: the cadre system and the self-regulated structures. Such a classification is an over simplification because there is overlapping, and sometimes the cadre system developed into a parallel self-regulated structure.

The Cadre

Little knowledge is available about the cadre system. It probably started informally from a labor pool or was improvised from necessity when it was financially impossible to hire staff. It probably was started in the renovating workshops when outstanding workers were promoted first to leadmen, then to foremen, and finally to department heads. Some even became directors of the workshops. As a rule, however, the worker was most often promoted to a leadman or assistant foreman. There are exceptions like the Disabled Employees of San Francisco where the handicapped workers occupied all supervisorial positions under absentee professional directors.

About the middle of the century and shortly thereafter, cadre-like situations are found at the Community Workshops of Boston and in many renovating workshops and long-term workshops.

The cadre remained when other workers left the shop. Because of their social and psychological proximity to the workers and their seniority, they often formed a lower echelon hierarchy which had informal influence far and beyond their official status. Their importance and distinction is that they are of the worker group and in a sense represent the workers in workshop organization.

Self-Regulated Structures

Somewhat different from the cadre form of structure is the self-regulated therapeutic community. In the cadre only the elite worker has a participatory role, and he has it by virtue of his superiority. In the therapeutic community every worker has a participatory role regardless of his ability or productive status. He has the role because as a person he is regarded just as important as any other person in the population of the workshop, including the director or the professional. In practice no organizational structure has been developed where each person in the population of the workshop has an equal voice in policy and decision making; but where the therapeutic community exists, efforts are made to provide for participation of each worker not only in matters concerning his individual problems but in the affairs of the workshop as an organization.

The therapeutic community concept became known to workshop personnel in this country mainly through the work of Maxwell Jones in England in the fifties, but self-regulated organizations have received other considerable study in this country (19). Since this democratic approach was applied usually in psychiatric hospitals, it became known to workshop personnel in hospital workshops and through them to other workshop personnel. Here we will be concerned not with the various theories of the therapeutic community but with the organizational implications of the theories which conjecture that aberrant or disordered behavior is related to the context or setting in which it occurs. This concept parallels the extrapsychic or environmental emphasis in many workshops. The therapeutic community would probably not be developed in workshops where the emphasis is on the intrapsychic approach, with emphasis on verbal therapies.

In the psychiatric hospitals where the therapeutic community concept exists, the workshop is usually considered a part of the total program. The overall role of the worker (the hospital patient) is the same as that which he plays in the total hospital setting. He participates in a group of his peers which may make choices for the workshop as well as other parts of the hospital. Since the mental hospital is usually in a public organization with legal mandates and an organizational structure of a formal administrative and functional nature, the choices of the workers in the workshop must at times be overridden. In practice, then, the self-regulative features are collaborative rather than administrative. From an administrative point of view, the therapeutic community is a collaborative communication system which enables those in authority to expand the choices and influence of the workers within legal and administrative limits. It requires that those exercising legal authority believe in the potential of the individuals served and be willing to take program risks by moving areas of decision making to those whose welfare is at stake (20).

The form of self-regulating systems in workshops in outpatient mental health organizations took a different form. These were, as far as is known, in private rather than public organization. This made greater exercise of authority possible among the workers. Using Fountain House in New York and Thresholds in Chicago as models, the structure may be described as follows: There is a dual administrative system. The nonprofit corporation is created with a board and a director. At the same time a membership organization is created which parallels the legal corporation. Only mentally ill persons receiving services in the organization may belong to the membership organization. These are referred to as members. The board and director administer the program, but the membership organization theoretically sets policies and can instruct the director. However, since the board raises the money and the director executes policy, the ability of the membership to implement policy is limited. As for the internal interrelations and activities in the workshop, the membership can determine how they will go. These and other matters are determined by a meeting of the entire membership, usually weekly.

In practice this type of therapeutic community structure amounts to a collaboration between the director and staff and the membership or workers. The membership is given *de facto* authority, and the staff is given operating responsibility. Thus the director and staff must win the membership consent for major program and must be able to dissuade the membership from actions which the staff considers impossible or nonfeasible. In this framework, the workers or members are the bosses, psychologically and sociologically, if not legally. The hierarchial triangle is reversed, with decision making theoretically initiated at the bottom rather than the top.

It is difficult to compare the structural characteristics because these organizations are new and they function informally. Professional and industrial staff is limited, and the work is simple or carried on in job sites. Similar to Alcoholics Anonymous and Synanon, which they resemble administratively, they are resistant to external pressures, though unlike Synanon, they will accept government support. The members respond negatively to status figures, to established social rituals, and to technical requirements. Informality, simplicity, and genuineness are the goals. Within this framework considerable give and take can occur. In essentials, this is a nonorganization, or an organization where informal and changing structures predominate.

The efforts made to involve workers, however, while interesting theoretically, have had little impact in American workshops generally. As a rule, the workshop used the professional-client relationships approach of clinical derivation or the industrial approach of a more informal foreman-worker relationship.

THE INFLUENCE OF IDEOLOGY ON ORGANIZATION

Workshops are established by sponsors who wish to solve groups of problems of handicapped persons. The solutions they have in mind are determined by their ideology. The organization of the workshop must be appropriate to their solution. The structure of the workshop must allow it to function to achieve the objectives of the sponsors. Thus by studying its function, the nature of the organization may be clarified.

Workshops function in three general ways to achieve their objectives. The first may be labeled the *rehabilitation-habilitation* function. The second may be called the *maintenance-prevention* function. The third may be designated the *amelioration-alleviation* function. A workshop may carry on each or any combination of these functions.

In the rehabilitation-habilitation function, the objective is to improve the performance of the individual. This function may be divided grossly into two parts. If the individual had a normal development, then suffers reduced functioning as a result of disability, the objective is to bring his performance up to or better than his previous level. This is rehabilitation. If the individual's functioning has never developed normally, the objective is to bring his performance to levels higher than he has ever experienced. This is habilitation. In either case, performance and behavior is improved vocationally and socially.

In the second function — maintenance-prevention — a program is carried on when there is no prospect of increasing performance. Performance can be maintained at an existing level, and this maintenance may prevent further deterioration. Whether the disfunction arises from underdevelopment because of disability or from subsequent disability, workshop services may support the existing level of performance and prevent decline of performance.

In the third situation — amelioration-alleviation — the individual's performance will inevitably decline because of a progressively worsening condition which cannot be reversed. The workshop cannot improve or maintain his condition, but it may be able to slow the rate of decline and mitigate or alleviate the physical and psychological trauma of an irreversible condition. In any case, the workshop makes the individual's condition more bearable.

In practice, workshops tend to emphasize one of the three functions. In such a case, the workshop acquires a constellation of ideology, resources, groups of functionally prejudged individuals labeled by the disability category or disadvantaged condition and a work setting; these together influence organization, but ideology plays a major and often unrecognized role.

The great majority of shops exercise the rehabilitation-habilitation function. This organization is relatively favored in support, since the social philosophy of the country is based on the belief that upward mobility and improved functioning is desirable and generally possible. The resources available, however, depend upon prevailing ideology. The shop is given money for professional staff or industrial staff or technical wherewithall such as plant and equipment. The character of the resources depends upon the nature of the influential ideology in relation to the rehabilitation-habilitation function. If the prevailing ideology is that professional staff creates rehabilitation, this resource is favored. Furthermore, the type of worker on the floor is determined by ideology. Since the function is improvement, only those who are expected to improve are accepted. Thus in the early history the mentally retarded and mentally ill were excluded, and now the alcoholic and the drug addict are usually excluded. Furthermore, some types of mentally retarded are excluded in the rehabilitation setting because they are given pejorative labels and others are included because they have been given more complimentary labels.

Depending upon ideology, a type of institutional framework is followed. This may be faithful to an original institutional model or it may represent a departure from an institutional format. However, the departure is often partial, and the main central structure may remain. For example, when the rehabilitation center revolted from the hospital model, it changed the outward framework but kept its core structure. The departure is more substantial when a therapeutic community or self-regulating structure is adopted. Usually the adaptation is complementary in nature, as when the work adjustment shop elaborated the vocational guidance structure.

In the exercise of the maintenance-prevention function, fewer resources are available. The constituents are parents of young adults or a few perceptive sympathetic humanitarians who give higher priority to human needs than to utilitarian criteria of a materialistic nature. The assumption is made that substantial increase in function is impossible and resources are thus limited because of low expectations. Disability labels often having little significance influence intake criteria, but they suggest low expectations which are reflected in assigned activities. Work is simple and unchallenging. The sociology of the shop is characterized by the relationship of teacher-caretaker and marginal performer. However, some improvement does take place, some learning occurs, but these are not sufficient usually to be regarded as significant in cultural terms. Thus the institutional prototype followed is that of the special school, the chronic care hospital, or the nursery.

The third function, that of amelioration-alleviation, is the stepchild function. The individuals served, whether chronically ill or aging, have a low priority in American culture. Thus the resources available to this kind of shop are minimal. The staff is meager and inadequate, the work is simple and routine. Thus the followed structure resembles the convalescent or home for the aged. However, because of inadequate staff, aged workers in nonresident facilities often assume cadre roles, and informal management roles are carried out by workers. This management role for the older worker is infrequent in alleviation types of shops in the United States, however, when compared to such European countries as the Netherlands (21).

In spite of the variability caused by ideology, each of the groups described above must respond somewhat to work and the work setting. The structure that results is a cross between the ideologically ascribed characteristics and the requirements of an industrial setting. As a rule, the ideological influences predominate, and thus at times skew the components of the workshop duality. The ideology, however, is not necessarily realistic or based on research findings. Thus it sometimes takes on the nature of mythology or folklore. For this reason, until research validation for workshop function and its results is achieved, quantitative or analysis measures of existing workshop structure may at times be expressions of ideology.

To sum up, in making a comparative analysis of workshops, it is difficult to find any prevailing theory which explains the development of the organizational structure of all of them. Some workshop groups have maintained the structure of their time of origin. Others have changed the organizational structure progressively. Some have maintained their organizational perceptions consistently and others have changed them from time to time. Some have resisted external influences at some times and accepted them at other times. Some have resisted technological change, and others have responded to such influences. Among the various groups reviewed, different subgroups have developed variously. Workshops are thus as diverse in structure as they are in scope and methods.

But if no theory can explain the development of workshop structure specifically, are there any factors or elements in them in consistent relationships? The universal characteristic of the workshop is its duality. It invariably has two elements, work and people services. Can a theory be formed by a statement of the duality relationship? This relationship expresses itself in a variety of proportions. One workshop has no distinct or separate people services, and what people services are provided arise as peripheral services or as by-products of its industrial process. Another has no industrial processes to speak of but pays workers for made work while occupying most of the time of the individual in a variety of psychosocial services. Others are in varying stages between these two extremes. The workshop duality, which always exists, is characterized by great variability — one part or the other may have greater magnitude. Thus the duality exists, but the proportional weight of the two parts varies tremendously.

Workshop organizations varied in structure for the reasons indicated, but the variability was often reinforced greatly internally by sponsorship as well. Sponsors often had fixed preoccupations about services to the groups of their interest. They often set up organizations in light of their history and resources and ideology. Thus sponsors and boards had great influence on structure. Undoubtedly, they constitute the most important internal influence in workshops. However, very little attention has been devoted to workshop sponsoring groups and boards. The role of boards in workshops is a neglected area in workshop study. Their importance is generally recognized but little is known that can be said in any systematic way about their influence on organizational structure.

TOWARDS A THEORY OF WORKSHOP STRUCTURE

From whatever point of view one approaches the study of workshops, one finds that its duality is central to understanding it. From an organizational point of view, the duality is expressed in the relationship between the things and services creating activities and the services to persons in the shop. It is therefore proposed to try to state a conceptualization of workshop structure that explains the duality by determining what influences it and how such influences affect it.

We begin with the proposition that the workshop duality is determined by external and internal forces. Such forces, however, cannot be understood by analyzing them at any point in time alone. They often have historical precedents which result in what may be called ideological lag. Since ideology is one of the important forces in the development of workshop structure, ideological lag may be imperceptible or may be disguised by outdated belief. For example, the early belief that the blind could do complicated tasks led to the development of a technology and structure that developed in an industrial direction. On the other hand, the belief that the mentally retarded were incapable of doing complex tasks led to a simple technology and the development of a structure resembling more nearly a school or custodial structure. In the same vein, the belief of sponsors of blind shops that sighted persons in controlled percentages should work with blind persons influenced their industrial development while the fears that sponsors of workshops for the mentally retarded maintained about persons with other handicaps working with the retarded inhibited their industrial development. We find that the refusal of boards of directors of some shops to accept government money because of political ideology prevented some

EXTERNAL AND INTERNAL FORCES IN THE WORKSHOP UNIVERSE

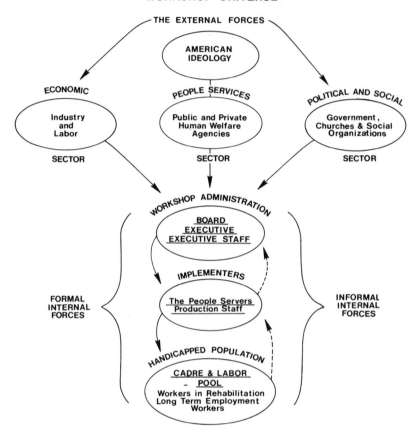

The above illustration shows how external and internal forces influence workshop programs. American ideology influences the economic sector, the political and religious sector, and the people services sector of American life. These in turn provide the ideology and resources of the workshop and set its general goals. These are accepted selectively by the executive system and interpreted to the staff. The staff reinterprets the policies and uses the resources selectively. The handicapped population adapts to the staff's activities with further modification of policies and use of resources.

An interaction takes place between the external forces and the internal forces through the executive system. A continuous interaction takes place between the executive system direction, the staff implementation, and the handicapped population response. It takes place formally through internal forces coming down from the executive system and the staff to the handicapped population, and informally up from the handicapped population and the staff to the executive system.

shops for decades from acquiring the resources they need to change their structure. In still another area, many workshop organizations embraced the holistic and team approach originated by prominent rehabilitation centers and the acceptance of this ideology influenced their organizational structure. The analysis of the structure of workshops should include their ideology, and if solutions to organizational problems are sought, the history of their ideological development.

The ideological force can be external or internal, and an external ideology can be internalized. The idea of the team approach was initially external but was then internalized. So also was the notion that taking money from government would result in control by government bureaucracy. Board members brought this concept to the shop from external sources and internalized it.

However, many external ideologic forces influencing structure remained external. In general, the ideology, attitudes, and customary practices of the various spheres of the local power structures influenced the resources and technology of workshops. In the economic area, industrial firms loaned shops machine tools or refused them, banks provided or refused capital for expansion, private enterprise ideology prohibited shops from engaging in repair services or in prime manufacture in competition with local industry, and shops were denied or allowed permission to set up local retail outlets in competition with local merchants. Local central charitable funding agencies gave shops lump sum allotment or refused them. School systems sometimes provided teachers or they did not. When they did, they dictated curriculum and class size or not depending on the concepts. The vocational rehabilitation agency might dictate the form of reports and the nature of the staff as a requirement for funding. And voluntary agencies concerned with special disability groups supported shops with money and participation or refused them, based on their beliefs on how services should be rendered. Workshop organizations responded differently to opportunities and constraints created by external power structure ideology, but the ideologies that existed greatly influenced their organization structure.

Internal ideological forces also influenced structure. The sources of internal ideas came from membership organization and boards, staff, and workers.

An important ideology which influenced structure was the eleemosynary stance of some memberships and boards. This view was that in a charitable, helping organization, staff should work for low wages and secure reward through satisfaction in their work, that efficiency was not to be expected, and that the organization should serve the few unfortunates who needed it without regard for the principles of organization which the members of the organization or of the board would apply in their own businesses or expect in government. Whether or not the organization was subject to this philanthropic view, ideology determined whether the director could obtain professionals or industrial personnel, buy expensive equipment, or plan to meet the needs of large numbers of handicapped persons who needed their services.

When the organization hired professional personnel, they sometimes brought into the organization an ideology which also created problems in skewing the workshop duality. When professional personnel held that only persons with certain training in certain fields were capable of making evaluations or decisions about people, they often created conflict with personnel essential to the coordination of the duality. And when they disregarded the practical necessities of the work processes on the principle that the community was obligated to enable their clients to reach their highest potential in all respects, they sometimes created a structure which was not native to the workshop setting. Basically they refuse to recognize that an imperfect man can create magnificently.

Finally, the effect of the ideology of the board and staff sometimes creates on the part of the workers on the floor, when they were mature adults, a counter ideology or influence which is subtle and informal but which expresses itself through the cadre and other informal organizational mechanisms to call attention to their conflicting attitudes with those of the staff. And at other times in some organizations, formal mechanisms such as grievance committees and labor unions are developed which openly influence organizations or create strains. These conflicts arise usually in long-term shops when the ideology of the staff is different from the ideology of the workers — when the staff see them as patients or clients and when they see themselves as persons who can initiate solutions to their own problems.

The discussion so far has concerned external and internal influences closely related to ideology. Other influences also exist, some of which possibly arose from ideology originally but are not currently ideologically based, and other forces which are not related to ideology. In the former group are the laws and the regulations on all levels of government, the culturally determined folkways of rendering services to people, and the financial subventions which exist as a result. In the second group are the geographic, economic, demographic, and transportation factors which influence structure.

In the first group, the laws and administrative regulations, examples are the various state laws requiring certain types of education for designated groups of minors, the county interpretations of the right of welfare recipients to work, and the state and federal wage and hour laws. The Federal Wage and Hour Law is a striking demonstration of how law can effect structure. Following the 1968 revision of the Fair Labor Standards, the regulations required that the workshop having a work activity center certificate must separate all workers in this group from the others to create a separate unit physically and administratively.

In the second group, an example of geographic and demographic nature is the surrounding territory with the public transportation system as an important factor. The need for a transportation system or of a branch system is determined by these factors (22). The number of people in the area and the number of other shops in the area determines many factors relating to the shop's structure. The nature of the economy also determines the technological necessities of the shop. Some industries subcontract more than others, and in some areas having the same industries, the marketing pattern is different than that in another. Nevertheless, all communities have an economic base, and the workshop usually develops a structure which is complementary to the economy in which it finds itself. A workshop in a forest area must develop woodworking capability, and a workshop in a resort area, service capability. This in turn influences structure.

The factors described above are generally external to the organization. Other internal forces not overtly ideological also influence the organization. The needs, abilities, aspirations, and informal goals of the organizational population exert various and subtle pressure internally also. These are difficult to describe because they are seldom formal, usually part of a "hidden agenda." For example, a workshop board to get community support may agree to take persons with all disabilities and even proclaim this ideology in its publications. Yet very few other persons than those with the disability of the group's interest are accepted, since it is understood that one group must be favored. This factor in turn influences its structure. The staff of a workshop may agree that work is the principal modality of a workshop but emphasizes social development rather than work competence because they are able to develop social goals but not work skills. Others emphasize work goals for similar reasons. Or some of the workers may come to the shop for a variety of reasons other than those stated and strive to show they do not belong there. These are but a few of the infinite variety of subtle influences that exist internally, often the counterinfluence of official goals and which, taken together, influence the structure of the shop.

The enumeration of but a few of the various external and internal forces which influence the structure of the workshop may give some inkling of the coordination, collaboration, and resource getting which must be done if the workshop is to respond appropriately to all of them. Of course it is highly improbable that all such forces will be accommodated perfectly. However, it is necessary to coordinate organizational activities in such a way that they will recognize and adjust to the most crucial influences and forces if the organization is to survive.

Currently it is customary to conceptualize a program by use of illustrations which resemble mathematical formulas borrowed from the physical sciences. Such illustrations have utility, but they harbor the hazard of suggesting that they are identical with those from the physical sciences, when in truth they are not. Those in the physical sciences deal with relatively finite concepts, while the essential nature of social sciences is the opposite. For this

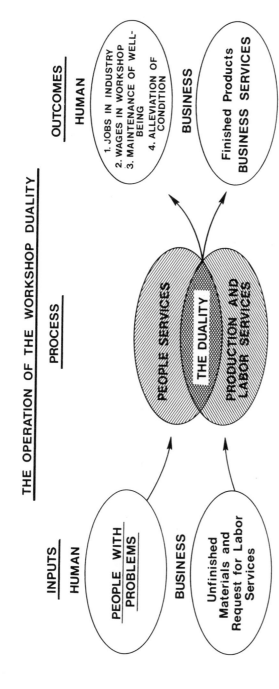

THE OPERATION OF THE WORKSHOP DUALITY

INPUTS   PROCESS   OUTCOMES

HUMAN

BUSINESS

PEOPLE WITH PROBLEMS

Unfinished Materials and Request for Labor Services

PEOPLE SERVICES

THE DUALITY

PRODUCTION AND LABOR SERVICES

HUMAN

1. JOBS IN INDUSTRY
2. WAGES IN WORKSHOP
3. MAINTENANCE OF WELL-BEING
4. ALLEVIATION OF CONDITION

BUSINESS

Finished Products
BUSINESS SERVICES

In the above illustration, the flow of people and products through the workshop is shown. People with handicaps come into the shop with requests for services. Materials are sent by contractors for processing or labor services are requested by them. The people who come seeking help are put to work on the materials or providing labor services. When this interprocess is successful, benefits accrue to the handicapped such as the ability to work in industry or the shop, or the increase of well-being. On the other hand, as a result of their work the business firm gets the labor services it desires.

reason, it is proposed to develop an illustration which will borrow the illustrative utility of the mathematic formula without implying the finite qualities which it suggests. Such a diagram will focus on function and objectives to show how the workshop duality becomes a synthesis. Its purpose is to show how the synthesis produces beneficial results for the handicapped person.

NOTES

1. For different definitions of organization see Cartwright, D.; Influence, Leadership, and Control (p. 1), and Udy, S. H.: The Comparative Analysis of Organizations (pp. 678-709), In March, J. G. (Ed.): Handbook of Organization, Chicago, Rand McNally, 1965.
2. An early discussion of administration of workshops may be found in a special feature section of the Journal of Rehabilitation, pp. 20-52, January-February, 1965. An early study of administrative problems was made by Smith N. P.: Operational techniques for sheltered work programs — a guide for planning and management. Rehabilitation Literature, August, pp. 230-239, 1966.
3. Button, W. H., Kimberly, J. R., Lubow, B. K. and Kimberly, R. P.: A Conceptual Framework for the Analysis of Work Behavior in Sheltered Workshops. Ithaca, Cornell University, 1969. Button, W. H.: Wage levels in Sheltered Employment. Ithaca, Cornell University, Rehabilitation Research Institute, 1967. Button, W. H.: Application of Systems Analysis in Sheltered Workshops. Ithaca, Cornell Rehabilitation Research Institute Report, undated. Kimberly, J. R.: Professional Staffing in Sheltered Workshops. Ithaca, Cornell University, Rehabilitation Research Institute, 1967. Kimberly, J. R.: Comparative Organizational Analysis: An Empirical Study of Rehabilitation Organizations. Masters thesis, Ithaca, Cornell University. Kimberly, J. R.: The Financial Structure of Sheltered Workshops. Ithaca, Organization and Administration of Sheltered Workshops, Research Report No. 3, 1968. Salkind, I. (Ed.): A Case Book in Rehabilitation Workshop Problems, San Francisco, University of San Francisco, 1968. Caddick, J.: A Manual of Production Improvement in a Rehabilitation Workshop. San Francisco, University of San Francisco, 1968.
4. Wessen, A. F.: The Apparatus of Rehabilitation: An Organizational Analysis. In Sussman, M. B. (Ed.): Sociology and Rehabilitation. Cleveland, American Sociological Association, 1965, pp. 152-153.
5. Nelson, N.: The industrial operation of the sheltered workshop. Journal of Rehabilitation, pp. 38-39, January-February, 1965.
6. Nelson, N.: The Economics of a subcontract and manufacturing workshop. Journal of Rehabilitation, July-August, 1964.

7. Wolinsky, D.: Developing Effective Business Practices in Relation to Sheltered Workshops. In Cohen, M. E. and Thiesse, N. H. (Eds.): The Sheltered Workshop. Manchester, New Hampshire, Massachusetts State, Association of Sheltered Workshops and Homebound Programs. 1968. See also, Black, B.: The workshop in a changing world. Rehabilitation Literature, Vol XXVI, No. 8, p. 235, August, 1965.

8. Christensen, J. W.: Sheltered Workshops — People and Profit. Chicago, DePaul University, Institute on Funding a Workshop Program, 1968.

9. Button, N. H.: Application of Systems Analysis in Sheltered Workshops, Ithaca, Regional Rehabilitation Research Institute, undated, pp. 2-3.

10. Wessen, A. F.: The Apparatus of Rehabilitation: An Organizational Analysis. In Sussman, M. E.: Sociology and Rehabilitation. Cleveland, American Sociological Association, 1965, pp. 159-164.

11. Stinchcombe, A.: Social Structure and Organization. In March, G. (Ed.): Handbook of Organizations. Chicago, Rand McNally, 1965, pp. 142-191.

12. Udy, S. H.: Comparative Analysis of Organizations. In March, J. G. (Ed.): Handbook of Organization. Chicago, Rand McNally, 1965, pp. 690-692.

13. Scott, R. A.: The Factory as a Social Service Organization: Goal Displacement in Workshops for the Blind. Social Problems, Fall, 1967, Vol. 15, No. 2, pp. 160-175.

14. Kimberly, J. R.: Comparative Organizational Analysis: An Empirical Study of Rehabilitation Organization. Masters thesis, Ithaca, Cornell University, 1967, pp. 29. Etzioni, A.: Modern Organizations. Englewood Cliffs, Prentice Hall, 1964, pp. 10-14.

15. This statement is based on the writer's attendance at bargaining sessions between management and workers at the California Industries for the Blind.

16. Compare with Scott, R. A.: The Factory as a Social Service Organization: Goal Displacement in Workshops for the Blind. pp. 160-175. Scott studied these workshops from 1900 to 1950. He does not trace their development from their beginning in 1838 to the present and thus gets a partial view of their development. The original goal of the workshops for the Blind was to train blind students for employment in industry. By 1900, when Scott indicates the original goals were developed as employment in industry, the shops had already had sixty years experience with training blind for industry without success. See Best, Harry, Blindness and the Blind in the United States, New York, MacMillan, 1934, pp. 496-518.

17. Standards for Rehabilitation Facilities (on accreditation of rehabilitation faculties), 1969, p. 10, 3.2.2.

18. Kimberly, J. R.: Financial Structure of Workshops (op. cit.), demonstrates this point for the shops in New York, New Jersey, and Pennsylvania.

19. Vitale, J. H.: The Therapeutic Community — A Review Article, In

Wessen, A. T. (Ed.): The Psychiatric Hospital as a Social System. Springfield, Charles C Thomas, 1964, pp. 91-106.

20. Ibid., pp. 105-106.

21. Roeder, A. E.: A Comparative Study of Dutch and California Sheltered Workshops for the Handicapped. A thesis submitted to the faculty of San Francisco State College in partial fulfillment of the requirements for the degree Master of Science, January, 1967.

22. Nelson, N.: The Planning for Workshops for the Handicapped. Presented at the National Association of Sheltered Workshops and Homebound Programs, San Francisco, California, November, 1968.

XIII

THE ADMINISTRATION AND
FINANCING OF WORKSHOPS

THE value of any of the organizational concepts described before depends upon the ways in which they are applied or implemented. The mechanisms which the organization sets up and the ways these mechanisms are used determine how well the organizations will achieve its objectives. Thus the description of organizational concepts needs to be followed by a narrative picture of administration — how it brings resources to the organization, the ways it coordinates activities, and the communication system it uses and how it makes decisions. Since no comprehensive nationwide field studies have been made of the organizational dynamics of workshops, the informal mechanisms which are important cannot be elucidated at the present time. A description of formal administration can be put together from clues arising out of history, financing, organization charts, and reports to which observations are added. The following description explains what appears to be happening in the formal administration of workshops so far as it can be determined from a few published works and personal observation (1).

The assumption is made that similar administrative elements exist regardless of the objectives of the workshop. Workshops in this discussion are not classified by objectives and discussed separately as has been done previously in connection with purposes or theories. The characteristics of organizations differ but the administrative elements are assumed to be the same. It is also assumed tentatively that organizations have different, specific objectives but that the similar administrative dynamics apply. Exceptions are the publicly operated government shops.

THE NATURE AND ELEMENTS
OF ORGANIZATION IN WORKSHOPS

Workshop organizations fall into two general groups: private, voluntary organizations, and public, government organizations. As a rule, the private organizations have more administrative flexibility than public organizations, at least formally or theoretically. Workshops in government programs find themselves bound by laws, regulations, and budgetary controls exercised outside of the workshop unit, while private workshops are related to boards which are closer at hand. Private workshops can create their own personnel structure while the public workshops are usually related to a governmental personnel structure contrived by bodies at state capitols for the state as a whole. The most important difference, however, is probably the financial one. The income of public workshops often goes into centralized general funds from which the money cannot easily be returned to the workshop for expenditures. To make expenditures, the shop must often initiate time-consuming purchasing and budgeting procedures.

However, while formally the public workshops suffer from relative administrative rigidity, informally their administrative possibilities vary depending upon the unit of government where they are located. For example, state hospital workshops may or may not have administrative flexibility depending upon the individual state hospital where they are located. The reason is that the state hospital often has more administrative autonomy than other units of government where workshops are located. Local county administrations also may vary in the extent of their controls on expenditures for workshops. The autonomy of the host unit may have disadvantages, however, when the administrator is unduly fearful of competing with local industry and thus handicaps the shop's work procurement procedures.

In other respects, however, both public and private workshops have administrative similarities. Both suffer from a similar competition between classes of personnel for power and prestige. Both have the problem of balancing the workshop duality of production and people services and suffer when there is an imbalance. Both have similar problems of meeting customer demands.

In availability of general financing, however, the public workshop has considerable advantage over the private shop. The public shop receives a relatively assured budget in advance of its fiscal year, while the private shop is not sure of its income until its users purchase services and its customers send it contract work or buy its commodities. Public shops, except perhaps those in mental hospitals, are not covered by the Fair Labor Standards Act and therefore do not have to meet minimum wage requirements, nor are they compelled to price in accordance with prevailing rates. The private shops have to meet both of these requirements.

The majority of the workshops in the United States, however, are privately operated nonprofit workshops. A study conducted by the National Association of Sheltered Workshops and Home-bound Industries in 1967 found that 92 percent of the shops were in the private nonprofit category (2). Perhaps the percentage of public shops is greater currently because of the many newly established workshops in mental hospitals, but the overwhelming majority of workshops are still private nonprofit corporations. For this reason, and because public workshops generally are made to conform with governmental organizational structure which is typical of the governmental agency and atypical of workshops, the rest of the discussion will consider primarily the private nonprofit sector in workshops.

ADMINISTRATION OF PRIVATE WORKSHOPS

The great art of administering a workshop consists of working with a series of elements externally and internally in such a way that its objectives can be achieved. Before discussing the process of administration, it is first necessary to identify the organizational elements which require the manipulation and coordination of administration. To achieve the objectives for people, administration must provide both the people services and product or service activities which will bring about desired results. This requires the development of resources from outside the shop and the coordination of the operating duality within the shop by the use of a communication system for both. Thus, to the dual functions of the shop must be added a third force which fuels and coordinates the goal-producing other two forces. This third administrative force must work through the traditional mechanisms and customs of a charitable agency format. We will begin by describing those mechanisms.

The External Forces Influencing Workshop Structure

The external forces influencing the workshop have been described in the previous chapter. In return for its submission to external influence, the workshop gets support. It is thus the function of administration to deal with specific outside organizations and persons to get that support in money, referrals, material donations and volunteer services. Administration must deal with local private agencies, both central community agencies and specialized health agencies, and service clubs to get from them the kind of support they are capable of giving. Administration needs also to secure from public agencies what resources they can provide. These latter are numerous and exist on local, state, and national levels. In addition, administration must deal with the economic world as sellers of labor or products or both.

The Internal Components in the Workshop Structure

Internally, administration must deal with or coordinate a variety of organizational components. These are the membership organization, the board, the staff, the cadre, and the handicapped persons served. These groups may create organizational strains whose dynamics are elusive or obvious but are seldom capable of solution by simple rules or arbitrary or unilateral decision. Each group requires understanding through communication. The nature of each component will first be described. The description will be illustrative; in reality the distinction between components is sometimes blurred.

The first component is the sponsorship. The sponsorship may consist of a charitable or religious organization or of a membership group or both. In rare instances neither exist, and the board serves in lieu of the sponsorship. Except in those instances where no sponsorship exists other than a board which is a legal fiction, the sponsorship makes the basic assumptions upon which the shop operates, and it sets the shop's limits. Sometimes when a workshop is a member of a state or national voluntary organization, the nature of its sponsorship authority may be limited. However, the importance of sponsorship varies.

Sponsoring organizations usually influence the organization financially and limit the scope of the program and goals. The crucial issues in workshops are usually decided by memberships or by boards. Whether the decision is left to boards depends on the nature of the membership group.

The Membership

Membership groups may be generally classified in two types: supportive and directive. In the supportive group, the members pay dues, attend meetings, elect officers, and serve as volunteers. The group does not generally make policy. The directive membership group makes policy or supervises operations or both. The directive membership group may be classified as an active group if it makes policy and an overactive group if the members attempt directly to supervise operations. The latter sort has existed most often in parent-dominated membership organizations. Finally, an exceptional kind of membership group is that which consists of the handicapped persons working in the shop. At present, their administrative roles cannot be classified without further study.

The Boards

In general however, the responsibility for the overall policy direction of the workshop is in the hands of a board of directors. If there is a directive membership group, the board may be subjected to its wishes. Usually, the board is the ultimate source of general policy decision making in the workshop. There are, however, exceptions, depending on the nature of the board.

Boards are of many varieties and probably cannot by classified with precision. However, groups of boards may be described based on their principal roles. As previously indicated, there are boards who serve primarily a legal function. In order to achieve the privilege of a nonprofit corporation, there must be a board of directors. An individual or individuals who wish to operate a workshop without restriction secure individuals who are sympathetic to their goals to play a legal nonparticipating role. In effect this board is a board in name only, or a nonboard.

Boards who exercise board functions may be generally divided into inactive boards and active boards. The inactive board is one which goes through the motions of holding meetings, with members lending their name and prestige to the organization. The board merely approves decisions of the administration and usually provides little support. Active boards may be supportive, responsible, or directive. The supportive board has confidence in administration and does little to initiate policy, but it supports the goals of the organization through fund-raising efforts, developing support in the community, and using influence to accomplish the shop's goals. The responsible board does all the supportive board does, but it also exercises final responsibility for the shop's policies and operation. The directive board adds to its supportiveness and responsibility the urgency to concern itself with the daily operations of the shop. It resembles in some respects the overactive membership organization.

Since the responsible board usually plays an appropriate role in influencing administration, its structure needs description. When the board functions responsibly, it usually has mechanisms to determine policy, receive adequate information about the organization, and carry out its planning on supportive functions. This is often done formally by use of committees. The nature of such committees vary but there is usually an executive committee and a finance and planning committee and other committees such as public relations committees, personnel committees, fund raising committees, work procurement or sales committees, and volunteer committees.

The Staff

The next administrative mechanism is the staff. The staff may be divided into two major groups: those who assist the director to provide resources and coordinate activities to enable the shop to meet its objectives, and those who create and supervise work activities or provide services to enable the handicapped persons to meet their objectives. The former is the administrative staff. The latter comprise the two wings of the operational duality. In one group are the personnel, usually professionals, who provide people services. In the other are the managers, salesmen, and work supervisors who find work and supervise work activity. Some personnel serve in both capacities. Their joint efforts create the dual program which achieves the objectives of the handicapped persons.

Although the two parts of the operational duality always exist, sometimes the design or the terminology of the shop disguises its operations. In the latter respect, the designation of a Director of Professional Services or a Director of Work Adjustment, who has ultimate responsibility for the procurement of work and its successful completion, may disguise the fact that he is performing a work management function. The designation of the floor supervisor or foreman as a training supervisor or a counseling foreman deemphasizes his work production role. Conversely, the designation as personnel officer of the chief of the section which includes social workers, psychologists, and counselors exercising their traditional functions, may disguise his responsibilities in the psychosocial services.

But the major reason for the lack of visability of the workshop operational duality in some shops arises from its imperfect implementation. One shop's ideology is that the demands of production must be completely subordinated to needs of clients. In this model, personnel with professional training make management decisions on work operations, and industrial personnel are either non-existent or have relatively little influence on decision making in the areas of their responsibilities. Conversely, in other shops, the ideology proclaims that the requirements of production best enhance the prospects of the disabled persons and that it must predominate both for the benefit of the individual and of the shop. In this event, work managers make decisions relating to the individual's needs and personnel with training in psychosocial fields are either nonexistent or have little influence on decision making in the areas of their responsibility. Thus relevant psychosocial problems of the individual may be disregarded.

The fact that job titles do not adequately describe function and that functions are carried out by people who are not trained to perform them does not mean that the twofold types of functions are not carried out in workshops. It may mean that one or the other of the two functions may be deemphasized or ineptly handled. Thus there are usually personnel performing both functions, but their job titles may be misleading, or personnel may be performing both functions simultaneously — one function well and the other not so well. One of the principal concerns of the workshop director is to develop a staffing pattern that will allow both functions to be carried on well.

The Handicapped Population

The third segment of persons in the shop that requires administrative concern is the handicapped population of the shop. This population can be classified into three groups depending upon the nature of the shop. The first group is a short-term group of handicapped persons who are often the clients of another agency such as vocational rehabilitation or the school district. This group is usually in the shop for evaluation and short-term training or adjustment. The short-term clients do not become part of the shop's social system in the same way that the long-term workers do. The shop is often performing services for another agency and they are temporary participants.

The other two groups are both long term. Both become part of the social structure of the shop in a more meaningful way. The majority of the handicapped persons who are the long-term workers become part of the administrative structure through their informal influence on decision making. They may often determine what can and cannot be accomplished and may often influence administration.

The Cadre and Labor Pool

Deserving special notice is that small minority of the handicapped population, the cadre. In addition to the managerial staff and the professional staff, there is usually in shops that have long term programs a small group of workers who are part worker and part supervisor, or an elite group of supervisory workers. The first step in the entry to this group may take place when a superior worker becomes a leadman. He continues working but exercises minor supervisorial functions. Another handicapped person, though he may not exercise foreman functions, is different from the average man on the floor in that he can be depended upon to work without supervision. In this class are sometimes intermittent workers who return to the shop in time of extra work volume. Sometimes they work part-time. They are sometimes called the labor pool. At a higher level of the elite group is the handicapped man on the level of an assistant foreman, working on special activities such as specialized quality control or time-keeping. This man also works without close supervision. Often the men in the categories described are aged men who are in semiretirement or persons with minimal physical handicaps who cannot adjust to industry and return to the shops. These relatively few core workers in effect take on some of the characteristics of an informal supervisory staff. They are often paid on a different basis than other floor workers.

Because of the influence of rehabilitation ideology, some shop personnel often fail to recognize the impact of these groups. In fact, however, they may contribute to administrative effectiveness and to good communication. Because of their usual status as handicapped workers, they are the group closest to the handicapped workers. In some places they have been called junior staff, but whatever their title they are important in the achievement of the shops' objectives, both in the area of people services and product creation. This special worker core constitutes a third force in the administrative structure, which because of its worker identification is neither professional staff or formal industrial staff. They may become coordinating and communications components in the sociology of the workshop.

THE BALANCE OF DEMAND AND CONTRIBUTION

We have seen that administration must deal with external forces — the social and economic forces previously indicated to get the resources it needs to achieve organization objectives. At the same time, it must deal with the internal mechanisms which use the resources brought into the shop to achieve its objectives. The external forces (the public and private agencies) make demands on administration but may not always willingly provide appropriate support. The internal mechanisms (the membership, board, and staff) make demands on administration without always providing appropriate returns in support or effective performance. And in both external and internal components, the demands may be competitive. One agency may wish the workshop to emphasize programs which exhaust the workshop resources and make it unable to respond to other demands. The professional and industrial personnel and the cadre may have conflicting demands for resources, power, and prestige, causing organization strains, and these demands may not always be demonstrably necessary if tested by the contribution of the contestants. But administration must arbitrate these various demands of organization components and allot the resources it provides them in keeping with their contribution to the workshop's objectives.

Although both external and internal forces make demands on administration, often the internal pressures are closer at hand than the external forces, which do not exert themselves as continuously. Thus, the tendency often is for the director or the administrative staff to respond with more time and attention to internal forces than to external forces. But external forces more often come up with resources, while as workshops are now constituted internal forces try to be resources consuming. Administration tries to find ways to balance demands and contribution — to get, from outside agencies and customers' adequate finances to pay for the services they ask for from staff, performance adequate enough to attract resources sufficient to meet staff demands.

To balance the demands and contributions of all the external and internal components enumerated is a difficult task. It is best accomplished by focusing on the general nature of the balancing problems — the securing of resources, principally money and work, and their appropriate use through the operational duality. When this is not accomplished, the workshop lives from crisis to crisis, managing to exist only because its utility is so great that minimal contribution is often externally engendered at the last moment.

The heart of the problem in the small or new workshop is that it lacks the resources which enable administration to operate a viable program, which can in turn attract additional resources. When administration should be seeking external resources, its energies are often required to be expended in meeting internal crises or demands. The phenomenon is understandable if the development of workshops is traced.

The Growth of Workshop Structure

The majority of workshops in the country were established in the last twenty years. Those established since 1950 were often established by a group of parents, or by small citizen or professional groups with few resources. The shops were administered initially sometimes by the boards whose members at first may have actually worked in the shop as contract getters, floor supervisors, and the like. When a director was hired he was usually from the people services professions and was engaged to perform practically all functions in the shop. The tradition that the new director had to arrive early to sweep the floor so that he could perform intake duties is symbolic of his origins. His initial energies were expended helping physically handicapped persons with or without real work in the shop. When he was able to hire additional staff, they were usually also from the people services professions and focused on individual problems of people. The management problems of the organization were initially handled by the board. Later an informal structure sometimes developed in which management and practitioner roles were intermingled. In time however, a more formal structure developed in which the director supervised almost every person on the staff and also carried on intake review and basic conference chairman responsibilities. This pattern of development did not take place in the same way when the shop was started by a well-established agency with substantial resources. Nevertheless, the early pattern of practitioner-director supervising many other practitioners predominated in many workshops with the educational, work adjustment, social welfare, or medical framework. When the director delegated functions to other personnel, it was often in the products-producing area. The people services professionals were longest kept individually reporting to the director.

The early manager-practitioner concept of administration had a number of characteristics and consequences. When the hierarchy developed, it often consisted of a flat pyramid with few levels and many personnel reporting to the director. Few responsibilities in operational decision making were delegated. The focus of the director was on people services, case management, or if in a large agency, on rationale and quality of services. The management of resources was neglected because the director was often too busy to give it the attention it needed. When finances became available they were usually expended for more practitioner staff, not for additional staff to assist the director with resource-producing activities. Often the resources that the shop received were expended on self-liquidating programs and not for growth engendering programs. Thus some of the private and government grants left the workshop in a condition of resources scarcity. Others given for plant, equipment, administration staff, industrial staff, vocational counseling staff and other income and growth-producing components gave the workshop added strength.

The Conflicts of the Unbalanced Structure

The importance of acquisition of external resources and their proper use is relatively easy to grasp. The same cannot be said for the proper use of internal resources. It has been pointed out that strains and conflicts can exist between classes of personnel in workshops. When these strains reach crisis proportions, the shop does not properly use its internal resources. When personnel spend great portions of time in conflict with other personnel, their value is diminished and a resource is wasted. This often happens when administration does not appreciate the requirements of balancing the operational duality. A social worker or an occupational therapist is brought into an industrially oriented shop and put in some position in the hierarchy and given such ambiguous, devalued functions that frustration and waste of time results. Or a production supervisor or contract procurement man is placed in a position reporting to professional people services staff who do not appreciate his role, so it becomes well nigh impossible for him to function. In a workshop, there needs to be a recognition and acceptance of the value of both wings of the program if internal resources are to be well used.

A Balanced Organization Chart

The chart on page 360 is shown to illustrate the principle of the operational duality. It is shown for a large industrially oriented shop to indicate the many ramifications of the duality. The chart can be rearranged and still respect the principle of the duality. For example, in a less industrially oriented shop the supervisor of the evaluation unit can report to the director of professional services.

This table of organization meets the requirements of the workshop duality but it does not show the communication that needs to exist between parallel echelons and it does not indicate the overlapping that takes place between business and people services activities. Neither does it show staffing meeting patterns. Another form of illustration shows the workshop duality both vertically and horizontally (p. 361).

This idealized illustration is based on the concept that considerable autonomy is delegated to the lower echelons and that it is exercised across organizational lines between the two parts of the duality at parallel levels. Thus the director and his assistants are at the head of the third or administrative force, which functions primarily as resource getters, distributors, policy interpretors, and arbitrators or coordinators. The two heads of people services and business activities are responsible for the coordination of their respective operations, for their distribution of resources, and the arbitration of all questions that cannot be resolved by the other levels. If they work successfully in tandem, the director is free to concentrate on resources getting and the activities required to achieve it. At the next level, the department chiefs coordinate the interrelationships between their staffs and arbitrate case decisions. At the next level where those closest to the handicapped persons meet, the individual services to them are planned and carried out. The handicapped population as a group receives signals from the

A BALANCED TABLE OF ORGANIZATION

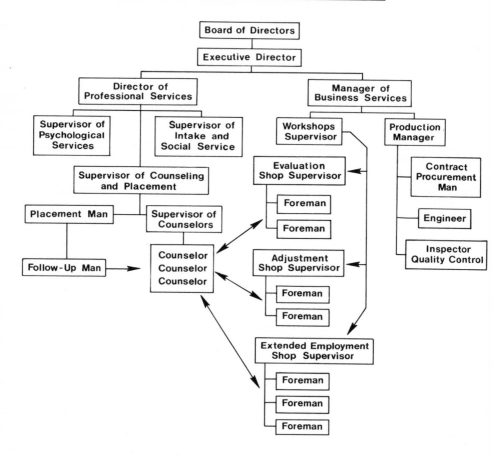

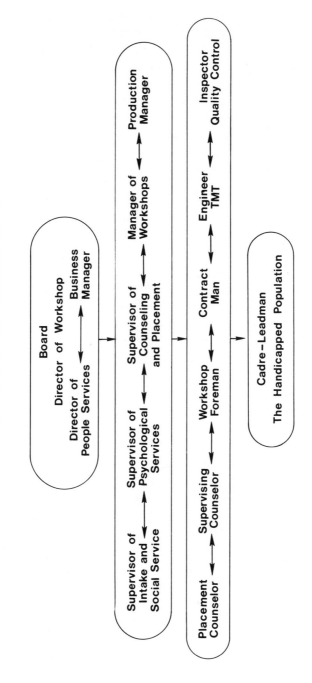

THE COORDINATION OF THE
WORKSHOP DUALITY FOR COMMUNICATION

Board
Director of Workshop

Director of People Services ←→ Business Manager

Supervisor of Intake and Social Service ←→ Supervisor of Psychological Services ←→ Supervisor of Counseling and Placement ←→ Manager of Workshops ←→ Production Manager

Placement Counselor ←→ Supervising Counselor ←→ Workshop Foreman ←→ Contract Man ←→ Engineer TMT ←→ Inspector Quality Control

Cadre–Leadman
The Handicapped Population

environment created by the operating duality and send out signals to the staff. In summary, the communication about the policies and resources goes down through the echelons and the unresolved problem goes up for arbitration. Because understanding and acceptance of policies and objectives are seldom complete, considerable coordination across echelous is necessary. This framework assumes that arbitration and accommodation should take place at a level where the decision makers are close to the problems and have intimate knowledge of the facts.

But tables of organization and flow charts cannot describe subtle factors arising out of staff philosophy, assumptions, and training, the influence of status or prestige, and the often potent influence of groups' attitudes and aspirations both of staff and the handicapped population. Thus, in a staffing which is representative of the duality, an opinion may predominate because it is more articulate but not necessarily more valid. And the attitudes and ideology of the director, his training and status, may condition the decisions and set patterns of priorities. Thus the domination of skewed ideology towards either part of the operational duality may make for an ineffective operation on one side or the other even when the table of organization or operational flow chart appears generally appropriate.

Another phenomenon that is not indicated by these illustrations is the overlapping created when personnel perform two functions in the duality at the same time, i.e. produce goods and provide people services at the same time. The principal staff person in this category is the foreman or floor supervisor. He is called by many names, but if he has direct responsibility for watching over a unit of handicapped persons at productive work, he usually performs both functions. Barton and Barton, in their pioneer study of floor supervisors, *The Requirements of Effective Workshop Supervision,* found that the floor supervisor exercised the following roles:

1. Manager of personnel and rehabilitation.
2. Human relations agent and leader.
3. Representative of the workshop duality.
4. Communicator.
5. Example for workers.

6. Manager of production.

7. Management and rehabilitation team member (3).

Also, it is surmised that counselors and others not supervising on the floor would influence outcomes on the floor. Thus there is usually overlapping between the two wings of the duality.

THE FINANCING OF PRIVATE WORKSHOPS

The resources of the workshop consist principally of funds, referrals, work, discards, equipment and plant, volunteer services and educational or promotional support. Here the discussion will involve primarily finances, since except in reconditioning shops, they are the major resources. This will be followed by a discussion of the appropriate identification of resources and costs.

The Sources of Funding

How does a workshop organization get financial resources? Since the workshop is both an economic and a charitable, service organization, perhaps the discussion should begin with consideration of resources getting by nonworkshop economic or charitable organizations. By such an analysis, we may discover the nature of workshop sources of funding and its capital problems.

The Nature of Workshop Resources

The Business Organization Resources

The economic or business organization gets capital resources from two general sources. It gets money from individuals or institutions who give or loan it money based on expectations that certain returns will acrue to them such as interest, dividends, or other types of gain. It gets money from the surplus resulting from the sale of products or services at rates in excess of its costs. We will oversimplify the situation by indicating that the sources of resources stem from investors and customers.

Investors generally provide money that is available before products and services are created. Customers provide resources which are generally available after the products or services are created. Both, however, expect to benefit, the customer from a desired product or service and the investor from some kind of economic gain.

The Economics of the Charitable Agency

The charitable service organization also gets resources from the same two general sources. However, there are differences between the kinds of customers and kinds of investors that the charitable agency gets. The charitable agencies' customers and investors usually buy services or invest to secure benefits for others – in the case of workshops, for handicapped persons. The economic investors, by contrast, buy or invest for their own interests. Another difference is that the benefits that the economic investors expect are concrete. They can sometimes require specific guarantees or safeguards before investing. The charitable or philanthropic investor, on the other hand, expects benefits which are more intangible. Nevertheless, he also sometimes specifies his expectations.

The Joint Resources

The workshop, being both an economic and charitable service organization, can get resources by selling its products or services or by getting philanthropic and government sources to make investments. A business investor is not likely to provide resources to a nonprofit corporation such as a workshop unless he is provided safeguards which are usually not available. The government investor is usually limited by legislation or local ordinances. The philanthropic investor has the most freedom to invest but he has a great variety of investment opportunities of considerable merit. The chance that he will invest in large amounts in workshops usually is not great. Thus the workshop is hard put to develop investments which make resources available beforehand without restriction. This condition would be alleviated if the workshop could acquire a surplus from its business operations, but this seldom happens. Here arises a problem in the development of resources, the inability of the workshop to develop nonrestricted capital.

The Dynamics of Resource Getting

Before discussing the means of acquiring resources, the principles discussed before need to be summarized. Resources become available from expectations. The customer expects that the product or services will meet his needs. The investor also must have some general belief that the resources he makes available will be used beneficially in the direction of his expectations. In the latter case, the situation is more fluid. The individual investor or contributor may provide resources relatively indiscriminately, but he also believes in some vague way that something good will happen. The foundation or community fund investor is more discriminating, and more specific in his expectations. The government investor is probably the most precise in his expectation. Thus resources are dependent upon the existence of expectations that their use will result in predetermined ends. Such expectations are developed by the administration.

How do expectations come about? They are generally the result of information or education and performance. In the first instance, they must be created. Once expectations are created and the organization gets the resources with expectations for their use, the continuance of expectation will depend in part on the successful accomplishment of such expectations. Sometimes scrutiny of accomplishment is slow in coming, but the trend both in private philanthropy and government is towards more precise evaluation of performance of expectations. Expectations must be created, and in the long run, successfully reinforced by performance.

The Time Span of Investments

The duration of investments in workshops falls into two categories, tempory and on-going. The majority are temporary. Usually sums are given for stated terms after which the workshop is expected to develop other resources. The ongoing investments are often given on an annual basis subject to review. They may not be continued if the shop does not meet requirements or if the source of funds is diminished or abolished. Very few funds are given in perpetuity and without conditions.

From what has been said about money given workshops beforehand, it is apparent that such funds are seldom a stable source of operating capital for workshops. These funds are called contributed revenue or income and do not constitute a large part of workshop capital generally.

Earned Income in Workshops

A major source of funds in workshops, although there are many exceptions, is the money which is earned by the sales of products, contract labor, or services, and from fees for services to handicapped persons. A principal characteristic of this phenomenon is that most of the money the workshop receives is available a considerable time after expenditures are made to earn it. Another is that the workshop cannot know ahead of time how large the earned income will be. This is, of course, not different from any business that depends upon sales, but the workshop has the added problem that part of its earned fee income depends upon the exigencies of local, state, and national politics. Thus when the workshop depends heavily upon fee income from services to agencies, its earned income may be partly as unstable as is its contributed income. This is important when its earned income is larger than contributed income, and constitutes the principal component in its resources.

The Specific Financial Resources of Workshops

One way to reduce the instability of workshop financing is to develop numerous sources of income. If the workshop depends upon a few large sources of income and one fails, the impact is greater than when it has numerous sources of income. It may therefore be useful to describe the various sources of contributed and earned income which are available to workshops in the United States.

The Sources of Contributed Income

The sources of contributed income are public and private, restricted and unrestricted. Public funds are usually more restricted than private funds. The public sources are national, state, and local. The private sources are most often local.

Public Sources of Contributed Income

The largest public source of contributed resources has been the federal government. Most grants which workshops received came from the Social and Rehabilitation Services of the Department of Health, Education, and Welfare. However, within the Department, grants have also been available from the National Institutes of Mental Health, the Public Health Service and the Office of Education. Workshops operated by county facilities can secure funds from the Social Security Amendments of 1965. Another possibility for workshops exists through the work incentive program of the Social Security Amendments of 1967. Among other departments the principal one making grants to workshops was the Department of Labor, principally under the Manpower Development and Training Acts.

Because the Social and Rehabilitation Services grants were in some instances especially established for workshops, their grant program is described. All of the grants are limited in time, with a usual duration of three years, and a maximum of five years. All of them, except the technical consultation program, require matching funds, although the matching for research and demonstration is minimal. The various grants provide money for new plants, remodeling of plants, equipment and staff for specified purposes. Grants are available for research and for demonstration as prescribed in an approved application. The applications for these grants are usually processed through the state vocational rehabilitation agency. All funds are restricted to the purposes for which they are given.

State funds are available in a few states in a number of ways. New York provides money to workshops based on staff positions that are approved. Missouri provides money based on a small per diem for each person in the shop. California provides money in similar manner but limits the number it covers. Lump sum payments are made by states such as Illinois and Wisconsin. In most of the states except New York, the money is relatively unrestricted.

Public contributions from counties to workshops are rare. Local school systems, however, often place teachers in workshops and pay their salaries. Counties and school systems operate workshops and pay their total costs.

Private Sources of Contributed Income

Private contributions have not been a great source of contributed income for workshops generally, but there are numerous sources of private contributions. National foundations have rarely supported workshops, but local and regional foundations have done so occasionally. Community chests and United Funds have provided funds occasionally, but usually not in large amounts. Parent or sponsoring organizations have more often provided funds, but also usually not in large amounts. Workshops have carried on their own fund drives and have made intermittent appeals for money without raising great sums as a rule. Occasionally, service organizations have contributed money but usually for specific purpose. Probably the largest contributions are those made through donated discards. These are used by reconditioning shops for conversion for sale and by contract shops for direct sale in thrift shops and bazaars. In general, contributed income is not restricted except for foundation grants.

The Sources of Earned Income

The principal sources of earned income come from sales of products and services or fees from services for handicapped persons. Under fees for services are included all other types of payments such as lump sum payments, per diem rates, and package payments. When purchasing services, the purchaser may designate the specific services desired or may leave this to the discretion of the workshop.

The Sources of Business Income

The largest amount of income for workshops as a whole probably comes from sales of products and from payments from subcontracts or services. Workshops manufacture products for sale or recondition discards for sale. They also take subcontracts from manufacturers, processors, or distributors. Although the sums received from these resources are large, the sums are received after the operation is over, and they contribute to future operations only if there is a surplus over costs. Thus, these sources may or may not create operating resources.

The Sources of Fee Income

The principal purchasers of services for handicapped persons are government, or public, agencies. Of this group, the state rehabilitation agency is usually the largest purchaser. The federal agencies which purchase services are the Veterans Administration and the Bureau of Hearings and Appeals of the Social Security Administration. Other state goverment agencies which purchase services are public health, social welfare, mental health, and corrections departments. On the local scene, the principal purchasers are the county welfare departments, the local health departments, and the public schools. Of the last group, the public schools are probably the largest source of support.

Private sources account for a relatively small share of workshop services. The largest group of private purchasers are probably the families of the handicapped persons. In addition, there are purchases of services by voluntary health agencies, service clubs, and by workmen's compensation carriers.

Percentage of Workshop Financing

Having indicated the various sources of financing, it might be useful to determine relative shares of income from various sources. There is no survey of sources of income on a national scale. However, John R. Kimberly has studied the financial structure of 123 workshops in New York, New Jersey, and

Pennsylvania. Table 1 gives his results for those states in December 1966, and Janaury 1967.

TABLE I

PERCENT CONTRIBUTION OF MAJOR SOURCES OF INCOME TO
TOTAL INCOME

Source of Income	New York	New Jersey	Pennsylvania	Total Sample
Sales, Services and Contracts	79.8	77.4	65.2	76.3
Fees from Clients	.2	2.0	.8	.4
Fees from Referring Agencies	6.6	11.9	10.1	7.7
Community Chest	3.0	2.5	6.1	3.7
Workshop Fund Drive	3.1	1.9	3.4	3.1
Parent Organizations	.2	1.2	2.1	.7
Grants	5.8	1.1	5.2	5.4
Other Income	1.3	2.0	7.1	2.7
Total Income	100.0	100.0	100.0	100.0

This table was taken from Kimberly's *The Financial Structure of Sheltered Workshops,* Region II Rehabilitation Research Institute, Cornell Univ. 1968, p. 6.

Kimberly pointed out that although as a whole income from business activities accounts for approximately three quarters of all income, the median proportion was 50 percent, since large workshops derive most of their income from sales, services, and contracts while smaller workshops tend to rely on other sources for their income (4).

William H. Button, working with data from 196 shops, principally in the eastern and central parts of the United States, found that their business income represented 55 percent of total income. The median among the shops was also 55 percent. He found also that business income was divided between subcontract income (57.2%), prime manufacturing (19.9%), salvage income (14.7%), and other income (7.8%) (5). Referral income represented 15 percent of total income on average, with a median of 5 percent.

The large percentages of sales, services and contract income indicated in these studies reflect larger involvement with prime manufacture than exists in some other regions of the country. The sales of manufactured products includes large percentages for materials. In the middle west for example, little prime manufacturing is done (6). In this region, the percentages from fee income would probably be higher. Also, the effect of the averaging phenomenon tends to diminish subgroup characteristics. Workshops for the mentally retarded would have relatively less business income and fee income and relatively more parent agency and other community support. Work adjustment shops, such as those operated by the Jewish Vocational Services, would have relatively less business income and relatively more fee income.

In spite of the limitations of the above information in precise description of regional and subgroup variations, it does provide general facts about the financial resources of workshops. Another study based on 194 workshops, conducted by the National Association of Sheltered Workshops and Homebound Programs, Inc., in 1967, resulted in similar findings in some respects (7). It found the following:

1. The major source of funds was sales and contracts.
2. The second source was fees for services.
3. The third major source was grants (public).
4. The fourth major source was local funds.

Based on available information, it may be stated that earned income is generally the largest source of funds, and that business income is generally a larger portion of earned income than fee income, though there are exceptions in individual shops (8). Contributed income is generally a much smaller portion of total income than earned income. Thus workshops generally get the larger portions of their income after they have earned it and minor portions of their revenue before they have expended it.

The only major resources that are generally available without strings come through fund drives and individual contributions. These are not found in all workshops and in any case constitute usually less than 10 percent of total income at best. The other principal sources of contributed income are from sponsoring or parent organizations and grants. Sponsoring organizations provide funds sometimes with general provisions and at other times with specific conditions. Grant money comes almost always with predefined specification as to use, except in cases where lump sums are provided for general purposes in a scattering of states. Thus on the whole, workshops get few unrestricted funds from contributed income.

The Major Resources: Business Income

The major source of funds is earned business income. Here the customer does not specify workshop objectives but does require that certain conditions be met, often in a purchase order or contract. Once the customer's conditions are met, he usually cares little what the shop does for handicapped persons. Thus, if workshops could generate funds in this category over those needed to meet customer demands, they could have resources available for allocation as they saw fit. Although statistics are not available, there is no reason to believe that workshops usually generate the equivalent of a profit, or a surplus, that they can use in their programs. It may be that they do not even recover enough costs to cover their expenses, since some workshops do not account for depreciation on donated items. The main handicap here is the workshop philosophy. Workshop personnel do not usually think in terms of earning a surplus from work. Thus often workshops forego the opportunity of using earnings for independent resources for programs. Unless the workshop is well endowed, it is usually dependent on purchasers of services for clients or on public or philanthropic investors.

The Resource Scarcity

Analysis of these facts together with other characteristics leads to the conclusion that the workshops live in a perpetual condition which may be called a resource scarcity. Another characteristic is that they often do not have complete autonomy over those scarce resources they do have. The workshops do not generate internally or usually do not get from without large sums of money which they can use as they see fit to achieve the objectives they choose. Thus they often allocate resources not in keeping with their internal needs but in response to outside influences.

The philosophy of the workshop which disposes it to shy away from an earned surplus also inhibits identification of costs. Since the workshop does not intend to make a "profit," and the workshop must have a "subsidy" in any case, the important thing is to find enough money from all sources to cover all costs no matter how engendered. This concept of showing all costs together is encouraged by volunteer accountants who consider workshops small operations not warranting functional accounting and who do not really understand the complex nature of the workshop economy. As a result, the workshop often is unable to identify the relationship between its resources and the ways in which they are used. This perpetuates its shortage of operating funds because it is not known why such shortages exist except in general terms.

The Identification of Workshop Costs

Workshops in the past have not usually identified their costs with the functions for which they were expended. They have generally listed costs by the most convenient rubrics available without respect to function. There is at present no way in most instances to determine the specific purposes for which money is spent in workshops. As shall appear, efforts are under way to correct this situation. Before considering these, it may be useful to indicate such categorical designations of expenditures as exist.

The Cornell Rehabilitation Research Institute in the publication indicated previously has recapped cost figure in workshops in the categories in which they are presently grouped. Button has indicated the aggregate expenses for 196 workshops as shown in Table II, p. 374.

Button also shows some classifications of capital costs, but since the original data from which the information is taken is not usually identified by expense objects, precise allocation of resources by objective cannot be determined. However, another general classification of income, expense, and costs per client gives significant information and is reproduced in Table III.

TABLE II

AGGREGATE EXPENSES FOR 196 WORKSHOPS

Type of Expense		Percent of Total	Mean	Median
Staff salaries	$11,168,490	21.6	56,982	32,500
Client wages	18,128,210	35.1	92,491	27,200
Material and supplies	12,383,820	24.0	63,183	7,800
Overhead and other	9,980,379	19.3	50,920	15,850
Total	$51,660,899	100.0	263,576	

Staff Salaries, by type		Percent of Total Staff Cost
Professional staff personnel	$ 3,495,737	31.3
Administrative, supervisory, and technical	4,701,934	42.1
Clerical and support personnel	2,970,818	26.6
Total	$11,168,490	100.0

This table has been compiled from tables 11 and 12 from Button (9).

TABLE III

AGGREGATED INCOME AND EXPENSE DATA FOR 196 SHELTERED WORKSHOPS WITH ESTIMATES OF PER CLIENT COSTS

A.	1.	Total expenses, 196 workshops*	$51,660,899
	2.	Expenses recovered through business operations†	40,963,080 (79.3%)
	3.	"Public costs" of workshop operation††	$10,697,819 (20.7%)
B.	1.	Total clients served annually	30,791
	2.	Average daily attendance	14,024
	3.	Total clients placed in competitive employment	4,931
	4.	Clients placed in competitive employment as a percent of total served	16%
C.	1.	Average public cost, total clients served in one year (Line A-3 ÷ B-1)	$ 347 per client
	2.	Average public cost for average number of clients served daily (Line A-3 ÷ B-2)	763 per client
	3.	Average public cost for each client placed in competitive employment (Line A-3 ÷ B-3)	2,170 per client
	4.	Average expense per client served daily (Line A-1 ÷ B-2)	3,684 per client

This table has been reproduced from Button, W. H. (10).

*Does not include capital costs (i.e. interest and/or depreciation in most cases) of facility, equipment and machines. Nonprofit organizations are restricted in the extent to which they can accumulate depreciation revenues.

†Assumes that returns from business operations cover costs of production including labor, materials, and overhead.

††"Public costs" include all costs borne by governmental units, particularly referral agencies purchasing services, and contributions and donations made to workshops from local community fund drives or distributed to workshops from charitable donations collected by parent or sponsoring associations.

The Separation of Costs of the Duality

The difficulty with most expenditure figures in workshop records has been that they do not separate the costs of production, the costs of services to people, and the costs of administering these two segments of workshops. As a result, it is impossible to determine how the income from business compares with the costs of doing business, and how the income from people services compares with the cost of people services. Thus the workshops which do not separate their costs cannot know how much they should be getting from their business customers and from their purchasers of services. Neither can they know how to allot resources to these respective activities with accuracy. To remedy this situation, several accounting systems have been suggested which attempt to identify costs by these functions.

In 1964, the writer suggested that workshops classify their expenditures under three headings — administrative expense, rehabilitation expense, and contract or manufacturing expense. The costs of administration could then be alloted to rehabilitation or production expense in proportion to the amounts spent in these categories. The total rehabilitation expense can then be compared with earned income from fees from agencies and parents and from contributed income, and the total business expense can be compared with business income (11). This of course would involve identifying the proportion of time a floor supervisor spent in production and rehabilitation.

The Analysis of Costs and Revenue in Workshops

The problem of separating costs was undertaken by James Caddick, who developed a comprehensive reporting system which separated and analyzed the business and people services expenses and revenues in workshops. By using his methods, many of the hidden costs of people services are identified.

Caddick's analysis begins with this introduction:

> Since a workshop is both a business enterprise and a social agency (a business with a heart), its director or manager must be able to isolate the activities in each sphere if he is to be successful in controlling its energies. Treating it as a financial whole will usually

result in no control at all, or even worse, in the workshop's problems so overwhelming the staff that they are forced to live from crisis to crisis (12).

Caddick's approach consists of distributing or allocating expense and revenue after analyzing each expense object and revenue item. One principle he stresses has to do with distribution of costs of personnel who have dual functions in business and people services. In dividing these costs between the two, he suggests that the proportion spent by private industry for personnel and training functions be used as a dividing mark for some personnel and the excess be allotted to people services costs. Supervisors or foremen are divided proportionate to the number of clients they supervise as compared to the number of workers supervised by their counterparts in competitive employment. He also developed the concept of "client productivity" as a base for allocating expense. A ratio is developed which expresses the "client productivity" as compared to industrial norms. If the client productivity is 60 percent of industrial norms, then 40 percent of certain costs such as supervision, occupancy, and administrative costs are shown as costs of services to people rather than business costs.

Caddick also provides guidelines for the analysis of revenue and especially of contributed income. He stresses the importance of including noncash contributions and of showing them as expenses as well. As examples, he cites free use of buildings, utilities paid by others, contributed materials, staff paid by others, and full-time volunteers. He also provides guidelines for separating depreciation between purchased assets and contributed assets.

To illustrate the way this kind of reporting would show up for a small shop, the operating statement for an imaginary shop is shown in Table IV, pp. 377-379.

For some time before Caddick had been working on his guidelines, the project advisory committee for the National Health Council — National Welfare Assembly Uniform Accounting Project had been studying a revision of the 1962 publication of the National Health Council, *Accounting and Financial Reporting for Voluntary Health Agencies.* In December 1964, the committee published a substantial revision, *Standards of Accounting and Financial Reporting for Voluntary Health and Welfare Organizations.* Because its title was long and it was published in a black

TABLE IV

OPERATING STATEMENT
(For the Month of July)

	Allo-cation Note	Total	Admin.	Rehab.	Business
Income					
Contracts		4,247			4,247
Product sales		2,510			2,510
Service fees		1,468		1,468	
Donations		604		604	
Foundation grant		2,250		2,250	
Other income		13			13
Total income		11,092	——	4,322	6,770
Accts Received Adjustment	1	(471)		(511)	40
Goods in process and finished					
Goods inventory adjustment	2	(1,295)	——		(1,295)
Adjusted Totals		9,326		3,811	5,515
Accounts Payable Increase	3	443			443
Expense					
Staff salaries	4	3,422	1,040	1,086	1,296*
Client wages	4	2,679	435	153	2,091
Payroll taxes	5	512	124	104	284
Product materials and supplies		1,255			1,255
Rent	6	300	39	33	288*
Insurance	6	27	4	3	20
Testing supplies		30		30	
Office supplies		45	45		
Postage		38	38		
Maintance supplies and repairs		51	51		
Utilities	6	189	25	21	143*
Telephone		68	68		
Freight		99			99
Travel		50	50		
Miscellaneous		131	131		
			2,050		
Allocate administrative	7		(2,050)	1,025	1,025*
Client productivity related to rehabilitation				1,614	(1,614)
Total expense		9,339	-0-	4,069	5,270
Net gain (loss)		(13)		(258)	245

*Clients are paid by piece rates. They worked 3,261 hours. All work is bid, and piece rates are set at the prevailing industrial rate of $1.60 per hour. The 64¢ per hour is 40% of $1.60, a productivity if compared with non-handicapped persons of 40%. Subtracting 40% from 100% gives the 60% rehabilitation factor to be applied to those business expense items which are exclusively related to the number of clients. The rehabilitation factor is deducted from business expenses and added to rehabilitation expenses since it arises out of the low productivity of clients and would not be a cost for a profit seeking business.

Source: James Caddick Associate Rehabilitation Workshop Administration University of San Francisco.

NOTES FOR OPERATING STATMENT

Note

1. From Schedule A. Accounts Receivable — Trade increased $40 (from $5,882 to $5,922) and Accounts Receivable — State agencies decreased $511 (from $1,624 to $1,113) for a net decrease of $471.

2. From Schedule A. Finished Goods Inventory decreased $1,309 (from $5,208 to $3,899) and Goods in Process increased $14 (from $513 to $527) for a net decrease of $1,295. This means that $1,295 of July's sales came from work done *before* the month of July.

3. From Schedule A. Accounts Payable increased $443 (from $417 to $860). This means that we have incurred $443 of expenses during July which have not yet been shown as expenses.

4. From Schedule B.

5. Payroll taxes of $512 are 8.4% of the $6,101 total wages. The amount of payroll taxes for each department will be 8.4% of the staff salaries and client wages charged in that department.

6. From Schedule B. The space used by each department is shown as a percentage. The expenses for the occupancy costs of rent, insurance and utilities are allocated to each department according to the percentage of space occupied by that department.

7. Administrative expense is allocated to the operating, income producing departments of Rehabilitation and Business in proportion to the estimate of time spent by administrative personnel. This is assumed to be 50% in each.

SCHEDULE B

Personnel Allocation

	Monthly Salary	Clients Supv'd	Function where time is spent					
			Admin		Rehab		Business	
			%	$	%	$	%	$
General Manager	857		35	300	35	300	30	275
Secretary	510		100	510				
Rehab Counselor	724				90	652	10	72
Bookkeeper (Part Time)	230		100	230				
Foreman	563	20**					100	563
Foreman	538	15**			25	134	75	404
	3,422	35		1,040		1,086		1,296
Client Wages								
(July)*	2,679			435		153		2,091

*Wages include $435 paid for clerical work and $153 of wage subsidy.
**Foreman in competitive employment would supervise 20 workers.

Space Utilization

	Total			
Square Feet	12,000	1,500	1,300	9,200
Percentage	100	13	11	76

hard cover, it became known as the Black Book. It was a financial landmark in the national voluntary movement. It provided standard forms for reporting for all private agencies in the country that wished to use it, including an Analysis of Functional Expenditures. Those workshops who were parts of health or welfare agencies who adopted it used its forms. Some other workshops who received funds from local private funding agencies were requested to use it.

Excellent as the Black Book is for health and welfare agencies, its forms were not ideally suited for workshop organizations who need to separate business and people services costs. The functional classifications of the Black Book related to programs or units of social welfare agencies who had separate programs. It is of course possible to use the Black Book and with supplementary reports separate production and people services costs. However, the forms were not designed for this purpose. The workshops needing to report in this manner and also to separate business and people services costs needed assistance in formal record keeping. For this reason the Social and Rehabilitation Services in 1967 funded a project of the Goodwill Industries of America to develop a uniform accounting system for workshops.

A Uniform Accounting System for Workshops

The Uniform Accounting Project of the Goodwill Industries of America first reported in 1968. It is based on the Black Book principles but is expanded to accommodate workshop reporting. It structured identification of activities under four headings: program services, supporting services, property and equipment acquisitions, and payments to affiliated agency. Under program services were shown rehabilitation training services and industrial program auxiliary services and research, and internship and training. Under supporting services were shown management and fund raising (13).

It also set up an evaluation system with inputs and outputs implemented by a computer model which analyzes the relationships of the human and financial resources that the agency takes from the community and the returns it provides.

The inputs to the system are the revenue data, functional data, and the community need data. The community data includes principally the population in the catchment area, geographic area description, services provided by neighboring agencies, potential competing services provided by commercial organizations, and surveys of handicapped population and of available trained professional personnel. The determination of good performance is developed by quantifiable measures related to the objectives of the workshop. The differences between allocation of resources by the community and the benefit it receives is stated. Some of the factors which are related are the cost and amount of services on a given budget, the numbers served, the size of the geographic area, and the sales volume (14).

A unique aspect of the Standard Accounting Project is its method of reflecting the costs of production and training. The Standard Accounting Project uses the term *training* or *training services* for the concept of services to people and also shows rehabilitation services as supportive services. It attempts to identify training costs in a "productive rehabilitation environment." The components are identified as: [1] training supervision, [2] department training, [3] training materials, [4] indirect or supportive costs, and [5] training maintenance.

The concept is based on the idea that there is a cost of training that is in excess of the cost of supervising production. It is assumed that the amount of increase in productivity is the result of training. The training element may be measured by the different levels of achievement of the trainee at stated times. This is his productivity increase factor. It is applied to total departmental costs less salaries and wages for production (15). On the other hand, the training maintenance cost is attributable to departmental expense for client/employees who have stabilized their productivity below the departmental average, but continue to work in the department. The amount of cost is determined by the productivity decrease factor.

The Standard Accounting Project system is probably more complex than the system suggested by Caddick. Also, it probably does not reflect some of the added costs required for people services. Moreover, workshop directors have complained that both systems require more skilled accounting personnel than they can afford. This problem always exists when small organizations need more resources than they can accumulate. It is essential, however, that workshops acquire adequate ability to account for their costs.

SUMMARY

Workshop organizations fall into two classifications — public and private organizations. The vast majority are private organizations. In general, they are administered more flexibly than public workshops.

Administration of the private workshop must deal with both external forces in the community and internal forces in the shop. Often administration pays more attention to the internal forces in the organization than the external forces in the community. The internal forces in the organization stem from the sponsoring organization, the staff, and the handicapped population of the shop. Of these forces, the most crucial are the boards of directors. Boards are generally active or inactive. Active boards are supportive, responsible, or directive.

The principal problems with staff is to minimize the strains between business and professional groups to achieve maximum contribution from them by arbitrating demands for prestige and power. This can be done by a balanced internal structure which allows each group opportunity for self expression and creativity. A necessary part of such a structure is a parallel communication system which provides equal opportunity for communication across hierarchial lines and provides feedback. With such a structure it is possible to allot resources adequately.

The resources of workshops are many. Their financial resources come from earned and contributed income. Contributed income is available beforehand but is small in workshops. Earned income comprises the largest resource but comes after services are rendered and seldom generates a surplus. Thus the workshop is often in a state of a resources scarcity.

Because of the resources scarcity, it is important for a workshop to identify its costs and sources of revenue and separate them in a function accounting system generic to workshops. Two such systems have been suggested, one by James Caddick and another by the Standard Accounting Project of Goodwill Industries of America. It is necessary that one of these or an equivalent system be utilized if workshops are to be able to account for their use of resources.

NOTES

1. These include the publications of the Cornell Rehabilitation Institute cited previously.
2. Suazo, A. E. (Ed.): A Study of the Characteristics and Practices of Sheltered Workshops, Washington, The National Association of Sheltered Workshops and Homebound Programs, undated.
3. Barton, E. H. and Barton, E. F.: The Requirements of Effective Sheltered Workshop Supervision, San Jose, Goodwill Industries of Santa Clara, Inc., 1965.
4. Kimberly, J. R.: The Financial Structure of Sheltered Workshops. Ithaca, Rehabilitation Research Institute, Cornell University, 1968, p. 5-6.
5. Button, W. H.: Sheltered Workshops in the United States — An Institutional Overview. Ithaca, Region II Rehabilitation Institute, Cornell University, 1970, Chart II, following p. 20, Table 10, following p. 24.
6. Economic Impact and Production Potential of Sheltered Workshops. Washington, NASWHP, 1969, p. 48.
7. Suazo, op. cit., Economic Impact and Production Potential of Sheltered Workshops, op. cit., pp. 4-8.
8. Barton and Barton, op. cit., table 4, pp. 14-15.
9. Button, op. cit., table 11 & 12, pp. 38-39.
10. Ibid., table 14, p. 43.
11. Nelson, N.: The economics of a subcontract and manufacturing workshop. Journal of Rehabilitation, July-August, 1964.
12. Caddick, J.: Procedures Used to Separate and Analyze Business and Services to People Expenses and Revenues in Rehabilitation Workshops. San Francisco, University of San Francisco, Rehabilitation Workshop Administration, undated, p. 1.
13. Identification of Activities, Washington, Standard Accounting Project, Goodwill Industries of America, 1969, p. 1.
14. Evaluation System Inputs and Outputs. Washington, Standard Accounting Project, Goodwill Industries of America, 1969, pp. 1-3.
15. Training Costs Accounting Procedures. Washington, Standard Accounting Project, Goodwill Industries of America, 1969, pp. 1.

Part Three

The Future of Workshops

"If a man does not keep pace with his companions, perhaps it is because he hears a different drummer. Let him step to the music which he hears, however measured or far away."

—*Henry David Thoreau*

XIV

THE FUTURE OF WORKSHOPS

To predict the future of workshops is probably impossible. Chances of forecasting accurately the course of all factors which will determine that future are negligible. Nevertheless, it is prudent to try to foresee opportunities and possible pitfalls.

To extrapolate into the future requires assessing the past and the present as they affect future possibilities. Such an assessment can indicate how existing programs will need to be modified to meet new conditions, or revised so that new and essentially different goals may be undertaken. Future changes are more likely to succeed, however, if they meet the aspirations of handicapped persons and are a part of the economic and social goals of the nation.

Consideration of the future of workshops may well begin, therefore, by scanning the directions the country has taken in the past in meeting the needs of its least successful people — the handicapped and disadvantaged.

THE CULTURAL INFLUENCES
AFFECTING WORKSHOPS

The central ideology of the United States has been that the greatest economic and social rewards, benefits, and prestige rightly go to those who are most successful in their economic or political performance. Those only moderately successful get fewer rewards or benefits and those who are least successful get scarcely any benefits at all. This economic and political system has proven acceptable because it has provided a relatively high level of benefits to the moderately successful majority of the people. It has little to offer those who cannot or do not perform well in the economic sphere or those who are not allowed to perform at an appropriate level because of social or psychological prejudices. The benefits to the least successful minority are kept low by design on the premise that if adequate benefits were available without great effort society would not make progress. The implicit assumption is that those who are least successful are not as worthy as those that are more successful. Thus, the least successful minority is kept on meager private charity or public assistance on the overall premise that each person receives benefits generally in keeping with his contribution to society. The American culture gives little consideration to the person whose economic contribution is minimal.

Flowing out of this ideology from its founding, the country has accepted the premise that government should not be involved in the efforts of its citizens to secure economic benefits. The idea was soon eroded, however, as the exigencies of circumstances induced the federal government to intervene on behalf of the most successful minority, providing tariffs, subsidies, land grants, and authorized monopolies during the course of the nineteenth century. These aids to the most successful were justified on the basis that they would benefit the majority of people indirectly by enhancing the economy.

The economic dislocations beginning with our urbanization at the close of the nineteenth century and culminating in the major depression of the 1930's made it clear that the intervention of the federal government on behalf of the most successful minority did not necessarily provide secure benefits for the majority of the productive population. The experience also brought into question the theory that each individual receives benefits in proportion to his contribution. There was recognition of the fact that the moderately successful majority of people were affected by factors beyond their control. This understanding redounded to the benefit of the least successful minority as well.

When as a result of the economic debacle of the 1930's new safeguards were instituted to protect the economic security of the majority of people, minor new benefits were made available to some groups of the handicapped. As a result of the Social Security Act of 1935, the unsuccessful minority was divided roughly into two groups: those whose lack of success was attributed to physical or mental disability or old age or desertion, and those whose failures were attributed to their unworthiness. The former were given increased money payments through federal financing. The latter were given the existing assistance payments through the counties or local jurisdictions.

The state-federal program of vocational rehabilitation, passed in 1920, provided another economic aid plan. This program gave handicapped persons opportunity to become employable and leave the unsuccessful minority. Originally established for the physically handicapped, by 1968 it was open to persons with all types of handicaps. As has been seen, the workshops which had been providing occupational training and sheltered employment many years before became part of the new program. Thus was provided opportunity for those who could compete in private employment. The state-federal program provided few employment opportunities for those who were not expected to engage in remunerative employment.

By 1970, clear legislative outlines of social programs have emerged for providing opportunities to become employable for all those who are physically and mentally handicapped. The legislative framework for rehabilitation programs for the disadvantaged is less clear but has been grossly formulated. Still no program national in scope was conceived for those handicapped or disadvantaged persons who could not be expected to engage in substantial employment, nor a national public system of work for those unacceptable to private industry.

The legislative limitations of the national programs for the solution of the employment problems of our least successful people need to be stressed. They were twofold: the programs did not serve the unemployables, nor all of those who could be prepared for work. The state-federal Vocational Rehabilitation Program completes services successfully to fewer persons each year than become handicapped in the year (1). In the fiscal year 1969, the program rehabilitated 241,390 persons, a small portion of the over 17 million people who were limited in life because of handicapping conditions. Of these 17 million over 5 million were unable to do their former job and over 6 million others were severely handicapped (2). The workshops of the country serve even a smaller segment of the unsuccessful population — about one fourth of those served by the government rehabilitation program (3).

OBSTACLES TO PARTICIPATION IN WORK

There are many reasons why the problems of the least successful handicapped persons remain largely unsolved. A major influence making solution difficult is the economic philosophy of the country which assumes generally that the economy will produce maximum benefits to all if it is left to operate automatically. Of course, many exceptions are made, and in the case of the handicapped, the vocational rehabilitation program is provided for limited numbers of those needing it. However, almost no effort is made to modify the working of the industrial system to enable the handicapped to participate in it. It is assumed that a solution to the problem is in force. Such an assumption ignores the millions of handicapped persons who are unable to secure rehabilitation services or who are deemed unable to work in industry. The prevailing economic philosophy of the country and the existence of the vocational rehabilitation program have had the effect of deterring the country from seeking a comprehensive and fundamental solution of the problems of all handicapped and disadvantaged persons. Consequently, the country has never given its major attention or committed sufficient resources to the vocational welfare of all handicapped persons.

A second deterrent to solving the problems of some handicapped groups lies in American attitudes, explicit or implicit, which have denied equal employment opportunity for psychological and social reasons or because of failure to understand the nature of the handicap. Thus the epileptic, mentally retarded, the mentally ill, the ethnic groups, and the culturally and educationally deprived have been unjustly excluded from economic participation in society.

Thirdly, in spite of the research carried on and the experience of many rehabilitators, very little is known definitively about the factors that make for the vocational success of handicapped persons. We do know from observation that some handicapped persons who receive services in keeping with the best methods known still fail to work successfully.

In summary, it seems most likely that in the foreseeable future there will be persons who cannot be employed within the framework of our present economic system and who can be helped to engage in useful work only by modifying the existing economic system by adding a nonprofit work appendage to it.

The inability of existing programs to meet the vocational needs of large groups of handicapped and disadvantaged persons is well described by Herbert Rusalem and Roland Baxt in a report for a Planning Committee of the National Citizens Conference on Rehabilitation of the Disabled (4). The groups include the homebound, the institutionalized, the severely handicapped and the aged. In addition to their disability, the handicapped often suffer additional deprivation as a result of lack of educational opportunity, lack of skills or work experience, or ethnic or migrant status. These conditions blunt motivation and cause distrust of the environment. Employer and labor union attitudes towards them are often negative or restrictive. Rehabilitation personnel engaging in stereotyped procedures fail to see possibilities for employment in persons coming to them from these groups of deprived outsiders.

A basic limitation of rehabilitation philosophy is pointed out by Rusalem and Baxt. They suggest that services may be restricted in the following way:

> ... by professional perspectives of rehabilitation as an adjusting mechanism. Virtually unchanged since the 1920's is the belief that rehabilitation has the mission of assisting clients to fit into existing society rather than changing society to make it more adapted to disabled persons. Moved by political conservatism and expediency, rehabilitation has sought to change the client and not the world. Yet, society is not altogether a desirable place for the disabled under the best of circumstances. Yet, we have failed to deliver what is perhaps the most needed service of all — social action to provide a better world for the deprived. Most rehabilitation workers do not perceive themselves as bearers of this responsibility. Consequently, they readily become apologists for a society which, in some respects, makes excessive demands upon the disabled and provides all too few benefits for them (5).

It is safe to predict that American society will probably provide more benefits to the handicapped and the disadvantaged in the future. It is doubtful, however, that American society will rapidly change its structure, especially its economic structure, to accommodate the handicapped. Its benefits to the handicapped will probably be augmented initially within the framework of existing social patterns. How much the benefits to the handicapped will be increased will depend on national priorities — the relative emphasis put on military goals as contrasted with goals for people. What is more difficult to predict is the nature of the increased benefits. Should the nature of money payments primarily be increased, to add a guaranteed annual income, the growth of workshops may be slowed or retarded. Should the expanded benefits consist of new and more rehabilitation or vocational training services, the growth of workshops may be hastened. If the expanded benefits will come in the form of a national nonprofit employment program for handicapped persons, and if workshops were given responsibility for such a program, the growth of workshops would be tremendous. Such a program might, however, be assigned to industry, in which case workshops would increase minimally.

Thus the future of workshops depends primarily upon what policies the nation adopts in augmenting benefits to the handicapped. If the nation maintains its present low priority for the welfare of handicapped persons, workshops will increase the numbers served at its characteristically slow pace. If the nation increases its benefits to handicapped persons through existing channels — by money payments and vocational rehabilitation services — the growth of workshop services will be greater, but it will consist of supplementary services to vocational rehabilitation programs. If the country should determine to provide the handicapped and disadvantaged with employment in extended employment workshops, then the numbers served in workshops would increase tremendously. The last mentioned alternative, however, is not likely. Should the nation decide to set up a national program to guarantee employment to handicapped persons, it is more likely such a program would be assigned to industry. It is most likely, however, that the United States will not attempt to provide a national employment program for handicapped persons but will continue to enable some of them to work in private industry through the services of the vocational rehabilitation program. If this conjecture is born out, the country will not in the near future be able to supply millions of handicapped and disadvantaged persons with employment.

THE FUTURE OF THE PRIVATE
AGENCY IN WORKSHOP EXPANSION

In the previous discussion, the nation and its public agencies were viewed as the possible source of funds for workshop expansion. However, in the past, private philanthrophy has also been a source of funds for services to the handicapped, often with substantial public funds. The workshops are operated mostly by private voluntary agencies. Can private funds be generated in increased amounts to expand workshop services to the extent needed? Will the private agencies develop an extended nonprofit employment system which will provide employment to those who cannot work in private industry?

It seems unlikely that private charity will assume a greater share of the cost of workshop programs. The trend in the recent past has been for the government to assume an increasingly larger share of workshop costs while the private agencies diminished their share. There is nothing to indicate that a reversal will take place. Since the private workshops dominate the field and increased services are probable, the present expectation is that the increased services will be supported in ever increasing amounts and in a larger share by government funds. Will government funds be available in ever increasing amounts without increasing controls in the operation of the private agency workshops?

Government agencies in the United States have shown little inclination to exercise administrative controls over privately operated workshops. In the few instances where the state vocational rehabilitation agency attempted to exercise administrative influence, there have been both successes and failures. State agencies have, of course, influenced the development of workshop services, but this has usually been in the role of a customer. If, however, a national high priority were to be given to employment of handicapped persons and the support came from tax sources, would there not be more influence or control by government agencies? Would there not be suggestions that since government was paying the costs, it should control or operate the programs?

In general, public agencies have shown little inclination to take over the operation of workshop programs. Government programs have been quite willing to fund parts of private programs without intensive oversight of the expenditures. Such oversight as has occurred routinely has been of an auditing rather than of an administrative nature. Thus the private workshop has been able to spend public money without submitting to substantial program supervision. This situation has existed because there has been little critical lay concern over a program which is generally considered to be doing good for disabled persons.

If the country should decide to provide training or employment to millions of handicapped and disadvantaged persons through private agencies which were spending public money and were at the same time producing goods and services entering into the economy, it is quite possible that a much greater degree of management oversight would be initiated. Yet review of policy decisions and administrative actions after they take place is often gratuitous and sometimes untenable. In the few instances where public funds principally finance private agency workshops, the public agency best exerts its influence before policies are made by naming representatives on the board of the private agency workshops. Such representatives may have an influence far in excess of their numerical importance, since they represent the principal source of funding. When they have a major influence, the private agency becomes a quasi-public agency.

The quasi-public agency is virtually unknown among American private workshops. It is unlikely that private agencies will accept this form of control, even though it presents a workable public-private partnership. The alternatives are to accept increasing oversight by the government bureaucracy or to acquire money from nonpublic sources.

WORK INCOME AS A SOURCE OF SUPPORT

Since the voluntary agencies have not been able or willing to raise massive funds for workshops from private giving, they may turn to sales or work income as a source of support. The prospect of engendering sales or work income as a principal source of support is frequently not given consideration by private workshops. When they operate short-term programs, the possibilities of substantial proportions of income from contract work seems remote. However, when long-term programs or extended employment programs are conducted, it is possible to engender internally substantial amounts of work income. To do so, workshops will need, by becoming more sophisticated industrially, to raise major revenue from their productive activities. To the extent that they do, they will move closer to the industrial community. Movement in this direction is inhibited, however, by a reluctance to do sophisticated industrial work because it is not considered a necessary part of rehabilitation services for the handicapped individuals. If workshop personnel should learn to use sophisticated or complex industrial processes, they may be able to enhance the prospects for employment of the handicapped in industry and will make a larger portion of their income from such processes. To the extent that they do so, they can minimize the necessity of government financing and ultimately of government control.

MAJOR PATHS TO WELFARE OF THE HANDICAPPED

The various paths which the country can take in serving the needs of handicapped persons have been described. Which of these paths the nation takes will influence the size of future workshop programs. If the decision is to emphasize money payment, the growth of workshop programs will be slowed. If the policy is to expand the vocational rehabilitation program, the growth of workshops will be speeded up moderately. If permanent employment in the workshop is included in the national goal, the growth will be tremendous. Permanent employment in workshops is currently the greatest need. To anticipate the possible growth in these categories, it is necessary to determine the numbers of persons in the United States who need workshop services.

THE NEED FOR WORKSHOP SERVICES

The need for workshop services may be interpreted variously depending upon how need is conceived. Different sponsors value certain services and objectives and underrate others. Some objectives which sponsors value highly are sometimes impossible to achieve. Need may thus be classified into actual need, felt need, and realizable or feasible need (6). The limiting factors in feasible need are usually money and sometimes work.

It is impossible to predict what services and objectives future sponsors will consider important. What can be done is to conceive the actual need without attempting to forecast what sponsors will consider important or will be willing to support. With the services and objectives in mind, it will then be possible to indicate the information which is available about the numbers and kinds of individuals who can benefit from all different kinds of services. The result will be a description of actual need.

The information about unsuccessful, marginal, and disadvantaged people in the United States has not been collected in a summary fashion. Thus, there is no grouping of people by demographic characteristics which includes all of the physically and mentally disabled, the uneducated, the depressed or stigmatized because of ethnic or social origin, and the deviate, the public offenders, and the inept, nomadic, antisocial, addicted populations. In recent years, some information has been obtained about the person with chronic conditions and disabilities, and more recently a good deal of information has been made available about the poor. Information about the other groups noted would need to be secured separately. The disability and poverty information, however, is useful as a base (7).

In a Public Health Survey (1963-1965) made by contacting family members, it was found that there were in the United States 12,347,000 persons of all ages with conditions which affected the amount or kind of major activity they undertook, 4,122,000 persons who were unable to carry on any major activity, and approximately 9,000,000 persons of working age with chronic disabilities which affected their work ability. A Social Security Survey of Disabled Adults (1966), made by contacting the disabled person found that there were 17,753,000 persons who had chronic conditions which affected their ability to work. Of this number, 5,014,000 were unable to do their former job and 6,100,000 were severely disabled (8). In 1967, a Social Security Survey found that 26,000,000 Americans lived below the poverty line ranging from 1,145 dollars for a single member household on a farm to 5,000 dollars for a household of seven or more in a city. It is assumed that some of the adults counted in the poverty group fall into some of the categories of the disadvantaged groups (9).

A rule of thumb yardstick which has been used by workshop personnel is that about 10 percent of the physically handicapped and chronically ill population will need the services of a workshop (10). Assuming this percentage for all groups of handicapped persons and that more than 10 million fall into the latter classification, this would leave more than 1,000,000 persons who need workshop services because of physical and mental disability. The European experience, where only sheltered work is emphasized, indicates that approximately .005 percent of the total population receives workshop services. Applying this yardstick to the United States population, we would arrive at a figure close to 1 million. This is a conservative estimate.

It is difficult to predict how many persons in disadvantaged categories who have no physical handicaps need workshop services. Of the 26 million in the poverty group, large numbers would not be able to attend workshops for a variety of reasons. However, from analysis of the experience of the public assistance workshops, it is believed that large numbers in the poverty group could benefit from workshops, and it appears that considerable numbers would accept workshop services under appropriate conditions. Because the wages in workshops and the regulations affecting retention of public assistance payments would influence workshop attendance greatly, it is extremely difficult to anticipate workshop utilization among the disadvantaged groups. All that can be said is that additional numbers of persons would seek workshop services if an industrial atmosphere was obtained and it was possible to retain substantial proportions of a substantial workshop wage. Much would depend upon the size of the workshop wage. One might hazard a guess that more than a half million more disadvantaged workers would attend workshops if the retainable income was considerable.

We have related that in 1968, the workshops served about 65,000 persons at any given time and provide services to about 175,000 persons during the year. Using these figures, workshops have served about 17.5 percent of the persons with physical or mental disabilities who are presumed to need their services. If needs of the disadvantaged are included, the percentage would be considerably less. Thus it appears that although the number of workshops have expanded rapidly in the United States in the last twenty years (from 800 to 1,500), they have not begun to meet the need for their services. If workshops were to retain approximately their present size, there would need to be about 7,500 workshops in the United States to serve all potential applicants. However, individual workshops have generally been increasing the numbers they serve, and it appears that with some exceptions this increase will continue. However, concurrent with the increase, workshop organizations have established satellite or branch shops. This trend will also probably continue. It is estimated that if workshops are to serve all the needs for their services, the number of work places would need to triple to somewhat less than 5,000.

Will workshops be able to expand to 5,000 shops and serve more than a million handicapped persons in the future? Will handicapped persons seek their services in such numbers? These questions must be answered along with others. Will the workshops add long-term employment to their programs? Will they provide substantial wages and fringe benefits? Will they provide workshop settings where men can work with dignity? If the answers to these questions are affirmative, the workshops may be able to expand greatly.

To do these things, however, three things primarily are needed: more financing, more work, and more public understanding of the nature of workshops and their contribution to society. Of these three needs, workshop personnel are usually more confident in their ability to secure financing and influence public opinion than in their ability to get work.

THE FUTURE OF WORK IN THE
UNITED STATES WORKSHOPS

Of all the resources the workshop needs, the most crucial is work. Work distinguishes the workshop from most other programs providing rehabilitative or social benefits. The future of workshops will depend greatly upon questions centering around work. Principal among such questions are the following: What will be the future of work and the work role in American society? Will workshops be able to generate enough work to support considerable expansion of workshop programs? What kinds of work will be required by the economy in the future?

The Influence of Technology
Upon the Future of Work

Recently, a number of social and economic thinkers began to visualize the prospect that work might some day be unnecessary for vast numbers of the population. Work, they point out, has been an onerous necessity throughout history. When man could find ways to escape work, he has done so. Nevertheless, cultural patterns have developed to give work both status and a cultural imperative. But modern technology will rid mankind of much of this ancient burden. The cultural imperative to work need no longer exist. Ways can be found to give men income or wherewithal to lead the good life without working.

The above projection applies to all people, not only the handicapped, and is conceived as applicable to future times. The concept is applied more immediately to handicapped persons specifically. Since the need for work is diminishing, say these social thinkers, let us not urge handicapped persons to work, especially the low producers who will never produce a great volume of work in any case. Let us teach them to seek rewarding social and recreational activities. Let us teach society to honor them for living graciously without work. Let us change the cultural emphasis on work and develop a new outlook more in keeping with modern technological developments. This approach appeals to those who believe in the importance of the individual and see the low producers among the handicapped as doing little productive work. It makes a virtue out of a seeming necessity.

It should be realized that the prediction that the necessity to work will disappear is largely a prediction for the future. There is no evidence that a lesser percentage of people are working now than formerly. Seymour L. Wolfbein, in Labor Trends, Manpower, and Automation, points out that in this century the portions of persons in the labor force has remained practically unchanged. Decennial census data show that 53.7 percent of all persons 14 years of age and over were in the labor force in 1900; by 1950 the figure was 54 percent; and by 1960, it was 55.3 percent. Not only has the percentage of persons in the labor force remained stable but people put in more years of work than they did previously. Since 1900, ten years of working life have been added by men and twelve by women. A group of 100,000 boys born in 1900 will produce 3,200,000 man-years of work; a similar number of boys born in 1960 will yield 4,200,000 man-hours of work during their lifetime. A comparable group of girls will triple the performance of their 1900 counterparts (11). There is nothing in the existing record to indicate that man's participation in work is diminishing.

There are, of course, changes in the nature of the work being done. A major shift has been from farm work to nonfarm work. In nonfarm work, the shift has been from goods-producing to service-producing work. In manufacturing, the shift has been in the direction of a more skilled work force. Automation and technical change has changed the nature of jobs and has moved persons into other jobs or unemployment. In spite of these changes, however, employment has increased and unemployment has declined (12). The conclusion which can be drawn, therefore, is that the nature and distribution of kinds of work will change but that there is no evidence that the amount of work done by man will diminish. Since both our work years and our educational and retirement years are increasing in length, it may be conjectured that the work time saved from technical change will be diverted into the ever-increasing areas of services.

It is unlikely that the value of work will diminish in the United

States in the foreseeable future even if technical forces should make it possible to reduce some of the kinds of work that is now being done. The acceptance of work is general in the United States. In the Full Employment Act of 1946, Congress made the employment of all Americans who wished to work the national goal. The majority of the people of the United States see work as the foundation of the American society. Too many essential human values derive from work, besides income, to persuade Americans to forgo work. If machines will produce the products man now makes, society will find other useful forms of work which will substitute for the work they are now doing. Work provides man with purpose. To propose that man exist happily without work is to propose that he exist without purpose. Thus it is likely that work will appeal to man both in industry and in the workshop and will continue as the central focus in our society in the immediate future.

It has been indicated that work is essential to workshops, and its volume sets the limits of services in workshops. It has also been pointed out that the procurement of work has been a problem in workshops. Furthermore, though work is not diminishing in general, it is diminishing in volume in production of products, and increasing in provision of services. If workshops are to expand their services, they will have to increase the volume of work in light of these circumstances.

The nature of work in shops changed greatly in general after 1950, when the new shops for the special disability groups spread rapidly over the country. Before 1950, workshops worked principally on renovation of discards, on manufacturing of household items, manufacturing on power machines, and on some simple assembling subcontracts. After 1950, the large volume of work sought was in simple assembly and subcontracts of manufactured products.

As important as the specific changes enumerated in respect to work accepted is the question of the willingness of more workshop personnel to change their philosophy in respect to work in shops. Such a change requires that the philosophy of the shop accept both social work behavior and work competence as the major determinants in employment success, rather than emphasize social behavior as the primary determinant. It also involves the principle that a more varied and complex work environment maximizes the potential for the development of both acceptable social behavior and work competence for persons from all levels of functioning and from all social backgrounds. If such a philosophy is accepted, the volume of work in workshops may increase considerably. For further comment, see Chapter XV, under work of shops in the future.

GOVERNMENT INFLUENCES ON GROWTH OF WORKSHOPS

In the preceding sections, the emphasis has been on the policies and actions of workshops as they will affect the growth of work. Even more influential could be the effect of action by government or by other public agencies.

The most immediate possibility for large expansion of work in workshops might come from the expansion of the Wagner O'Day Act to include other workshops and other products or by the passage of a new law setting aside other products the government buys for the prior purchase from workshops. The Wagner O'Day Act which was passed for the workshops for the blind has worked very well. There is no logical reason why the same benefits should not be extended to persons with other disabilities. Such a legislative enactment would make available on an ongoing basis large amounts of work now not available to workshops. It would also have the added effect of giving the workshops opportunity to develop increased capability in manufacturing skills which could be used for private manufacturing operations or contracting operations involving producing complete products.

Other prospects for the strengthening and growth of workshops are found in the proposals of Secretary of Labor W. Willard Wirtz in his recommendations to Congress in September, 1967. The Secretary recommended (13):

> 1. There should be provision for wage payments to supplement the meager earnings of sheltered workshop clients, and also to help pay for such overhead costs as training, supervision, and management counseling.

2. There should be broadened authority under the Manpower Development and Training Act to facilitate opportunities for the participation of sheltered workshops.

3. The vocational rehabilitation training programs should be expanded to provide larger amounts than are currently allocated to the States to help sheltered workshops.

4. Federal public assistance laws should provide that income for work performed in a sheltered workshop must not be counted against the amount given by the public welfare authorities at least up to a specific point.

The Secretary of Labor's proposals involve the inclusion of more federal money to workshops or to handicapped workers. A similar possibility exists in the subsidization of workshop programs by state and local government. A beginning has been made in a few states which participate in the costs of operating workshops but these are in the minority. A few counties have provided small percentages of workshop costs but this has usually happened when such funds may be used to match federal or state funds.

Another source of funding which has been generally overlooked is the educational system. While school systems have paid for services from workshops for half-day students or provided teachers, few school systems have provided ongoing lump sum funds for staff and administration costs. The traditional acceptance by the American people of public education makes the school system a potential partner in workshops or an operator of them. It is possible that the educational system may become an important factor in the development of workshops in the future.

SUMMARY AND COMMENT

In general, the future of workshops will depend upon the decisions American society makes about the economic welfare of its least successful people. Of great importance will be the priority given subsidized employment as a means of providing economic well-being. It is anticipated that the great value placed on work will continue. The necessity for man to work to have what he wants will not disappear. The nature of the work done, however, may change considerably.

The objectives of the Full Employment Act of 1946 will not be achieved as long as the economic system imposes the obstacles of social prejudice and psychological misunderstanding in the way of handicapped and disadvantaged persons. Those obstacles may reduced somewhat, but that they will be eliminated quickly is unlikely, and in any case the obstacles inherent in disability will remain. It is anticipated that more than a million handicapped and disadvantaged persons will need to participate in workshop programs so that their vocational welfare may be assured.

To serve as work places for the country's least successful people, privately sponsored workshops will need public support. The forms this support could take are federal funds for the costs of services to people in workshops, wage supplements, and the provision of work set aside for workshops by state and federal purchasing agencies. The infusion of larger amounts of public money will require greater accountability on the part of workshops. If accountability is not effectively achieved, there may be a trend towards publicly operated workshops.

The great need for more workshop services and the problems in developing them adequately present both challenges and opportunities to workshops of the country. To these challenges and opportunities we turn in the concluding chapter.

NOTES

1. Selected Facts and Figures about the Disabled and the Disadvantaged. Washington, National Citizens Conference on Rehabilitation of the Disabled and Disadvantaged, U.S. Department of Health, Education, and Welfare, Social and Rehabilitation Service, 1969, p. 2.
2. Ibid. Number of Persons Rehabilitated, Rate, and Rank per 100,000 Population. Washington, U.S. Department of Health, Education, and Welfare, SRS, 1969.
3. Vocational Rehabilitation Agency Program Data. Washington, U.S. Dept. of Health, Education, and Welfare, SRS, 1969, p. 140.
4. Rusalem, H. and Baxt, R.: Emerging Patterns of Rehabilitation Delivery Service. Washington, U.S. Department of Health, Education, and Welfare, SRS, 1970, p. 6-12. Hipkens, T. P.: Rehabilitation has outlived its usefulness. Journal of Rehabilitation, pp. 12-13, March-April, 1970.
5. Rusalem and Baxt, op. cit.
6. Nelson, N.: Planning for workshops for the handicapped. Rehabilitation Literature, pp. 71-73, March, 1969.

7. Selected Facts and Figures about the Disabled and Disadvantaged, op. cit.
8. Ibid., p. 1.
9. Ibid., p. 5-9.
10. Black, B. J.: A workshop in a changing world. Rehabilitation Literature, August 1965.
11. Wolfbein, S. L.: Labor Trends, Manpower, and Automation. In Man in a World at Work. Boston, Houghton Mifflin Company, 1964, p. 157.
12. Ibid., pp. 160-172.
13. Sheltered Workshop Report of the Secretary of Labor, Washington, U.S. Dept of Labor, Wage and Hour and Public Contracts Divisions, 1967, pp. 5-8.

XV

OPPORTUNITIES FOR
FUTURE DEVELOPMENT

In the preceding chapter we have discussed the American cultural framework within which workshops have developed and which will probably circumscribe their future activities. The general outline of this social structure will probably remain as described, but it is quite possible that modifications or changes may take place within it as the American people extend the definitions of their goals to create opportunity and benefits for more of the total population. Workshop personnel can stimulate this process by showing in realistic terms how opportunity may be extended to the handicapped and disadvantaged. They can influence the diminishing of unnecessary rejections of such individuals and further their claims for equal treatment with other groups in society, for equal access to employment and other benefits of the country. In the process, workshop personnel may modify the nature of their institution and make an additional contribution to the welfare of the country.

It is improbable that workshop personnel will be able to persuade American society to alter its folk ways by logical or common sense appeals for justice or compassion. It may be possible, however, to demonstrate how meaningful work programs can meet some of the needs of America's least successful people. If this can be done in keeping with American ideals of what is worthwhile and also admirable, it is possible that additional resources of the country will become available for work programs for handicapped and disadvantaged people. Workshops will have to demonstrate that they could teach individuals to be creative, productive money makers, the kind of individuals that the country admires. And the workshop will have to be an efficient and useful part of the economic process, like the profit-making business firm, a credit to American enterprise.

It is not suggested that American workshops can become exact duplicates of American industrial plants or produce the ideal American worker. What does seem apparent, however, is that workshop organizations and personnel should change their orientation if they wish to become a more potent force in American society. They may not be able to achieve the exact goals of industry, but they must strive to attain similar goals if they are to be respected. They must stress creativity, productivity, and independence. They may not be able to give their long-term people equivalent wages to those paid in private employment, but they must be able to give them the status and dignity of such employment and the basic fringe benefits associated with private employment. If workshops are to be more highly respected they must deemphasize their charitable orientation and aspire to a more socially accepted reputation as an employment facility.

The identification of the workshop as a charitable organization fixes it in an aura of impotence in the public mind. The individual who attends a sheltered workshop has failed in life. Indeed the sheltered workshop is a substitute when the real thing is not available. Even industrialists on boards of workshops sometimes conceive workshop employment as a sop to unfortunates unable to muster the fortitude to make it in the real world. To become a major force in American society, the workshop will need to substitute a picture of potency for that of impotence. To do this, it will need to move into the orbit of industry and business. It should be able to do this without severing its ties to the rehabilitation movement in the United States.

To move into a closer relationship with the outside world of work and make a larger contribution to the solutions of some of the country's most difficult problems, the workshop movement needs to take advantage of existing opportunities. Among the major tasks that need doing are these:

1. Expand the perspective and add new dimensions to its scope and methodology.
2. Assume an advocate role as a spokesman for handicapped and disadvantaged persons.
3. Restate its concepts of dysfunction and its relationship towards handicapped and disadvantaged persons.
4. Develop a nonprofit work system.
5. Adjust work capability to the changes of the economic system.

6. Identify the organizational components of a work-oriented welfare program and the various skills needed by staff.
7. Adopt a new approach for new kinds of people.

EXPANDING WORKSHOP HORIZONS

Most workshops adopted the philosophy of rehabilitation by the middle of the century. The philosophy of rehabilitation held that every individual had the right to reach his highest potential. After the middle of the century, many workshops joined a partnership with the public vocational rehabilitation program. The public program, however, usually helped him only if that potential was for private employment. As a consequence many workshops emphasized improvement towards employment in private industry. There were also many shops who had other goals, such as sheltered employment, but these were principally shops which had existed before mid-century or served relatively small numbers of persons with special disabilities. At no time did any organization visualize serving all handicapped persons in the community regardless of their disability and irrespective of their potential level of functioning.

The statement that each individual should be enabled to reach his highest potential, admirable though it is, had a rather serious limitation in implementation. It was usually interpreted to mean that the individual should be enabled to improve his condition or his situation. In practice no ideologic concept existed for all those who could not improve their situation or for those whose condition was getting worse. Such persons were usually considered candidates for medical or custodial care. This is in decided contrast to such European countries as Great Britain or the Netherlands, where people are given work not because they will improve their function necessarily but because they need to work for their health and welfare. In American ideology, many individuals incapable of improving are left in a workless limbo.

The neglect of the workless deteriorating or static handicapped person is unintentional. American rehabilitation practitioners, outside of public assistance, usually select out of large numbers a few they choose to serve. Their focus is on the individual. If they serve the few well, they are content. There are large numbers not served. Rarely do individual practitioners concern themselves with epidemiological or demographic studies of handicapped persons or with social statistics. Usually evaluation of outcomes are of a clinical nature and made by the practitioner who rendered the service at the time he terminates the case. The emphasis of workshop methodology since mid-century has been clinical and therapeutic. There has been little study of how the total population of handicapped persons perform, earn, or live in the community and how they may be served in workshops.

The opportunity for workshop personnel is to expand their dimensions and scope to encompass the welfare of all handicapped and disadvantaged persons regardless of the severity of their handicapping condition and their prognosis. The opportunity in methodology is to develop group methods of improving functioning and enhancing well-being both in and outside of workshops, not only in verbal discussion groups but in work teams in workshops, in industry and commerce, and in open air domestic employment. Work groups may totally man retail and industrial units, and workshop organizations should try to operate industrial plants employing both handicapped and nonhandicapped individuals. Workshop personnel may test the effectiveness of their existing and future techniques, as some are now doing, by making quantitative evaluations of the functioning of their individuals in industrial sites and in workshops by extensive follow-up studies. By these efforts they will develop impressive programs both in and out of workshops which will win the admiration and support of the American people.

TOWARDS AN ADVOCACY ROLE

If the changed philosophy and theory of workshops are to have practical significance, the workshop community will need to assume an advocacy role quite different from anything they have tried previously. In the past, workshops through their organization have supported federal vocational rehabilitation legislation. Quite often such legislation was justified on the premise that the expenditures would save the taxpayer money in the long run. In general, this legislation has never encompassed nearly all the needs of handicapped persons. The legislation was generally in keeping with the ideology which assumes that success in the competitive economy is the only goal to be achieved.

Another characteristic of the past role of rehabilitation and workshop organizations is that they have not always been in harmony with organizations of the handicapped persons they served. Although handicapped persons have not, with the exception of the blind, participated in organizations, to a great extent, such organizations which existed have not usually worked in harmony with the workshop and rehabilitation organizations. In general, the handicapped organizations have felt that rehabilitation legislation has not been directed to the objectives of providing direct benefits to them. Often handicapped persons felt that rehabilitation personnel did not understand that their difficulties were not caused by their disabilities but by society's unjustified assumptions about them.

The funding of programs serving all the needs of the handicapped population cannot turn on the argument that these services will rid the public of their support. If the handicapped who cannot work in industry are given employment in workshops rather than direct money payments in public assistance, the workshops will need additional public funds if they are to put to work all those individuals rejected by industry. The only financial claims that can be made is that such funding will be less than their public assistance payments. The main justification that can be made is that such funds will be less in total than the huge subsidies paid to the other segments of society such as industry, farming, and the like. Thus workshop personnel and organizations can assume an advocacy role to persuade society to provide employment in industry or at adequate wages under acceptable conditions in workshops in a nonprofit employment system. To do so, they need to understand society's part in the rejection of the handicapped and the handicapped person's feeling about such rejection.

DYSFUNCTION, DEVIANCE, AND THE HANDICAPPING CONDITION

With the increase of the kinds of people served in workshops, new concepts of disability and handicap will arise. When physical disability was the primary source of the handicapping condition, the rationale was relatively simple. In general, but not always, there was a direct relationship between the disability and the handicap. It was clear that there was something about the person that could be expressed as a relatively objectively determined deviance from a physical norm. When, however, the nature of the disabilities changed to emotional disturbance and social or cultural elements, there was no longer as clear a deviance from a quantitative norm. The futility of complete dependence on a medical diagnosis as the sole basis for prediction became more clear. Even the diagnosis of mental retardation, which had some quantitative components, became increasingly questionable as a means of prognosis. In place of categorical classification, dependence was more often placed on functional descriptions.

Thus a person's potential was judged principally by the nature and level of his functioning. In relating his functioning to his handicap, however, a curious phenomenon became apparent. Individuals who functioned at a given level or in a given way were unacceptable for employment at one time and acceptable at another time. Examples are times of war and prosperity as opposed to times of depressions. And one kind of social deviance from accepted standards was unacceptable at one time and acceptable at another. Many handicapped persons who were not hired fifty years ago are acceptable now. External forces such as available funds or national social pressures changed requirements at different times. What became clear was that dysfunction or deviance as a barrier to employment is influenced by the changing requirements of society and is not solely a function of the individual condition. Another opportunity for the workshop community is to advocate only necessary and objective requirements for employment. They should also redefine a handicap as resulting from disability or deviance as socially evaluated from time to time.

The allowances that industry sometimes makes for handicapped persons is not always made out of reasonableness but out of necessity. Industry usually withdraws its allowances when circumstances do not require them. While workshop personnel can learn from this experience that the impact of deviance is socially established, they cannot determine when social allowances may be withdrawn. Thus if they are to be true advocates of handicapped individuals, they must provide a more extensive workshop employment system while they are trying to influence the economic system to treat our least successful people more objectively.

A NONPROFIT SOCIAL EMPLOYMENT SYSTEM

Perhaps the greatest opportunity facing workshops is to create a more extensive nonprofit work system that will provide permanent employment for our least successful population. The objective of such an employment system is to provide social employment. By social employment is meant work which will provide a reasonable wage, at least the minimum wage, and provide a wholesome environment conducive to creative work and social activities. Such a system should emphasize the dignity and status of the worker and give him an opportunity to participate in its direction in the same way that nonhandicapped workers participate in industry, through labor unions or grievance committees.

Past experience with sheltered employment might lead one to question the possibility of achieving an acceptable social employment system. In light of the low average wage paid in sheltered employment currently (70 cents an hour in 1968) and the unsatisfactory conditions which have sometimes characterized sheltered workshop programs in the past, it may be said that it is impossible to develop such a system on an acceptable basis. It is indeed difficult to provide such a system on an acceptable basis without a wage supplement from a social source and resources enabling the shop to develop a high level of industrial capability. It is also necessary to develop an increased volume and variety of types of work if the social employment system is to prove satisfactory to the individual served.

THE NATURE OF THE SOCIAL EMPLOYMENT SYSTEM

Assuming that workshops will be part of it, that is a social employment system, how will they be included? Now workshops are divided into a number of systems serving different types of individuals and having different kinds of objectives. Long-term employment is now concentrated generally in three parts in the workshop system. The first are workshops serving persons whose production is inconsequential and who are getting a variety of supportive services at the same time. The second are workshops serving persons at a variety of productive levels who are receiving few additional services. A third and smaller group of shops are those who move many of their workers into private employment, but also keep a portion in long-term employment. Gellman envisions that the total rehabilitation system will be fluid, with movement from the transitional workshop to activity centers, to training, to competitive employment and to the noncompetitive work system (1).

Undoubtedly, many of the existing workshops will continue as presently constituted and will move individuals into employment or into social employment workshops. However, if a national wage subsidy and work allotment program come into being, it will have to be settled whether long-term work activity centers and short-term adjustment centers will be included. If they are not, the social employment system will be conducted primarily by workshops having substantial extended employment programs with many marginal and high producers capable of doing complex work. These will be in the main large shops. If work activity centers are included the majority of handicapped persons can be included in a social employment system.

Recently, an incipient development towards merger of different types of workshops has taken place in the United States. Six had been recorded by 1970. The most prominent example has been the Detroit merger of the League for the Handicapped and the Goodwill Industries. When major workshops in a community merge, the new organization operates all types of workshop programs for the community. Such workshops would usually be expected to assume responsibility for the social employment program. Where such multiprogram agencies do not exist, the social employment program would usually be carried on by the workshop having the largest extended employment program, or by a number of shops having social employment objectives.

THE NATURE OF WORK IN SHOPS

In addition to securing financial resources and funding, getting and accomplishing more and varied forms of work is the principal problem facing workshops. The success the social employment system has in performing varied and complex types of remunerative work will determine the amount of financing they will need for wages supplement and overhead expenditures. If the public financial contribution is small, the chances of securing it are enhanced. Thus an early question to be answered is how great are the prospects of American workshops to secure and accomplish an increased volume of varied, complex, and reasonably remunerative work.

There are no published national statistics summarizing the characteristics and volume of work in workshops. The conjectures made subsequently are based on observations of about two hundred workshops during the last twenty years. There is no intent to imply that the observations have statistical validity. It is believed, however, that such observations may be useful in future planning in the absence of published data.

In general, the problem relating to work since 1950 has been that the workshops, especially those serving the single disability groups, have not been able to secure enough work of a simple nature to expand their programs as necessary. They have been offered subcontract work of a complex nature but have not accepted such work for a number of reasons. The reasons why they have not accepted such work is at the heart of the work problem.

A frequent reason given for the rejection of complex work is that the handicapped persons cannot do the more difficult work. A secondary reason is that complex work often requires the use of machine tools shops do not have or are not inclined to secure. Often complex work requires training in occupational skills which the workshops do not wish to undertake. Sometimes complex work involves more time in the shop. More capital funds are often needed. In general, workshops have not accepted complex work because it conflicts with their philosophy and rationale. That philosophy sees psychosocial behavior as the principal determinate in successful employment and gives less stress to physiological components such as work competence and work skills.

Do the workshops have to accept simple work exclusively and reject complex work? Where workshops have attempted complex work with industrial know-how, they have found ways to enable their most severely handicapped person, including the severely mentally retarded, to perform the most difficult kinds of work adequately. Where there has been a desire to perform complex work, shops have secured use of machine tools from contractors or have purchased them with grant funds or charitable contributions. Where they have desired to do so, they have been able to bring in production supervisors with industrial experience and to train handicapped persons in occupational skills. Furthermore, European workshops such as those in the Netherlands have demonstrated that complex work can be done in workshops (2).

Workshops can develop greater work capacity and thus secure more varied types of work. With greater work capacity will also come greater ability in accommodating to types of work and varying services and products which change rapidly in response to commercial demands. This kind of flexibility will be necessary whether the work undertaken is manufacturing, subcontracting, or service work. The development of greater capability and flexibility is essential if workshops are to develop long term employment and a social employment system.

IDENTIFICATION OF COMPONENTS OF THE SOCIAL EMPLOYMENT SYSTEM

Wherever the social employment system exists, however, an organizational component and staff must exist with characteristics designed for it. In social employment programs, the individual will work indefinitely and is regarded as having a permanent job. Those he works for are his bosses and he is a worker. His job is good if his wages are high, his fringe benefits good, his job-related perquisites good, and he is treated with the respect due an able and competent worker. The work done must therefore be meaningful and indicative of his worth. He communicates with management as an equal through his union or grievance committee. He is not a client receiving counseling, casework, or psychotherapy, but a handicapped worker who is unable to work in industry because of circumstances which will not usually change substantially.

The staff of the social employment program must therefore include industry-oriented managers, supervisors, and foremen who understand the problems and attitudes of handicapped and disadvantaged individuals. They must be skilled in the training and supervision of industrial workers. While several training programs are available for managers, no substantial training programs are available for supervisors and foremen. Thus a prime requisite for a social employment system is the training of supervisors and foremen. The foreman in particular is a key man, since he is the staff man closest to the handicapped person. He is to be distinguished from the counselor-foreman or the counselor-aid. This foreman's role is not to change the worker's condition but to accept him as he is and to train him to be as creative and productive as he can be in light of his limitations. This foreman adjusts workshop conditions to meet each worker's need for fulfillment. The development of such a foreman presents a major opportunity to workshop personnel.

TOWARDS A NEW WORKSHOP

Redefining the Handicap

Finally the great challenge to workshop personnel is to expand their basis for entry or stay in workshops. We have seen that the workshops have increased the kinds of persons with physical and mental handicaps in their programs. In the future their eligibility concepts will probably expand to include in larger numbers individuals in two other groups.

The first is composed of individuals described as disadvantaged in the Vocational Rehabilitation Act Amendments of 1968. These include individuals disadvantaged by reason of youth or advanced age, low educational attainments, ethnic or cultural factors, and prison or delinquency records. Gellman identifies many of the above described and others who cannot enter employment because of disability as the "disemployed" (3). These individuals are rejected in the main by industry.

A second group of the above individuals are those who reject the conditions or rewards of the private employment system. The difference between them and those in the first group is that the latter could meet the conditions of industries if they desired to do so. They are potentially placeable but lack willingness to become employed in the circumstances available to them. They are unable to secure employment which they regard as appropriate. They prefer other social alternatives such as public assistance or antisocial money-making activities.

Both these groups present a challenge and an opportunity to workshops. In all probability, the workshops will attempt to deal with the first-named disadvantaged group in ever increasing numbers. What is not certain is if workshops will be able to engage the disadvantaged in a relationship based on an appreciation of their social philosophy and traditional value systems. If the history of workshops is a guide, they will probably be able to do so.

The opportunity to serve the first-named disadvantaged group will rest primarily with shops having short-term programs to move individuals into employment. If these shops can forsake their individual, counseling relationships exclusively and use also indigenous shop groups and community work approaches, they may find a new avenue for workshop expansion. They will also contribute to an important problem facing American society.

The second group who reject private employment will provide opportunities for long-term shops to create acceptable social employment systems. Here the challenge will be great because they will have to change, not "clients," but their own institutions to meet those just requirements which provide for their workers adequate income, satisfactory work, social acceptability, and dignity and respect.

Finally, the challenge to workshop personnel is to change their way of thinking about the people in their shops. They will view them in the future not as individuals with disabilities but as people with varying levels of handicaps. The handicaps are created in part by their conditions, or in part by their responses to our work systems, and in part by the society in which they live. Workshop personnel will assume that they need opportunities to solve their problems in their own ways. Sometimes they will need help and this help should be given in the ways they want it given. They may want it given individually for them to solve their own problems, or socially to respond to circumstances they cannot or do not wish to change. In this way, workshops will in the future provide opportunities to people who have problems in securing and remaining in employment which is satisfactory to them.

NOTES

1. Gellman, W.: New directions for workshops meeting the rehabilitation challenge of the future. Rehabilitation Literature, p. 287, September, 1967.
2. Roeder, A. E.: A Comparative Study of Dutch and California Sheltered Workshops, Master's thesis, San Francisco, San Francisco State College, 1967, p. 64.
3. Gellman, W.: New perspectives in rehabilitation. American Psychological Association Bulletin, p. 42, November, 1966.

Appendix

SUMMARY OF STANDARDS
FOR THE OPERATION OF WORKSHOPS
FOR HANDICAPPED
AND DISADVANTAGED PERSONS

THE following summary of workshop standards is a concise restatement of desirable practices determined by standard-setting organizations. They are the Goodwill Industries of America, the Commission of Standards and Accreditation of Services for the Blind, the Commission on Accreditation of Rehabilitation Facilities, and the Vocational Rehabilitation Services of the Department of Health, Education, and Welfare.

The summary combines and paraphrases common elements on a selective basis of the standards of the above organizations. In a very few instances, new statements have been added. Occasionally, major statements have been omitted because they were narrowly specific to the organization's special program emphasis. In other instances, principles were omitted when they were abstract and were better expressed more specifically. The summary is therefore not a collection of standards of all standard setting groups or of any single one of them. It is a selective and interpretive restatement of what appears to be accepted standards.

It should therefore not be assumed that those who apply these standards will achieve accreditation from any group. The summary is designed as an educational tool to help those who use the standards develop better workshops.

THE PURPOSE OF A WORKSHOP

The general purpose of a workshop is to help the handicapped persons to whom it offers services, and all its operations are carried on towards that end. The specific objectives are a matter of

419

record for the information of the persons in the shop, for community agencies, and the public generally.

There is a periodic review of the operations of the workshop by the staff and governing body to determine if the objectives are achieved and to ascertain if the objectives are adequate in nature and scope to meet the needs of the persons in the workshop. Recommendations of the staff in relation to the character of the case load and program effectiveness shall be regularly transmitted to and considered by the chief executive officer. He shall in turn submit appropriate reports of program effectiveness regularly to the governing body.

There shall be an established program for follow-up in terms of outcomes as compared with goals.

POLICIES OF THE WORKSHOP

The principal thrust of the workshop is the use of paid work to help the handicapped persons in it, but it assumes the responsibility to discover if other services may be needed and to make those services available to those it serves within the workshop or through other agencies as may be possible.

The workshop specifies the kind of persons it takes into the shop and describes the services it renders to them in a public document.

INTAKE AND TERMINATIONS

Only those incapable of working in private industry or unable to secure jobs there because of their disabling conditions are admitted to the workshop. Individuals ineligible for services are informed as to the reasons and, if possible, appropriate referrals are made.

When a person becomes capable of working in industry and is able to find a job there, he is helped to leave the workshop. A periodic review of the capabilities of those in the workshop is made to determine who can leave for industry. Those who leave the shop for employment are given the opportunity to return if they lose their jobs through no fault of their own. When a person ceases to benefit from his stay in the shop, he is helped to change to a beneficial situation of a different kind.

To bring about the optimum development of the persons in the workshop, attempts are made to achieve the maximum efficiency in workshop operations consistent with the conditions of the persons in it.

WAGES AND WORKING CONDITIONS

The workshop complies with all local, state, and federal laws applicable to workshops, including minimum wage and overtime laws, minimum age laws, equal rights and equal pay laws, and others. Wages are paid in accordance with the productivity of the workers commensurate with pay for similar levels of productivity in industry. Payment is made in accordance with productivity while the worker is undergoing evaluation or training. Periodic reviews of production records are made to assure that wages are in keeping with productivity. If incentive wages are paid in excess of productivity, an explanation of the reasons for the excess payment is made.

The organization treats everyone in the workshop equally with regard to employment, promotion, pay, or place of work without regard to race, sex, creed, or national origin.

ADMINISTRATION AND ORGANIZATION

The organization is incorporated as a nonprofit organization with an exemption from the payment of income tax under Section 501 of the Internal Revenue Code. The charter or constitution and by-laws identify the corporation and its purposes, and establishes membership meeting times, qualifications of members, quorum requirements, and methods of amending the bylaws.

The bylaws shall in additon do the following:

1. Provide for a governing body.
2. Provide for the election and specification of duties of officers.
3. Establish regular and special meetings of the governing body, in no event less than three meetings a year.
4. Provide for committees of the governing body.
5. Describe the parliamentary procedures which shall be followed in

the conduct of business meetings.
6. Require the recording of minutes.

THE COMPOSITION OF THE
GOVERNING BODY

The members of the governing body are representatives of varied interests of the community and provide direction, support, and stability for the workshop. Members serve staggered terms on a rotating basis to provide opportunities for the appointment of new members continuously. The qualification for membership, election, and tenure are described in the bylaws. Members serve without pay. No one on the board should be in a relationship to the workshop which creates a conflict of interests.

THE RESPONSIBILITIES OF THE
GOVERNING BODY

The governing body establishes policies for the operation and management of the workshop and formulates long-range plans for its future development and public relations.

It approves the organizational structure of the workshop and its rules and regulations. It adopts the budgets and develops adequate financial support for the workshop. It establishes standards for the operation of the workshop and approves personnel policies and salary schedules. It makes a periodic review of the nature of the workshop's program of services, its administrative and professional effectiveness, and its public relations.

THE GOVERNING BODY–DIRECTOR RELATIONSHIPS

The governing body appoints a full-time administrator and delegates to him authority and responsibility to manage the workshop in keeping with its policies. The director is an ex officio member of the governing body and attends all its meetings and those of its committees. He assists the body in its formulation of policies and plans and in such other matters as the body may require. He keeps the body informed on the operations and problems of the workshop and of such matters outside the workshop which are important to its welfare.

The Chief Executive shall carry out his responsibilities in the following manner:

1. He shall be present at all meetings of the governing body and standing committees, except when his personal status is under consideration.
2. He shall be an ex officio member of the governing body without voting privileges.
3. Staff members other than the chief executive shall not serve as members of the governing body.
4. The chief executive officer shall orient new members of the governing body.
5. He shall assist the governing body in formulation of policy and interpretation of operating reports and financial statements, plans, and changing concepts.
6. He shall assist the governing body as required in such functions as fund raising, community relations, and related duties.

STAFF ORGANIZATION

The Workshop Director

The director carries on the regular business and program of the workshop in keeping with the policies of the governing body. He directs the day-by-day operations at the workshop and authorizes expenditures in keeping with the budget. He employs all staff, sets forth their duties in writing, designates lines of communication and authority, and provides an organization chart. He reviews the operations of the workshop by analyzing reports and records and comparing their findings with the objectives, budget, and standards of the workshop. He takes steps to improve operations to effect approved goals. He reviews the effectiveness of the public relations of the workshop and works with the governing body to achieve maximum effectiveness. He initiates, reviews, and improves as required the financial operations and records. He encourages the staff to experiment to effect improvements.

Senior Staff

The executive director designates a person to be in charge of the shop when he is absent. The director delegates specific authority and responsibility to senior staff. Each department or unit head has assigned duties in a written job description for which he is responsible to his superior as shown in the organization chart. Each department or unit head participates in decisions affecting his department or unit. Coordination of activities between departments or units is effected through regularly scheduled meetings. Professional staff attend when appropriate. Senior staff conferences for short-term and long-range planning are scheduled away from work duties at least annually. Minutes are kept of all senior staff meetings.

Each senior staff member is responsible for the supervision and training of those who report to him as shown in the organization chart, for rating of their effectiveness and for their accomplishment of the assigned tasks in keeping with the policies of the governing body and instructions of the executive director. He is responsible for interns, trainees, and volunteers assigned to him.

Junior staff, floor supervisors, foremen, and lead men employees have written job descriptions which specify their duties. They participate in all staff meetings in which handicapped workers under their supervision are discussed.

Performance

The director gets a weekly report on attendance, production, and cash. Professional services are covered by fee or contributed income. Production income from work shows effective pricing and production. Quality control reports show accomplishment within specifications. Review of contract flow shows reasonable retention of customer satisfaction. Public relations feedback shows reasonable compliance with ethical and sound business practices in sale of products and subcontracting.

The layout and work flow are planned to produce maximum efficiency. The quality of work meets industrial standards.

FINANCIAL MANAGEMENT

The workshop's financial operations conform with all legal

requirements. Generally accepted accounting procedures appropriate to the facility are used. Financial operations are conducted in a manner appropriate to the purposes of the workshop. Sound ethical practices are observed in the payment of obligations and collections. Fund-raising programs conform to established ethical standards in the community. Capital commitments are not made at the expense of equitable wages to the handicapped in the shop.

Budget and Reporting

The director prepares an annual budget which is approved by the governing body. He reviews the budget and the financial experience of the shop at least quarterly with the governing body and senior staff. He prepares a balance sheet for the governing body quarterly. An annual fiscal report is published and made available to the public. At least a weekly cash report is made to the director.

The Accounting System

An accurate, double-entry system is used which includes [1] a daily cash journal, [2] general ledger of accounts, [3] accounts receivable, and [4] accounts payable records. All operating funds are disbursed from a single operating account, through which all funds are transferred by check. Records are maintained to provide evidence that federal, state, and local tax payments and reporting are in compliance with the law.

Internal Control

All checks except individual payroll checks are signed by more than one person as determined by the governing body. All wages are paid by check. Records of purchasing and distribution are maintained.

Cost System

Records are maintained which enable the director to identify the expenditures for rehabilitation services and for business costs. Records of departmental costs are maintained, and also for the costs of each contract of over 1000 dollars per year. Financial records shall make it possible to identify separately at least the following operating costs: worker earnings, wage supplements, direct labor, indirect labor, payroll taxes, raw materials, insurance, maintenance, occupancy, receiving and shipping, administration, product development, and marketing and selling.

Auditing

The financial operation of the workshop is audited by a qualified auditor who has no office, membership function, or connection with the workshop. He makes a statement in his report that depreciation is reported in keeping with standard auditing practices as determined by C.P.A. procedures.

Sales and Pricing

A markup for overhead over direct labor is charged to cover overhead costs; in no case is it less than 80 percent of direct labor costs. Contributed income is not used to pay overhead costs in connection with subcontracting. Selling prices for products are in line with prevailing price ranges in the area. When products are sold by outside outlets, the workshop obtains assurance that the products are sold on a fair basis. Contract and product pricing is reviewed annually to assure an adequate pricing structure and conformity with fair practice.

INDUSTRIAL PRACTICES

The workshop shall not knowingly accept struck work. Bidding for work shall be based on adequate knowledge of costs involved including the following:
1. Knowledge of local industry prevailing piece rates or time rates for comparable work.
2. Production rate norms established when industry rates are not available.

3. Costs of supplies, special equipment for the work, and administrative overhead.

Wages and Working Conditions

All workers shall be paid at least the applicable certificate minimums required by wage and hour regulations and overtime pay as required by law.

The workshop complies with legal minimum age requirements.

Wage payments shall be of a monetary nature and not payments in kind.

Each worker shall receive a written statement for each pay period indicating his gross pay, hours worked and deductions.

Insurance

The workshop carries workmen's compensation insurance or is self-insured for workmen's compensation. It bonds all employees who handle money. It has public liability on all its property including trucks and cars and to compensate people in the shop for events for which it may be liable. It has fire and extended coverage on all property including equipment in adequate amounts. It has liability insurance to cover the property belonging to other companies or persons while it is in the shop. It has burglary, payroll, safe, inside hold-up, outside employee service, products, and sprinkler damage insurance.

It has a written record of review of insurance by the governing body in its minutes every three years plus annual review by the director of the workshop.

PHYSICAL FACILITIES

The physical plant is located in the community so that it is readily accessible and has adequate parking. It is adequate in size and design to promote efficiency and flexibility in operations. It meets all legal requirements in design and construction. The staff is consulted in selection of tools and equipment which meet industrial standards. Work production areas have layouts designed to expedite flow of materials and finished work into and out of building, and to promote time and motion economy. Storage areas are located to expedite handling of raw materials, work in process, and finished products. Lighting meets acceptable industrial standards. Reception areas and offices are easily accessible and adequate in size. Conference rooms are available within the plant.

HEALTH AND SAFETY

An established first aid system is described in writing in a personnel brochure. A designated first aid area is maintained at each plant. Each station is supplied with a first aid kit, resting equipment and a person trained in first aid is available.

One wash basin with hot and cold water is provided for every twenty persons in or adjacent to toilet rooms. Suitable cleansing agents are provided in each space. Hand towels and receptacles for used towels are available. Rest rooms are clean, well painted, with dispensers and waste receptacles, adequate lighting, and privacy. Food service personnel are clean, uniformed, and have health cards. Required public inspections are made and inspection permits are posted.

Separate toilets are available for each sex. Each toilet is not more than one flight of stairs from work areas. Toilets have water closets as follows: for ten persons, one water closet; for twenty-five persons, two water closets; and one additional water closet for each twenty-five persons. In men's toilets, urinals may be used in lieu of water closets at one urinal for each ten men, provided water closets are two thirds of the numbers specified above. Every water closet is separately enclosed.

Separate changing or dressing rooms are provided for each sex. Where change to work clothes is required, a locker and key is provided. Retiring rooms with privacy are provided for women workers.

Written plans covering fire and disaster evacuation are available in a personnel brochure. An evacuation drill shall be conducted at least annually, and preferably three times a year. Annual inspections by local fire control agencies are requested and reports are kept on record. A system of security control is established with a watchman on duty all closed hours, burglar alarms are required, and an operative fire alarm system. Inspection permits are current on elevators, boilers, and other equipment requiring them. Daily inspection is made at closing time of extension cords and electric appliances, lighted tobacco items, and other potential fire hazards.

Safety goggles or face shields are provided to all persons in the vicinity where there is a hazard to the eye. Belts, fly wheels, and moving parts of machinery are enclosed with appropriate guards. Points of operation, when necessary and practicable, are covered with movable shields when work is not in process.

Guard rails are establshed when necessary and are strong, securely fastened, and free from sharp edges. Sprinkler or other approved systems are installed. Fire doors are installed as required by building codes and fire exits are clearly marked.

DISASTER PLAN

The workshop shall establish plans for its participation, if it is part of a community disaster plan, which shall include emergency casuality care in times of external disaster.

WORK AREAS AND EQUIPMENT

The work production area shall be designed to ensure the most efficient flow of materials in and out of the facility. Provision shall be made for storage of raw materials and of finished products.

The facility shall use labor-saving tools, equipment and machinery comparable to those used in industry, unless there are clearly defined reasons for exceptions in dealing with specific groups of clients.

In the presence of unusual hazards, such as dust, fumes and noise, arising from certain operations, appropriate precautions shall be taken to ensure the protection of clients and staff.

Suitable first aid facilities shall be readily available. A sufficient number of appropriate persons shall be trained in administering first aid services to ensure the presence of at least one such individual in the workshop during all working hours.

A formal plan shall be established for the referral of persons who have required and received first aid to a local hospital or physician's office for further care. An outline of such a plan shall be posted at the first aid station and at other appropriate places in the workshop.

A formal plan shall be established for the reporting of all accidents occurring in the workshop or on its premises, whether or not they give rise to injuries requiring medical treatment.

The accident report shall contain, but not be limited to, the following information:

1. Identification of persons involved.
2. Place of accident within the premises.
3. Time of accident.
4. Name of responsible supervisor present.
5. Circumstances under which accident occurred, such as equipment in use at time, type of operation being performed, etc.
6. Description of first aid services given to any injured persons.
7. Data on referral of injured persons, if such referral is necessary.
   a. Where sent or taken.
   b. Time of departure of workshop.
   c. Means of transportation used.

A plan shall be established for the review of accident reports by management representatives, with a view to improving the workshop's safety programs and its plans for the handling of accidents. This plan shall be reduced to written form.

The workshop shall provide a minimum of sixty square feet of floor space per worker, exclusive of space used for storage, but including aisle space within the work area. All ceilings shall be a minimum of nine feet in height.

All floors shall be kept clean and dry and free of holes or projections which constitute hazards.

All areas of the sheltered workshop shall have not less than two means of egress, exclusive of ladders and elevators, as remote from each other as possible. On the street floor, at least one exit shall lead directly outside the building. On upper floors and in basements, at least one of the exits shall lead to an enclosed smoke-proof stairwell, with direct access to the outside of the building. All exit doors shall be accessible through unobstructed aisles; they shall be equipped with panic bolts and swing in the direction of exit in a manner that does not obstruct passages of egress.

There shall be no variation in the width of treads and height of risers in any flight of stairs. Where variation of heights of risers in different flights is necessary, such variations shall not exceed three sixteenth of an inch. All treads shall be at least ten inches wide and in good repair, free from tripping or slipping hazards. No storage shall be allowed on stairs.

All single steps which protrude into passageways shall be provided with railings on each side. All stairways with two or more risers shall be equipped with a railing on the right side descending, and all stairways with four or more risers shall be equipped with railings on both sides of the stairway. Double rails, a hand rail and an intermediate rail shall be provided on all open sides of stairways.

All step and stair railings shall be solidly anchored, strong enough to support the weight of a heavy individual, with a distance no more than thirty-four inches, not less than thirty inches, above the tread when measured in line with the riser. Intermediate rails shall be equally secure and strong, and approximately midway between the hand rail and stair tread. Stair railings, including their terminal posts, shall extend at least as far as the top and bottom risers of the stairway.

Permanent aisles and passageways shall be clearly defined by painted lines, curbings or other methods of marking and shall be kept clear and in good repair, with no obstructions across or in the aisles that would cause tripping.

Where industrial trucks are used, one-way traffic aisles shall be at least two feet wider than the widest vehicle. Where aisles are regularly used for two-way traffic, they shall be at least three feet wider than twice the width of the widest vehicle.

All material in bags, containers, or bundles, stored in tiers, shall be stacked and limited in height so as to be stable and secure against sliding or collapse.

Where automatic sprinkler protection is provided, clearance of at least eighteen inches shall be maintained between the tops of materials and the underside of the lowest beams or other overhead structures.

The sheltered workshop shall have illumination throughout the work areas of no less than thirty foot candles of illumination, and where clients are engaged in work that requires the use of vision to its maximum capacity, a higher level of supplementary illumination shall be provided.

Places in which combustible or flammable materials are stored shall be effectively separated from the rest of the workshop in such a way as to minimize the hazard of fire spread.

Fire alarm systems will be in the following areas:

1. Combustible or flammable storage areas.
2. Laboratories.
3. Trash collection rooms.
4. Trash chutes.
5. Employee locker rooms.
6. Kitchens.
7. Attic space when used for combustible storage or for heating or air conditioning equipment.
8. Basement corridors.

Responsibility for the observance of the foregoing safety and health standards, and for the maintenance and implementation of the workshop's safety programs shall be vested in specified members of the staff.

PERSONNEL

Personnel policies and practices are established, maintained, and made available to each staff member in written form. These policies are reviewed periodically. Qualifications required of staff members are available in written form.

Each staff member is provided with a written job description. Staff members shall meet legal requirements when such exist.

The governing body shall have final responsibility for standards and/or qualifications of staff. It shall delegate authority and responsibility for implementing standards to the chief executive.

Personnel policies cover the basic relationships between employer and employee, the responsibilities and obligations of each, and general working arrangements.

STAFF QUALIFICATIONS FOR POSITIONS WHEN USED

The director. The workshop has a full-time director. The workshop director has a bachelor's degree from an accredited college with eight years' paid employment of which four years are directing professional or supervisory personnel. Two years of supervision may be substituted for each year of education to make eight years of supervisory experience the equivalent of a bachelor's degree. Graduate training may be substituted for up to three years' experience. A master's degree in workshop administration, business administration, or industrial administration may be substituted as the equivalent of one year's experience.

The plant superintendent or *production supervisor* is a high school graduate with five years' paid employment in regular industry or a workshop including at least two years' supervisory experience. Two years' supervisory experience may be substituted for each year of required education.

The workshop foreman or *floor supervisor* is a high school graduate with four years' paid employment and one year's experience in industrial work or office supervision. Up to three years of military service, education or business experience may be substituted for either education or experience requirements.

The contract procurement specialist is a high school graduate with at least four years' paid employment in industrial sales, sales engineering, or similar fields including experience in estimating and bidding practices.

The work evaluator has a master's degree in appropriate field and one year's experience in rehabilitation or a related field, or a bachelor's degree and three years' experience in education, industrial arts, occupational therapy, rehabilitation counseling, psychology, and manual arts therapy.

The job placement specialist has a bachelor's degree plus two years' personnel experience or other placement experience.

The occupational skill instructor has been accredited by an appropriate state agency, qualifies as a journeyman and has one year's experience teaching his trade, or has a combination of experience and teaching which is equivalent to the above requirements.

Supportive Staff

The vocational rehabilitation counselor has completed a vocational rehabilitation counseling curriculum or has a bachelor's degree and two years' experience in a vocational rehabilitation agency, or has completed a graduate curriculum in counseling and guidance or psychology.

The psychologist has a master's degree in psychology from a recognized university.

The social worker shall have graduated from an accredited school of social work.

Other supportive staff members and consultants meet the requirements of their recognized professional groups. When volunteers work in above listed staff positions, they have the same qualifications.

A physician and an industrial engineer shall be available through formal affiliation or consultation.

WORKER-STAFF RATIOS

In extended employment programs, the workshop shall employ a minimum of three supervisory or administrative staff for the first fifteen workers, plus an additional employee for each fifteen workers.

In evaluative and work adjustment programs, the workshop shall employ a minimum of three supervisory and administrative staff for the first ten clients, plus an additional employee for each additional ten clients.

STAFF DEVELOPMENT

The workshop carries on a planned in-service training program for its staff. Staff are encouraged to attend training institutes and the workshop pays tuition and costs. Staff are encouraged to belong to professional organizations and to attend meetings and conferences. The workshop subscribes to professional journals and makes them available to the staff. Staff members are encouraged to experiment and carry on research.

An evaluation of the workshop is made every three years by outside, competent personnel such as an accreditation team, local welfare council representatives, or by independent consultants.

WORKER-CLIENT WORKING CONDITIONS

The workshop provides each worker with a manual with information on services, benefits, working conditions, and other matters of interest to its handicapped persons. Meetings of workers are held at regular intervals to discuss plans of the shop which affect their welfare, to answer their questions, to receive their suggestions, and to enlist their cooperation in the affairs of the shop. Prior to a change in the worker's status, the reasons for the change will be explained to him. There will be a written grievance procedure described in the workshop manual.

The workshop provides workers with fringe benefits consistent with good personnel practice and includes, in addition to workmen's compensation, old age and survivors and disability insurance or its equivalent, vacations for workers in extended employment of at least five days a year. There shall be a minimum of five holidays with pay.

The workshop shall comply with federal laws concerning rights and equal pay.

The workshop shall not discriminate with regard to employment opportunities in respect to promotion, pay or place of work because of race, creed, or national origin.

COMMUNICATION AND GRIEVANCES

Handicapped persons who are concerned about policies of the workshops shall be given an opportunity to discuss their concern through a regular meeting where their questions may be answered.

Individuals who take exception to the decision of a staff member shall have the right and be given an opportunity to appeal such a decision.

The workshop shall establish an effective mechanism for dealing with group concerns and individual appeals.

REPORTS AND RECORDS

The workshop maintains adequate and complete records necessary to the conduct of its program and makes reports which reflect the performance of the organization in the achievement of its objectives. Its records and reports meet all legal requirements and the requirements of accepted professional and administrative practice. A records committee reviews at least annually an appropriate sample of records to assure that they meet record-keeping requirements and to make recommendations for improvement. Records include minutes of administrative and professional staff meetings.

Records are maintained for periods necessary to meet legal, professional, and administrative requirements.

Administrative records and reports guide the operations of the facility, measure performance productivity, and provide an account of the accomplishments of the workshop. Controls exist so that the location of records are known at all times. An indexing and filing system and a correspondence file are maintained.

Appropriate safeguards are maintained to protect all records and to assure they are kept confidential. Records are stored under lock and key and protected from fire and other hazards. Access to records is limited to personnel authorized by the workshop director to use them. Records are made available to outside agencies or persons as authorized by persons concerned or by their legal representatives.

A central case record is maintained for each person admitted to the workshop. The records include [1] reports from referring sources, [2] identifying data, [3] a pertinent history including a medical report not more than two years old, [4] evaluation reports and a plan for workshop activities towards stated goals, [5] the designation of a staff member responsible for each worker's activities in the workshop, [6] progress reports of performance and progress and a record of attendance, [7] report of untoward events or noteworthy accomplishments, [8] signed release forms for information to outsiders, [9] a discharge summary of disposition or referral, [10] follow-up reports.

PAYROLL AND WORK RECORDS

The workshop maintains records of local prevailing wage rates paid nonhandicapped persons for the same or similar types of work done in the shop. The records show dates, the source of information, such as commercial or industrial establishments, time studies, or other sources. The workshop pays wage rates commensurate with prevailing rates for the quantity of work done. Records show that wage payments are in keeping with state and federal minimum wage laws and for those not covered by the laws by wages commensurate with minimum wage requirements.

For each worker paid at piece rates or whose productivity can be measured, there is a continuing production record. Reports reflect the productivity of each worker on a continuing, periodic basis at intervals not exceeding six months.

Files on work methods and quality control are maintained. Work tolerance reports with statements of work progress are made.

A payroll record is maintained for every worker which includes [1] worker identification, [2] time of day and day of week work begins, [3] daily and weekly hours worked, [4] regular overtime earnings. For any period, the record shows gross pay, additions or deductions and net pay, date of payment, and pay period covered. Each worker receives a written statement for each pay period showing gross pay, hours worked, and deductions. Information concerning work tolerance, productivity, and pay amounts is given to supervisory personnel.

For each person who works on the floor of the workshop in the production process, the following information shall be recorded:
1. Regular hourly rate of pay.
2. Hours worked each work day and work week.
3. Total daily or weekly straight time earnings.
4. Total overtime pay.
5. Total additions to or deductions from wages paid each pay period.
6. Total wages paid each pay period.
7. Total amount of bonus, if any.

8. Day of payment and pay period covered by the payment.
For each handicapped person employed:
1. Special work considerations to be taken into account in assignment.
2. Statement on work progress.
3. Production record.
4. Identification on payroll.

Records of handicapped persons who have been placed in outside employment include the following:
1. Place of employment.
2. Job title.
3. Rate of pay.
4. Date on which employment commenced.
5. Employment status at the end of the first ten weeks.

SERVICES

The services are planned to serve the needs of the handicapped persons in the shop. The workshop describes in writing the services which it renders, and this document is available to the public. The workshop has available a current description of other services for handicapped persons rendered by other resources in the community.

There shall be written criteria and procedures for admission. There is a policy of nondiscrimination on the basis of race, sex, creed, or national origin. The procedures for intake are enumerated.

The workshop has a check list for orientation and induction. The staff member responsible for program of each inductee is indicated.

Written procedures are established to determine the individual's evaluation and program at the shop. The staff who participate in the evaluation determine the services and the objectives for him. They are explained to the individual and to his family when indicated. Individuals who are not served are informed of the reasons for the decision, and if possible, referrals are made elsewhere. All referrals are given a personal interview and a review of application forms as a minimum.

Work evaluation is an integral part of the services, and is continuous during the stay of the worker. The evaluation includes assessment of psychological and social traits and physical capacities. Other appropriate measures as written tests, job tryouts, and staff interviews are used as needed.

The program is organized to develop work tolerance and work adjustment. The work adjustment program is graduated and activities modified to meet client needs. The workshop program motivates the worker to do productive work, to be self-reliant, to accept supervision, and to work with speed and accuracy. There is a periodic review of the work program.

Instructional activities are designed to develop skills, knowledge, and work habits comparable to those required in private employment. There is an organized plan of instruction for each training course. Follow-up data is used in revising the training.

Extended remunerative employment in the shop includes instruction in work activities and observation of safety principles in a realistic work environment. Supportive services, such as counseling or social services, are provided as needed. Referrals are made to outside programs for supportive services when indicated.

The workshop provides a placement program through its own means or through existing community services as the public employment service, the vocational rehabilitation agency, and industrial companies. The placement process includes orientation to the demands of the job and information to the employer when indicated. The placement program is reviewed at least annually and reports are maintained.

The workshop follows an established procedure for discharge from the shop. Separation is preceded by consultation with appropriate members of the staff. The handicapped person, his family when indicated, and the referring source are given prior notice of the decision to discharge.

Follow-up contacts are scheduled and carried out after discharge. Follow-up contacts are made with the family when indicated and other agencies. Follow-up information is used to improve services in the shop.

Throughout the program of service, staff conferences are held as needed to review progress, to develop further plans, and to coordinate individual programs. The staff member responsible for the program evaluates the program and is responsible for needed services in the facility or elsewhere. Written notations in the case record are made. Assurance of priority in return to the workshop in case of loss of job is made.

Work orientation shall be provided to encourage good work habits, including proper care of equipment and materials, correct handling of tools and machines, good attendance, punctuality and safe work practices, to afford disciplined interpersonal relations with supervisory personnel and co-workers, and to promote work tolerance and work pace consistent with the handicapped person's potential.

The layout of work positions and the assignment of operations shall be so planned as to allow for efficient flow of work and appropriate relationship of each operation to all other operations in its sequence with respect to the time required for its completion. The organization of work shall embody an awareness of safe practices and of the importance of time and motion economy.

Files on work methods and quality control shall be maintained and actively used by supervisory personnel.

Written specifications shall be prepared and available for each article produced. Products shall be made in conformance with relevant specifications, and meet the standards of competitive products in the open market.

The workshop shall maintain a formal system of quality control, responsibility for which is vested in specified members of the staff. The quality of workshop products shall meet competitive industrial standards.

Information concerning health and special work considerations which should be taken into account in the assignment of handicapped persons shall be clearly communicated to supervisory personnel.

The workshop shall obtain and utilize rehabilitation diagnostic and training data from cooperative programs, whether within its parent organization or other community sources. The following services shall be provided either by facility staff, or through formal affiliation, or by consultation.

A general medical examination is to be obtained prior to planning any workshop service for a handicapped person, and repeated annually following employment. The report on the examination is to include a statement of the handicapped person's physical and other limitations, need for treatment and conditions under which the handicapped person may work.

When indicated, examinations by appropriate medical specialists are to be arranged. Reports shall be obtained, clearly reflecting the findings and recommendations.

At least annually, vocational assessment shall be made by a professional rehabilitation specialist, and a report obtained, clearly reflecting the findings and recommendations.

When indicated, a psychological evaluation shall be made, and a report obtained, clearly reflecting the findings and recommendations.

As indicated, social casework services and vocational counseling shall be available.

The workshop shall maintain provisions, either within its parent organization or through cooperative agreements with appropriate community services, for the placement in regular industry of any of its handicapped persons who may qualify for such placement.

Handicapped persons shall be informed, through the personnel manual of the workshop and by other means, of the availability of such services for placement in competitive industry.

If the handicapped person is placed in regular industry from a sheltered employment program, and if circumstances beyond his control result in the loss of his job, the handicapped person's return to a position in the workshop shall be guaranteed for a period of thirty days. He shall be assured of priority for reemployment in the workshop for a period of ninety days.

The workshop shall make referrals of clients to programs for supportive services outside the workshop function, when indicated.

There shall be adequate provision for handling referrals to and from the agency. All possible pertinent data shall be obtained at the time of referral and intake. Information shall be secured from sufficient and appropriate sources, and shall be current, reliable and complete. All referral data shall be kept in the handicapped person's case record.

The workshop shall make no charge to the handicapped person for the privilege of employment per se in the workshop.

If the handicapped person or his legal guardian elect to purchase opitional services (such as room and board) at standard fees, payroll deductions shall be made only with his written authorization.

With respect to such other changes as may be levied upon the handicapped person, payroll deductions shall be made only with the written authorization of the client or his legal guardian.

COMMUNITY RELATIONS

The workshop develops broad community and professional acceptance in order to effect its goals. It participates actively in community planning organizations in fields related to its program. It maintains working relations with other community, health, and welfare organizations, business, labor, and civic groups who contribute to programs for the handicapped.

The workshop develops and expands its service program based on objective studies of needs of the community for service to handicapped persons. These studies are carried out in cooperation with established community groups in health and welfare. The content of such studies is reported to the governing body.

The workshop conducts a planned public information program using accepted forms of communication to engender understanding by and support from the community. This includes a scheduled program of press, radio, and TV presentations. Special scheduled events for education and promotion are carried out with the cooperation of the governing body and volunteer assistance.

The workshop shall maintain a program designed to provide opportunities for participation by members of the community in its work.

There shall be an established procedure for providing acknowledgment and donation and receipts for income tax purposes upon the receipt of any gift, donation, or bequest.

The workshop and its representatives shall employ only ethical methods of publicity, promotion and solicitation of funds.

Promotional materials shall not contain portrayals of the disabled as helpless. No use shall be made of any living disabled person's name or picture without prior permission of the individual concerned. No rights shall be granted to profit-making or nonprofit groups to couple their support of programs for the disabled with their sales promotions in such a manner as to exploit the handicapped.

When applicable, the workshop shall maintain a systematic procedure for the collection of discards.

There shall be no representation of products as made by the disabled unless the workshop employs the labor of disabled persons in 75 percent of the total man-hours worked in the direct labor of production of manufactured products.

INDEX